Chartered
Institute of
Housing

Help with Housing Costs:

Universal Credit and Council Tax Rebates

2018-19

Sam Lister and Martin Ward

Shelter

Help With Housing Costs: Guide to Universal Credit and Council Tax Rebates
Sam Lister and Martin Ward, 2014-19

Sam Lister is policy and practice officer at the Chartered Institute of Housing *(email: sam.lister@cih.org)* and a founding director of Worcester Citizens Advice Bureau and Whabac. He has specialised in housing benefit and social security since 1993.

Martin Ward is an independent consultant and trainer on housing and benefit related matters *(e-mail: mward@knowledgeflow.org.uk).* He has provided consultancy services and training for several national organisations as well as many local authorities and large and small housing providers across the UK since 1982.

ISBN 978-0-9934984-6-6

Edited and typeset by Davies Communications
(www.daviescomms.com)

Printed by MBA Group Ltd

Chartered Institute of Housing

The Chartered Institute of Housing (CIH) is the independent voice for housing and the home of professional standards.

Our goal is simple – we want to transform lives. We want everyone to have a decent, affordable home in a thriving, safe community. We passionately believe that our contribution as housing professionals is vital to making communities great places to live. Our work is rooted in three main objectives – learn, improve and influence. We provide opportunities for learning and improving and we champion housing to influence the direction of policy.

Chartered Institute of Housing
Octavia House
Westwood Way
Coventry
CV4 8JP

Telephone: 024 7685 1700
E-mail: *customer.services@cih.org*
Web site: *www.cih.org*

Shelter

Shelter helps over a million people a year struggling with bad housing or homelessness – and we campaign to prevent it in the first place.

We're here so no-one has to fight bad housing or homelessness on their own.

Please support us at *shelter.org.uk*

For more information about Shelter, please contact:

88 Old Street
London
EC1V 9HU

Tel: 0300 330 1234
shelter.org.uk

For help with your housing problems, phone Shelter's free housing advice helpline on 0808 800 4444 (open from 8am to 8pm on Mondays to Fridays and from 8am to 5pm on weekends: calls are free from UK landlines and main mobile networks) or visit *shelter.org.uk/advice*

Contents

Preface

This guide explains universal credit and council tax rebates, focusing on help with housing costs. It gives the rules which apply from 1st April 2018, using information available on 15th May 2018.

We welcome comments and criticisms on the contents of our guide and make every effort to ensure it is accurate. However, the only statement of the law is found in the relevant Acts, regulations, orders and rules (chapter 1).

This guide has been written with the help and encouragement of many other people. We wish to thank the following in particular:

Julia Service (Housing Systems), John Zebedee, Linda Davies and Peter Singer (editing and production) as well as staff from the Department for Work and Pensions and the Rent Service. Their help has been essential to the production of this guide.

Sam Lister and Martin Ward

May 2018

List of tables

Abbreviations

The principal abbreviations used in the guide are given below.

ADM	Advice for Decision Makers (DWP manual)
CTC	Child tax credit
CTR	Council tax rebate
DCLG	The Department for Communities and Local Government
DLA	Disability Living Allowance
DWP	The Department for Work and Pensions in Great Britain
ESA	Employment and support allowance
ESA(C)	Contributory employment and support allowance
ESA(IR)	Income-related employment and support allowance
GB	England, Scotland and Wales
HB	Housing benefit
HMRC	Her Majesty's Revenue and Customs
HMCTS	Her Majesty's Courts and Tribunals Service
IB	Incapacity benefit
IS	Income support
JSA	Jobseeker's allowance
JSA(C)	Contribution-based jobseeker's allowance
JSA(IB)	Income-based jobseeker's allowance
LCW	Limited capability for work
LCWRA	Limited capability for work and work-related activity
LHA	Local housing allowance
NISR	Northern Ireland Statutory Rules
PIP	Personal independence payment
SAR	Second adult rebate
SDA	Severe disablement allowance
SI	Statutory instrument
SMI	Support for Mortgage Interest
SPC	State pension credit
SSI	Scottish Statutory Instrument
UC	Universal credit
UK	England, Scotland, Wales and Northern Ireland
WTC	Working tax credit

Key to footnotes

For further information about footnotes see para 1.30.

AA	The Social Security Administration Act 1992
art	Article number
C&P	The Universal Credit, Personal Independence Payment, Jobseeker's Allowance and Employment and Support Allowance (Claims and Payments) Regulations 2013, SI No 380
CTP	The Council Tax Reduction Schemes (Prescribed Requirements) (England) Regulations 2012, SI No 2885
CTPW	The Council Tax Reduction Scheme and Prescribed Requirements (Wales) Regulations 2013, SI No 3029
CTR	The Council Tax Reduction Schemes (Default Scheme) (England) Regulations 2012, SI No 2886
CTRW	The Council Tax Reduction Schemes (Default Scheme) (Wales) Regulations 2013, SI No 3035
CTS	The Council Tax Reduction (Scotland) Regulations 2012, SSI No 303
CTS60+	The Council Tax Reduction (State Pension Credit) (Scotland) Regulations 2012, SSI No 319
D&A	The Universal Credit, Personal Independence Payment, Jobseeker's Allowance and Employment and Support Allowance (Decisions and Appeals) Regulations 2013, SI No 381
DDO	The Council Tax (Discount Disregards) Order 1992, SI 1992 No 548
DDR	The Council Tax (Additional Provisions for Discount Disregards) Regulations 1992, SI 1992 No 552
EEA	The Immigration (European Economic Area) Regulations 2006, SI No 1003
FTPR	The Tribunal Procedure (First-tier Tribunal) (Social Entitlement Chamber) Rules 2008, SI No 2685
IAA99	The Immigration and Asylum Act 1999
LGFA	The Local Government Finance Act 1992
IAA99	The Immigration and Asylum Act 1999
NIAA	The Social Security Administration (Northern Ireland) Act 1992
NIC&P	The Universal Credit, Personal Independence Payment, Jobseeker's Allowance and Employment and Support Allowance (Claims and Payments) Regulations (Northern Ireland) 2016, NISR No 220
NID&A	The Universal Credit, Personal Independence Payment, Jobseeker's Allowance and Employment and Support Allowance (Decisions and Appeals) Regulations (Northern Ireland) 2016, NISR No 221

NIHB	The Housing Benefit Regulations (Northern Ireland) 2006, NISR No 405
NIHB60+	The Housing Benefit (Persons who have attained the age for state pension credit) Regulations (Northern Ireland) 2006, NISR No 406
NIOP	The Social Security (Overpayments and Recovery) Regulations (Northern Ireland) 2016, NISR No 224
NIPOA	The Social Security (Payments on Account of Benefit) Regulations (Northern Ireland) 2016, NISR No 223
NIWRO	The Welfare Reform (Northern Ireland) Order 2015, SI No 2006 (NI 1)
NIUC	The Universal Credit Regulations (Northern Ireland) 2016, NISR No 216
NIUCED	The Universal Credit Housing Costs (Executive Determinations) Regulations (Northern Ireland) 2016, NISR No 222
NIUCTP	The Universal Credit (Transitional Provisions) Regulations (Northern Ireland) 2016, NISR No 226
OP Regs	The Social Security (Overpayments and Recovery) Regulations 2013, SI No 384
para	Paragraph number
POA	The Social Security (Payments on Account of Benefit) Regulations 2013, SI No 383
reg	Regulation number
RR	The Rate Relief Regulations (Northern Ireland) 2017, NISR No 184
s	Section number
sch	Schedule number
SI	Statutory instrument [year and reference number]
SSA	Social Security Act 1998
TCEA	Tribunals, Courts and Enforcement Act 2007
UC	The Universal Credit Regulations 2013, SI No 376
UCROO	The Rent Officers (Universal Credit Functions) Order 2013
UCTP	The Universal Credit (Transitional Provisions) Regulations 2014, SI No 1230
UTPR	The Tribunal Procedure (Upper Tribunal) Rules 2008, SI No 2698
WRA	The Welfare Reform Act 2012

Chapter 1 **Introduction**

1.1   Welcome to this guide, which explains the new system of getting help with your housing costs. The guide is for people claiming benefit, their landlords and mortgage lenders, advisers and those making decisions.

1.2   Universal credit (UC) is being introduced throughout the UK. If you are a renter, UC helps you meet basic living needs and pay your rent. If you are an owner, UC helps you meet basic living needs and DWP loans help you pay your mortgage interest.

1.3   Council tax rebate (CTR) helps you pay your council tax. It applies throughout Great Britain but the details vary locally. In Northern Ireland the rate rebate scheme helps with your rates.

1.4   Many people continue to get help with their rent (and/or rates in Northern Ireland) from housing benefit (HB). See the *Guide to Housing Benefit 2018-19,* which is the companion to this guide.

1.5   The rules in this guide apply from April 2018. The next edition will give the rules from April 2019. For basic definitions of the main terminology in this guide, see table 1.1.

Examples: Help with housing costs: UC and CTR

1. A single tenant

A single person rents her home. If she meets the conditions:

- she can get UC towards her living needs and her rent;
- she can get CTR towards her council tax.

2. A home owner couple

A couple are buying their home on a mortgage. If they meet the conditions:

- they can get UC towards their living needs;
- they can get a DWP loan towards their mortgage interest;
- they can get CTR towards their council tax.

Table 1.1 **UC and CTR terminology**

Claimant (UC and CTR)

A claimant is someone who is making a claim (in CTR law called an 'application') for UC/CTR or someone who is getting UC/CTR.

Joint claimant (UC)

If you are claiming UC as a couple you are joint claimants. In CTR one of you is the claimant (in CTR law you are called the 'applicant'), but the claim covers you both.

Couple (UC and CTR)

You are a couple if you are two people who are married, in a civil partnership, or living together as a couple.

Single person (UC)

In UC you are a single person if you are not in a couple or not claiming as a couple (whether or not you have children or young persons).

Single claimant and lone parent (CTR)

In CTR you are a single claimant if you are not in a couple and have no children or young persons, or a lone parent if you are not in a couple and have one or more children or young persons.

Benefit unit (UC) and family (CTR)

In UC your benefit unit means the people you are claiming for. In CTR law this is called your family.

Child and young person (UC and CTR)

A child is someone aged under 16. A young person is someone aged 16 to 19 who is in secondary education.

Working age and pension age (UC and CTR)

You are working age if you are under state pension credit (SPC) age. You are pension age if you have reached SPC age. During this benefit year (2018-19) SPC age is rising from 64½ to 65¼. From 6th December 2018 SPC age matches (and rises in line with) state retirement age.

Assessment period (UC)

UC is calculated on a monthly basis. Each monthly period is called an assessment period. Your first assessment period begins on the day your UC starts (this can be any date in the month) and the following ones start on the same date each month.

Benefit week (CTR)

CTR is calculated on a weekly basis. Each weekly period is called a benefit week (in CTR law it is called a 'reduction week'). Benefit weeks always begin on a Monday.

Maximum UC, allowances and elements (UC)

The calculation of your UC is based on your income and capital and your maximum UC. Your maximum UC is made up of a standard allowance and other elements you qualify for, including a housing costs element.

Maximum CTR, applicable amount, personal allowances, premiums and components (CTR)

The calculation of your CTR is based on your income and capital, your maximum CTR and your applicable amount. Your maximum CTR is the weekly amount of your council tax. Your applicable amount is made up of the personal allowances, premiums and components you qualify for.

Housing costs element (UC)

In UC the housing costs element is the part of your maximum UC which is for your housing costs. It can help with rent and service charges. But mortgage interest and similar payments can be met instead by DWP loans.

Eligible council tax (CTR)

In CTR your eligible council tax is the weekly amount of council tax you are liable to pay.

Housing cost contributions (UC) and non-dependant deductions (CTR)

If you have one or more non-dependants they may be expected to contribute towards your UC housing costs and/or your council tax. In UC this is called a housing cost contribution. In CTR it is called a non-dependant deduction.

Non-dependant (UC and CTR)

A non-dependant is an adult son, daughter, or other relative or friend who lives with you on a non-commercial basis.

Renter and tenant (UC and CTR)

Renter (mainly in UC) and tenant (mainly in CTR) both mean someone who is liable to pay rent (including for example a licensee).

Owner and shared owner (UC and CTR)

Owner means someone who owns or is buying their home. Shared owner means someone who is part renting and part buying their home.

DWP and DFC

The DWP (Department for Work and Pensions) deals with claims for UC in Great Britain. The DFC (Department for Communities) deals with claims for UC in Northern Ireland. In this guide, references to the DWP include the DFC.

Authority (CTR)

An authority means any local council that issues bills for council tax and deals with claims for CTR.

The UC scheme

1.6   The key features of the UC scheme are as follows:

  (a)   UC is for working age claimants who meet the conditions of entitlement: see chapter 2;

  (b)   it can help meet your living costs and housing costs: see paras 1.7-8;

  (c)   you claim UC from the DWP or DFC: see para 1.9;

  (d)   it applies throughout the UK;

  (e)   UC replaces several other social security benefits and currently there are transitional rules about who can claim: see paras 1.13-33;

  (f)   it was first introduced in Ashton-under-Lyne on 29th April 2013.

The amount of your UC

1.7   Depending on your financial and other circumstances, you can get UC towards:

  (a)   your basic living needs; and

  (b)   your housing costs.

The amount of your UC takes into account whether you have a partner and/or children or young persons who live with you. It also takes into account whether you have limited capability for work, are a carer, and/or have childcare costs. For further details see chapters 2, 9 and 10.

UC and your housing costs

1.8   Being on UC means you can get help with your housing costs:

  (a)   UC itself includes a 'housing costs element' which helps you pay your rent and/or service charges;

  (b)   separate DWP loans help you pay your mortgage interest or similar costs.

In each case there are limits to how much you can get. Also the amount towards your rent can be reduced if you have one or more non-dependants living with you. And you cannot get help with your mortgage interest or similar costs if you have any kind of earned income. For further details see chapters 3 to 8.

How to get UC

1.9   To get UC, you make a claim (usually by a free telephone call) to:

  (a)   the DWP (Department for Work and Pensions) in Great Britain;

  (b)   the DFC (Department for Communities) in Northern Ireland.

If you are claiming UC as a couple you make a joint claim. UC is a monthly benefit based on 'assessment periods' which begin on the same day each month. It is paid to you at the end of each assessment period, or in some cases to your landlord or mortgage lender. If you are overpaid you may have to repay it. You can ask the DWP to reconsider your UC if you think it is wrong, and appeal to an independent tribunal. For further details see chapters 3 and 11 to 14.

The CTR scheme

1.10 The key features of the CTR scheme are as follows:

(a) CTR is for claimants of any age who meet the conditions of entitlement: see chapter 15;

(b) it can help meet your council tax: see para 1.11;

(c) you claim CTR from your local authority: see para 1.12;

(d) it applies throughout Great Britain, but the details vary in England, Scotland and Wales, and in England and Wales from local authority area to area: see chapter 15;

(e) CTR was introduced on 1st April 2013, when it replaced council tax benefit.

The assessment of CTR

1.11 CTR can help you pay your council tax. How much you get depends on your financial and other circumstances:

(a) you get maximum CTR if you are on a passport benefit (JSA(IB), ESA(IR), IS or guarantee credit of SPC), and also if your only income is from UC;

(b) you can get CTR in other circumstances, for example if you receive other income as well as UC.

The amount you get can be reduced if you have one or more non-dependants living with you. For further details see chapters 17 and 18.

How to get CTR

1.12 To get CTR, you make a claim to the local authority that sends your council tax bill. If you are in a couple your claim covers both of you. CTR is a daily benefit, though most of the calculation rules are based on 'benefit weeks' (in the law called 'reduction weeks'). It is awarded as a credit to your council tax bill, so you have less council tax to pay (see chapter 16). If you are overpaid you may have to repay it. You can ask your local authority to reconsider your CTR if you think it is wrong, and appeal to an independent tribunal. For further details see chapters 19 and 21.

The UC transitional rules

1.13 This section explains the transitional rules that apply until UC is fully introduced. These depend on whether the 'full service' or 'live service' rules apply to you (paras 1.14-15). They affect:

(a) whether you can get UC or legacy benefits (paras 1.16-32); and

(b) UC assessment periods (paras 3.39 and 3.43), reclaims and re-awards (paras 3.45-49), backdating (paras 3.53-54), housing costs for under 18s (para 4.84), and childcare costs (para 9.45).

Table 1.2 shows how UC has expanded during its first five years.

Table 1.2 **Households on UC (2015-2017)**

	All households	With housing costs element
November 2015	141,140	50,635
May 2016	260,172	98,311
November 2016	398,079	159,836
May 2017	494,809	228,580
November 2017	623,439	314,644

■ Source: DWP, Stat-Xplore

UC full service and live service rules

1.14   The full service rules apply if:

(a) you live in a UC full service area (also called a 'digital service area') – see para 1.15; or

(b) you move from a full service area to a live service area while you are on UC; or

(c) you become a couple with someone the full service area rules apply to; or

(d) you reclaim UC within six months of receiving it in a full service area (para 3.45); or

(e) your UC is for any other reason administered on the DWP's full service (digital service) computer system.

The live service rules apply if you live in a live service area (para 1.15) except as described in (b) to (e).

Full service and live service areas

1.15   In Great Britain, everywhere is either a full service area or live service area, and live service areas are being converted to full service areas over the period to December 2018. In Northern Ireland, UC is being introduced over the period to December 2018, and every area that has UC is a full service area (there are no live service areas). Appendix 5 gives the planned dates for the introduction of UC full service for the whole of the UK.

1.14   Commencement orders (see appendix 1);
        www.gov.uk/government/publications/universal-credit-national-expansion

The legacy benefits

1.16   UC is gradually replacing the 'legacy benefits' (para 1.17). Paras 1.19-32 explain when and how this is done.

1.17   The legacy benefits (also called 'existing benefits' in the law) are:

(a) housing benefit (HB) for working age claimants, unless you live in specified supported accommodation or temporary accommodation (see para 1.32);

(b) income-based JSA (JSA(IB));

(c) income-related ESA (ESA(IR));

(d) income support (IS);

(e) child tax credit (CTC); and

(f) working tax credit (WTC).

1.18   UC doesn't replace other benefits. For example the following continue alongside UC:

(a) state pension credit (para 1.33);

(b) housing benefit for pension age claimants;

(c) CTR, rate rebates and discretionary housing payments;

(d) contribution-based JSA (JSA(C)) and contributory ESA (ESA(C) (also called 'new style' JSA and ESA).

Claims for UC and legacy benefits

1.19   In UC full service areas, you can make a claim for:

(a) UC unless you have more than two children or young persons (para 9.22); but

(b) legacy benefits if you have more than two children or young persons.

For HB, see also paras 1.31-33.

1.20   In UC live service areas, you can only make a claim for legacy benefits. Since 1st January 2018, no one can make a claim for UC until your area becomes a full service area.

Continuing entitlement to UC and legacy benefits

1.21   If you are already on UC, you can continue to get it for as long as you meet the basic financial conditions (paras 2.2-3). This applies whether you are in a full service area or live service area. But if you are in a live service area you can choose to transfer from UC to legacy benefits – by 'terminating' your UC award and making a claim for them (DWP circular HB U4/2017 para 5 confirms this for HB).

1.22   If you are already on legacy benefits, you can continue to get them (if you meet their conditions) until you transfer to UC as described in paras 1.23-30.

1.17   WRA 33; UCTP 2(1) definition: 'existing benefit', 5(1); NIWRO 39; NIUCTP 2(1), 3(1)

1.19-22 UCTP 4-8,8A,10; commencement orders; NIUCTP 3-6, 8

Migration from legacy benefits to UC

1.23   This section explains how and when you move from the old system (where you can get legacy benefits but not UC) to the new system (where you can get UC but not legacy benefits). This is often called 'migration'.

Natural migration

1.24   'Natural' migration occurs when:

(a) you stop being entitled to a legacy benefit (under the rules for that benefit) and can only claim UC (or be worse off): see para 1.25; or

(b) you claim UC for other reasons (whether or not you are on a legacy benefit): see paras 3.2-3; or

(c) you become a couple with someone who is already on UC: see para 3.5.

Any of (a) to (c) can apply if you live in a full service area, but only (c) can apply if you live in a live service area (or have more than two children: paras 1.19 and 9.22). See paras 1.28-30 for how natural migration affects you.

1.25   Natural migration can result from the loss of a legacy benefit (para 1.24(a)) if you claim UC when:

(a) you lose JSA(IB)/ESA(IR)/IS because of starting work or increasing your hours or earnings (see example 1);

(b) you lose JSA(IB) because of being unfit for work;

(c) you lose ESA(IR) because of becoming fit for work (see example 2);

(d) you lose WTC because of ending work or reducing your hours (see example 3);

(e) you lose IS because your child reaches the age of five or you stop being responsible for them;

(f) you lose HB because of moving areas (see example 4); or

(g) you lose a legacy benefit for other reasons.

1.26   But natural migration doesn't occur if the only change in your legacy benefits is that:

(a) you are on WTC and start qualifying for CTC (or vice versa); or

(b) you are on JSA(C)/ESA(C) and start qualifying for JSA(IB)/ESA(IR) (respectively).

Managed migration

1.27   'Managed' migration will occur when the DWP/DFC begins to transfer whole groups of people from legacy benefits to UC. This is expected to begin at some point after April 2019 on an area by area basis. See paras 1.28-30 for how managed migration is likely to affect you.

1.22-23 UCTP 4-8, 10; commencement orders; NIUCTP 3-6, 8

Examples: natural migration to UC

All the examples are claimants who lose legacy benefits, and all take place in UC full service areas (paras 1.24-25).

1. Getting a job

A claimant on JSA(IB). and HB gets a new job working 16 hours per week and this means his JSA(IB) ends.

- In the past he could have claimed WTC but he can no longer do so.
- He claims UC so his HB ends.
- He can't in the future claim any of the legacy benefits.

2. Becoming fit for work

A claimant on ESA(IR), CTC and HB becomes fit for work and this means her ESA(IR) ends..

- In the past she could have claimed JSA(I but she can no longer do so.
- She claims UC so her CTC and HB also end.
- She can't in the future claim any of the legacy benefits.

3. Losing a job

A claimant on WTC, CTC and HB loses his job this means his WTC ends.

- In the past he could have claimed JSA(IB), ESA(IR) or IS (depending on his circumstances) but he can no longer do so.
- He claims UC so his CTC and HB also end.
- He can also claim JSA(C) or ESA(C) (depending on his circumstances) (para 1.18).
- He can't in the future claim any of the legacy benefits.

4. Moving home to a new job

A claimant on HB moves to a new area and this means his HB ends.

- In the past she could have claimed HB in the new area but she can no longer do so.
- She claims UC so if she is on any other legacy benefits they also end.
- She can't in the future claim any legacy benefits.

How migration affects you

1.28   When you migrate to UC, this means that:

(a) you can claim UC now or in the future; but

(b) you can't claim any of the legacy benefits now or in the future (except HB for specified supported or temporary accommodation: para 1.32).

The law does this by saying that the legacy benefits are 'abolished' for you.

1.28-30 UCTP 4-8,8A,10; commencement orders; NIUCTP 3-6, 8

1.29   Migrating to UC can make you better off. One example is that if you have a working non-dependant, UC is reduced by a lower figure than HB is (para 9.61). But it can make you worse off. One example is that HB, JSA(IB), ESA(IR) and IS include additions (such as the severe disability premium) that don't have an equivalent in UC. Managed migration (para 1.27) is expected to have some kind of transitional protection to help compensate for these losses, but natural migration (paras 1.24-25) has no transitional protection.

The date of migration

1.30   Whenever you claim UC (for any reason), any legacy benefits you are getting end on the day before your UC starts (para 3.27). But when you become a couple with someone already on UC, they end on the day before the start of your first assessment period as a couple (para 3.39). For HB, see also paras 1.31-33.

HB run on

1.31   If you make a claim for UC while you are on HB, you can get two weeks' extra HB overlapping with the beginning of your UC. For the details see the *Guide to Housing Benefit*.

HB for specified supported and temporary accommodation

1.32   You can claim (or continue to receive) HB for 'specified supported accommodation' or 'temporary accommodation' while you are on UC. In this case your UC is awarded only for your living costs. For the details see paras 4.11-14 and table 4.2.

State pension credit

1.33   Once the introduction of UC is completed, the government plans to transfer help with rent for pension age claimants from HB to state pension credit. The planned 'housing credit' of SPC is likely to be similar to the UC housing costs element. (See also paras 2.10-11 and 8.47.)

Using this guide

1.34   The UC and CTR rules in this guide apply from April 2017. For UC changes during 2017 and 2018, see table 1.3.

UC and CTR benefit figures

1.35   The UC figures in this guide apply from 6th or 9th April 2018 (see table 1.3) and the CTR figures apply from 1st April 2018. Many figures aren't increased this year, and the government plans to freeze most working age benefits until April 2020.

UC and CTR terminology

1.36   Table 1.1 summarises the main terms used in this guide, and shows the similarities and the differences between those used in UC and in CTR.

1.31   UCTP 8(2A),8A

Table 1.3 **Summary of UC changes from 2017**

3rd May- 28th Jun 2017 SI 2017/584	Full service commencement in selected postcode areas: see appendix 5 for details
5th Jul- 27th Sep 2017 SI 2017/664	Full service commencement in selected postcode areas: see appendix 5 for details
27th Sep 2017 NISR 2017/190	Start of UC roll out in Northern Ireland. Commencement in selected postcode areas: see appendix 5 for details
19th Jun 2017 SI 2017/689 30th Oct 2017 NISR 2017/219	New disregards relating to compensation payments (para 10.67(d)
4th Oct 2017 SSI 2017/227	New claimants in Scotland can choose to have their UC paid twice-monthly and/or to have their housing costs paid to themselves rather than their landlord (para 12.18)
4th Oct 2017- 24th Jan 2018 SI 2017/952	Full service commencement in selected postcode areas: see appendix 5 for details
3rd Nov 2017 SI 2017/901	Amendments to take account of up-to-date social care law in Wales
10th Nov 2017 SI 2017/1015	Clarification of information the DWP can obtain from pension fund holders (para 3.24) and of time limit for late applications for a revision (para 14.12)
1st Jan 2018 SI 2014/1230	No new claims for UC in live service areas (so new claims are for HB and other legacy benefits). (Determination made by the Minister for Employment on 11th December 2017 under Regulation 4)
26th Jan 2018 SI 2017/1323 NISR 2018/2	Rent officer rules altered to allow for increases in LHA figures in some areas from April 2018. Change to (frozen) LHA rate if it goes down due to a lower 30th percentile figure: it cannot go back up again (whereas previously it could go back up to the 2015 rate)
31st Jan 2018 SSI 2017/436	Rules introduced on 4th October 2017 (above) extended to all claimants in Scotland
7th Feb- 25th Apr 2018 SI 2018/138	Full service commencement in selected postcode areas: see appendix 5 for details

14th Feb 2018 SI 2018/65	Abolition of 'waiting days' which had stopped claimants getting UC for the first seven days of their UC claim (para 3.33). Clarification of rules relating to tax and national insurance contributions (paras 10.21 and 10.29) and when future changes in UC law will take effect (para 11.36).
6th Apr 2018 SI 2018/65 SI 2018/281 NISR 2018/58	Benefits up-rating. Most working rates remain frozen except amounts for disability. Changes to deductions for non-dependants etc
SI 2017/725 SI 2017/111 NISR 2017/176 NISR 2018/66	Help with mortgage interest for out-of-work households in UC, SPC and legacy benefits abolished. Instead claimants will be offered a DWP equity loan to help with these. Transitional rules for existing awards – existing claimants can accept or refuse loan payments (chapter 8)
11th Apr 2018 SI 2018/65 SI 2015/345 8th May 2018 NISR 2018/92	New transitional payment of two weeks further HB for people transferring from HB to UC (para 1.23). Housing costs of UC claimants living in temporary accommodation for homeless people transferred from UC to HB (paras 4.13-14), with related changes to the work allowance (table 10.1) and discretionary housing payments. Housing costs of 18-21 year olds on armed force independence payment can now be met by UC (table 4.7(j)). Foreign state retirement pensions and PPF periodic payments are counted in full as retirement pension income (para 10.34). Changes relating to claimant commitment for students (table 2.4(k)) and assessment periods when UC is backdated in live service areas (para 3.54). New rules in full service areas for 'surplus earnings' and self-employed 'unused losses' (paras 10.12 and 10.29)
2nd May-25th July 2018 SI 2018/532	Full service commencement in full service areas: see appendix 5 for details
6th Dec 2018 SI 2017/1015 SI 2017/1187	Various consequential changes arising from state pension credit age rising to age 65

Planned changes

2018	All areas are expected to be UC full service areas by the end of December 2018: see appendix 5 for details. When this is complete, HB (except as described below) and other legacy benefits will no longer be available to new working age claimants (paras 1.19-22)

2018-19	Claimants whose home is specified supported accommodation or temporary accommodation for homeless people (paras 4.11-14) can continue to get HB while they are on UC. This is expected to end in or after 2019, when housing costs in this accommodation are likely to be included in UC with top-up funds (to reflect the higher costs) administered by local authorities in England and national governments in Scotland, Wales and Northern Ireland. (The precise arrangements may differ from those described here and will follow after consultation)
2019-22	People of working age who are still on HB and other legacy benefits are expected to be transferred to UC, probably on an area by area basis, with transitional protection against losses
Later	The possible transfer of pension age claimants from HB to SPC, with SPC meeting housing costs in a similar way to UC (called 'housing credit')

Abbreviations and footnotes

1.37   The tables at the front of this guide give:

(a) a list of abbreviations used in the text; and

(b) a key to the abbreviations used in the footnotes.

1.38   The footnotes throughout this guide refer to UC and CTR law (see paras 1.39 and 1.41). All the references are to the law as amended. CTR law is different in England, Scotland and Wales – the footnotes give the law for England (except where the paragraph relates only to Scotland or Wales). The equivalent footnotes for the law in Scotland and Wales are in appendix 4.

Law and guidance

UC law

1.39   The law governing the UC scheme is in the Welfare Reform Act 2012 (in Great Britain), and the Welfare Reform (Northern Ireland) Order SI 2015/2006 (which is made under the powers in the Northern Ireland (Welfare Reform) Act 2015). The regulations and orders giving the details of the UC scheme are listed in appendix 1. These are called statutory instruments in Great Britain (SIs) and statutory rules in Northern Ireland (NISRs). The main ones are the Universal Credit Regulations SI 2013/376 (in Great Britain), and the Universal Credit Regulations (Northern Ireland) NISR 2016/216.

1.39-43 UC regulations with amendments: www.gov.uk/government/policies/simplifying-the-welfare-system-and-making-sure-work-pays/
supporting-pages/welfare-reform-act-2012-regulations
All other UC and CTR legislation: www.legislation.gov.uk
UC guidance: www.gov.uk/government/publications/advice-for-decision-making-staff-guide
CTR guidance (England): www.gov.uk/government/collections/localising-council-tax-support

UC guidance

1.40   Government guidance on the UC scheme in Great Britain is the responsibility of the DWP and is contained in its Advice for Decision Makers (ADM). The DWP also issues UC circulars to local councils which you can obtain.

CTR law

1.41   The Act of Parliament governing the CTR schemes is the Local Government Finance Act 1992 (as amended by the Local Government Finance Act 2012). The regulations and orders giving the details of the schemes are listed in appendix 1. They are called statutory instruments (SIs). The main ones are the six Council Tax Reduction Regulations listed there.

CTR guidance

1.42   Government guidance on the CTR scheme is the responsibility of the DCLG (Department of Communities and Local Government) in England, and of the Scottish and Welsh Governments.

Obtaining the law and guidance

1.43   The Acts, regulations, orders and government guidance are available online [www].

Case law

1.44   'Case law' means decisions of courts and Upper Tribunals which interpret the law. These set a precedent and are binding on DWP, DFC and local authority decision makers, and First-tier Tribunals. There is little case law about UC or CTR themselves. The cases referred to in this guide are usually about HB or other benefit law, and are relevant because of similarities with UC or CTR law. Most Upper Tribunal decisions are available online [www]. For further details about how decisions should be made, see chapter 1 of the *Guide to Housing Benefit*.

1.44   www.osscsc.gov.uk/aspx/default.aspx (decisions before January 2016)
        www.gov.uk/administrative-appeals-tribunal-decisions (decisions from January 2016)

Chapter 2 **Who can get universal credit**

- General rules: see paras 2.1-4.
- Entitlement to UC: see paras 2.5-8.
- Age limits: see paras 2.9-17.
- Students: see paras 2.18-25.
- Presence in the UK: see paras 2.26-32.
- Migrants, prisoners, hospital detainees and religious orders: see paras 2.33-39.
- The claimant commitment: see paras 2.40-44.

General rules

2.1   You can only get universal credit (UC) if:

(a) you meet the basic and financial conditions; and

(b) you make a claim and meet the transitional conditions.

Basic conditions

2.2   The basic conditions for getting UC relate to your personal circumstances. The details are in this chapter: see table 2.1 for the main rules.

Financial conditions

2.3   The financial conditions for getting UC are:

(a) your capital must not be over £16,000; and

(b) your income must be low enough for you to qualify.

The details are in chapter 9.

Claims and transitional conditions

2.4   To get UC you must make a claim: see chapter 3. While UC is being introduced there are also transitional conditions. In general terms:

(a) anyone in a UC 'full service' area can claim UC (unless you have more than two children/young persons: para 9.22);

(b) people in a UC 'live service' area cannot currently claim UC;

(c) but once you are on UC you can usually continue to get it even if you move, etc.

The details are in paras 1.13-22.

Table 2.1 **Basic conditions for UC**

If you are single	You must meet all the basic conditions:
	(a) you must be under state pension credit age
	(b) you must be aged 16 or more
	(c) if you are aged 16 or 17 you must be in an eligible group (see table 2.2)
	(d) if you are a student you must be in an eligible group (see table 2.3)
	(e) you must in most cases be in the UK (see para 2.26)
	(f) you must not be an excluded migrant (see para 2.34)
	(g) you must not be a prisoner, hospital detainee or member of a religious order (but for single prisoners' housing costs see paras 4.80-81)
	(h) you must accept a claimant commitment if required to do so
If you are in a couple	You can get UC as a couple if:
	▪ you both meet all the basic conditions or
	▪ you both meet them all except that (only) one of you does not meet condition (a) or (d)
	You can get UC as a single person if:
	▪ you meet all the basic conditions and
	▪ your partner meets them all apart from condition (c), (e), (f) or (g)

Entitlement to UC

2.5   You can get UC as a single person or as a couple. Table 2.1 summarises the rules. For whether you count as a 'single person' or a 'couple' see paras 3.57-69. For polygamous marriages see paras 3.70-71.

UC for single people

2.6   To get UC as a single person you must meet all the basic and financial conditions (see table 2.1 and chapter 9). You count as single if you are the only person in your benefit unit or if you are a lone parent (paras 3.57-58).

T2.1   WRA 4; UC 3(2),(3), Part 2; NIWRO 9; NIUC 3(1),(2), Part 2

2.5   WRA 1(1),(2); NIWRO 6(1),(2)

2.6   WRA 2(1)(a), 3(1); NIWRO 7(1)(a), 8(1)

UC for couples

2.7   To get UC as a couple (or 'joint claimants') you must:

(a) both meet all the basic conditions (see table 2.1); or

(b) both meet all those conditions except that (only) one of you is:

■ over state pension credit age, or

■ an excluded migrant.

And you must jointly meet the financial conditions (see chapter 9).

In a couple but claiming UC as a single person

2.8   If you are in a couple you can get UC as a single person if:

(a) you both meet all the basic conditions; except that

(b) your partner (but not you) is:

■ a 16/17 year old who is not in an eligible group, or

■ not in the UK, or

■ an excluded migrant, or

■ a prisoner, hospital detainee or member of a religious order.

And you must jointly meet the financial conditions (see chapter 9).

Age limits

2.9   This section gives the UC basic conditions relating to age, including the maximum age, minimum age and the rules for 16/17 year olds. (For 18-21 year olds' housing costs, see para 4.84.)

Maximum age

2.10   To get UC you must be under state pension credit age ('SPC age') or if you are in a couple at least one of you must be under SPC age. During the year from 6th March 2018 to 6th March 2019, SPC age is gradually rising from 64½ to 65¼. Appendix 3 gives the precise date you reach SPC age.

2.11   If you are over SPC age (or are in a couple and at least one of you is) you can get SPC instead of UC (para 1.33).

Minimum age

2.12   To get UC you must have reached the minimum age. This means you must be:

(a) aged 18 or more; or

(b) aged 16 or 17 and in an eligible group (see para 2.14).

2.7   WRA 2(1)(b), 3(2); UC 3(2); NIWRO 7(1)(b), 8(2); NIUC 3(1)

2.8   WRA 2(2), 3(1); UC 3(3); NIWRO 7(2), 8(1); NIUC 3(2)

2.10   WRA 4(1)(b),(4); UC 3(2)(a); NIWRO 9(1)(b),(4); NIUC 3(1)(a)

2.12   WRA 4(1)(a),(3); NIWRO 9(1)(a),(3)

2.13   If you are in a couple you can get UC if at least one of you meets condition (a) or (b) in para 2.12. If you meet condition (a) or (b) but your partner is a 16/17 year old who is not in an eligible group, you can get UC as a single person (see para 2.8).

16/17 year olds

2.14   If you are aged 16 or 17, you can get UC if you fall within one (or more) of the eligible groups in table 2.2.

Table 2.2 **16/17 year olds: the UC eligible groups**

All 16/17 year olds including care leavers	(a) You have a limited capability for work and meet the LCW (or LCWRA) condition (see para 9.26), or are waiting for an assessment about this and a registered medical practitioner has stated you are not fit for work
	(b) You are responsible for a child, or your partner (if you are in a couple) is responsible for a child or young person
Only 16/17 year olds who are not care leavers	(c) You are pregnant and it is no more than 11 weeks before your expected date of confinement, or you were pregnant and it is no more than 15 weeks after your baby's birth (including a still-birth after 24 weeks of pregnancy)
	(d) You meet the conditions for a carer element, or would do so except that you share your caring responsibilities with someone who gets the carer element instead of you (see para 9.35)
	(e) You are without parental support and are not being looked after by a local authority

Care leavers

2.15   You count as a 'care leaver' if you used to be looked after by a local authority and responsibility for supporting you continues to belong to them. If you are a 16/17 year old care leaver you can get UC if you fall within group (a) or (b) in table 2.2 (but if you live in a 'full service' area you cannot get a UC housing costs elements towards your rent until you are 18: see para 4.84).

Looked after by a local authority

2.16   You count as being 'looked after by a local authority' if you are in local authority care.

2.13   UC 3(3)(a); NIUC 3(2)(a)

2.14   UC 8; NIUC 8

T2.2   UC 8, 30; NIUC 8, 31

2.15   UC 8(2),(4); NIUC 8(2),(4)

2.16   UC 2 definition: 'looked after by a local authority'; NIUC 2

Without parental support

2.17   You count as being 'without parental support' if you:

(a) have no parent or guardian (i.e. someone acting in the place of your parent); or

(b) cannot live with them because:

■ you are estranged from them, or

■ there is a serious risk to your physical or mental health or of significant harm to you if you did; or

(c) are living away from them, and they cannot support you financially because they:

■ have a physical or mental impairment, or

■ are detained in custody, or

■ are prohibited from entering or re-entering the UK.

If you are without parental support you can get UC even if you are a 16/17 year old or a student in non-advanced education (see tables 2.2 and 2.3).

Students

2.18   This section gives the UC basic conditions for students. The law refers to people who are 'receiving education' but in this guide we use 'students' to mean the same thing.

Who is a student

2.19   You are a student if you are undertaking:

(a) non-advanced education (or have recently left): see paras 2.20-21; or

(b) full-time advanced or funded education: see paras 2.22-23; or

(c) any other course which is not compatible with your claimant commitment: see para 2.24.

For whether you can get UC as a student, see para 2.25.

Non-advanced education

2.20   This means education or training which:

(a) you have been enrolled or accepted on; and

(b) is not above GCE A level or equivalent (national standard level 3) [www]; and

(c) is provided at a school or college, or elsewhere if approved by the DWP; and

(d) takes up more than 12 hours per week on average during term-time of tuition, practical work, supervised study or taking examinations; and

(e) is not provided under a contract of employment; and

(f) in the case of training, is approved by the DWP. But this does not include government-sponsored work-preparation training schemes.

2.17   UC 8(1)(g),(3),(4); NIUC 8(1)(g),(3),(4)

2.19   UC 12(1),(1A),(2); NIUC 12(1),(2)

2.20   UC 5(1)(b),(2)-(4), 12(1A),(1B) definition: 'relevant training scheme'; NIUC 6(1)(b),(2)-(4)
        https://www.gov.uk/what-different-qualification-levels-mean

2.21   You count as being in non-advanced education:

(a)   until the 31st August following your 16th birthday (whether or not you have in fact left education); and

(b)   from then until the 31st August following your 19th birthday, but:

■   only while you remain in the education, and

■   if you are 19, only if you were enrolled or accepted on your course before you were 19.

Full-time advanced or funded education

2.22   This means:

(a)   a full-time course of advanced education. It is advanced if it leads to a first or postgraduate degree or comparable qualification, a diploma of higher education or a higher national diploma; or is any other course above GCE A level, advanced GNVQ or higher or advanced Scottish national qualification; or

(b)   any other full-time course of study or training at an educational establishment, for which you get a student loan, grant or award for your maintenance.

2.23   You count as being in this education from the day you start the course to the day it ends or you abandon it or are dismissed from it, including any vacations during that period. The same applies to a full-time module within a modular course, and in this case also includes any vacation after the full-time module but before the end of the course, and any time taken to complete the full-time module or re-take exams relating to it.

Incompatible courses

2.24   This means a course of study that is not compatible with any work-related requirement included in your UC claimant commitment (see para 2.43). You count as being on the course for the period described in para 2.23.

Which students can get UC

2.25   The rules are as follows:

(a)   if you are a single person and you are a student, you cannot get UC unless you fall within one (or more) of the eligible groups in table 2.3;

(b)   if you are in a couple and only one of you is a student, you can get UC (whether or not the student is in an eligible group);

(c)   if you are in a couple and both of you are students, you cannot get UC unless at least one of you falls within one (or more) of the eligible groups in table 2.3.

2.21   UC 5(1),(2); NIUC 6(1),(2)

2.22   UC 12(2),(3), 68(7); NIUC 12(2),(3), 68(7)

2.23   UC 13(1)-(3); NIUC 13(1)-(3)

2.24   UC 12(4); NIUC 12(4)

2.25   WRA4(1)(d),(6); UC 3(2)(b), 13(4), 14; NIWRO 9(1)(d),(6); NIUC 3(1)(b), 13(4), 14

Table 2.3 **Students: the eligible groups**

(a) You are:

  ▪ without parental support (see para 2.17), and

  ▪ aged under 21, or aged 21 and reached that age while on your course, and

  ▪ not in full-time advanced education (para 2.22(a)).

(b) You:

  ▪ are on disability living allowance, personal independence payment or attendance allowance or a benefit equivalent to attendance allowance (para 10.37), and

  ▪ have limited capability for work, or for work and meet the LCW (or LCWRA) condition (see para 9.26).

(c) You or your partner are responsible for a child or young person.

(d) You or your partner are a foster parent and have a child placed with you.

(e) You or your partner have reached state pension credit age.

(f) You took time out of your course with the consent of your educational establishment because you were ill or caring for someone, and have now recovered or are no longer providing the care, but you have not resumed your course and are not eligible for a student loan or grant.

Presence in the UK

2.26   This section gives the UC basic conditions about being in the UK. This means Great Britain (England, Wales and Scotland) or Northern Ireland, but not the Republic of Ireland, the Channel Islands or the Isle of Man.

2.27   To get UC you must be in the UK. This means you must be physically present here. If you are in a couple, and you are in the UK but your partner is not, you can get UC as a single person (see para 2.8). Exceptions to this rule are in paras 2.28-32. See also the rules for migrants in para 2.34.

Crown servants and HM Forces

2.28   You do not have to be in the UK to get UC if you are absent for the following reasons, nor does your partner if they are accompanying you:

(a) you are a Crown servant or member of HM Forces; and

(b) you are posted overseas to perform your duties; and

(c) immediately before you were posted overseas you were habitually resident in the UK.

T2.3   UC 2 definition: 'foster parent', 12(3), 13(4), 14; NIUC 2, 12(3), 13(4), 14

2.27   WRA 4(1)(c); UC 3(3)(b); NIWRO 9(1)(c); NIUC 3(2)(b)

2.28   UC 10; NIUC 10

Temporary absence abroad: first month

2.29   If you are on UC, you can continue to get UC during a temporary absence from the UK of up to one month (so long as it is not expected to exceed one month) whatever the reason for your absence – for example you could be on holiday.

Temporary absence abroad: a death in the family

2.30   You can then continue to get UC for up to one further month during a temporary absence from the UK, if your absence is in connection with the death of:

    (a)   your partner; or

    (b)   a child or young person you or your partner are responsible for; or

    (c)   a close relative (see para 4.45) of you or one of the above.

But this applies only if the DWP considers it would be unreasonable to expect you to return within the first month.

Temporary absence abroad: medical treatment etc

2.31   If you are on UC, you can continue to get UC during a temporary absence from the UK of up to six months (so long as it is not expected to exceed six months) if your absence is solely in connection with you:

    (a)   being treated by (or under the supervision of) a qualified practitioner for an illness or physical or mental impairment; or

    (b)   undergoing convalescence or care which results from treatment for an illness or physical or mental impairment which you had before you left the UK; or

    (c)   accompanying your partner or a child or young person you are responsible for, if their absence is for one of the above reasons.

Temporary absences abroad: mariners etc

2.32   If you are on UC, you can continue to get UC during a temporary absence from the UK of up to six months (so long as it is not expected to exceed six months) if you are:

    (a)   a mariner with a UK contract of employment; or

    (b)   a continental shelf worker in UK, EU or Norwegian waters.

2.29   UC 11(1)(a),(b)(i); NIUC 11(1)(a),(b)(i)

2.30   UC 11(2); NIUC 11(2)

2.31   UC 11(1)(a),(b)(ii),(3),(5); NIUC 11(1)(a),(b)(ii),(3),(5)

2.32   UC 11(1)(a),(b)(ii),(4),(5); NIUC 11(1)(a),(b)(ii),(4),(5)

Special groups

2.33 This section is about the UC basic conditions for migrants, prisoners, hospital detainees and members of religious orders.

Migrants

2.34 Some migrants are eligible for UC and some are excluded from UC. Chapter 22 explains:

(a) who counts as a 'migrant' (for example some returners to the UK are included); and

(b) which migrants are eligible and which are excluded.

2.35 If you are a single person and you are an excluded migrant you cannot get UC. But you can get UC if you are an eligible migrant (or don't count as a migrant).

2.36 The rules for couples are as follows:

(a) if both of you are excluded migrants, you cannot get UC;

(b) if only one of you is an excluded migrant, the other one can get UC as a single person (see para 2.8);

(c) if neither of you are excluded migrants, you can get UC as a couple.

For example, (b) applies if the other one is an eligible migrant (or doesn't count as a migrant); and (c) applies if both of you are eligible migrants (or don't count as migrants).

Prisoners and hospital detainees

2.37 You are a prisoner if you are detained in custody or on temporary release, unless you are serving a sentence of imprisonment detained in hospital, in which case you are a hospital detainee.

2.38 You cannot get UC if you are a prisoner or a hospital detainee. The only exception is if you are single and a prisoner you may be able to get UC for your housing costs for up to six months: see para 4.80. If your partner is a prisoner or a hospital detainee and you are not, you may be able to get UC as a single person (see para 2.8).

Members of religious orders

2.39 You cannot get UC if you are a member of a religious order and are fully maintained by them. If this applies to your partner but not you, you can get UC as a single person (see para 2.8).

2.35-36 WRA 4(1)(c),(5); UC 3(3)(b),(e), 9

2.38 WRA 6(1)(a); UC 2 definition: 'prisoner', 3(3)(c),(d), 19(1)(b),(c),(4); NIWRO 11(1)(a); NIUC 2, 3(2)(c),(d), 19(1)(b),(c),(4)

2.39 WRA 6(1)(a); UC 3(3)(d), 19(1)(a); NIWRO 11(1)(a); NIUC 3(2)(d), 19(1)(a)

The claimant commitment

2.40   Accepting a claimant commitment is one of the UC basic conditions. This section gives a summary of the rules about this. You can get further details of the rules online [www].

Who must accept a claimant commitment

2.41   To get UC you must accept a claimant commitment, or if you are in a couple you both must, unless the DWP considers that:

(a)   you lack the capacity to do so; or

(b)   there are exceptional circumstances which make it unreasonable to expect you to do so.

What a claimant commitment contains

2.42   Your claimant commitment includes your duties in relation to your UC claim (for example to notify changes in your circumstances) and which work-related requirements (if any) you are expected to carry out.

Work-related requirements

2.43   You may be required to carry out one or more of the following 'work-related requirements':

(a)   a work search requirement;

(b)   a work availability requirement;

(c)   a work-focused interview requirement;

(d)   a work preparation requirement.

If you fail to carry out a requirement you may be subject to a sanction and you may or may not be able to get UC hardship payments: see paras 9.75-83.

2.44   You do not have to carry out any work search or work availability requirement if you fall within any of groups (a) to (t) in table 2.4 (but if you fall only within (a)(ii), (b) or (e) to (g), you may have to carry out a work-focused interview or work preparation requirement). If you are claiming UC as a couple, table 2.4 applies separately to each of you.

2.40   www.gov.uk/government/publications/universal-credit-and-your-claimant-commitment-quick-guide

2.41   WRA 4(1)(e),(7); UC 16; NIWRO 9(1)(e),(7); NIUC 16

2.42   WRA 14(1),(4); UC Part 8; NIWRO 19(1),(4); NIUC Part 8

2.43   WRA 14; UC Part 8; NIWRO 19; NIUC Part 8

Table 2.4 **UC work-related requirements: exceptions**

Earnings level, work capability, work preparation, unfit to work	(a) You and/or your partner have earned income (paras 10.7-8) equal to at least:
	
	   (i) the national minimum wage for your expected hours or
	
	   (ii) if lower £78.10 pw (single people) or £124.85 pw (couples)
	
	(b) You have a limited capability for work, and meet the LCW (or LCWRA) condition (see para 9.26)
	
	(c) You are carrying out required or voluntary work preparation and the DWP agrees
	
	(d) The DWP accepts you are unfit for work. This applies for up to two periods of up to 14 days in any 12 months, or for more periods and/or days if the DWP agrees

Children, fostering, adoption, pregnancy *If you are in a couple, (e), (f) and usually (g) can only apply to one of you: you jointly choose which of you this is*	(e) You and/or your partner are responsible for a child under three years old; or (for up to 12 months) for a child under 16 whose parents can't care for them and who would otherwise be likely to go into local authority care (f) You are the foster parent of a child under 16 years old (g) You have adopted a child under 16 years old and it is within 12 months of the date of adoption (or the date 14 days before the expected date of placement if you request the 12 months to begin then), but this does not apply if you are the child's close relative (see para 4.45) or foster parent (h) You are pregnant and it is no more than 11 weeks before your expected date of confinement, or you were pregnant and it is no more than 15 weeks after your baby's birth (including a still-birth after 24 weeks of pregnancy)
Pension age, carers, students, domestic violence	(i) You have reached state pension credit age (j) You meet the conditions for a UC carer element, or would do so except that you share your caring responsibilities with someone who gets the carer element instead of you (see para 9.35), or you do not do so but the DWP agrees you have similar caring responsibilities

T2.4   (a)   UC 6(1A),90, 99(6),(6A); NIUC 7(2), 89, 97(14),(15)   (b)   WRA 19(2)(a), 21(1)(a); NIWRO 24(2)(a), 26(1)(a)
     (c)   UC 99(5)(a); NIUC 97(11)(a)   (d)   UC 99(4),(4ZA),(4ZB),(5)(c); NIUC 97(11)(c)
     (e)   WRA 19(2)(c),(6), 20(1)(a),21(1)(aa); UC 86,91(2)(e),(3);   (f)   UC 2,85,86, 89(1)(f), 91(2)(a)-(d);
          NWRO 24(2)(c),(6), 25(1)(a), 26(5); NIUC 85,90(2)(e),(3),91   NIUC 2,84,85, 88(1)(f), 90(2)(a)-(d)
     (g)   UC 89(1)(d),(3); NIUC 88(1)(d),(3)   (h)   UC 89(1)(c); NIUC 88(1)(c)
     (i)   UC 89(1)(a); NIUC 88(1)(a)   (j)   WRA 19(2)(b); UC 30, 89(1)(b),(2); NIWRO 24(2)(b); NIUC 31, 88(1)(b),(2)

	(k) You are a student and you fall within eligible group (a) in table 2.3, or you have a student loan, grant or award (other than a part-time postgraduate master's degree loan) and fall within any of the groups in that table
	(l) You have been a victim of actual or threatened domestic violence within the past six months from a partner, former partner, or family member you are not (or no longer) living with. A 'family member' includes any close relative (see para 4.45). It also includes a grandparent, grandchild, step-brother/sister or brother/sister-in-law, or if any of them are in a couple, their partner. This applies for 13 weeks from when you notify the DWP about it, but only if it has not applied to you during the previous 12 months. It can apply for a further 13 weeks if you are responsible for a child
Treatment abroad, drug/alcohol programmes, emergencies etc, death in the family	(m) You are temporarily absent from GB in connection with treatment, convalescence or care for you, your partner or a child or young person, and you meet the conditions in para 2.31
	(n) You are in an alcohol or drug dependency treatment programme and have been for no more than six months
	(o) You temporarily have new or increased child care responsibilities (including when a child is affected by death or violence) or are dealing with a domestic emergency, funeral arrangements etc, and the DWP agrees
	(p) Your partner, or a child or young person you or your partner are responsible for, or a child of yours (even if not included in your benefit unit) has died within the past six months
Prisoners, court proceedings, police protection, public duties	(q) You are a prisoner claiming UC for housing costs
	(r) You are attending a court or tribunal as a party to proceedings or witness
	(s) You are receiving police protection and have been for no more than six months
	(t) You are engaged in activities which the DWP agrees amount to a public duty

T2.4   (k) UC 68(7), 89(1)(da),(e); NIUC 68(7), 88(1)(e)   (l) UC 98; NIUC 96
       (m) UC 99(3)(c); NIUC 97(6)(c)   (n) UC 99(3)(e); NIUC 97(6)(e)
       (o) UC 99(4A)-(4C),(5)(b),(5A); NIUC 97(8)-(10),(11)(b),(12) (p) UC 99(3)(d); NIUC 97(6)(d)
       (q) UC 99(3)(b); NIUC 97(6)(b)   (r) UC 99(3)(a); NIUC 97(6)(a)
       (s) UC 99(3)(f); NIUC 97(6)(f)   (t) UC 99(3)(g); NIUC 97(6)(g)

Chapter 3 **UC claims**

- Making a claim: see paras 3.1-11.
- How to claim: see paras 3.12-18.
- Information and evidence: see paras 3.19-26.
- When your UC starts: see paras 3.27-33.
- Decisions, notifications and awards: see paras 3.34-37.
- Assessment periods (and reclaims and reawards): see paras 3.38-49.
- Backdating: see paras 3.50-55.
- Your benefit unit: see paras 3.56-79.
- Non-dependants: see paras 3.80-87.

Making a claim

3.1   You can only get UC if:

   (a) you make a claim for it (see paras 3.2-3); or

   (b) you are treated as having claimed it (see paras 3.4-7 and 3.48-49); or

   (c) someone claims it on your behalf (see paras 3.8-11).

In each case you (or the person claiming on your behalf) must provide appropriate information and evidence.

Claiming as a single person

3.2   You make your claim yourself if:

   (a) you are a single person (see paras 2.6 and 3.57-58); or

   (b) you are in a couple or polygamous marriage and are eligible for UC as a single person (see paras 2.8 and 3.71).

Claiming as a couple (joint claimants)

3.3   You make your claim jointly with your partner if:

   (a) you are a couple (see para 2.7); or

   (b) you are in a polygamous marriage and are eligible for UC as a couple (see para 3.71).

The law also calls you 'joint claimants'.

3.1   AA 1,5; NIAA 1,5

3.2   WRA 2(1)(a),(2); UC 3(3),(4); NIWRO 7(1)(a),(2); NIUC 3(2),(3)

3.3   WRA 2(1)(b),(2); UC 3(4); NIWRO 7(1)(b),(2); NIUC 3(3)

If you should have claimed as a couple or as a single person

3.4   The DWP:

(a)   can treat you as having claimed UC as a couple if:

- you each made a claim as a single person, but
- the DWP decides you are a couple;

(b)   must treat you as having claimed UC as a single person if:

- you made a claim as a couple, but
- you are only eligible for UC as a single person (paras 2.8 and 3.71).

If you become a couple or a single person

3.5   UC continues without you having to make a new claim when:

(a)   you become a couple; and

(b)   you or your partner (or both of you) have been getting UC (either as a single person or as a couple with someone else); and

(c)   you qualify for UC based on your new circumstances.

This also applies when you are a couple but have (until now) only been eligible for UC as a single person (paras 2.8 and 3.71).

3.6   And UC continues without you having to make a new claim when:

(a)   you become a single person; and

(b)   you have been getting UC as a couple; and

(c)   you qualify for UC based on your new circumstances.

This applies whether your relationship has ended or your partner has died. It also applies when you are a couple but are now only eligible as a single person (paras 2.8 and 3.71).

3.7   Paras 3.5-6 apply whether you fall within the 'full service' or 'live service' rules (para 1.14), and for assessment periods in these cases see para 3.40. But if a couple separate it is possible, in live service areas only, that one of the partners may have to make a claim.

If you are unable to act: attorneys, appointees, etc

3.8   The following may act on your behalf in connection with your UC:

(a)   a person who has power of attorney for you;

(b)   a deputy appointed for you by the Court of Protection;

(c)   a receiver appointed for you;

(d)   in Scotland, a judicial factor or any guardian acting or appointed for you.

3.4   C&P 9(1)-(4); NIC&P 8(1)-(4)

3.5-7   C&P 9(6),(8)(a),(10); NIC&P 8(6),(8)(a),(10); SI 2014/2887 reg 5

3.8   General law about incapacity etc

3.9   The DWP can appoint someone to act on your behalf in connection with your UC (known as an 'appointee') if:

(a) they apply in writing to do so (for example in a letter or online); and

(b) unless they are a firm or organisation, they are over 18 years old; and

(c) you do not have an attorney etc (see para 3.8).

They can be someone who already acts on your behalf in connection with HB or a social security benefit.

3.10   Your appointee has all the rights you have in connection with UC, including making a claim, receiving payments, and requesting a reconsideration or appeal. They continue to act on your behalf until:

(a) they resign their appointment. They must give the DWP one month's written notice of this; or

(b) the DWP ends their appointment; or

(c) the DWP is notified that you now have an attorney etc (see para 3.8).

If your partner is unable to act

3.11   If you are claiming UC as a couple and your partner is unable to claim jointly with you, you can make the UC claim yourself on behalf of both of you.

How to claim

3.12   You can make your claim for UC:

(a) online; or

(b) by telephone if the DWP agrees to this.

Once you have submitted a claim you may subsequently be asked to provide evidence to confirm information you have given, to attend an interview, and to agree to conditions set out in a claimant commitment: see paras 2.40-44. In some areas, local councils and other organisations can help with UC claims.

Online claims

3.13   Online claims are made to the DWP [www]. The website tells you what information you should have before you start the claim process. The DWP says that 'you need to allow up to 40 minutes for your online application because you must complete it in one session' [www]. Depending on your circumstances the DWP can provide you with assistance to do this in a DWP office or in your home. Your local council may also be able to help you with claiming UC.

3.9   C&P 2(1) definition: 'writing', 57(1)-(3),(6); UCTP 16; NIC&P 2(1),52(1)-(3),(6); NIUCTP 15

3.10   C&P 57(4),(5),(7),(8); NIC&P 52(4),(5),(7),(8)

3.11   C&P 9(5); NIC&P 8(5)

3.12   C&P 8(1),(2), 35; NIC&P 7(1),(2),34

3.13   C&P 8(1), sch 2; NIC&P 7(1), sch 1
         www.gov.uk/apply-universal-credit

Telephone claims

3.14   The DWP can agree to accept a telephone claim from particular groups of claimants or in individual cases. If you are not able to go online yourself you can contact an adviser on 0845 6000 723 or text phone 0845 6000 743 between 8am and 6pm, Monday to Friday (closed on bank and public holidays). Note that this call is not free and if it 'ends suddenly it is up to you to call back'.

Properly completed claims

3.15   Your claim for UC must be 'properly completed'. If it is an online claim, this means it must be in the approved form and completed in accordance with the instructions. You may also be required to provide appropriate authentication of your identity and other information, and maintain records of your claim. If it is a telephone claim, it is properly completed if you provided all the information during the call needed to decide your claim. See also paras 3.16-17.

Defective claims

3.16   A claim which does not meet the conditions in para 3.15 is called 'defective'. If this applies to you, the DWP must tell you how you can properly complete your claim and what the time limits are for doing so (see para 3.17).

Properly completing a defective claim

3.17   You can properly complete a defective claim as follows:

(a) if it is an online claim, you re-submit the claim with the missing information, etc, now included;

(b) if it is a telephone claim, you need only provide the information, etc, that was missing.

If you do this within one month of when you were first informed that your claim was defective, or longer if the DWP considers it reasonable, your claim counts as having been made on the date you originally made it.

Amending or withdrawing a claim

3.18   Before the DWP decides your claim you can:

(a) amend it: the DWP then decides your claim on the amended basis; or

(b) withdraw it: the DWP then takes no further action on your claim.

You can amend or withdraw a claim by writing to the DWP (online or in a letter, etc), by telephoning them, or in any other way they agree to.

Information and evidence

From you

3.19   The DWP can require you to provide information and evidence in order for it to decide:

(a) whether you are entitled to UC;

(b) whether your entitlement to UC should be changed;

(c) who your UC should be paid to.

If you're in a couple this applies to both of you, even if you are claiming UC as a single person. If you are claiming UC as a couple, information you have given to the DWP can be passed on to your partner.

3.20   The DWP must tell you what information and evidence it requires, and whether you should provide it online, by telephone, by personally attending a DWP office, or in some other way. It must also tell you when you should provide it by. If it is required for a UC claim, the time limit is one month from when the DWP first requested it, or longer if the DWP considers it reasonable.

3.21   UC law does not list what information or evidence you can be asked to provide (except as described in paras 3.23-26). Examples include details about yourself, your partner, your children/young persons, your housing costs, your non-dependants, and your and your partner's income, capital and entitlement to the various UC elements. You also need to provide your rent agreement (para 9.53), your child benefit reference number, and the reference number for your bank, building society, or credit union account (para 12.1).

From third parties

3.22   The DWP can require:

(a) your landlord to provide information and evidence about your rent;

(b) your childcare provider to provide information and evidence relating to the UC childcare costs element (see para 9.43);

(c) a person you are caring for to confirm information relating to the UC carer element (see paras 9.34-35);

(d) a pension fund holder to provide information: see para 3.24;

(e) a rent officer to provide information: see para 3.25.

They have one month to do this, or longer if the DWP considers it reasonable.

National Insurance numbers

3.23   You must provide your NI number and, if you are claiming UC as a couple, your partner's NI number. If you do not know it, you must provide information enabling the DWP to find it out. If you do not have one, you must apply for one.

3.19   C&P 37(1),(2),(4),(5),(8),(9), 38(1),(2),(6); NIC&P 36(1),(2),(4),(5),(8),(9), 37(1),(2),(6)

3.20   C&P 35, 37(3), 38(3); NIC&P 34, 36(3), 37(3)

3.22   C&P 37(6),(7), 38(7),(8); NIC&P 36(6),(7), 37(7),(8)

3.23   AA 1(1A); NIAA 1(1A); C&P 5; NIC&P 5

Pension fund holders

3.24　　If you or your partner:

(a) have a personal or occupational pension scheme; and

(b) are aged 60 or over; and

(c) are not claiming personal independence payment,

the DWP can require you to provide information about the pension scheme, including the name and address of the holder and the policy or reference number. The DWP can then require the pension fund holder to provide information about how much is being paid or could be paid (for example if you have deferred your pension).

Rent officers

3.25　　If you are a social renter, the DWP can refer your rent and/or service charges to the rent officer if these are unreasonably high (see paras 5.21-26). The DWP tells the rent officer your and your landlord's name and address, your rent and/or service charge details, and the number of bedrooms you have. The rent officer can require your landlord to provide information and evidence not obtainable from the DWP.

Income and capital

3.26　　You should provide information about your:

(a) earnings from employment – but only if the DWP can't get the details from HMRC (para 10.22);

(b) earnings from self-employment (para 10.30);

(c) unearned income – but not usually social security benefits (table 10.3);

(d) capital (para 10.53).

If you are in a couple you should provide this information for both of you – even if you are claiming UC as a single person (para 10.3).

When your UC starts

Your first day of entitlement

3.27   The general rule is:

(a) your first day of entitlement to UC is your date of claim (paras 3.28-32);

(b) so your UC starts on your date of claim even though you don't get paid straight away.

Different rules can apply if you claimed before 14th February 2018 (para 3.33), or were on UC within the past six months (paras 3.44-49) or qualify for backdating (para 3.50).

3.28   Your date of claim is the day your UC claim is received (online or by telephone) by the DWP. This includes the day a defective claim is received if you then properly complete it within the time limit (see para 3.17). Paras 3.29-32 give further rules.

If you receive assistance making an online claim

3.29   If you receive assistance making an online claim (see para 3.13), your date of claim is the date you first notified the DWP of your need for assistance.

If the DWP cannot take your telephone claim

3.30   If you telephone the DWP to make a claim but they cannot take your telephone claim until a later date, your date of claim is the day of your first telephone call if the later date is within one month of that.

Advance claims

3.31   If you do not qualify for UC when you claim it but will do so within one month, the date of claim is the day you first qualify. The DWP can agree to apply this rule for particular groups of claimants or in individual cases.

3.32   You can also choose to claim UC from a date in the future, for example if you claim in advance of losing a job or some other event. In this case, your date of claim is the day you are claiming from.

Waiting days for claims made before 14th February 2018

3.33   If your date of claim was before 14th February 2018, there were 'waiting days' that meant your entitlement to UC began seven days after your date of claim. The details and the exceptions are in the 2017-18 edition of this guide.

3.27   C&P 26(1); NIC&P 25(1)

3.28   C&P 10(1)(a),(c),(2); NIC&P 9(1)(a),(c),(2)

3.29   C&P 2(1) definition: 'appropriate office', 10(1)(b); NIC&P 2(1), 9(1)(b)

3.30   C&P 10(1)(d); NIC&P 9(1)(d)

3.31   C&P 32; NIC&P 31

3.32   C&P 10(1); NIC&P 9(1)

Decisions, notifications and awards

Decisions about your UC

3.34   The DWP makes a decision about your UC:

(a) when you claim – about whether you are entitled and (if you are) how much you qualify for and how it will be paid;

(b) when your circumstances change while you are on UC (para 11.5); and

(c) when it changes a wrong decision (para 11.41).

Chapter 11 explains how you can ask for a decision to be changed and chapter 14 explains how you can then go on (in most cases) to make an appeal.

The DWP's notification to you

3.35   The DWP tells you about decisions relating to your UC claim and about any changes it makes to your UC. The law requires this if you have the right of appeal, but in practice the DWP notifies all decisions. It normally notifies you via your online account (para 3.13) but can also do so by telephone (para 3.14) or by post. The time limit that can apply when you ask for a decision to be changed (para 11.53) starts from when the decision is notified. For online notifications, this is said to mean the day the decision becomes available to view.

3.36   The DWP also notifies:

(a) your partner if you are claiming UC as a couple. It does this even if the notification is about sanctions or fraud, but has said it intends to protect sensitive information about your health and similar matters;

(b) your landlord etc if it decides to pay UC to them (para 12.11). It normally does this by post, saying how much they will receive but not what your personal or financial details are.

Awards of UC

3.37   There is no fixed time limit for an award of UC. It continues for each of your assessment periods until you stop being entitled to it. For the rules about when UC changes or ends, see chapter 11; and for reclaims and rewards, see paras 3.45-49.

Assessment periods and the monthly basis of UC

3.38   UC is calculated, awarded and paid for monthly 'assessment periods'. This section explains assessment periods and how the monthly basis of UC may affect you.

Your assessment periods

3.39   UC assessment periods are always one month, but different people's assessment periods begin on different days of the month. Yours depend on when your UC starts (paras 3.27-33):

3.34   SSA 8,10

3.35   D&A 4,51; C&P 38(6), sch 2; NIC&P 37(6), sch 1
        ssac.independent.gov.uk/pdf/uc-pip-decisions-appeals-draft-regs-2012-memorandum.pdf – see annex 2 para 5(b)-(d)

3.37   C&P 36(1); NIC&P 35(1)

(a) your first assessment period begins on the day your UC starts;

(b) after that, your assessment periods begin on the same day of each following month except as shown in table 3.1.

In full service areas (para 1.14), if your UC start date changes (other than due to backdating: paras 3.53-54), the DWP doesn't have to change your assessment periods, but can instead lengthen or shorten the first one as necessary and calculate your UC in it on a daily basis (in the same way as in para 3.55).

Table 3.1 **UC assessment periods**

If your first assessment period starts on the day of the month in column 1, your following assessment periods start on the day of the month in column 2 (a), (b) or (c).

1 – Start of first assessment period	2 – Start of following assessment periods		
	(a) Except February	(b) February not in a leap year	(c) February in a leap year
1st to 28th	Same as 1	Same as 1	Same as 1
29th	29th	27th	28th
30th	30th	27th	28th
31st	Last day (30th or 31st)	28th	29th

Assessment periods when you become a couple or a single person

3.40   Your assessment period periods continue with the same start date each month when you become a couple or a single person (paras 3.5-6). But if you become a couple and both of you were previously getting UC:

(a) under the 'full service' rules (para 1.14) the DWP uses the assessment periods of whichever of you means your UC as a couple starts earlier; and

(b) under the 'live service' rules (para 1.14) you choose whose assessment periods will be used (otherwise the DWP chooses).

The monthly calculation of UC

3.41   The amount of your UC in each assessment period is based on your personal, financial and other circumstances in that assessment period (para 9.2). So when your UC is calculated:

(a) the following are already monthly figures:

- your UC standard allowance and any elements that apply to you (table 9.2), and
- any housing cost contributions that apply (para 9.60);

3.39   WRA 7: 21(1),(2),21A; NIWRO 12: NIUC 22(1)-(3), 22A

T3.1   UC 21(2); NIUC 22(2)

3.40   UC 21(3)-(3B),(3D),(4); SI 2014/2887 reg 5; NIUC 22(4)-(8)

   (b) the following are converted to a monthly figure as necessary:

- your eligible rent and service charge payments (para 9.54), and
- your unearned income (para 10.33);

   (c) but your unearned income is not converted to a monthly figure or averaged out in any way – this applies to:

- employed earnings (para 10.17), and
- self-employed earnings (para 10.24).

See also paras 3.43-44.

Calculating UC when your circumstances change

3.42　Most changes of circumstances after your UC from the beginning of the assessment period in which they take place. Chapter 11 gives the detailed rules, but the main rule is:

   (a) if your circumstances change in a way that means your entitlement to UC increases or reduces or ends;

   (b) then your award of UC (the amount you are paid) is higher or lower or nil from the whole of the assessment period in which that change takes place.

For example, this also applies if you stop meeting the UC basic conditions (chapter 2), or have a change in your personal circumstances that affects your UC (chapter 9), or your rent, service charges, capital, or unearned or earned income goes up or down. See also paras 3.43-44.

How monthly assessment periods can affect you

3.43　In the past, state benefits were usually assessed and paid on a weekly or fortnightly basis. Assessing and paying UC on a monthly basis is a significant change. This 'whole month' approach simplifies the administration of UC, because the DWP doesn't have to deal with a lot of change dates or split changes across the assessment period. It can also affect you financially:

   (a) it can help you if a change that increases your UC takes place near the end of your assessment period, because the increased amount is paid for the whole of the assessment period;

   (b) it may cause you budgeting difficulties if a change that reduces (or ends) your UC takes place near the end of an assessment period, because the reduced amount (or no UC) is paid for the whole of the assessment period.

See examples 2 and 3.

3.44　If you are working, the monthly basis of UC can affect you in another way, by making your earned income seem to vary more than it does (or even seem to vary when it is constant). If you are paid weekly, some assessment periods contain four pay days and some contain five. Because earned income isn't averaged out but is taken into account in the assessment period in which you receive it (para 3.41), your UC is lower in a month with five pay days than in a month with four. Although you shouldn't lose out financially (over a year), some people find this hard to manage. And in some cases, the level of your income may mean you don't qualify for any UC in the months with five pay days. So (in full service areas) you have to reclaim UC after each month this happens (paras 1.14 and 3.45-47). See examples 4 and 5.

Examples: UC assessment periods

1. A claim

Mason claims UC on 5th May 2018 and the DWP decides he qualifies for £375 per month.

- His first assessment period starts on 5th May. He should receive UC of £375 for this assessment period by about 12th June (para 12.2).
- His following assessment periods start on the 5th of each month.

2. A rent increase

Mason's rent goes up on 1st August, and the DWP increases his UC.

- His UC increases for the whole of his assessment period starting on 5th July, and for his following assessment periods.

3. An increase in unearned income

Mason's unearned income increases on 29th October, and the DWP reduces his UC.

- His UC reduces for the whole of his assessment period starting on 5th October, and for his following assessment periods.

4. Weekly earned income

Margaret claims UC on 19th September 2018. She works part-time for net pay of £100 per week which is paid to her each Saturday, She doesn't qualify for a UC work allowance.

- In her first assessment period (beginning 19th September) she has four pay days, so her earned income is £400.
- In her second assessment period (beginning 19th October) she has five pay days, so her earned income is £500.
- In each assessment period with five pay days her earned income is £100 higher, so her UC is £63 lower (para 9.8).

5. Frequent UC reclaims

If the reduction in Margaret's UC reduces her entitlement to nil, then she qualifies for UC only for the assessment periods in which she has four pay days.

- Her UC stops for her second assessment period (beginning 19th October), which has five pay days.
- She has to reclaim UC for her third assessment period (beginning 19th November), which has four pay days.
- Her UC continues for her fourth assessment period (beginning 19th December), which has four pay days.
- Her UC stops for her fifth assessment period (beginning 19th January), which has five pay days.

And so on.

Note:

Margaret doesn't have to reclaim if the live service rules apply to her (paras 1.14 and 3.48-49).

Full service rules: reclaims within six months

3.45　　When the 'full service' rules apply to you (para 1.14), there are special rules about reclaiming within six months of your UC ending. They affect your assessment periods and the amount of your UC: see paras 3.46-47. (If you reclaim UC in any other circumstances, the normal UC rules apply.)

3.46　　Your assessment periods continue with the same start date as when you were last on UC if:

(a) you claim UC within six months of your (or your partner's) UC ending; and

(b) throughout that period, you (or in a couple, at least one of you) met the UC basic conditions (a) to (d), (f) and (g) in table 2.1.

If you are a couple and each of you previously had different assessment periods, the DWP uses the assessment periods of whichever of you means your UC starts earlier.

3.47　　But the amount of your UC is affected if you (or your partner if you are in a couple) stopped receiving earned income (para 10.7) within the six months described in paras 3.46. In this case if:

(a) the date of your UC claim is more than six days after the earned income ended; and

(b) the DWP doesn't consider you have 'good reason' for taking longer to make your claim;

then in your first assessment period you get UC on a daily basis (para 3.55) only from the date of your claim. 'Good reason' isn't defined in UC law, but it isn't confined to the situations in table 3.2. It is possible it will be interpreted in a similar way to 'good cause' (paras 16.34-35).

Live service rules: re-awards within six months

3.48　　When the 'live service' rules apply to you (para 1.14), there are special rules about becoming entitled to UC within six months of your UC ending or being refused. They affect whether you have to make a claim and your assessment periods: see para 3.49. (If you become entitled to UC in any other circumstances, the normal UC rules apply.)

3.49　　The DWP must award you UC without you having to make a claim if:

(a) you were getting UC within the past six months, but it ended because you began to receive earned income or your earned income increased; or

(b) you claimed UC within the past six months, but didn't qualify because of the level of your earned income;

(c) and (in either case) the DWP receives information about your income from you or HMRC (paras 10.22 and 10.30) showing you qualify for UC.

In these cases your UC starts again, and the DWP uses assessment periods with the same start date as when you previously claimed. This rule applies when your earned income (para 10.7) reduces or ends, or when some other change in your circumstances means you now qualify (even if your earned income hasn't changed). See the examples.

3.46　　UC 21(3C),(3D); C&P 26(5); SI 2014/2887 reg 5; NIUC 22(7),(8); NIC&P 25(5)

3.47　　UC 22A, 52; SI 2014/2887 reg 5; NIUC 24, 51

3.49　　UC 21(1),(3), 52; SI 2014/2887 reg 5; NIUC 22(1),(4), 51

Examples: UC reclaims and re-awards when earned income ends

Lesley was awarded UC from 3rd January when she had earned income, and her assessment periods begin on the 3rd of each month. Her UC stopped from 3rd July because her earned income increased. But her earned income ended on 20th November, and she continues to meet the conditions for UC.

If the 'full service' rules apply (paras 3.45-47)

Lesley has to make a new claim for UC.

- If she claims on 24th November (within six days after her earned income ended), she gets a full month's UC for 3rd November to 2nd December.

- If she claims on 28th November (more than six days after her earned income ended) and doesn't have 'good reason' for her delay, she gets five days of UC for 28th November to 2nd December.

- In either case, her assessment periods start on the 3rd of each month.

If the 'live service' rules apply (paras 3.48-49)

Lesley is awarded UC without having to make a claim (so long as she or HMRC provide DWP with details of her income).

- She gets a full month's UC for 3rd November to 2nd December.

- Her assessment periods start on the 3rd of each month.

Backdating

3.50   You can get UC for a period before you claim it if you meet the qualifying conditions in para 3.51. The UC regulations say that the DWP must 'extend the time for claiming' UC if you meet these conditions. In this guide, the term 'backdating' is used to mean the same thing.

Qualifying for backdating

3.51   You qualify for backdating if:

  (a) one or more of the circumstances in table 3.2 applies to you; and

  (b) as a result, you 'could not reasonably have been expected to make the claim earlier'.

If you are claiming UC as a couple, one or more of the circumstances in the table must apply to each of you (and (b) above must apply).

The backdating time limit

3.52   The maximum period for which UC can be backdated is one month. For example, if you claim UC on 25th January, it cannot be backdated before 25th December.

3.50   C&P 26(2); NIC&P 25(2)

3.51   C&P 26(2)(a),(b),(4); NIC&P 25(2)(a),(b),(4)

3.52   C&P 26(2); NIC&P 25(2)

How backdating affects assessment periods

3.53   When your UC is backdated, the DWP can alter the start dates of your assessment periods so that the first one starts on the first day of your backdated UC and the others start on the same day each month (table 3.1).

3.54   Alternatively:

   (a) if the 'full service' rules apply to you (para 1.14), the DWP can lengthen your first assessment period to include the backdated period;

   (b) if the 'live service' rules apply to you (para 1.14), the DWP can assess your UC for the backdated period separately.

The DWP calculates your UC for these periods on a daily basis (para 3.55).

3.55   When UC is calculated on a daily basis (para 3.39 and 3.54):

   (a) work out how much UC you would qualify for if the assessment period was one month;

   (b) multiply the result by 12;

   (c) then divide by 365;

   (d) then multiply by the number of days in the period.

Table 3.2 **Backdating UC: qualifying circumstances**

To qualify for backdating one or more of the following must have meant you could not reasonably have claimed UC earlier.

   (a) You were previously on JSA(IB), JSA(C), ESA(IR), ESA(C), IS, HB, CTC or WTC, and you were not told about the ending of that benefit until after it had ended.

   (b) You have a disability.

   (c) You had an illness that prevented you from making a claim and you have given the DWP medical evidence that confirms this.

   (d) You were unable to make a claim on-line because the official computer system wasn't working.

   (e) You were getting UC as a couple, but are now a single person and the DWP required you to make a claim because the 'live service' rules apply to you (para 3.7).

   (f) You were in a couple and the DWP decided not to award you UC (or ended your UC) because your partner didn't accept the claimant commitment, and you are now making a claim as a single person.

3.53-54   UC 21(1),(2), 21A; SI 2014/2887 reg 5; NIUC 22(1),(2)

T3.2(a)   C&P 26(3)(a), (aa); UCTP 2(1) definition: 'existing benefits', 15(2); NIC&P 25(3)(a); NIUCTP 2(1),14(2)

T3.2(b)-(d) and (f)   C&P 26(3)(b)-(d) and (f)-(g) respectively; NIC&P 25(3)(b)-(f)

T3.2(e)   C&P 26(3)(e); SI 2014/2887 reg 5

UC claims   41

Example: Backdating UC

A single person gets a letter from her local council on 9th February saying her HB will end on 14th February. She is blind, and the friend who normally reads her letters to her is away on holiday from 7th to 21st February. He reads the letter to her on 22nd February. She makes an online claim for UC that day and qualifies for UC. She asks the DWP to backdate her UC.

The DWP's decision

The DWP agrees that from 9th February she meets the conditions for qualifying for backdated UC (see para 3.51) as follows.

Qualifying circumstances

Her circumstances do not fall within (a) in table 3.2, because the council notified her before her HB ended. But they do fall within (b) in the table, because she has a disability.

Ability to claim earlier

Her blindness, and the unavailability of her friend, meant she could not reasonably have been expected to claim UC earlier.

Your benefit unit

3.56 This section explains who is included in your 'benefit unit'. Your entitlement to UC is based on this (see para 9.4)

Single people

3.57 For UC purposes you are a 'single person' if you are not in a couple.

3.58 If you are a single person, your benefit unit is:

(a) you; and

(b) any children or young persons you are responsible for.

Couples

3.59 For UC purposes you are a 'couple' if you are two people who are members of the same household (see para 3.62) and are:

(a) a married couple (of opposite sexes or the same sex) or civil partners (of the same sex); or

(b) living together as a married couple or civil partners (see para 3.64).

3.60 If you are in a couple and are claiming UC as a couple (see para 2.7), your benefit unit is:

(a) both of you; and

(b) any children or young persons either (or both) of you are responsible for.

3.57   WRA 40; NIWRO 46
3.58   WRA 1(2)(a), 9(1)(a), 10(1); NIWRO 6(2)(a), 14(1)(a), 15(1)
3.59   WRA 39, 40; UC 2 definition: 'partner'; NIWRO 45, 46; NIUC 2
3.60   WRA 1(2)(b), 9(1)(b), 10(1); NIWRO 6(2)(b), 14(1)(b), 15(1)

3.61   If you are in a couple but claiming UC as a single person (see para 2.8), your benefit unit is:

(a) you; and

(b) any children or young persons you are responsible for.

Members of the same household

3.62   You are only a couple for UC purposes if you are members of the same household. (This applies to married couples and civil partners as well as couples who are living together: [2014] UKUT 186 (AAC).) You are not a couple if you:

(a) live in different dwellings and maintain them as separate homes (R(SB) 4/83); or

(b) live in the same dwelling but lead separate lives rather than living as one household (CIS/072/1994).

And you cannot be a member of two (or more) households at the same time (R(SB) 8/85).

3.63   A 'household' generally means a domestic arrangement involving two or more people who live together as a unit (R(IS) 1/99), even when they have a reasonable level of independence and self-sufficiency (R(SB) 8/85). It requires a settled course of daily living rather than visits from time to time (R(F) 2/81). So if you keep your eating, cooking, food storage, finances (including paying your housing costs), living space and family life separate you are unlikely to be members of the same household.

Living together

3.64   If you are not married or in a civil partnership you are only a couple for UC purposes if you are living together as though you were. This means considering:

(a) your purpose in living together (Crake and Butterworth v the Supplementary Benefit Commission); and

(b) if your purpose is unclear, your relationship and living arrangements.

3.65   What matters is your relationship as a whole (R(SB) 17/81) taking account of the following factors (Crake case and [2013] UKUT 505 (AAC)):

(a) whether you share the same household;

(b) the stability of your relationship;

(c) your financial arrangement;

(d) whether you have a sexual relationship;

(e) whether you share responsibility for a child;

(f) whether you publicly acknowledge you are a couple;

(g) the emotional element of your relationship.

The last two points were emphasised in [2014] UKUT 17 (AAC), which held that 'a committed loving relationship must be established and publicly acknowledged'.

3.61   WRA 1(2)(a), 2(2), 9(1)(a), 10(1); NIWRO 6(2)(a), 2(2), 14(1)(a), 15(1)

3.62   WRA 39(1)(a),(c); NIWRO 45(1)(a),(c)

3.64   WRA 39(1)(b),(d),(2); NIWRO 45(1)(b),(d),(2); Crake and Butterworth v SBC 21/07/80 QBD 1982 1 ALL ER 498

3.66   There are many reasons why two people might live in the same household or same dwelling. They might be a couple. But they might be landlord/lady and lodger, house sharers, etc. Even living together for reasons of 'care, companionship and mutual convenience' does not by itself mean you are a couple (R(SB) 35/85).

Ending a relationship

3.67   If you were a couple but your relationship has ended, your shared understanding that it has ended and your actual living arrangement are more important than any shared responsibilities and financial arrangements you still have (CIS/72/1994). But if you remain married or in a civil partnership, a shared understanding may not be enough by itself to show you are no longer a couple (CIS/2900/1998).

If your partner is temporarily absent

3.68   If your partner is temporarily absent from your household you continue to count as a couple, unless their absence exceeds or is expected to exceed six months.

3.69   This means you stop counting as a couple if and when your partner:

(a)   decides not to return or decides to be absent for more than six months (whether they decide this at the beginning of the absence or during it); or

(b)   has been absent for six months

For absences outside the UK see paras 2.28-32.

Polygamous marriages

3.70   For UC purposes you are in a 'polygamous marriage' if you or your husband or wife are married to more than one person under the laws of a country which permits polygamy.

3.71   The members of the polygamous marriage who live in your household can get UC as follows:

(a)   the two who were married earliest count as a couple;

(b)   each other person in the marriage counts as a single person.

The earlier rules about entitlement to UC and the benefit unit then apply: see paras 2.6-8 and 3.56-61.

Children and young persons

3.72   Your benefit unit includes the children and young persons:

(a)   you are responsible for, if you are:

■   a single person, or

■   in a couple but claiming UC as a single person;

(b)   you or your partner are responsible for, if you are:

■   in a couple and claiming UC as a couple.

3.68   UC 3(6); NIUC 3(5)

3.70   UC 3(5); NIUC 3(4)

3.71   UC 3(4); NIUC 3(3)

3.72   WRA 10(1); NIWRO 15(1)

3.73   A 'child' means someone under the age of 16.

3.74   A 'young person' means someone aged 16 or more but under 20 (other than your partner) who:

    (a)   is in non-advanced education (see paras 2.20-21); and

    (b)   is not on UC, ESA, JSA, HB, CTC or WTC.

Responsibility for a child or young person

3.75   For UC purposes you are responsible for a child or young person if he or she:

    (a)   normally lives with you (see paras 3.76-77); and

    (b)   is not being looked after by a local authority (see para 3.78); and

    (c)   is not a prisoner (see para 4.79).

3.76   Whether a child or young person 'normally lives with you' is a question of fact and is usually straightforward. For example they could be your son or daughter, adopted by you, a step-child, a grandchild or any other child or young person (whether related to you or not), so long as they normally live with you.

3.77   A child or young person can only be the responsibility of one single person or couple at any one time. If they normally live with two or more single persons or couples, they are the responsibility of the single person or couple with the main responsibility. You can choose ('nominate') who this is to be. But the DWP makes the choice instead if:

    (a)   you do not choose or cannot agree; or

    (b)   your choice does not reflect the arrangements between you.

If a child or young person is in local authority care

3.78   A child or young person is not included in your benefit unit if they are being 'looked after by a local authority' (this means in local authority care) unless this is for a planned short-term break to give you time off from caring for them, or one of a series of such breaks.

If a child or young person is temporarily absent

3.79   If a child or young person you are responsible for is temporarily absent from your household they continue to be included in your benefit unit, unless their absence exceeds or is expected to exceed:

    (a)   six months if they remain in Great Britain during the absence;

    (b)   one month if they are outside Great Britain;

    (c)   one further month if they remain outside Great Britain and this is in connection with the death of their close relative (see para 4.45) and it would be unreasonable for them to be expected to return within the first month;

3.73   WRA 40; NIWRO 46

3.74   WRA 10(5); UC 4(3), 5(1),(5); UCTP 28; NIWRO 15(5); NIUC 4(3), 5(1),(5)

3.75   UC 4(1),(2),(6); NIUC 4(1),(2),(6)

3.77   UC 4(4),(5); NIUC 4(4),(5)

3.78   UC 2 definition: 'looked after by a local authority', 4(6), 4A; NIUC 2, 4(6), 5

3.79   UC 4(7); NIUC 4(7)

(d) six months if they are outside Great Britain in connection with treatment, convalescence or care which meets the conditions in para 2.31.

Non-dependants

3.80   This section explains who counts as a non-dependant. If you are a renter and have one or more non-dependants living with you, this can affect the amount of UC you get for your housing costs: see paras 7.8 and 9.58.

Who is a non-dependant

3.81   A 'non-dependant' is anyone who:

(a) normally lives in the accommodation with you; and

(b) is not in any of the groups in table 3.3.

For example, a non-dependant is usually an adult son, daughter, other relative or friend who lives with you on a non-commercial basis, whether they are single or in a couple.

'Normally living in the accommodation with you'

3.82   To count as a non-dependant a person must 'normally live in the accommodation with you'. For example:

(a) someone who shares essential living accommodation with you, even if you each have your own bedroom, is likely to count as 'living with you' (CH/542/2006, CH/3656/2005, though the HB regulations in these cases have a different wording); but

(b) a short-term visitor does not count as 'normally' living with you. Nor does someone you take in temporarily because they have nowhere else to go (CH/4004/2004), though this may change as time goes by (CH/3935/2007).

Non-dependants and children/young persons

3.83   A child or young person (see paras 3.73-74) never counts as a non-dependant, whether you, your partner, anyone else or no-one is responsible for them. The only exception is that a child or young person of a non-dependant counts as a non-dependant (and this can be relevant to the size criteria: see para 7.14).

Non-dependants and lodgers

3.84   If you have a lodger who pays you rent on a commercial basis, the lodger does not count as a non-dependant.

3.85   The difference between a lodger and a non-dependant is as follows:

(a) a lodger is someone who makes payments to you on a commercial basis (see table 4.4(a));

(b) a non-dependant may or may not pay their way. If they do pay you, it is on a non-commercial basis.

3.81   UC sch 4 paras 3, 9(1),(2); NIUC sch 4 paras 3, 8(1),(2)

3.83   UC sch 4 para 9(1)(b),(2)(a),(c),(g); NIUC sch 4 para 8(1)(b),(2)(a),(c),(g)

3.84   UC sch 4 para 9(2)(d); NIUC sch 4 para 8(2)(d)

Table 3.3 **People who are not non-dependants**

(a) You and your partner, whether you are claiming UC as a couple or as a single person.

(b) Any child or young person (see para 3.83).

(c) A foster child placed with you or your partner.

(d) A resident landlord/landlady and members of their household.

(e) Anyone who is liable to make payments on a commercial basis on the accommodation including:

- a lodger of yours (see paras 3.84-85)

- a joint tenant of yours (if you rent your accommodation jointly) (see para 3.86)

- a separate tenant of your landlord's (if your accommodation is rented out in separate lettings).

(f) A non-dependant of anyone described in (e) above (see para 3.87).

Non-dependants and joint tenants

3.86　　If you rent your accommodation jointly, your joint tenants are not your non-dependants. For example, if two sisters, a father and son, three friends (and so on) are joint tenants, they are not non-dependants of each other.

3.87　　If you jointly rent your accommodation and there is also a non-dependant living there, the non-dependant is included in the UC claim of only one of the joint tenants, as follows:

(a) the non-dependant may normally live with only one of the joint tenants. In that case, they are included in the UC claim of only that joint tenant;

(b) the non-dependant may normally live with more than one of the joint tenants. In that case, once they have been included in the UC claim of one joint tenant they are not included in the UC claim of any of the others.

T3.3　　UC sch 4 paras 3, 9; NIUC sch 4 paras 3, 8

3.86　　UC sch 4 para 9(2)(d); NIUC sch 4 para 8(2)(d)

3.87　　UC sch 4 para 9(2)(f); NIUC sch 4 para 8(2)(f)

Chapter 4 **UC for housing costs**

- Summary of housing costs: UC and loans: see paras 4.1-4.
- Rent, owner-occupier and service charge payments: see paras 4.5-32.
- Liability for housing costs: see paras 4.33-36.
- People who are treated as liable or not liable: see paras 4.37-58.
- Occupying a dwelling as a home: see paras 4.59-62.
- Moving home, having two homes and temporary absences: see paras 4.63-77.
- Prisoners, care leavers and 18-21 year olds: see paras 4.78-86.

Summary of housing costs

4.1 This chapter explains the help you can get with your housing costs while you are on UC. It includes:

(a) the UC housing costs element for rent and service charges; and

(b) DWP loan payments for mortgage interest or related costs.

The rules in this chapter apply from the 6th April 2018. Before then, mortgage interest or related costs could be met by the UC housing costs element. If you were on UC before 6th April 2018, see paras 8.50-55.

The main conditions

4.2 To get a housing costs element or DWP loan payments (paras 4.3-4) you must satisfy all the following conditions:

(a) the payment condition, which says which payments can be met for your dwelling. See table 4.1 and paras 4.5-32;

(b) the liability condition, which says you must be liable for these payments. In some cases you can count as liable even if you are not, or count as not liable even though you are. See paras 4.33-58;

(c) the occupation condition, which says you must occupy the dwelling as your home. In some cases you can get a housing costs element or DWP loan on two homes or during a temporary absence. See paras 4.59-77.

For prisoners, care leavers and 18-21 year olds, see also paras 4.78-86.

Table 4.1 **The housing costs UC can meet**

Rent payments

Renters and shared owners can get help with:

- rent under a tenancy
- rent under a licence or permission to occupy
- houseboat mooring charges
- caravan or mobile home site charges
- payments to charitable almshouses

Owner-occupier payments

Owner-occupiers and shared owners can get a DWP loan towards:

- loan interest payments
- alternative finance payments

Service charge payments

Renters, owner-occupiers and shared owners can get help with service charge payments.

Exceptions

You can't get UC (or a DWP loan) towards:

- a bail or probation hostel
- specified supported or temporary accommodation where HB can be paid instead
- a care home
- a tent or its site
- ground rent

The UC housing costs element

4.3   The UC 'housing costs element' can help you with:

  (a) your rent payments (paras 4.5-16); and/or

  (b) your service charge payments (paras 4.23-32).

If you qualify, the housing costs element is included in the calculation of your UC. The result of the calculation may be that you get all, some or none of your rent or service charges met by UC. If you don't qualify, your UC is calculated without a housing costs element. The calculations are explained in chapter 9.

T4.1   UC 26, sch 1 paras 1-3,7; LMI 3, sch 1 para 5; NIUC 27, sch 1 paras 1-8

4.3   UC 25

Loans for mortgage interest

4.4   If you have claimed UC, the DWP can make loan payments to help you with:

(a)   your mortgage interest or interest on other loans secured on your home (para 8.8); and/or

(b)   alternative finance arrangements (para 8.9).

If you qualify, the DWP loan payments are separate from your UC and are repayable: see chapter 8.

Rent payments

4.5   If you are a renter or shared owner you can get UC towards your rent and service charge payments. Chapters 5-7 explain how much of these UC can meet. This section describes which payments count as 'rent payments'. For service charges, see paras 4.23-32.

Tenancies, licences, etc

4.6   Rent, licence payments and payments for permission to occupy all count as rent payments in UC. For example, this includes most social and private rented housing, whether self-contained or shared, and also bed and breakfast, co-operative and Crown lettings.

Houseboats, caravans and mobile homes

4.7   If you live in a houseboat (including a canal narrow boat: CH/4250/2007), caravan or mobile home you can get UC towards your rent payments. Both the following count as rent payments in UC:

(a)   the mooring or site charges (whether you rent or own it);

(b)   the rent (if you rent it).

Charitable almshouses

4.8   If you live in an almshouse provided by a housing association (table 5.1 and para 6.3) which is a registered charity or exempt from registration, you can get UC towards your maintenance contributions there. But different rules apply if your landlord also provides you with support (paras 4.11-14).

Bail, probation and other hostels

4.9   If you live in a bail or probation hostel (also called 'approved premises') you cannot get UC towards your rent or service charge payments there.

4.10   If you live in any other kind of hostel you can get UC towards your housing costs (see para 4.6) unless it is specified supported accommodation.

4.4   LMI 3

4.5   UC 25(2)(a),(c); NIUC 26(2)(a),(c)

4.6   UC sch 1 para 2(a),(b); NIUC sch 1 para 2(a),(b)

4.7   UC sch 1 para 2(c),(d); NIUC sch 1 para 2(c),(d)

4.8   UC sch 1 para 2(e); NIUC sch 1 para 2(e)

4.9   UC sch 1 paras 1,3(c), 7(3)(b)(ii); NIUC sch 1 paras 1,3(c), 8(3)(b)(ii)

4.10   UC sch 1 para 2(a),(b); NIUC sch 1 para 2(a),(b)

Specified supported accommodation

4.11   If you live in 'specified supported accommodation' (called 'specified accommodation' in the law) you cannot get UC towards your rent or service charges there. Instead you can get HB towards these as described in the *Guide to Housing Benefit*.

4.12   Table 4.2 lists all the types of specified supported accommodation. Your landlord should be able to tell you whether your home is included. Sometimes this is not straightforward: for a summary of the case law see the *Guide to Housing Benefit*.

Table 4.2 **Supported accommodation types**

This table lists the types of 'specified supported accommodation' (see para 4.11). In this table 'CSS' means care, support or supervision.

(a) Exempt accommodation[1]

Accommodation provider:[2]

- a housing association, registered or unregistered; or
- a registered charity; or
- a not for profit voluntary organisation; or
- an English county council that doesn't administer HB.

Condition:

- the accommodation provider, or someone on its behalf, provides the claimant with CSS.

(b) General supported accommodation[3]

Accommodation provider:[2]

- a housing association, registered or unregistered; or
- a registered charity; or
- a not for profit voluntary organisation; or
- an English county council that doesn't administer HB.

Conditions:

- the claimant receives CSS from the accommodation provider or someone else; and
- the claimant was admitted into the accommodation in order to meet a need for CSS.

4.11   UC sch 1 para 1 definition: 'exempt accommodation', 3(h), 3A, 7(3)(b)(iv); UCTP 2(1) definition: 'specified accommodation', 5(1)(b), (2)(a); NIUC sch 1 para 1, 3(e), 4, 8(3)(b)(iv)

T4.2   As para 4.11

(c) Domestic violence refuges

Accommodation provider:[2]

- a housing association, registered or unregistered; or
- a registered charity; or
- a not for profit voluntary organisation; or
- an English county council that doesn't administer HB; or
- an authority that administers HB.

Conditions:

- the building (or relevant part of it) is wholly or mainly used as non-permanent accommodation for people who have left their home as a result of domestic violence;[4] and
- the accommodation is provided to the claimant for that reason.

(d) Local authority hostels

Accommodation owner/manager:

- the building must be owned or managed by an authority which administers HB.

Conditions:

- the claimant receives CSS from the accommodation provider or someone else; and
- the building provides non-self-contained domestic accommodation with meals or adequate food-preparation facilities (and is not a care home or independent hospital).

Notes

1. *Exempt accommodation:* This also includes resettlement places where the provider was previously getting a grant for the provision or maintenance of such accommodation under s30 of the Jobseekers Act 1995.

2. *Accommodation provider:* In exempt accommodation this must be the tenant's immediate landlord, and this is likely to be the case in types (b) and (c).

3. *General supported accommodation:* This differs from exempt accommodation in two main ways:
   - the CSS can be provided or commissioned independently of the landlord;
   - the claimant must have been 'admitted' into the accommodation in order to receive CSS.

4. *Domestic violence:* This is defined as including controlling or coercive behaviour, violence, or psychological, physical, sexual, emotional, financial or other abuse, regardless of the gender or sexuality of the victim.

Temporary accommodation

4.13   Since 11th April 2018, if you live in 'temporary accommodation' you cannot get UC towards your rent or service charges there. Instead you can get HB towards these as described in the *Guide to Housing Benefit*. But if you were on UC on 10th April 2018 and it included a housing costs element towards temporary accommodation on that day, your UC continues to include this (and you can't get HB instead) until the amount of your rent or service charge payments changes or you stop qualifying for a housing costs element.

4.14   'Temporary accommodation' means accommodation that you rent from a social landlord that was provided to you:

(a)   under part 7 of the Housing Act 1996, or part 2 of the Housing (Scotland) Act 1987, or part 2 of the Housing (Northern Ireland) Order 1988, because you were homeless; or

(b)   under the same legislation to prevent you from becoming homeless.

And it counts as 'temporary' regardless of how long you live in it.

Care homes etc

4.15   If you live in a care home (in Scotland a care home service) or independent hospital you cannot get UC towards your rent or service charge payments there.

Tents

4.16   If you live in a tent or similar moveable structure you cannot get UC towards your rent or service charge payments for the tent or its site.

Owner-occupier payments

4.17   If you are an owner-occupier or shared owner, you can get a DWP loan towards your owner occupier payments: see paras 4.19-22. Chapter 8 gives the full details and explains how much of these payments the loan can meet.

4.18   You can get UC towards your service charge payments (owner-occupiers and shared owners) and rent payments (shared owners only): see paras 4.5-16.

Loan interest payments

4.19   You can get DWP loan payments towards the interest on a loan secured on your home. This could be a mortgage or a similar loan from a bank or building society or any other organisation or individual (para 8.8).

Alternative finance payments

4.20   You can get DWP loan payments towards the cost of 'alternative finance arrangements' you entered into to purchase your home. These are typically schemes designed to avoid the payment of interest (para 8.9 and table 8.2).

4.13   UC sch 1 paras 1, 3B; UCTP 2(1) 'temporary accommodation', 5(1)(b),(2)(a); SI 2018/65 reg 8; NIUC sch 1 paras 1, 3(d), 8(3)(b)(iii)

4.15   UC sch 1 paras 1,3(d),7(3)(b)(iii); NIUC sch 1 paras 1,3(d), 8(3)(b)(iii)

4.16   UC sch 1 paras 1, 3(b), 7(3)(b)(i); NIUC sch 1 paras 1, 3(b), 8(3)(b)(i)

4.18   UC 25(2)(c); NIUC 26(2)(b),(c)

4.19-20 LMI sch 1 para 5; NILMI sch 1 para 5

Crofts and croft land

4.21   If you live in a croft in Scotland, you can get help towards your housing costs on the croft and on any associated land. This means a DWP loan towards owner-occupier payments and/or UC towards rent and service charge payments.

Ground rent

4.22   You can't get UC (or a DWP loan) towards any ground rent you pay on your home.

Service charge payments

4.23   This section describes which payments count as 'service charge payments' in UC. It applies whether you are a renter, owner-occupier or shared owner. It also applies if you only pay service charges.

Definition

4.24   For UC purposes:

(a)   services means 'services or facilities for the use or benefit of persons occupying accommodation'; and

(b)   'service charge payments' means:

   ▪ payments for all or part of the costs or charges relating to services or facilities, or

   ▪ amounts which are fairly attributable to the costs or charges relating to available services or facilities.

4.25   Payments which meet the above definition are service charge payments whether they are:

(a)   named in an agreement or not;

(b)   paid in with the other payments you make on your home or separately;

(c)   paid under the agreement under which you occupy your home or under a separate agreement.

Service charges and renters

4.26   If you are a renter you can get UC towards your service charge payments as well as your rent payments. But you cannot get help with these if you live in a bail or probation hostel, specified supported accommodation, care home or tent (see paras 4.9-16).

4.27   If you are a social renter the distinction between rent and service charge payments is important as not all service charge payments can be included in your eligible rent (see paras 5.9 and 5.27). It is the law which decides whether a particular payment you make is rent or

---

4.21   UC sch 3 para 2; LMI sch 3 para 12(3)

4.22   UC sch 1 para 3(a); NIUC sch 1 para 3(a)

4.24   UC sch 1 para 7(1)(a),(b),(2); NIUC sch 1 para 8(1)(a),(b),(2)

4.25   UC sch 1 para 7(4) ; NIUC sch 1 para 8(4)

4.26   UC 26(2)(b), sch 1 para 7(3)(b), sch 4 para 3; NIUC 27(2)(b), sch 1 para 8(3)(b), sch 4 para 3

4.27   UC sch 1 para 3(g), 8(7), sch 4 paras 3,31; NIUC sch 1 para 3(g), 9(7), sch 4 paras 3,30

Guide to Universal Credit 2018-19

service charge, not your landlord or your letting agreement ([2009] UKUT 28 AAC, CH/3528/2006). For example, a landlord's normal overheads (such as maintenance, insurance, management costs, council tax and charges for voids in certain types of accommodation) count as rent, not services.

4.28 If you are a private renter, your rent and service charge payments are combined together in the calculation of your eligible rent, so the distinction between them is less important (see para 6.10).

Service charges and owner-occupiers

4.29 If you are an owner-occupier you can get UC towards your service charge payments as well as a DWP loan towards your owner-occupier payments (see paras 5.27 and 8.10). The distinction between them is important as not all service charge payments can be included in your eligible housing costs (see paras 5.27 and 8.10).

4.30 If you have taken out a loan for your service charge payments, the interest on the loan counts as an owner-occupier payment (see para 4.19), not a service charge payment.

Service charges and shared owners

4.31 If you are a shared owner you can get UC towards your rent and service charge payments (see para 5.27) as well as a DWP loan towards your owner-occupier payments.

Service charges only cases

4.32 You can get UC towards your service charge payments (see para 5.27) even if you are not liable for owner-occupier or rent payments. This could apply if you own your home outright, live in a charitable almshouse where only service charges are payable, etc.

Liability for housing costs

4.33 To get UC for your housing costs you must be liable for rent or service charge payments, and to get DWP loan payments you must be liable for owner-occupier payments. In each case:

(a) if you are single, you yourself must be liable for them;

(b) if you are in a couple, either of you or both of you jointly must be liable.

4.34 You are 'liable' for rent, owner-occupier or service charge payments if you are:

(a) actually liable to pay them on a commercial basis (see paras 4.35-36); or

(b) 'treated as liable' to pay them (see paras 4.37-42).

But you cannot get UC for housing costs or DWP loan payments if you are 'treated as not liable' to pay them (see paras 4.43-58).

4.28   UC sch 1 para 3(g), sch 4 para 3; NIUC sch 1 para 3(g), sch 4 para 3

4.29   UC 26(3)(b)(i), sch 1 paras 4(2), 7(1)(c), 8(7), sch 5 para 3; NIUC 27(3)(b)(i), sch 1 paras 5(2), 8(1)(c), 9(7), sch 5 para 3

4.30   UC sch 1 para 7(3)(a); NIUC sch 1 para 8(3)(a)

4.31   UC 26(4),(5), sch 4 para 3; NIUC 27(4),(5), sch 4 para 3

4.32   UC 26(3)(b)(ii), sch 5 para 3; NIUC 27(3)(b)(ii), sch 5 para 3

4.33   UC 25(3); LMI 3(2)(b), sch 2 para 5(1); NIUC 26(3)

Liability

4.35   You are liable to make payments if you have a legal obligation or duty to pay them, whether you are:

   (a)   solely liable for them; or

   (b)   jointly liable with your partner; or

   (c)   jointly liable with others.

If you are an owner-occupier this should be in your loan and/or service charge agreement and is usually straightforward. If you are a renter, see table 4.3.

Table 4.3 **Liability of renters**

   (a)   *Your letting agreement:* Although letting agreements are often in writing, an agreement by word of mouth can be sufficient to create a liability (R v Poole BC ex parte Ross).

   (b)   *Your landlord's circumstances:* To grant a letting and create a liability your landlord must have a sufficient legal interest in the dwelling (e.g. as an owner or tenant), but there can be exceptions (CH/2959/2006).

   (c)   *Your circumstances:* If you already have the right to occupy your home (e.g. as a joint owner) no-one can grant you a letting on it (e.g. another joint owner) so you cannot be liable.

   (d)   *If you are under 18 or unable to act:* If you have someone appointed to act for you they can enter a letting for you thus making you liable. If you do not and you are incapable of understanding an agreement you entered, the agreement may be void under Scottish law ([2011] UKHT 354 AAC) but not English and Welsh law (CH/2121/2006, ([2012] UKUT 12 AAC). If it is void, you are not liable.

   (e)   *Arrears, etc:* If you have arrears (even large arrears) or are paying less rent than your agreement says (whether or not your landlord has agreed to this), this does not by itself mean you are not liable ([2010] UKUT 43 AAC). But very large arrears would normally lead a landlord to end a letting, so they may suggest you are not liable (CH/1849/2007).

   (f)   *If your letting breaks your landlord's occupation agreement:* If by granting your letting your landlord has broken their own occupation agreement on your dwelling (e.g. because it says they must not rent it out), your own letting agreement is still valid so you are liable (Governors of Peabody Donation Fund v Higgins) until and unless your landlord's right to occupy is terminated.

   (g)   *If your landlord breaks the law:* If by granting your letting your landlord has committed a criminal offence (e.g. because a Housing Act prohibition order bans them from renting out your home), your letting agreement is unlikely to be valid and you are unlikely to be liable.

T4.3   R v Poole BC ex parte Ross 05/05/95 QBD 28 HLR 351
             The Governors of Peabody Donation Fund v Higgins 20/06/83 CA [1983] 1 WLR 1091

Commerciality

4.36 Whether your liability is on a commercial basis is a question of fact and judgment based on your individual circumstances. If you are an owner-occupier this is usually straight-forward. If you are a renter see table 4.4.

Table 4.4 **Commerciality and renters**

(a) *What makes a letting commercial:* Not only the financial arrangements between you and your landlord but all the terms of your agreement should be taken into account (R v Sutton LBC ex parte Partridge). Each case must be considered on its individual facts and is a matter of judgment (R(H) 1/03). The arrangements between you should be 'arms length' (R v Sheffield HBRB ex part Smith). It is their true factual basis which matters. If these show your letting is 'truly personal' it is not commercial regardless of what is written in your letting agreement (CH/3282/2006).

(b) *Personal and religious considerations:* If your letting is in fact commercial, friendliness and kindness between you and your landlord does not make it non-commercial (R v Poole BC ex parte Ross, CH/4854/2003, [2009] UKUT 13 AAC). If your letting is non-commercial, the fact that it was drawn up in a way that meets your religious beliefs does not make it commercial (R(H) 8/04).

(c) *Lettings between family members:* A letting between family members may or may not be commercial. The family arrangement is not decisive by itself. If the letting enables a disabled family member to be cared for more easily, this is not decisive by itself. Each case depends on its individual circumstances (CH/296/2004, CH/1096/2008, CH/2491/2007).

(d) *If the circumstances of your letting change:* If your letting was commercial when it began, it can become non-commercial if there is an identifiable reason for this (CH/3497/2005).

Treated as liable

4.37 If you are treated as liable to make rent, owner-occupier or service charge payments, you can get UC or DWP loan payments towards them in the same way as if you were actually liable. This section gives the rules about this.

T4.4   R v Sutton LBC ex p Partridge 04/11/94 QBD 28 HLR 315; R v Sheffield HBRB ex p Smith 08/12/94 QBD 28 HLR 36;
         R (Ross) v Poole BC see footnote T4.3

4.37   UC 25(3)(a)(ii); LMI sch 2 para 5(2); NIUC 26(3)(a)(ii); NILMI sch 2 para 5(2)

If a partner, child or young person is liable

4.38   You are treated as liable if:

(a) you are in a couple but claiming UC as a single person (see para 2.8) and your partner (not you) is liable (for other couple cases see para 4.33); or

(b) you are single or in a couple and a child or young person is liable. This means a child or young person you are responsible for or your partner (even if they are not included in your UC claim) is responsible for.

This rule does not apply if you are in a polygamous marriage.

When the liable person is not paying

4.39   You are treated as liable if:

(a) the person who is actually liable is not making the payments (whether they are an individual, a company or some other body: R(H) 5/05); and

(b) you have to make the payments in order to continue occupying your home; and

(c) it would be unreasonable in the circumstances to expect you to make other arrangements; and

(d) it is reasonable in all the circumstances to treat you as liable. In the case of owner-occupier payments, what is 'reasonable' can be affected by the fact that the liable person may benefit if their housing costs are paid.

4.40   If you meet the above conditions, this rule may help you if (for example) your partner was liable to make the payments and has died, left you, or is absent for too long to get UC or DWP loan payments for them (see paras 4.74-81). But if the liable person cannot pay because they have been treated as not liable for the housing costs (see paras 4.43-58) it may not be 'reasonable' for you to be treated as liable (CH/606/2005).

When payments are waived in return for repair works

4.41   You are treated as liable for payments if the person they are due to has allowed you not to pay them as reasonable compensation for reasonable repairs or redecorations you have done (and which otherwise they would or should have done).

Rent free periods

4.42   If you are a renter, you are treated as liable for rent and/or service charge payments during any rent free periods allowed under your letting agreement (see para 9.56 for how this is calculated).

4.38   UC sch 2 para 1; LMI sch 2 para 5(1),(2)(a),(3); NIUC sch 2 para 1; NILMI sch 2 para 5(1),(2)(a)

4.39   UC sch 2 para 2; LMI sch 2 para 5(2)(b); NIUC sch 2 para 2; NILMI sch 2 para 5(2)(b)

4.41   UC sch 2 para 3; LMI sch 2 para 5(2)(c); NIUC sch 2 para 3; NILMI sch 2 para 5(2)(c)

4.42   UC sch 2 para 4, sch 4 para 7(4); NIUC sch 2 para 4, sch 4 para 6(5)

Treated as not liable

4.43   If you are treated as not liable to make rent, owner-occupier or service charge payments, you cannot get UC or DWP loan payments towards them. This section gives the rules about this.

Related to you

4.44   Some of the following rules refer to people who are related to you. This means:

(a) your partner, whether you are claiming UC with them or as a single person; or

(b) a child you or your partner are responsible for; or

(c) a young person you or your partner are responsible for; or

(d) a close relative (see para 4.45) of you, or of any of the above, who lives in the accommodation with you (see para 4.46).

Close relative

4.45   A close relative means:

(a) a parent, step-parent or parent-in-law; or

(b) a brother or sister, including a half-brother or half-sister (R(SB) 22/87) but not a step-brother or step-sister; or

(c) a daughter, son, step-daughter, step-son, daughter-in-law or son-in-law; or

(d) if any of the above is in a couple, their partner.

Living in the accommodation with you

4.46   Some of the rules in this section refer to a person who 'lives in the accommodation' with you. This is likely to include any arrangement in which they share some essential living accommodation with you, even if you each have your own bedroom (CH/542/2006, CH/3656/2004, though the HB regulations in these cases had a different wording).

Renters with a resident landlord who is related to you

4.47   You are treated as not liable to make rent payments (and so cannot get UC towards them) if they are due to a landlord who:

(a) is related to you (see para 4.44); and

(b) lives in the accommodation with you (see para 4.46).

If this applies to you, you are also treated as not liable to make service charge payments due to that landlord.

4.43   UC 25(3)(b); LMI sch 2 para 6; NIUC 26(3)(b)

4.44   UC sch 2 paras 5(1), 6(1), 7(1); NIUC sch 2 paras 5(1), 6(1), 7(1)

4.45   UC 2 definition: 'close relative'; NIUC 2

4.47   UC sch 2 para 5; NIUC sch 2 para 5

Renters whose landlord is a company connected with you

4.48 You are treated as not liable to make rent payments (and so cannot get UC towards them) if they are due to a company and:

(a) you are an owner or director of the company; or

(b) at least one of its owners or directors is related to you (see para 4.44 (a), (c) and (d)).

If this applies to you, you are also treated as not liable to make service charge payments due to that company or another company which meets the above conditions.

4.49 This rule is likely to apply only to registered companies. Details of these and their directors can be checked online with Companies House [www].

4.50 An 'owner' of a company is defined in detailed terms based on company law. In broad terms it means someone who has at least 10% of the shares in, or otherwise has significant control of, the company or a parent company, whether alone or with or through associates.

Renters whose landlord is a trust connected with you

4.51 You are treated as not liable to make rent payments (and so cannot get UC towards them) if they are due to a trustee of a trust and:

(a) you are a trustee or beneficiary of the trust; or

(b) at least one of its trustees or beneficiaries is related to you (see para 4.44)

If this applies to you, you are also treated as not liable to make service charge payments due to a trustee of that trust or another trust which meets the above conditions.

4.52 A trust is an arrangement whereby the legal ownership of property, money, etc, is separated from its benefits (such as the right to live in it or receive income). Ownership (title) is held by the 'trustees' who ensure that its benefits are delivered for use by someone else, the 'beneficiary'.

Owners etc whose liability is to a household member

4.53 You are treated as not liable to make owner-occupier payments (and so cannot get DWP loan payments towards them) if they are due to someone who lives in your household. If this applies to you, you are also treated as not liable to make service charge payments due to that person.

4.54 If you are liable for service charge payments only (see para 4.32), you are treated as not liable if they are due to someone who lives in your household.

4.55 A 'household' generally means a domestic arrangement involving two or more people who live together as a unit (R(IS) 1/99), even when they have a reasonable level of independence and self-sufficiency (R(SB) 8/85). It requires a settled course of daily living rather than visits from time to time (R(F) 2/81).

4.48   UC sch 2 para 6(1),(2); NIUC sch 2 para 6(1),(2)

4.49   www.gov.uk/get-information-about-a-company

4.50   UC sch 2 para 6(3)-(8); NIUC sch 2 para 6(3)-(8)

4.51   UC sch 2 para 7; NIUC sch 2 para 7

4.53   UC sch 2 para 8(1),(2); LMI sch 2 para 6(a); NIUC sch 2 para 8(1),(2)

4.54   UC sch 2 para 8(3); NIUC sch 2 para 8(3)

Renters, owners, etc: increases to recover arrears

4.56   If your rent, owner-occupier or service charge payments have been increased in order to recover arrears or other charges on your current or former home, you are treated as not liable for the amount of that increase (and so cannot get UC or DWP loan payments towards it). This applies only to increases to recover your own arrears or charges, not when increases are imposed across-the-board to recover arrears and charges generally.

Renters, owners, etc: contrived liability

4.57   You are treated as not liable to make rent, owner-occupier or service charge payments (and so cannot get UC or DWP loan payments towards them) if the DWP is satisfied that your liability 'was contrived in order to secure the inclusion of the housing costs element in an award of universal credit or to increase the amount of that element' (but only when the other rules in this section do not apply).

4.58   This can only apply if there is evidence that you and/or someone else (such as your landlord or mortgage lender) have 'contrived' your liability as a way of gaining UC or DWP loan payments. This is different from saying you are not 'liable' for housing costs (see para 4.35), though in practice the two things can be hard to distinguish. If you are a renter, see table 4.5.

Table 4.5 **Contrived liability and renters**

(a) *What makes a letting contrived:* You must be liable for rent but the liability must have been contrived as a way of gaining UC. The word 'contrived' implies abuse of the UC scheme (CH/39/2007). There must be evidence of this (R v Solihull HBRB ex parte Simpson), and the circumstances and intentions of both you and your landlord should be taken into account (R v Sutton HBRB ex parte Keegan).

(b) *No liability vs contrived liability:* These are separate considerations and should not be confused (CSHB/718/2002). If your landlord is unlikely to evict you if you do not pay, this can be evidence that you are not liable (see table 4.3(e)) or that your liability is contrived (Solihull case).

(c) *Lettings between family members:* If your landlord is a relation of yours (e.g. your parent) this does not by itself mean your letting is contrived (Solihull case). But see para 4.47 and table 4.4(c) for other rules which may affect you.

(d) *Lettings to people on low incomes:* If you cannot afford your rent, this is not evidence that your letting is contrived (Solihull case). And there is no objection to landlords letting to people on low incomes in order to make a profit unless their charges and profits show abuse (CH/39/2007, R v Manchester CC ex parte Baragrove Properties).

4.56   UC sch 2 para 9; LMI sch 2 para 6(b); NIUC sch 2 para 9

4.57   UC sch 2 para 10; LMI sch 2 para 6(c); NIUC sch 2 para 10

T4.5   R (Simpson) v Solihull HBRB 03/12/93 QBD 26 HLR 370; R (Keegan) v Sutton HBRB 15/05/92 QBD 27 HLR 92;
        R (Baragrove Properties) v Manchester CC 15/03/91 QBD 23 HLR 337

Occupying a dwelling as your home

4.59　　You can get a UC housing costs element or DWP loan payments towards the dwelling you normally occupy as your home: see paras 4.60-62.

A dwelling

4.60　　A 'dwelling' has the same meaning as in council tax law (para 15.4). It can be a house, flat, etc, or a houseboat or mobile home used for domestic purposes. It must be in Great Britain.

Normally occupied as your home

4.61　　Whether you 'normally occupy' a dwelling as your 'home' is a question of fact which is decided in your individual circumstances, and is not restricted to where your 'centre of interests' is (CH/1786/2005). It usually means more than simply being liable for housing costs: it means being physically present – though exceptions can arise (R(H) 9/05). However, accommodation you occupy only for a holiday cannot be a home and is not included.

4.62　　If you occupy more than one dwelling, the question of which one you normally occupy as your home is decided by having regard to 'all the circumstances… including (among other things) any persons with whom [you occupy] each dwelling'. For example, if you are a couple and one of you occupies one home with children at school nearby, and the other is temporarily occupying another home to be near work, the first is likely to be your normal home.

Moving home and having two homes

4.63　　This section explains how your UC housing costs element or DWP loan payments can be affected when you move home and when you have two homes. See paras 11.23-24 for when your UC changes, and paras 8.35-36 for loan payments.

Fear of violence

4.64　　The rules in paras 4.65-66 apply to you if:

(a)　you have left your normal home and are occupying other accommodation; and

(b)　it is unreasonable to expect you to return to your normal home because you have a reasonable fear of violence in your normal home or from a former partner, whether that violence would be towards yourself, your partner, or a child or young person you are responsible for (see para 4.67); but

(c)　you intend to return to your normal home (see para 4.68).

4.59　　UC 25(4), sch 3 para 1; LMI 3(2)(c), sch 3 para 1; NIUC 26(4), sch 3 para 1

4.60　　WRA 11(2); UC sch 3 para 1(4); LMI 2(1); NIWRO 16(2); NIUC sch 3 para 1(4)

4.61　　UC sch 3 para 1(1); LMI sch 3 para 12(1); NIUC sch 3 para 1(1)

4.62　　UC sch 3 para 1(3); LMI sch 3 para 12(2); NIUC sch 3 para 1(3)

4.64　　UC sch 3 para 6(1); LMI sch 3 para 15(1); NIUC sch 3 para 6(1)

4.65   If you meet the conditions in para 4.64, and are liable to make payments (as a renter or owner-occupier) on both your normal home and the other accommodation, you can – if it is reasonable – get a UC housing costs element or DWP loan payments covering both dwellings for a maximum of 12 months. For the amount, see table 4.6. If one of the addresses is in 'specified supported accommodation' (see paras 4.11-12), a similar rule allows you to get HB for that address while you are getting a UC housing costs element for the other one.

4.66   If you meet the conditions in para 4.64, and are liable to make payments (as a renter or owner-occupier) on only one dwelling (whether this is your normal home or the other accommodation), you can – if it is reasonable – get a UC housing costs element or DWP loan payments for only that one, unless your absence exceeds or is expected to exceed 12 months: see paras 4.74-77.

4.67   You do not need to have suffered actual violence for the rules in paras 4.64-66 to apply. You need only have a reasonable fear that it may occur. If the fear is of violence in your normal home, it could be from anyone whether or not they are related to you. If the fear is of violence outside your normal home, it must be from a former partner. You do not need to have formally ended the relationship with them, but they must no longer count as your 'partner' for UC purposes (see para 3.59). In each case, the fear of violence must be such that it is unreasonable to expect you to return to your normal home.

4.68   However, you must have an intention to return to your normal home. This can include an intention to return when it becomes safe to do so. If at any point you decide not to return, you can from that point get a UC housing costs element or DWP loan payments only on what is now your normal home – which is likely to be the dwelling you are currently occupying.

Waiting for adaptations for a disability

4.69   You can get a UC housing costs element or DWP loan payments for a maximum of one month before you move into a new home if:

(a) you, your partner, or a child or young person you are responsible for is getting:

   ▪ the daily living component of PIP, or

   ▪ the middle or highest rate of the care component of DLA, or

   ▪ attendance allowance (or equivalent benefit: para 10.37); and

(b) the delay in moving was necessary to enable your new home to be adapted to meet that person's disablement needs, and was reasonable; and

(c) you were liable to make payments on your new home (as a renter or owner-occupier) during that period.

The adaptations can include furnishing, carpeting or decorating as well as structural changes, provided that the change makes it more suitable for the needs of the disabled person: R (Mahmoudi) v Lewisham LBC.

4.65   UC sch 3 paras 6(2),(4), 9(3); LMI sch 3 para 15(2),(4);
         reg 7(6)(a)(i) of SI 2006/213 The Housing Benefit Regulations 2006; NIUC sch 3 paras 5(2),(4), 8(3)

4.66   UC sch 3 para 6(3); LMI sch 3 para 15(3); NIUC sch 3 para 5(3)

4.69   UC sch 3 para 7; LMI sch 3 para 14; NIUC sch 3 para 6; R (Mahmoudi) v Lewisham CA (2014)
         www.bailii.org/ew/cases/EWCA/Civ/2014/284.html

4.70 If you meet the conditions in para 4.69, and were also getting a UC housing costs element or DWP loan payments on your old home, you can get a UC housing costs element or DWP loan payments covering both dwellings for a maximum of one month. See also table 4.6.

Table 4.6 **Calculating a UC housing costs element for two homes**

Fear of violence and waiting for adaptations (see paras 4.65 and 4.70)

(a) Calculate the UC housing costs element separately for each dwelling in the normal way (see chapter 9), making any deductions for housing costs contributions applicable in each case.

(b) Add the two amounts together.

(c) If deductions for housing costs contributions were made for both dwellings, add back to figure (b) the deductions made for:

- the accommodation which is not your normal home, in fear of violence cases;

- your new home, in waiting for adaptations cases.

Large families housed in two dwellings (see para 4.73)

(a) Calculate the UC housing costs element as if the two dwellings were one dwelling by:

- adding together the two eligible rents;

- adding together the two lots of bedrooms;

- making any deductions for housing cost contributions only once.

(b) If the rent on both dwellings is due to a social landlord (see para 5.4), and neither is temporary accommodation (see para 5.5), make the calculations in (a) using the rules in chapter 5.

(c) In all other cases, make the calculations in (a) using the rules in chapter 6.

Leaving hospital or a care home

4.71 You can get a UC housing costs element or DWP loan payments on a new home for a maximum of one month before you move into it if:

(a) you have now moved in; and

(b) you were liable to make payments on it (as a renter or owner-occupier) during that period; and

(c) you were in a hospital (or similar institution) or a care home when the liability to make those payments arose. If you are in a couple, this must apply to both of you.

4.70   UC sch 3 para 5; LMI sch 3 para 16; NIUC sch 3 para 4

T4.6   UC sch 4 paras 17-19, 25(3),(4); NIUC sch 4 paras 16-18, 24(3),(4)

4.71   UC sch 3 para 8; LMI sch 3 para 17; NIUC sch 3 para 7

Moving out for repairs to be done

4.72　If you are required to leave your normal home because essential repairs are being done to it, and you intend to return there afterwards, you can get a UC housing costs element or DWP loan payments towards only one dwelling:

(a)　if you are liable to make payments (as a renter or owner-occupier) on only one dwelling (whether this is your normal home or the other accommodation), you can get a UC housing costs element or DWP loan payments for only that one;

(b)　if you are liable to make payments (as a renter or owner-occupier) on both dwellings, you can get a UC housing costs element or DWP loan payments only for your normal home.

Large families housed in two dwellings

4.73　You can get a UC housing costs element covering two dwellings (with no time limit) if:

(a)　you were housed in them both by a social landlord (see para 5.4) because of the number of children and young persons living with you; and

(b)　you normally occupy both dwellings with children or young persons; and

(c)　you are liable to make rent payments on both dwellings.

See also table 4.6. (You can't get DWP loan payments on two homes in this situation.)

Temporary absences

4.74　You can get a UC housing costs element or DWP loan payments during a temporary absence from your normal home, unless your absence exceeds or is expected to exceed:

(a)　12 months if the absence is because of fear of violence: see para 4.66;

(b)　six months if the absence is for any other reason. For example, this could be on holiday, to work or look for work, in hospital, trying out a care home, going to care for (or be cared for by) a friend or relative, and so on. For exceptions, see para 4.76.

The six months rule also applies if you are temporarily absent from accommodation which is not your normal home but which you are occupying because of fear of violence (see para 4.64).

4.75　The rules do not apply if you are absent for repairs to be done: in that case, see para 4.72. For prisoners, see paras 4.79-81. For absences from Great Britain, see paras 2.26-32.

When is an absence 'temporary'?

4.76　Whether your absence is 'temporary' is a question of fact. For example, it cannot be temporary if you do not intend to return – nor if it is objectively impossible for you to do so (CSHB/405/2005).

4.72　UC sch 3 para 3; LMI sch 3 para 13; NIUC sch 3 para 2

4.73　UC sch 3 para 4; NIUC sch 3 para 3

4.74-76　UC sch 3 para 9(1),(3); LMI sch 3 para 18; NIUC sch 3 para 8(1),(3)

The length of absence

4.77   When you begin a temporary absence, the question is whether it is 'expected to exceed' the time limit (six months or 12 months: see para 4.74). If it is, no UC housing costs element or DWP loan payments can be awarded. The question is reconsidered as and when your situation changes. If, during your absence, it becomes clear that it will exceed the time limit, your UC housing costs element or DWP loan payments stop. They also stop when your absence reaches the time limit. See paras 4.39-40 for whether someone else may be able to claim during your absence.

Special groups

4.78   This section gives the extra rules for prisoners, care leavers and 18-21 year olds. If you are a renter or shared owner, the rules (in paras 4.79-86) affect your entitlement to a UC housing costs element towards your rent and/or service charges. If you are an owner-occupier or shared owner, they don't stop you getting DWP loan payments towards your owner-occupier payments (chapter 8).

Prisoners

4.79   For UC purposes, you count as a 'prisoner' if you are:

(a) detained in custody – whether pending trial, pending sentence, on conviction, or sentenced by a court; or

(b) on temporary release (also called home leave or ROTL – release on temporary licence).

But you do not count as a 'prisoner' if you are detained in hospital: see para 2.37.

4.80   You can get a UC housing costs element for the first six months that you are a prisoner if:

(a) you were entitled to UC as a single person immediately before you became a prisoner (whether you were actually single, or in a couple but claiming UC as a single person: see para 2.8); and

(b) the calculation of that award of UC included a UC housing costs element; and

(c) you have not been sentenced, or have been sentenced to a term that is not expected to extend beyond six months.

You cannot get UC for anything else while you are a prisoner: see para 2.38. But if you can get UC (even just a housing costs element), you can also get DWP loan payments (para 8.4 and table 8.1).

4.81   The rule in para 4.80 means that you cannot get UC at all if you claim it after you become a prisoner. You can get a UC housing costs element only if you claimed it before you became a prisoner:

4.79   UC 2 definition: 'prisoner'; NIUC 2

4.80   UC 19(1)-(3); NIUC 19(1)-(3)

(a) if you have not been sentenced, you can get this for a maximum of six months (regardless of the possible length of any sentence you may get);

(b) once you are sentenced, the test is whether your term in prison is expected to exceed six months. If it is, your UC housing costs element stops. In considering this any remission you could get must be allowed for. So if your sentence is no longer than one year you are likely to qualify (and your sentence can be longer than this if you are eligible for Home Detention Curfew).

See paras 2.37 and 4.39-40 for whether someone else may be able to claim a UC housing costs element (or DWP loan payments) during your absence.

Care leavers

4.82   You count as a 'care leaver' if you used to be in local authority care and responsibility for supporting you continues to belong to them.

4.83   The following rules apply if you are a care leaver:

(a) if you are aged 16 or 17 and you are liable for rent (see paras 4.33-34):

- you cannot get a UC housing costs element towards your rent or service charge payments,

- but you can get UC (apart from the housing costs element) if you are in group (a) or (b) in table 2.2;

(b) if you are aged 16 or 17 and you are liable for service charges but not rent:

- you can get UC including a housing costs element towards your service charge payments (see para 4.32) if you are in group (a) or (b) in table 2.2;

(c) if you are aged 18 or more:

- you can get UC including a housing costs element towards your rent and/or service charge payments (but see also paras 4.84-86).

And if you can get UC, you can also get DWP loan payments (para 8.4 and table 8.1). See paras 2.12-16 for further details, including the rules for couples.

18-21 year olds

4.84   From a date later in 2018 (yet to be decided at the time of writing), all 18-21 year olds can get a UC housing costs element [www]. But until then there are restrictions (para 4.85), which apply if you:

(a) are aged 18 or over but under 22;

(b) are single, or claiming UC as a single person (paras 2.7-8);

(c) live in a full service area (paras 1.14-15); and

(d) aren't in an eligible group (table 4.7).

4.82   UC 2 definition: 'looked after by a local authority'; NIUC 2

4.83   UC 8(2),(4), 26(3)(b)(ii), sch 4 para 4; NIUC 8(2),(4), 27(3)(b)(ii), sch 4 para 4

4.84-85 WRA 11(1),(5); UC sch 4 paras 1(1),4A-4C
           www.gov.uk/government/news/housing-support-for-young-people

4.85   In these cases:

(a) if you are a renter, you can't get UC towards your rent or service charges, so you don't qualify for a UC housing costs element;

(b) if you are a shared owner, you can't get UC towards your rent or service charges, so you don't qualify for a UC housing costs element, but you can get DWP loan payments towards your owner-occupier payments, (chapter 8);

(c) if you are an owner-occupier, you get DWP loan payments towards your owner-occupier payments, and a UC housing costs element towards your service charge payments (chapter 8).

4.86   If you are in an eligible group (table 4.7), you can get UC towards your rent and service charges and/or DWP loan payments towards your owner-occupier payments (paras 4.2-4).

Table 4.7 **18-21 year olds who can get UC towards rent**

If you are aged 18-21 and are a renter or shared owner, you can get UC towards your rent and service charge payments if you are in one or more of the following eligible groups.

(a) You are claiming UC as a couple (but not if you are in a couple and claiming as a single person: paras 2.7-8).

(b) You are responsible for at least one child or young person (para 3.75).

(c) You have a foster child or adopted child or are pregnant, as described in table 2.4(f) to (g).

(d) You don't fall within the UC 'full service' rules (para 1.14).

(e) You were getting UC with a housing costs element or HB immediately before your UC award begins or before you start to fall within the UC 'full service' rules, and have been getting a UC housing costs element continuously since then.

(f) Your earned income (paras 10.7-8) is at least £94.40 per week (£59.20 if you are an apprentice or £118.08 if you are aged 21) or was at least that amount throughout the past six months. These figures increase whenever the minimum wage increases.

(g) You have limited capability for work or work-related activity (para 9.26).

T4.7(a)   UC sch 4 para 4A(c)

T4.7(b)   UC sch 4 para 4B(1)(a)

T4.7(c)   UC 89(1),(3), 91(2),(3), sch 4 para 4A(b)

T4.7(d)   SI 2017/252 reg 3

T4.7(e)   SI 2017/252 reg 4

T4.7(f)   UC sch 4 para 4C

T4.7(g)   WRA 19(2)(a), 21(1)(a); UC 30, 89(1),(2), sch 4 para 4A(b)

(h) The DWP has decided that you are expected to work less than 35 hours per week, because of your caring responsibilities for a child, a foster child or a person with physical or mental impairment, or because you have a physical or mental impairment.

(i) You are unfit for work, but this only applies for up to two periods of up to 14 days in any 12 months.

(j) You are in receipt of:

- the daily living component of personal independence payment, or

- the middle or highest rate of the care component of disability living allowance, or

- (from 11th April 2018), attendance allowance or the equivalent benefits in para 10.37 (e.g. armed forces independence payment).

(k) You meet the conditions for a UC carer element or the related conditions in table 2.4(j).

(l) You are a student and meet the conditions in table 2.4(k).

(m) You have had actual or threatened domestic violence inflicted on you (at any time) from a partner, former partner or family member. 'Family member' means the same as in table 2.4(l).

(n) You were a care leaver before you reached the age of 18.

(o) You have no parents or neither of your parents has a home in Great Britain.

(p) The DWP agrees it is inappropriate for you to live with your parents, because there would be serious risk to your physical or mental health or you would suffer significant harm if you did, or for other reasons (table 4.8).

(q) Your home is temporary accommodation provided to you because you were homeless or threatened with homelessness (para 5.5).

(r) You are an ex-offender managed under a multi-agency (MAPPA) agreement because you pose a serious risk of harm to the public.

T4.7(h)	UC 85, 86, 88, sch 4 para 4B(1)(f)
T4.7(i)	UC 99(4), sch 4 para 4B(1)(g)
T4.7(j)	UC sch 4 paras 4B(1)(b), 29(5)(a),(c)
T4.7(k)	WRA 19(2)(b); UC 30, 89(1),(2), sch 4 para 4A(b)
T4.7(l)	UC 68(7), 89(1), sch 4 para 4A(b)
T4.7(m)	UC 98(4), sch 4 para 4B(1)(h)
T4.7(n)	UC 8(4), sch 4 paras 4B(1)(b), 29(2)
T4.7(o)	UC sch 4 para 4B(1)(d)
T4.7(p)	UC sch 4 para 4B(1)(e)
T4.7(q)	UC sch 4 para 4B(1)(c)
T4.7(r)	UC sch 4 paras 4B(1)(b), 29(6)-(9)

(s) You meet the conditions relating to:

- treatment abroad: table 2.4(m),
- drug/alcohol programmes: table 2.4(n),
- death in the family: table 2.4(p),
- prisoners: table 2.4(q),
- court proceedings: table 2.4(r),
- police protection: table 2.4(s), or
- public duties: table 2.4(t).

Note:

For guidance on all of the above and in particular if you are homeless or unable to live with parents see DWP ADM memo 6/17 [www].

Table 4.8 **18-21 year olds who cannot live with parents**

The law does not say when it is inappropriate to live with your parents (table 4.7(p)) but some guidance is given in ADM memo 6/17 [www]. The main reasons are given here (and the guidance stresses this list is not exhaustive). The guidance says it is inappropriate to live with your parents if:

(a) Your parents' home is so remote it presents a serious barrier to finding work.

(b) Your parents' home would be overcrowded if you lived there.

(c) You are estranged from your parents as a result of their religion, etc.

(d) You have been asked to leave the family home.

(e) You are a former gang member attempting to withdraw from your involvement in it or you are at risk of threats from it.

(f) You are homeless including if you are a 'sofa surfer', or you are owed a prevention or relief duty by your local council under homelessness legislation.

(g) You are moving on from temporary or supported accommodation.

(h) You are being supported by a third party or your need to live independently is part of an agreed support plan.

(i) You would be at risk of reoffending if you returned to the family home.

T4.7(s)   UC 99(3), sch 4 para 4B(1)(g)

T4.7 note   www.gov.uk/government/publications/advice-for-decision-making-staff-guide

T4.8   https://www.gov.uk/government/publications/advice-for-decision-making-staff-guide

Chapter 5 **Eligible rent: social renters**

- Social renters: see paras 5.1-6.
- The amount of your eligible rent: see paras 5.7-15.
- Reductions for under-occupation: see paras 5.16-20.
- Unreasonably high rents etc: see paras 5.21-26.
- Service charges (for social renters and owner-occupiers): see paras 5.27-33.

Social renters

5.1   This chapter explains how your UC housing costs element is worked out if you are a social renter. For renters, the housing costs element is also called your eligible rent.

5.2   To qualify for a housing costs element you must meet the conditions in chapter 4 as well as this chapter. Chapter 9 explains how your housing costs element affects the amount of your UC, and how it can be reduced if you have one or more non-dependants.

Who is a social renter

5.3   You are a social renter if you are liable to pay rent (with or without service charges) to a social landlord. The rules in this chapter also apply if you are a shared owner (para 8.6) with a social landlord.

Social landlords

5.4   All local authorities and most housing associations and housing trusts are social landlords. The full list is in table 5.1.

Exceptions

5.5   You cannot get UC towards your rent or service charges for:

(a) 'specified supported accommodation' (see paras 4.11-12 and table 4.2); or

(b) 'temporary accommodation' for people who are or were homeless (see paras 4.13-14); or

(c) certain other accommodation (paras 4.9-10 and 4.15-16).

5.6   You may not be able to get UC towards your rent or service charges if you are single and are:

(a) a care leaver aged 16 or 17 (see paras 4.82-83); or

(b) aged 18-21 and don't fall in an eligible group (see paras 4.84-86).

5.3   UC sch 4 para 30; NIUC sch 4 para 29

5.4   UC 2 definition: 'local authority', sch 4 para 2; NIUC sch 4 para 2

Table 5.1 **Social landlords**

All the following are social landlords (in UC law 'a provider of social housing'). If you rent your home from any of them this chapter applies to you.

(a)   Local authorities and public bodies

- in England: county, district and parish councils, London boroughs, the City of London and the council of the Isles of Scilly

- in Wales: county, county borough and community councils

- in Scotland: the council that issues your council tax bill

- in Northern Ireland: the Northern Ireland Housing Executive

(b)   Housing associations, trusts, etc

- in England: registered providers of social housing (i.e. any landlord who is registered with the Homes and Communities Agency: but see note)

- in Wales and Scotland: registered social landlords, i.e. any landlord that is registered with the Scottish or Welsh Government

- in Northern Ireland: a housing association registered with the DFC

Note:

Registered providers of social housing can be profit making or non-profit making. If they are profit making:

- their social housing falls within the rules in this chapter. This means housing let below a market rent (such as part of the Affordable Rent Programme) and shared ownership tenancies;

- their other housing is commercial, and falls within the rules in chapter 6.

If they are non-profit making, all their housing falls within the rules in this chapter.

The amount of your eligible rent

5.7   The rest of this chapter explains how to work out your eligible rent. The rules are summarised in table 5.2.

5.8   The amount of your eligible rent depends on whether you are:

(a)   a sole tenant – in other words, you are the only person liable for rent on your home; or

(b)   a joint tenant with only your partner and/or a child or young person you are responsible for – in other words, you are all in the same benefit unit; or

(c)   a joint tenant with at least one person who is neither your partner nor a child or young person you are responsible for – in other words, you are in different benefit units.

If (a) or (b) applies to you, see the general rule in paras 5.9-10. If (c) applies to you, see paras 5.11-13. (For more on who is in your benefit unit, see paras 3.56 onwards.)

T5.1   UC 2 – definition: 'local authority', sch 4 para 2 – definition: 'a provider of social housing'; NIUC sch 4 para 2

Table 5.2 **Eligible rent: social renters**

Step 1: Rent and eligible service charges (see paras 5.8-10)

Your eligible rent is the monthly total of your:

- rent payments (including any discounted amounts: see paras 5.14-15); and
- eligible service charge payments (if any).

But this is reduced if any of the following steps apply to you.

Step 2: Certain joint tenancies (see paras 5.13-15)

If you are in a joint tenancy (for example a house-share) and at least one joint tenant is not in your benefit unit, the eligible rent is split between you and the other joint tenant(s).

Step 3: Reductions for under-occupation (see paras 5.11-13)

If your home has more bedrooms than the UC rules say you are entitled to, your eligible rent is reduced by:

- 14% if you have one extra bedroom;
- 25% if you have two or more extra bedrooms.

But this does not apply if Step 2 applies to you.

Step 4: Reductions for high rents (see paras 5.21-26)

If the amounts in Step 1 are unreasonably high, they can be referred to the rent officer, and this may mean your eligible rent is reduced. If this applies to you, this reduction is made before Step 2 or 3.

Eligible rent: the general rule

5.9   The general rule is that your eligible rent is the monthly total of:

(a) your rent payments (including any DWP-approved discount: paras 5.14-15); and

(b) your eligible service charge payments (if any).

See chapter 4 for which rent and service charge payments count, and paras 5.27-33 for which service charges are eligible. For how to convert payments to a monthly figure, see para 9.54.

5.10   But your eligible rent is reduced if you are under-occupying (see paras 5.16-20) and/or if your rent or service charge payments are unreasonably high (see paras 5.21-26).

T5.2   UC sch 4 paras 3,5,6,31,32A,34,35; NIUC sch 4 paras 3,5,30,33,34

5.9   UC sch 4 paras 3,5,6,32A,34,35; NIUC sch 4 paras 3,5,33,34

Eligible rent: joint tenants not in the same benefit unit

5.11   If you have at least one joint tenant who is not in your benefit unit, the general rule in paras 5.9-10 applies to you, with two differences:

(a)   your eligible rent is your share of the monthly total of rent and eligible service charge payments;

(b)   the rules about under-occupation do not apply to you.

5.12   Your share is worked out as follows:

(a)   start with the monthly total of your rent and eligible service charge payments;

(b)   divide this by the total number of joint tenants (including yourself);

(c)   multiply the result by the number of joint tenants (including yourself) who are in your benefit unit.

The last step is only needed in the kind of situation illustrated in example 4.

5.13   But if the above produces an unreasonable result, the DWP can agree to split the eligible rent in some other way, taking account of all the circumstances, including how many joint tenants there are and how you actually split your rent and service charges. See example 5.

Rent discounts

5.14   Some social landlords have a rent discount scheme which reduces your rent as a payment incentive (e.g. for prompt payment or online payment).

5.15   If you get such a discount, and your landlord's scheme is approved by the DWP, the discount is not deducted from your eligible rent. For example, if your eligible rent is normally £800 but your rent is reduced by £25 for prompt payment, your eligible rent is still £800.

Examples: the amount of eligible rent

In all these examples, the eligible rent for the dwelling (including eligible service charges) is £600 per month, the tenants are not under-occupying, and the rent is not unreasonably high.

1. **A sole tenant**
   - The tenant's eligible rent is simply £600 per month.

2. **A couple who are the only joint tenants**
   - Their eligible rent is simply £600 per month.

3. **Three joint tenants who are not related**
   - Each one's eligible rent is £200 per month.

4. **Three joint tenants two of whom are a couple**
   - The couple's eligible rent is £400 per month (two-thirds of £600).
   - The single person's eligible rent is £200 per month (a third of £600).

5.11   UC sch 4 para 35(1),(2),(4); NIUC sch 4 para 34(1),(2),(4)

5.12   UC sch 4 paras 2 definition: 'listed persons', 35(4); NIUC sch 4 paras 2, 34(4)

5.13   UC sch 4 para 35(5); NIUC sch 4 para 34(5)

5.15   UC sch 4 para 32A

5. **A different split of the eligible rent**
    - The couple in example 4 have one bedroom and have always paid half the rent. The same applies to the single person. The DWP agrees it is reasonable to split the eligible rent the same way.
    - So the couple's eligible rent is £300 per month, and so is the single person's.

Reductions for under-occupation

5.16   Your eligible rent is reduced if you are under-occupying your home. You count as under-occupying if you have more bedrooms in your home than the UC rules say you are entitled to. Other rooms (such as living rooms) are not taken into account.

Exceptions

5.17   The rules about under-occupation do not apply to you if:

(a) you have a joint tenant who is not in your benefit unit (see para 5.11); or

(b) you are a shared owner (see para 8.6).

How many bedrooms you are entitled to

5.18   You qualify for one bedroom for each of the following occupiers of your home: a couple, a single person over 16, two children under 16 if they are of the same sex, or under 10 if they are of opposite sexes, and each other child. You may also qualify for an additional bedroom if you are a foster parent, or for someone who requires overnight care, or whose disability means they can't share a bedroom. See chapter 7 for the full rules. See also paras 11.34-35 for the 'bereavement run-on', which can mean you continue to qualify for a bedroom for up to three months for a member of your household who has died.

The amount of the reduction

5.19   Your eligible rent is reduced by:

(a) 14% if you have one bedroom more than you are entitled to;

(b) 25% if you have two or more bedrooms more than you are entitled to.

See the following examples.

Reductions and discretionary housing payments (DHPs)

5.20   If your eligible rent is reduced because you are under-occupying (para 5.19), or because your rent is unreasonably high (para 5.26), you may be able to get a DHP from your local council. For details of the DHP scheme, see chapter 21 of the *Guide to Housing Benefit*.

5.16   UC sch 4 para 36(1); NIUC sch 4 para 35(1)

5.17   UC sch 4 paras 35(4), 36(5); NIUC sch 4 paras 34(4), 35(5)

5.18   UC sch 4 paras 8-12; NIUC sch 4 paras 7-11

5.19   UC sch 4 para 36(2)-(4); NIUC sch 4 para 36(2)-(4)

Examples: reductions for under-occupation

1. **One extra bedroom.**
   A couple have two children under 10. They rent a three bedroom house and no-one else lives with them. The eligible rent for the dwelling is £1,000 per month.

   They qualify for two bedrooms, one for themselves and one for the children. Because their home has one bedroom more than this, their eligible rent is reduced by 14% (£140) to £860 per month.

2. **Two extra bedrooms.**
   A single person rents a three-bedroom house and no-one else lives with her. The eligible rent for the dwelling is £1,000 per month.

   She qualifies for one bedroom. Because her home has two bedrooms more than this, her eligible rent is reduced by 25% (£250) to £750 per month.

For further examples, see chapter 7.

Reductions for unreasonably high rents

5.21   This section explains how your eligible rent could be reduced if the rent officer makes a 'housing payment determination' saying that your rent and/or service charge payments are unreasonably high. The rent officer can only do this if the DWP requests it. This in practice is rare.

5.22   Rent officers are independent of the DWP. They are government employees in the Rent Service (in England), the Rent Officer Service (in Wales) or the Rent Registration Service (in Scotland).

Housing payment determinations

5.23   The DWP can request a housing payment determination if it considers that your:

(a) rent payments; and/or

(b) eligible service charge payments (see table 5.3),

are 'greater than it is reasonable to meet by way of the [UC] housing costs element'. DWP guidance (ADM F3253) says this could happen if your rent is higher than the LHA figure that would apply if you were a private sector renter, but also says that any special circumstances should be taken into account.

5.24   When making a housing payment determination, the rent officer:

(a) bases this on the whole of your accommodation (even if you are a joint tenant);

(b) looks separately at each rent and/or service charge payment the DWP has asked them to consider;

(c) decides whether the amount is reasonable (see para 5.25); and

(d) if it is not, tells the DWP what amount is reasonable.

If your home is in the Affordable Rent Programme, the rent officer must agree that your rent payments (but not necessarily your service charge payments) are reasonable.

5.23   UC sch 4 paras 3, 32(1),(2); NIUC sch 4 paras 3,31

5.25   The rent officer takes account of the level of rent and/or service charge payments which a landlord could 'reasonably be expected to obtain' on accommodation which:

(a)   has the same number of bedrooms as yours;

(b)   has the same kind of landlord as yours (see table 5.1(a) or (b));

(c)   is in a similar reasonable state of repair to yours; and

(d)   is in the same council area as yours. If this area doesn't have enough accommodation meeting these conditions, the rent officer includes accommodation in an adjoining council area (or areas).

The rent officer excludes the cost of care, support or supervision and other excluded services (see table 5.3).

How the reduction applies

5.26   if the rent officer decides your rent and/or service charge payments are unreasonably high, the DWP:

(a)   uses the amount the rent officer says is reasonable (rather than the amount you actually pay) to work out your eligible rent; but

(b)   can agree not to do this if it wouldn't be 'appropriate'.

And if the rules about joint tenants or under-occupying your home (see paras 5.11-19) also apply to you, they apply after this rule (see table 5.2).

Service charges

5.27   This section is about service charges. It applies if:

(a)   you are a social renter (see para 5.3);

(b)   you are a shared owner (see paras 8.6 and 8.11) in a scheme run by a social landlord (see para 5.4);

(c)   you are an owner-occupier (see paras 8.5 and 8.10);

(d)   you are only liable for service charges (see para 4.32).

If you are a private renter, or shared owner in a scheme run by a private landlord, different rules apply: see paras 6.9-10.

Which service charges are eligible for UC

5.28   A service charge is eligible for UC if it meets all the following conditions:

(a)   it is for an eligible kind of service, not an excluded kind (see paras 5.29-30);

(b)   you have to pay it in order to occupy your home (see para 5.31); and

(c)   the service and amount are reasonable (see paras 5.32-33).

5.24-25 art 5 and sch 2 of SI 2013/382;

5.26   UC sch 4 para 35(3),(4); NIUC sch 4 para 34(3),(4)

5.28   UC sch 1 para 8(2)-(6); NIUC sch 1 para 9(2)-(6)

Eligible and excluded services

5.29   Table 5.3 lists the kinds of service charges which are eligible for UC, and those which are excluded from UC.

5.30   If a service charge is:

(a) 'eligible', this means it is included in your eligible rent (if you are a social sector renter) or eligible housing costs (if you are an owner-occupier, shared owner, or only liable for service charges);

(b) 'excluded', this means you cannot get UC for it. See also para 4.27 about distinguishing eligible and excluded services from rent.

A condition of occupying your home

5.31   To be eligible for UC, a service charge must be one you have to pay in order to have the right to occupy your home (see para 4.35). This does not need to have applied since you moved in so long as, when you agreed to pay it, the alternative was that you could lose your home.

Unreasonable kinds of service charges

5.32   A service charge can be excluded from UC if the services or facilities are of a kind which it is not 'reasonable to provide'. Although the rules about which service charges are eligible are already strict (table 5.3), this rule could, for example, apply to maintenance and/or repairs, and DWP guidance (ADM para F2065) gives the example of maintaining a luxury item such as a swimming pool.

Table 5.3 **Service charges**

Eligible service charges

Categories A to D are listed in the law as being eligible for UC.

Maintaining the general standard of accommodation (Category A)

- External window cleaning on upper floors.
- For owner-occupiers and shared owners only, separately identifiable payments for maintenance and/or repairs.

General upkeep of communal areas (Category B)

- Ongoing maintenance and/or cleaning of communal areas.
- Supply of water, fuel or other commodities to communal areas.

'Communal areas' include internal areas, external areas and areas for reasonable facilities such as laundry rooms and children's play areas. DWP guidance (ADM para F2072) says that ground maintenance (e.g. lawn mowing, litter removal and lighting for access areas) and tenant parking (excluding security costs) should be included.

5.29   UC sch 1 paras 8(4),(6); NIUC sch 1 paras 9(4),(6)
5.31   UC sch 1 para 8(3); NIUC sch 1 para 9(3)
5.32   UC sch 1 para 8(5); NIUC sch 1 para 9(5)

Basic communal services (Category C)

- Provision of basic communal services.

- Ongoing maintenance, cleaning and/or repair in connection with basic communal services.

'Basic communal services' are those available to everyone in the accommodation, such as refuse collection, communal lifts, secure building access and/or TV/wireless aerials for receiving a free service. DWP guidance (ADM paras F2073-74) says that communal telephones (but not call costs) should be included, as should a fair proportion of the staff management and administration costs of providing communal services.

Accommodation-specific charges (Category D)

- Use of essential items in your own accommodation, such as furniture and domestic appliances.

Excluded service charges

The first two items are listed in the law as being excluded from UC. The others are excluded from UC because they do not fall within categories A to D, and are based on DWP guidance (ADM para F2077).

- Food of any kind.

- Medical or personal services of any kind, including personal care.

- Nursing care, emergency alarm systems or individual personal alarms.

- Equipment or adaptations relating to disability or infirmity.

- Counselling, support or intensive housing management.

- Fuel, water or sewerage charges for your own accommodation.

- Living expenses such as heating, lighting or hot water.

- Cleaning your own accommodation or having your laundry done.

- Gardening your own garden.

- Recreational facilities or subscription/fee-based TV.

- Transport, permits, licences or maintenance of unadopted roads.

- Any other service or facility not included in categories A to D.

Special cases

The following are listed in the law as being excluded from UC, even if they are for items falling within categories A to D.

- Services or facilities that could be met by public funds (e.g. Supporting People) even if you do not yourself qualify for such help.

- Payments which result in an asset changing hands (e.g. if you pay for furniture but after a period it will become yours).

See also paras 5.31-33.

T5.3   UC sch 1 para 8(4),(6); NIUC sch 1 para 9(4),(6)

Examples: Eligible housing costs and service charges

In these examples, the basic communal services are eligible for UC (table 5.3).

1. **A social sector renter**
   A social sector renter (who is not under-occupying) pays rent of £500 per month, plus service charges of £40 per month for basic communal services. So his eligible rent is £540 per month.

2. **An owner-occupier**
   An owner-occupier pays interest on her mortgage (see chapter 8). She also pays £20 per month on her lease for basic communal services. So her eligible housing costs are £20 per month.

Unreasonably high service charges

5.33   A service charge can be excluded from UC if the costs and charges relating to it are not of a 'reasonable amount'. But:

(a) if you are a social sector renter or shared owner, the service charge must be referred to the rent officer for a determination (paras 5.21-26). DWP guidance (ADM para F2068) confirms that this means the reasonable part of the amount for the service charge is eligible for UC (and only the unreasonable part is excluded);

(b) if you are an owner-occupier, DWP guidance (ADM para F2066) is that service charges should not be excluded from UC under this rule.

5.33   UC sch 1 para 8(5); NIUC sch 1 para 9(5)

Chapter 6 **Eligible rent: private renters**

- Private renters: see paras 6.1-6.
- The amount of your eligible rent: see paras 6.7-14.
- The local housing allowance (LHA) figures: see paras 6.15-21.
- The size of accommodation you qualify for: see paras 6.22-27.

Private renters

6.1　This chapter explains how your UC housing costs element is worked out if you are a private renter. For renters, the housing costs element is also called your eligible rent.

6.2　To qualify for a housing costs element you must meet the conditions in chapter 4 as well as this chapter. Chapter 9 explains how your housing costs element affects the amount of your UC, and how it can be reduced if you have one or more non-dependants.

Who is a private renter

6.3　You are a private renter if you are liable to pay rent (with or without service charges) to anyone other than a social landlord (see table 5.1). The rules in this chapter also apply if you are a shared owner (para 8.6) with anyone other than a social landlord.

6.4　For example, your landlord could be a private landlord, a lettings agency, a company, a registered charity or a not-for-profit organisation.

Exceptions

6.5　You cannot get UC towards your rent or service charges for:

  (a) 'specified supported accommodation' (see paras 4.11-12 and table 4.2); or

  (b) 'temporary accommodation' for people who are or were homeless (see paras 4.13-14); or

  (c) certain other accommodation (paras 4.9-10 and 4.15-16).

6.6　You may not be able to get UC towards your rent or service charges if you are single and are:

  (a) a care leaver aged 16 or 17 (see paras 4.82-83); or

  (b) aged 18-21 and don't fall in an eligible group (see paras 4.84-86).

The amount of your eligible rent

6.7   The rest of this chapter explains how to work out your eligible rent.

6.8   The amount of your eligible rent depends on whether you are:

(a)   a sole tenant – in other words you are the only person liable for rent on your home; or

(b)   a joint tenant with only your partner and/or a child or young person you are responsible for – in other words, you are all in the same benefit unit; or

(c)   a joint tenant with at least one person who is neither your partner nor a child or young person you are responsible for – in other words, you are in different benefit units.

If (a) or (b) applies to you, see the general rule in paras 6.9-10. If (c) applies to you, see paras 6.11-13. (For more on who is in your benefit unit, see paras 3.56 onwards.)

Eligible rent: the general rule

6.9   The general rule is that your eligible rent equals:

(a)   your actual monthly rent (see para 6.10); or

(b)   if it is lower, the local housing allowance (LHA) figure which applies to you (see para 6.17).

Actual monthly rent

6.10   Your actual monthly rent is the monthly total of your:

(a)   rent payments; and

(b)   service charge payments (if any).

See chapter 4 for which rent and service charge payments count. Unlike the rules for social renters, no service charges are excluded. For how to convert payments to a monthly figure, see para 9.54.

Eligible rent: joint tenants not in the same benefit unit

6.11   If you have at least one joint tenant who is not in your benefit unit, the actual monthly rent (see para 6.10) is split between you and the other joint tenant(s). Your eligible rent equals:

(a)   your share of the actual monthly rent; or

(b)   if it is lower, the LHA figure which applies to you.

6.12   Your share is worked out as follows:

(a)   start with the actual monthly rent on your dwelling;

(b)   divide this by the total number of joint tenants (including yourself);

(c)   multiply the result by the number of joint tenants (including yourself) who are in your benefit unit.

The last step is only needed in the kind of situation illustrated in example 4.

6.9   UC sch 4 para 22; NIUC sch 4 para 21

6.10   UC sch 4 paras 3,5,6,23,24; NIUC sch 4 paras 3,5,22,23

6.11   UC sch 4 para 24(1),(2),(4); NIUC sch 4 para 23(1),(2),(4)

6.12   UC sch 4 paras 2 definition: 'listed persons', 24(4); NIUC sch 4 paras 2, 23(4)

6.13   But if the above would produce an unreasonable result, the DWP can agree to split the actual monthly rent in some other way, taking account of all the circumstances including how many joint tenants there are and how you actually split your rent and eligible service charges. See example 5.

Legal terminology: 'core rent' and 'cap rent'

6.14   UC law and guidance uses these terms:

(a) 'core rent' means your actual monthly rent (or share of it);

(b) 'cap rent' means the LHA figure which applies to you.

Examples: Actual monthly rent and eligible rent

1. A sole tenant

- ■ A sole tenant's actual monthly rent is £900.
- ■ If her LHA figure is £800, her eligible rent is £800.

2. A couple who are the only joint tenants

- ■ Their actual monthly rent is £700.
- ■ If their LHA figure is £800, their eligible rent is £700.

3. Three joint tenants who are not related

- ■ The actually monthly rent for their dwelling is £1,200.
- ■ So each one's share of it is £400 (⅓ of £1,200).
- ■ If the LHA figure (for each of them) is £350, each one's eligible rent is £350.

4. Three joint tenants, two of whom are a couple

- ■ The couple are claiming UC, but the single person is not.
- ■ The actual monthly rent for the dwelling is £1,200.
- ■ So the couple's share is £800 (⅔ of £1,200).
- ■ If their LHA figure is £1,000, their eligible rent is £800.

5. A different split of the actual monthly rent

- ■ The couple in example 4 have the use of three of the four bedrooms (they have children) and have always paid ¾ of the rent. The DWP agrees it is reasonable to split the actual monthly rent the same way.
- ■ So their share is now £900 (¾ of £1,200).
- ■ If their LHA figure is £1,000, their eligible rent is £900.

6.13   UC sch 4 para 24(5); NIUC sch 4 para 23(5)

The local housing allowance (LHA) figures

6.15   LHA figures are used in deciding your eligible rent (see paras 6.9 and 6.11). They are monthly figures set by the rent officer, and are available for the whole of Great Britain online [www].

6.16   Rent officers are independent of the DWP. They are government employees in the Rent Service (in England), the Rent Officer Service (in Wales) or Rent Registration Service (in Scotland).

Which LHA figure applies to you

6.17   The LHA figure which applies to you is the one for:

(a) the size of accommodation the UC rules say you are entitled to (see paras 6.23-27); and

(b) the area your home is in. In the law this is called a 'broad rental market area' (BRMA).

Your LHA figure changes whenever you become entitled to a different size of accommodation (e.g. when someone moves in or out) or move to an area with different LHA figures. See paras 11.14-24 for the date your UC changes.

6.18   Each year the rent officer sets LHA figures for the sizes of accommodation listed in table 6.1. These vary from area to area but can never be greater than the national maximum amounts shown in the table. The rent officer sets the figures on the last working day in January, and you can view them online from then (para 6.15). But they take effect:

(a) on the first Monday in the tax year (9th April in 2018); or

(b) if you are already on UC, from the first day of your assessment period beginning on or after that date.

6.19   In the year from 9th April 2018:

(a) for certain sizes of accommodation in certain areas (these are listed in the regulations), each LHA figure is:

■   3% higher than last year's figure, or (if lower)

■   the national maximum amount (see table 6.1);

(b) in all other cases, each LHA figure is:

■   the same as last year's, or (if lower)

■   the rent officer's current valuation of the rent at the 30th percentile (see para 6.20).

6.20   The rent at the 30th percentile means the highest rent within the bottom 30% of rents in the rent officer's data. This data is taken from actual rents (including service charges) payable during the year ending on the preceding 30th September, on accommodation which:

6.15   https://lha-direct.voa.gov.uk/search.aspx
          http://www.nihe.gov.uk/index/benefits/lha/current_lha_rates.htm

6.17   UC sch 4 para 25(1),(2),(5); NIUC sch 4 para 24(1),(2),(5)

6.18-20 arts 3,4 and sch 1 of SI 2013/382;arts 3,4 and sch 1 of NISR 2016/222

(a)   is rented on an assured tenancy;

(b)   is in a reasonable state of repair;

(c)   is the correct size and in the correct area (see para 6.17). If that area doesn't have enough accommodation of that size, the rent officer can include accommodation from a comparable area (or areas).

The rent officer excludes rents paid by people on UC or HB (this is to avoid the effect UC/HB could have on rent levels) and very high or very low rents (rents which a landlord couldn't 'reasonably be expected to obtain'). The UC rules are slightly different from those used in HB (see chapter 11 of the *Guide to Housing Benefit*) but the LHA figures for UC and HB are usually the same.

Table 6.1 **LHA figures: sizes of accommodation and maximum amounts**

Size of accommodation	National monthly maximum
(a) one-bedroom shared accommodation	£1163.30
(b) one-bedroom self-contained accommodation	£1163.30
(c) two-bedroom dwellings	£1349.43
(d) three-bedroom dwellings	£1582.09
(e) four-bedroom dwellings	£1861.28

Notes:

In practice actual LHAs for (a) are lower than those for (b) (though the national maximums are the same).

For which size of accommodation applies to you, see paras 6.23-27.

The above national maximums are 3% higher than last year, in order to allow for the 3% increase in para 6.19(a).

LHAs and discretionary housing payments (DHPs)

6.21   If your LHA figure is lower than your actual monthly rent you may be able to get a DHP from your local council. For details of the DHP scheme, see chapter 21 of the *Guide to Housing Benefit*.

T6.1   SI 2013/382 sch 1 para 4, SI 2017/1323 art 4(3)(b)

The size of accommodation you qualify for

6.22   This section explains what size of accommodation you are entitled to if you are a private sector renter. This affects which LHA figure is used in assessing your eligible rent (see para 6.17).

Examples: LHAs and size of accommodation

1. A single person aged 24

■ Unless she is in an excepted group (see table 6.2), she qualifies for the LHA for one-bedroom shared accommodation.

2. A single person aged 58

■ He qualifies for the LHA for one-bedroom self-contained accommodation.

3. A couple

■ They qualify for the LHA for one-bedroom self-contained accommodation.

4. A couple with a son aged 9 and a daughter aged 7

■ The couple qualify for the LHA for a two-bedroom dwelling.

5. The son in example 4 reaches the age of 10

■ Because the children are no longer expected to share a bedroom (see para 6.25), the couple qualify for the LHA for a three-bedroom dwelling.

6. Three joint tenants who are not related

■ They are all under 35 and none of them is in an excepted group (see table 6.2). So each one qualifies for the LHA for one-bedroom shared accommodation.

7. Two brothers who are joint tenants

■ They are in their 40s, and the daughter of one of them lives with him. So that brother qualifies for the LHA for a two-bedroom dwelling. The other brother qualifies for the LHA for one-bedroom self-contained accommodation.

For further examples about size of accommodation, see chapter 7.

Sizes of accommodation

6.23   The sizes of accommodation are given in table 6.1. The size you qualify for is worked out as follows:

(a)   you qualify for accommodation with the appropriate number of bedrooms for the occupiers of your home: see para 6.25. Other rooms (such as living rooms) are not taken into account;

(b)   but the maximum number of bedrooms is always four;

(c)   and if you are a single person under 35, you may qualify for one-bedroom shared accommodation (rather than self-contained): see para 6.26.

Joint tenants not in the same benefit unit

6.24   If you have at least one joint tenant who is not in your benefit unit, the size of accommodation you qualify for is worked out separately for each single joint tenant or joint tenant couple. See examples 6 and 7.

How many bedrooms you are entitled to

6.25   You qualify for one bedroom for each of the following occupiers of your home: a couple, a single person over 16, two children under 16 if they are of the same sex, or under 10 if they are of opposite sexes, and each other child. You may also qualify for an additional bedroom if you are a foster parent, or for someone who requires overnight care or whose disability means they can't share a bedroom. See chapter 7 for the full rules. See also paras 11.34-35 for the 'bereavement run-on' which can mean you continue to qualify for a bedroom for up to three months for a member of your household who has died. But (unlike social sector tenants) the maximum number of bedrooms for private sector tenants is always four.

Single people under 35

6.26   You qualify for one-bedroom shared accommodation (rather than self-contained) if you are:

(a)   a single person, or in a couple but claiming UC as a single person (see paras 2.6 and 2.8); and

(b)   under 35 years old; and

(c)   not in any of the excepted groups in table 6.2.

This rule never applies to you if you are claiming UC as a couple.

6.23   UC sch 4 paras 8-12, 26-29; NIUC sch 4 paras 7-11, 25-28

6.24   UC sch 4 paras 8,9; NIUC sch 4 paras 7,8

6.25   UC sch 4 paras 8-12, 26; NIUC sch 4 paras 7-11, 25

6.26   UC sch 4 paras 27, 28(1),(2); NIUC sch 4 paras 26, 27(1),(2)

Table 6.2 **Single people under 35: the UC excepted groups**

If you are single and are in any of these groups, you qualify for self-contained accommodation (para 6.26).

(a) You are responsible for one or more children or young persons (see paras 3.72-79).

(b) You have one or more non-dependants (see paras 3.80-87).

(c) You are in receipt of:

- the middle or highest rate of the care component of disability living allowance, or

- the daily living component of personal independence payment, or

- a benefit equivalent to attendance allowance (see para 10.37).

(d) You are aged 18 or over but under 22, and were a care leaver before you reached the age of 18.

(e) You are an ex-offender managed under a multi-agency (MAPPA) agreement because you pose a serious risk of harm to the public.

(f) You are aged 25 or over, and:

- you have occupied one or more hostels for homeless people (see para 6.27) for at least three months. This does not need to have been a continuous three months, and it does not need to have been recent; and

- while you were there, you were offered and you accepted support with rehabilitation or resettlement within the community.

Hostels for homeless people

6.27   A hostel for homeless people (see table 6.2(f)) means a building which meets all the following conditions:

(a) it provides non-self-contained domestic accommodation, together with meals or adequate food-preparation facilities;

(b) its main purpose is to provide accommodation together with care, support or supervision, in order to assist homeless people to be rehabilitated or resettled in the community;

(c) it is:

- managed or owned by a social landlord other than a local authority (table 5.1), or

- run on a non-commercial basis, and wholly or partly funded by a government department or agency or local authority, or

- managed by a registered charity or non-profit-making voluntary organisation;

(d) it is not a care home (see para 4.15).

T6.2   UC 2 definition: 'attendance allowance', sch 4 paras 28(3),(4), 29; NIUC 2, sch 4 paras 27(3),(4), 28

6.27   UC 2 definition: 'local authority', sch 4 para 29(10); NIUC sch 4 para 28(6)

Chapter 7 **The size criteria**

- The size criteria and your eligible rent: see paras 7.1-4.
- The number of bedrooms you qualify for: see paras 7.5-7.
- Which occupiers are included: see paras 7.8-18.
- Qualifying for an additional bedroom: see paras 7.19-28.

The size criteria and eligible rent

7.1 This chapter explains how many bedrooms you qualify for in the calculation of your UC if you rent your home. The rules about this are known as the size criteria. Opponents of the rules say they are a 'bedroom tax'; supporters say they prevent a 'spare room subsidy'. The rules are not always the same as those used in HB (see the *Guide to Housing Benefit* chapter 11).

How the number of bedrooms affects your UC

7.2 If you rent your home, the housing costs element of your UC depends on the amount of your eligible rent (see paras 9.46-56). This in turn depends on how many bedrooms you qualify for, as follows:

(a) if you are a social renter:
- the UC size criteria say how many bedrooms you qualify for (see para 7.5 onwards),
- your eligible rent is reduced if you have more bedrooms than you qualify for (see paras 5.16-20),
- whether a particular room is a bedroom can therefore be important (see paras 7.6-7);

(b) if you are a private renter:
- the UC size criteria say how many bedrooms you qualify for (see para 7.5 onwards),
- your eligible rent is limited to the local housing allowance figure which applies to you (see paras 6.9-27),
- whether a particular room is a bedroom is not relevant, because your LHA figure is based on how many bedrooms you qualify for, not how many there are in your home.

7.3 If you are a shared owner the rules in para 7.2(a) or (b) apply (depending on whether your shared ownership scheme is run by a social or private landlord), but only to your eligible rent, not to your owner-occupier payments (see chapter 8). The size criteria do not apply if you are an owner occupier.

7.4 If the size criteria mean your eligible rent is lower than your actual rent, you may be able to get a discretionary housing payment from your local council (see paras 5.20 and 6.21).

The number of bedrooms you qualify for

7.5   Table 7.1 shows how to work out the number of bedrooms you qualify for. If you are a private sector renter, the maximum number is four. (This limit does not apply if you are a social renter.)

Table 7.1 **The UC size criteria**

The size criteria are based on the occupiers of your home (paras 7.8-18).

General rules

One bedroom is allowed for each of the following occupiers of your home:

- yourself, or yourself and your partner if you are claiming UC as a couple;
- each young person aged 16 or over;
- each non-dependant aged 16 or over;
- two children under 16 of the same sex;
- two children under 10 of the same or opposite sex;
- any other child aged under 16.

Children are expected to share bedrooms in whatever way results in the smallest number of bedrooms. See examples 5 and 6.

Additional bedrooms

One or more additional bedrooms can be allowed for:

- a foster parent (para 7.21);
- a person who requires overnight care (paras 7.22-24);
- a disabled person who can't share a bedroom (paras 7.25-28).

What counts as a bedroom

7.6   Whether a particular room in your home is a bedroom (rather than a living room, storage room, etc) can be important if you are a social renter (see para 7.2). Neither UC law nor DWP guidance (ADM paras F3110-38) define what a bedroom is (but see para 7.7). In practice, the DWP is likely to follow your landlord's description of whether a room is a bedroom (for example in your letting agreement), but you can ask the DWP to reconsider this and appeal to a tribunal if you disagree (see chapter 14).

7.7   There have been a number of court and Upper Tribunal decisions about what is a bedroom, and these are summarised in table 7.2.

7.5   UC sch 4 paras 8,10; NIUC sch 4 paras 7,9

T7.1   WRA 40 definition: 'child'; UC sch 4 paras 10,12; NIWRO 46; NIUC sch 4 paras 9,11

Table 7.2 **What counts as a bedroom: case law**

The use and suitability of the room. The Court of Session (the Scottish equivalent of the Court of Appeal) has decided that whether a room is a bedroom is determined by 'an objective assessment of the property as vacant which is not related to the residents or what their actual use or needs might be.' ([2017] CSIH 35.) However, the Upper Tribunal has held that this is persuasive but not binding in England and Wales, and that (in any case) a bedroom must be capable of being used by the category of occupiers in question (so a room that couldn't fit two beds in wasn't suitable for two boys under 16). ([2017] UKUT 471 (AAC).) Apart from that, actual, former or planned use of the room is not likely to be relevant ([2014] UKUT 525 (AAC) paras 27-28; CH/2512/2015). However, a bedroom can stop counting as a bedroom if exceptional circumstances relating to physical or mental disability mean it is now used as a living room ([2015] UKUT 282 (AAC)).

Applying the undefined term 'bedroom'. The word 'bedroom' has its ordinary or familiar English meaning. It should not be paraphrased, but should be understood and applied 'having regard to the underlying purpose of the legislation' which is 'to limit the HB entitlement of those under-occupying accommodation'. Like an 'elephant', a 'bedroom' is capable of description rather than definition. And in an individual case, the authority's understanding of what is a bedroom 'is best provided by the reasons given for [its] decision'. ([2014] UKUT 525 (AAC) paras 19-24.) The description of a bedroom required by an overnight carer (see para 11.32) as a room with a bed or beds in and/or a room suitable for sleeping in ([2014] UKUT 48 (AAC)) is unlikely to be a conclusive general definition.

The description of the room by the landlord or in the building's plans. The council can take account of the description of the room by the original or current landlord (for example in the letting agreement or marketing materials) or in the plans or designs for the building. But this is 'a starting point' and is not conclusive. ([2014] UKUT 525 (AAC) para 30.)

Relevant practical considerations. The council should consider practical factors including '(a) size, configuration and overall dimensions, (b) access, (c) natural and electronic lighting, (d) ventilation, and (e) privacy', taking account of the adults and children referred to in the regulations (paras 7.8-16). For example, it should not be necessary to 'jump from a passage through an outward opening door in order to get into bed'. It should be possible to get into bed from within the room, and there should be somewhere to put clothes and a glass of water ([2014] UKUT 525 (AAC) paras 31-44; [2016] UKUT 164 (AAC)). A bedside cabinet with drawers can be sufficient for these purposes, rather than there needing to be both a bedside table and somewhere separate to store clothes ([2017] UKUT 443 (AAC)).

Underoccupation and overcrowding. Underoccupation is not 'the flip side of overcrowding'. The two sets of rules are different, and overcrowding law takes account of living rooms as well as bedrooms (Housing Act 1985 s326, Housing (Scotland) Act 1987 s137). But over-crowding rules (for example if a room has very small dimensions) can sound 'warning bells' that a room may not be a bedroom ([2014] UKUT 525 (AAC) paras 53-55; [2016] UKUT 164 (AAC); ([2017] UKUT 443 (AAC)). In practice, direct conflict between overcrowding law and the HB size criteria is rare.

Examples: How many bedrooms you qualify for

1. A single person who is the only occupier

She qualifies for one bedroom. If she is a private renter under 35, see para 6.26 for whether she qualifies for shared or self-contained accommodation.

2. A couple who are the only occupiers

They qualify for one bedroom.

3. A single person with three children

He has sons aged 15 and 8 and a daughter aged 13. The sons are expected to share a bedroom. So the household qualifies for three bedrooms.

4. The older son in example 3 reaches 16

Now none of the children are expected to share a bedroom. So the household qualifies for four bedrooms.

5. A couple with four children

They have daughters aged 13 and 4 and sons aged 14 and 8. The children are expected to share bedrooms in the way that results in the smallest number of bedrooms (the daughters sharing, and also the sons). The household qualifies for three bedrooms.

6. The couple in example 5 have a baby

The couple now qualify for four bedrooms. No way of sharing bedrooms can result in a lower number.

7. A single person with two non-dependants

The household qualifies for three bedrooms. This is the case even if the non-dependants are a couple: see para 7.14.

Examples including additional bedrooms are later in this chapter.

Which occupiers are included

7.8   The following occupiers of your home are taken into account in deciding how many bedrooms you qualify for:

   (a)   the people in your benefit unit (see paras 7.10-13); and

   (b)   non-dependants (see paras 7.14-16).

In the law these are called the members of your 'extended benefit unit'. See also paras 11.34-35 for the 'bereavement run-on' which can mean you continue to qualify for a bedroom for up to three months for a member of your extended benefit unit who has died.

7.9   The DWP decides which occupiers to include, not (for example) the rent officer. Decisions about this are appealable to a tribunal: [2010] UKUT 79 AAC.

7.8   UC sch 4 para 9(1); NIUC sch 4 para 8(1)

People in your benefit unit

7.10 Your benefit unit is yourself, your partner if you are claiming UC as a couple, and any children or young persons you are responsible for. For more on who is in your benefit unit, see paras 3.56-79. Table 7.1 shows how many bedrooms you qualify for.

7.11 A child or young person is included as an occupier even if the 'two child limit' means they are not included in your maximum UC (paras 9.4 and 9.17). But a child or young person who spends time in more than one home (for example with each parent) can only be included as an occupier in one of these (para 3.77).

If you or your partner are temporarily absent

7.12 If you and/or your partner are temporarily absent, you are included as an occupier during:

   (a) an absence from Great Britain which meets the conditions in paras 2.29-32; or

   (b) the first six months that you are a prisoner if you meet the conditions in para 4.80.

If a child or young person is temporarily absent

7.13 A child or young person who is temporarily absent is included as an occupier during:

   (a) any period they are included in your benefit unit (see para 3.79);

   (b) the first six months they are in local authority care (see para 3.78); or

   (c) the first six months they are a prisoner (see para 4.79).

But (b) and (c) only apply if they were included in your benefit unit immediately before their absence, and you then qualified for the housing costs element in your award of UC.

Non-dependants

7.14 Non-dependants are normally adult sons, daughters or other relatives or friends who live with you on a non-commercial basis. For more on who is a non-dependant, see paras 3.80-87. If you have one or more non-dependants the rules are as follows:

   (a) you are allowed one bedroom for each non-dependant over 16 (see table 7.1). This means two bedrooms for two non-dependants over 16 even if they are a couple;

   (b) one bedroom is allowed for each young person over 16 who is the responsibility of a non-dependant (rather than of you or your partner) – because they also count as a non-dependant (see para 3.83);

   (c) a child under 16 who is the responsibility of a non-dependant is taken into account as a child in the normal way (table 7.1).

7.10   UC sch 4 para 10(1)(a),(b),(d)-(f); NIUC sch 4 para 9(1)(a),(b),(d)-(f)

7.12   UC sch 4 para 11(1),(3); NIUC sch 4 para 10(1),(3)

7.13   UC sch 4 para 11(1),(2); NIUC sch 4 para 10(1),(2)

7.14   WRA 40 definition: 'child'; UC sch 4 para 10(1)(c); NIWRO 46; NIUC sch 4 para 9(1)(c)

If a non-dependant is temporarily absent

7.15   A non-dependant who is temporarily absent is included as an occupier during:

  (a) an absence from Great Britain which meets the conditions in paras 2.39-32; or

  (b) the first six months that they are a prisoner if they meet the conditions in para 4.79; or

  (c) the first six months in any other circumstances so long as their absence is not expected to exceed six months. (For example they could be away studying.)

But these only apply if they were your non-dependant or included in your benefit unit (e.g. as a child or young person) immediately before their absence, and you then qualified for the housing costs element in your UC.

Non-dependants in the armed forces

7.16   A non-dependant who is temporarily absent is included as an occupier if they are:

  (a) your or your partner's son, daughter, step-son, or step-daughter; and

  (b) a member of the armed forces who is away on operations (para 2.28).

There is no time limit to this rule so long as they intend to return. But it only applies if they were your non-dependant or included in your benefit unit immediately before their absence (whether or not you then qualified for the housing costs element in your UC).

Other people in your home

7.17   Bedrooms are not allowed for anyone other than those described above (paras 7.8-16). For example they are not allowed for:

  (a) your partner if you are in a couple but claiming UC as a single person (see para 2.8);

  (b) your husbands and wives in a polygamous marriage, other than the one you are claiming UC with (see para 3.71);

  (c) lodgers of yours;

  (d) separate tenants of your landlord (if your accommodation is rented out in separate lettings);

  (e) a resident landlord/landlady;

  (f) joint tenants who are not in your benefit unit (see para 7.18);

  (g) non-dependants of any of the above (but see para 3.87 for non-dependants of joint tenants);

  (h) children and young persons for whom any of the above are responsible;

  (i) children for whom a non-dependant of yours is responsible (but see para 7.14);

  (j) foster children (but see para 7.21 for when an additional bedroom is allowed for a foster parent).

7.15   UC sch 4 para 11(1),(4),(5)(a)-(c),(6); NIUC sch 4 para 10(1),(4),(5)(a)-(c),(6); https://tinyurl.com/l32edcu

7.16   UC sch 4 paras 2 definition: 'member of the armed forces', 11(1),(4),(5)(d); NIUC sch 4 paras 2, 10(1),(4),(5)(d)

Joint tenants not in the same benefit unit

7.18   The following rules apply if you are in a joint tenancy (for example a house share) and at least one joint tenant is not in your benefit unit:

(a)   if you are a private renter, the size criteria apply separately to each single joint tenant or joint tenant couple: see para 6.24;

(b)   if you are a social renter, the size criteria do not apply to you at all: see para 5.17.

Additional bedrooms

7.19   You may qualify for an additional bedroom for an occupier of your home who:

(a)   is a foster parent or has a child placed with them for adoption (see para 7.21); or

(b)   requires overnight care from a non-resident carer (see paras 7.22-24); or

(c)   can't share a bedroom due to their disability (see paras 7.25-28).

You could qualify for one additional bedroom under each of (a) and (b), and two under (c) (one for you/your partner and one for a child). But if you are a private renter, the maximum number of bedrooms (under the general rules in table 7.1 and these rules) is always four.

7.20   The Upper Tribunal ([2017] UKUT 393 (AAC)) has held it to be unlawful discrimination that the additional bedroom in para 7.19(a) doesn't apply to disabled adults placed with the claimant under an adult placement scheme. Former discrimination between adults and children ([2016] UKSC 58) has been ended because the additional bedroom in each of para 7.19(b) and (c) now applies to both adults and children.

Fostering/kinship and pre-adoption

7.21   You qualify for an additional bedroom if you, or your partner if you are claiming UC as a couple:

(a)   are a foster parent (in Scotland a kinship carer) and:

- have a child placed with you, or
- are waiting for placement or between placements, but this only applies for up to 12 months in each period in which you don't have a placement; or

(b)   have a child placed with you for adoption (unless you are the child's close relative: see para 4.45).

Only one additional bedroom is allowed, even if you have more than one child placed with you. But if any child requires overnight care, see paras 7.27-28.

7.19   UC sch 4 paras 12(9), 26; NIUC sch 4 paras 11, 25

7.21   UC 2 definition: 'foster parent', 89(3)(a), sch 4 para 12(1)(b),(4),(5),(9); NIUC 2, 88(3)(a), sch 4 para 11(1)(b),(4),(5),(9)

Example: A foster parent

A couple are foster parents. They have two sons of their own aged 13 and 11, and two foster daughters aged 12 and 9.

The couple qualify for one bedroom for themselves, and one for their two sons. Although they do not qualify for a bedroom for the foster daughters under the general rules (table 7.1), they qualify for one additional bedroom as foster parents. So they qualify for three bedrooms in all.

People who require overnight care

7.22   You qualify for an additional bedroom if an occupier of your home (see para 7.23):

(a) is in receipt of:

   ▪ the daily living component of personal independence payment, or

   ▪ the middle or highest rate of the care component of disability living allowance, or

   ▪ constant attendance allowance or armed forces independence payment paid as part of an industrial injury or war disablement pension; and

(b) is provided with overnight care on a regular basis (see para 7.24) by one or more people who stay in your home and are engaged for this purpose, but who do not live with you.

Only one additional bedroom is allowed, even if more than one occupier meets these conditions.

7.23   For this rule, the occupiers of your home are:

(a) the people in your benefit unit (you, your partner, children and young persons: see paras 7.10-13); and

(b) non-dependants (see paras 7.14-16); and

(c) any child placed with you or your partner as their foster child (or kinship carer) or prior to adoption (see para 7.21).

7.24   It is not necessary for an actual bedroom to be available for your overnight carer(s). And the care does not have to be every night or on the majority of nights; but must be provided regularly –which means 'habitually, customarily or commonly', not just 'on occasion' or 'when needed': [2014] UKUT 325 (AAC).

Example: A person who requires overnight care

A husband and wife live alone. The husband receives the daily living component of personal independence payment, and a rota of carers stay every night of the week to care for him. At the weekend his wife provides overnight care for him.

The couple qualify for one bedroom under the general rules (table 7.1), and one additional bedroom because the carers provide regular overnight care. So they qualify for two bedrooms in all.

7.22-23 UC sch 4 para 12(A1),(3),(9); NIUC sch 4 para 11(A1),(3),(9)

Disabled people who can't share a bedroom

7.25   You qualify for an additional bedroom for:

(a) you and your partner if you meet the conditions in para 7.26;

(b) a child under 16 in your home who meets the conditions in para 7.27.

You can qualify under (a) or (b) or both.

7.26   You and your partner meet the conditions if:

(a) you are claiming UC as a couple (para 2.7); and

(b) one or both of you is in receipt of:

  ■ the daily living component of personal independence payment, or

  ■ the middle or highest rate of the care component of disability living allowance; or

  ■ the higher rate of attendance allowance; and

(c) due to your or your partner's disability, you are 'not reasonably able to share a bedroom' with each other.

7.27   A child under 16 meets the conditions if he or she:

(a) is the responsibility of:

  ■ you, or your partner if you are claiming UC as a couple (see paras 3.75-79 and 7.13), or

  ■ a non-dependant who is an occupier of your home; and

(b) is in receipt of the middle or highest rate of the care component of disability living allowance; and

(c) due to his or her disability, is 'not reasonably able to share a room with another child'.

But an additional bedroom is only allowed if this is needed to ensure the child has their own bedroom. (Young persons aren't included because they qualify for their own bedroom under the general rules in table 7.1.)

7.28   DWP guidance (ADM para F5135) gives examples of a child who 'disrupts the sleep of and may pose a risk to' or 'would significantly disturb the sleep of' another child; but this does not suggest that these are the only two situations in which an additional bedroom can be allowed.

Examples: Disabled people who can't share a bedroom

  1. A couple live alone. One partner is disabled.

  Under the general rules (table 7.1) they qualify for one bedroom. An additional bedroom is needed and allowed, so they qualify for two bedrooms.

  2. A couple have one child aged 14 who is disabled.

  Under the general rules they qualify for two bedrooms. No additional bedroom is needed or allowed.

7.25-27 UC sch 4 paras 1(2) definition: 'joint renter, 12(1)(c),(d),(6),(6A),(8),(9); NIUC sch 4 paras 1(2),11(1)(c),(d),(6),(6A),(8),(9)

3. A single person has two children aged 12 and 10. One child is disabled.

    Under the general rules they qualify for two bedrooms. An additional bedroom is needed and allowed, so they qualify for three bedrooms.

4. A couple have two children aged eight and six. One partner in the couple is disabled and one child is disabled.

    Under the general rules they qualify for two bedrooms. Two additional bedrooms are needed or allowed, so they qualify for four bedrooms.

Chapter 8 **Loan payments for mortgage interest**

- Who can get loan payments: see paras 8.4-17.
- The qualifying period: see paras 8.18-22.
- How to get loan payments: see paras 8.23-29.
- The amount of your loan payments: see paras 8.30-38.
- Payments, repayments and appeals: see paras 8.39-46.
- Loan payments if you are on other benefits: see paras 8.47-49.
- Transitional rules: see paras 8.50-55.

Introduction

8.1   This chapter applies to owner-occupiers and shared owners. It explains the loan payments the DWP can make towards mortgage interest or related payments on your home. It gives detailed rules for people who have claimed UC (paras 8.4-46) and summarises the rules for people who have claimed SPC or a legacy benefit (paras 8.47-49).

8.2   Before 6th April 2018, UC, SPC and the legacy benefits (JSA(IB), ESA(IR) and IS) included non-repayable amounts towards mortgage interest etc. Except in transitional cases (paras 8.50-55) these owner occupier benefit payments are replaced by loan payments from 6th April 2018.

8.3   Loan payments are legally separate from UC and other benefits. In Great Britain the law is made under sections 18-21 of the Welfare Reform and Work Act 2016, and is in the Loans for Mortgage Interest Regulations 2017 (SI 2017/725). DWP guidance is in ADM memo 8/18 [www]. In Northern Ireland the law is made under articles 13-16 of the Welfare Reform and Work (Northern Ireland) Order 2016 and the Loans for Mortgage Interest Regulations (Northern Ireland) 2017 (NISR 2017/176).

Who can get loan payments

8.4   Table 8.1 explains who can get loan payments. It applies if you are claiming UC. If you are claiming another benefit, see paras 8.47-49.

8.3   https://www.gov.uk/government/publications/advice-for-decison-making-staff-guide

8.4   LMI 3(1)-(2),(4), 5; NILMI 3(1),(2),(4),5

Table 8.1 **Loan payments for mortgage interest: conditions**

To get loan payments if you are claiming UC, you must meet all of the following conditions.

(a)　You are an owner occupier or shared owner (paras 8.5-6).

(b)　You are liable to make owner occupier payments on your home (para 4.34).

(c)　You have claimed UC or are treated as having claimed it (paras 3.2-11).

(d)　You meet all the conditions for UC (chapter 2).

(e)　You qualify for UC (paras 9.1-10) or would do except that your unearned income is too high (para 8.17).

(f)　You don't have any earned income (paras 8.15-16).

(g)　You have completed a qualifying period (para 8.18).

(h)　You consent to the DWPs loan offer and to a charge being placed on your home (para 8.26).

Owner occupiers and shared owners

8.5　　You can get loan payments if you are:

(a)　an owner occupier and buying your home; or

(b)　a shared owner and are part-buying and part renting your home.

In either case, you must be liable to make owner occupier payments (paras 8.7-9) on your home. Paras 4.59-78 explain when a dwelling counts as your home.

8.6　　In England and Wales 'shared owner' means you own a percentage of the value of your home (typically 25%, 50% or 75%) on a shared ownership lease. In Scotland it means you jointly own your home with your landlord and have the right to purchase their share.

Owner occupier payments

8.7　　'Owner occupier payments' (for both owner occupiers and shared owners) are:

(a)　interest on a mortgage or loan secured on your home (para 8.8); or

(b)　payments under an alternative finance arrangement (para 8. 9).

Mortgages and other loans

8.8　　You can get loan payments towards any mortgage or other loan that is secured on your home. In the case of a loan, this applies even if it was taken out to purchase items other than your home (e.g. a car loan or a loan for home improvements). If there is more than one mortgage/loan secured on your home, these are added together (up to the capital limit: para 8.33).

8.5-6　　LMI 3(1)-(2),(4), 5; UC 26(6); NILMI 3(1)-(2),(4),5; NIUC 27(6)

8.7-9　　LMI 3, schs 1-3; NILMI 3, schs 1-3

Alternative finance arrangements

8.9   You can get loan payments towards any 'alternative finance arrangement' that is recognised by UK law and was undertaken to purchase your home (either full ownership or shared ownership). Alternative finance arrangements are defined in Part 10A of the Income Tax Act 2007 (as amended). They are usually designed for religious purposes but can be used by anyone. Although they are structured to avoid the payment or receipt of interest, the lender's return is equivalent to the finance costs of borrowing. Many different types of product are recognised by UK law: the most common examples are in table 8.2.

Table 8.2 **Examples of alternative finance arrangements**

Purchase and resale (Murabaha)

The finance provider buys the home and immediately re-sells it to the home-owner at an agreed higher price, payable either in instalments or in one lump sum at a later date.

Diminishing shared ownership (Musharaka)

This is a partnership contract used to purchase a property. The bank and a customer usually both acquire beneficial interests in the asset. The home owner may pay a fee for the use of the asset, while also making payments in stages to gradually acquire an increasing share in, and ultimately all, the ownership of the home.

Profit share agency (Mudaraba/Wakala)

The customer deposits money with a finance institution (usually a bank) and either allows the bank to use it or appoints them as their agent to invest it. Any profits made are shared by the bank and the customer as agreed. The customer may pay a fee to the bank for its services.

Investment bonds (Sukuk)

These are similar to corporate bonds or a collective investment scheme. The finance institution provides the money to the customer to acquire the home in return for a share certificate in the ownership of the property. The property is used and managed by the home owner on behalf of the certificate holders.

Housing costs of owner occupiers

8.10   If you are an owner occupier, you can get:

(a)   loan payments towards your owner occupier payments; and

(b)   UC towards your eligible service charges (if any): see para 5.27.

No deduction is made from either of these for non-dependants (para 9.57).

8.10-13 LMI 3, schs 1-3; UC 26, sch 5; NILMI 3, schs 1-3; NIUC 27, sch 5

Housing costs of shared owners

8.11   If you are a shared owner, you can get:

(a) loan payments towards your owner occupier payments; and

(b) UC towards your eligible rent including eligible service charges: see chapters 5 and 6.

Deductions can be made from your eligible rent for non-dependants (para 9.58) but not from your owner-occupier payments.

Joint owner-occupiers and joint shared owners

8.12   The rules about joint owner occupiers and joint shared owners depend on whether you are jointly liable with:

(a) just your partner; or

(b) at least one person who is not your partner (for example if you and a friend are jointly buying your home).

8.13   If you are jointly liable with just your partner, the rules in paras 8.10-11 apply to you.

8.14   But if you are jointly liable with at least one person who is not in your benefit unit you can only get:

(a) loan payments towards your share of the owner occupier payments. The DWP decides this 'by reference to the appropriate proportion of the payments for which [you are] responsible'. So if there are two of you, your share could be half or could be some other reasonable proportion; and

(b) UC towards your share of the eligible service charges (owner occupiers and shared owners) and eligible rent (shared owners). This is decided as described in paras 5.11-13 or 6.11-13.

In practice the shares in (a) and (b) are normally the same.

If you have earned income

8.15   You can't get loan payments during any UC assessment period (para 3.39) in which:

(a) you are single and you have earned income; or

(b) you are a couple and either of you have earned income (whether you are claiming UC as a couple or as a single person).

If you are an owner occupier, you also can't get UC towards your service charges (para 5.27), but if you are a shared owner, you can get UC towards your eligible rent and service charges (chapters 5 and 6).

8.16   There are no exceptions to the rule in para 8.15. It applies to any kind of earned income you or your partner have (paras 10.3 and 10.7), irrespective of the nature of the work, its duration or the level of earnings. Working for only one day, or for just one hour during your assessment period disqualifies you.

8.14   LMI 3(3); UC sch 5; NILMI 3(3); NIUC sch 5

8.15   LMI 3(4); UC sch 5; NILMI 3(4); NIUC sch 5

If you have unearned income

8.17 If you or your partner have unearned income, this reduces the amount of your UC (paras 10.31-32). Then:

(a) if you qualify for at least some UC (paras 9.8-9), your unearned income doesn't affect the amount of your loan payments; but

(b) if you don't qualify for UC because your unearned income is too high (paras 9.8-9), your loan payments are reduced by the excess of your unearned income (see example 4).

The rules about (b) are not quite clear. But the DWP confirms it is correct, saying 'loan payments will be available to claimants who would have received support… pre-6th April 2018' (para 7.4 of explanatory memorandum to SI 2018/307).

Examples: Loan payments for mortgage interest

1. An owner occupier

Anna owns her home and has a mortgage on it. She is on UC and has no other income.

Once she completes her qualifying period, she can get loan payments from the DWP towards her mortgage interest (paras 8.10 and 8.19).

2. A shared owner couple

Kevin and Lucy are buying their home in a shared ownership scheme. They are on UC and have no other income.

Once they complete their qualifying period, they get loan payments from the DWP towards their mortgage interest. And both during and after their qualifying period, they can get UC towards their eligible rent and service charges (paras 8.11 and 8.19).

3. Earned income

Kevin gets a job with low income and he and Lucy continue to qualify for UC.

Because they now have earned income, their loan payments stop. But they continue to get UC towards their eligible rent and service charges (para 8.15).

4. Unearned income

Curtis owns his home and has a mortgage on it. He has been on UC for over nine months and gets UC of £317.82 per month and DWP loan payments of £50 per month.

He starts to receive unearned income of £330 per month from an annuity. His UC stops because his unearned income exceeds his maximum UC (para 9.4) by £12.18 per month.

His loan payments are reduced by the £12.18 per month 'excess' income, so he now gets loan payments of £37.82 per month (para 8.17).

Note on council tax rebates

In 1 and 2, the claimants are likely to receive maximum CTR (because their only income is from UC). But in 3 and 4, the claimants are likely to get less than maximum CTR.

8.17   LMI 2(1) definition: 'applicable amount', 11(1), 12(1); UC sch 5; NILMI 2(1),11(1),12(1); NIUC sch 5

The qualifying period

8.18   You can't get loan payments until you have completed a 'qualifying period'. The qualifying period is nine consecutive UC assessment periods (para 3.39) in each of which you have received UC. It can include assessment periods before 6th April 2018 and/or periods you were on JSA(IB), ESA(IR) or IS (paras 8.50-55).

Your housing costs during and after the qualifying period

8.19   During your qualifying period, you can't get loan payments, and:

(a) if you are an owner occupier, you also can't get UC towards any service charges (para 5.27); but

(b) if you are a shared owner, you can get UC towards your eligible rent and service charges (chapters 5 and 6).

8.20   After your qualifying period, you can get loan payments (so long as you meet the conditions in table 8.1) and UC payments towards your other housing costs as described in paras 8.10-14.

8.21   If you stop being entitled to UC (either during or after the qualifying period), you have to complete a full new qualifying period before you get loan payments (but if you move onto SPC, see paras 8.47-49).

Becoming a couple or a single person

8.22   When you become a couple or a single person (paras 3.5-6):

(a) your qualifying period continues to run, so long as you continue to receive UC; or

(b) if you have completed your qualifying period, your loan payments continue so long as you meet the conditions in table 8.1.

In live service areas (para 1.14), this is the case even if you have to reclaim UC (para 3.7), so long as you do so within one month.

How to get loan payments

8.23   You shouldn't have to make a separate claim for loan payments. The DWP should offer them to you whenever you qualify for them. This section explains the offer and how it could affect you. (See also paras 8.50-52 if you were on UC, JSA(IB), ESA(IR) or IS on 5th April 2018.)

8.24   However, you should inform the DWP if you become liable for owner occupier payments during your award of UC, and/or when the amount of capital you owe changes (para 8.35).

The DWP's offer

8.25   The DWP's offer should be sent to you or, if you are a couple, it should be sent to both of you.

8.18-22 LMI 2(1) definiitions: 'claimant', 'joint claimants', 'single claimant', 'qualifying period', 8(1)(b), 21; UC sch 5; NIUC sch 5

8.23-27 LMI 2(1) definition: 'benefit unit', 3(1)-(2), 4-6; NILMI 2(1),3(1),(2),4-6

8.26 The DWP's offer contains:

(a) a summary of the terms and conditions relating to the loan payments;

(b) the fact that there will be a charge on your home (para 8.27); and

(c) details of where you can get further information and independent legal and financial advice.

The charge on your home

8.27 If you accept the DWP's offer, the charge on your home will be registered with the Land Registry. You must 'execute' (sign) the relevant documentation about this. If you are a couple who are joint owners (or joint shared owners) both of you must do this (even if you are claiming UC as a single person).

Accepting or refusing the offer

8.28 If you accept the DWP's offer, you are awarded loan payments once your qualifying period is complete: see paras 8.18-22.

8.29 If you refuse the DWP's offer or don't reply to it, you can't get loan payments. But:

(a) if you are an owner occupier, you can get UC towards eligible service charges (para 5.27); and

(b) if you are a shared owner, you can get UC towards your eligible rent and service charges (chapters 5 and 6).

If you later change your mind about loan payments, the DWP should issue you with a new offer if you request this.

The amount of your loan payments

8.30 Your loan payments are worked out in two steps:

(a) assess the amount of capital you owe (para 8.31); and

(b) from this, calculate the amount of your loan payments (para 8.32).

Because the calculation uses a standard rate of interest (para 8.37), your loan payments are unlikely to match what you actually pay (and they can never cover capital repayments).

The capital you owe

8.31 Your loan payments are based on the capital you owe on:

(a) mortgages and other loans secured on your home (para 8.8); and

(b) alternative finance arrangements used to buy your home (para 8.9);

but only up to the capital limit (para 8.33). See also paras 8.12-14 if you are a joint owner or joint shared owner.

8.31   LMI 10, 11(1), 12(1),(3); NILMI 10,11(1),12(1),(3)

The calculation of your loan payments

8.32   Your monthly loan payment is calculated as follows:

(a) multiply the lower of

 - the capital you owe (para 8.31), or
 - the capital limit (para 8.33),

by the standard rate of interest (paras 8.37-38);

(b) divide the result by 12;

(c) if you have a mortgage or loan protection policy (e.g. to help you pay your mortgage when you lose your job or are ill), subtract the amount paid (in that month) to you or your lender;

(d) then subtract the whole of any unearned income you have (in that month) that is not used in the calculation of your UC.

Step (d) is only needed in the circumstances described in para 8.17 and the example there.

Example: Calculating loan payments

A single claimant is an unemployed home owner who meets the claimant commitment and qualifies for UC.

She purchased her home for £140,000 with a £120,000 repayment mortgage from her bank. The term of the loan is 25 years. At the time of her claim she has repaid £20,000 of the outstanding capital. The interest rate currently charged by her bank on her mortgage is 4.00%. Her current mortgage payments are £640.12 per month (including capital and interest).

She has completed her initial qualifying period (para 8.18) and qualifies for loan payments. On the date she completes her qualifying period the standard rate of interest is 2.61%.

Her loan payments are calculated as follows:

Total outstanding capital (£120,000 – £20,000)	£100,000
Standard rate of interest	2.61%
Annual loan payments (2.61% x £100,000)	£2,610
Monthly loan payments (£2,610 divided by 12)	£217.50

The capital limit

8.33   The capital limit is £200,000. This can only be increased for disability adaptations (para 8.34).

8.32   LMI 10,11(1),12(1),14A; NILMI 10,11(1),12(1),14A
8.33   LMI 11(2), 12(2); NILMI 11(2),12(2)

Adjusting the capital limit for disability adaptations

8.34 The following applies if:

(a) you, your partner, or a child or young person you are responsible for is getting:

- the daily living component of PIP, or
- the middle or highest rate of the care component of DLA, or
- attendance allowance or equivalent benefit (para 10.37); and

(b) you have a mortgage, loan or alternative finance arrangement (paras 8.8-9) which was to pay for adaptations that were necessary to meet that person's disablement needs; and

(c) as a result, the total capital you owe is greater than £200,000.

In this case, all the other amounts you owe (para 8.31) are added together and are subject to the £200,000 limit. The capital you owe for the adaptations is added (even if this takes the total above £200,000) and this (higher) figure is multiplied by the standard rate of interest in the calculation in para 8.32.

Changes in the capital you owe

8.35 Once you are entitled to loan payments, their amount is recalculated when the amount of capital you owe changes. This applies whether the capital you owe increases (e.g. because you have taken out a new mortgage/loan or alternative finance arrangement) or decreases (e.g. because you have made a capital repayment). But the change in your loan payment doesn't take effect until the first anniversary date on or after the change in the capital you owe. 'Anniversary dates' are counted from the first day you were entitled to:

(a) loan payments; or

(b) if earlier, owner occupier benefit payments in your UC or JSA(IB)/ESA(IR)/IS (paras 8.51-52).

8.36 If you first become entitled to loan payments while you are on UC (e.g. you take out your first mortgage/loan or alternative finance arrangement), the rules aren't quite clear. It seems that your loan payments begin when you notify the DWP and accept its offer or (if later) once your qualifying period is complete (para 8.28).

The standard rate of interest

8.37 The standard rate of interest is used to calculate your loan payments (para 8.32). It is the average mortgage rate published by the Bank of England [www]. On 6th April 2018 it was 2.61%.

8.38 The standard rate of interest only changes when the Bank of England publishes an average mortgage rate that differs from it by 0.5% or more. This new standard rate applies in the calculation of loan payments from the date six weeks later. At least seven days before that, the DWP must publish the new standard rate on a publicly accessible website, along with the date it will apply from.

8.34   LMI 2(1): 'disabled person', 11(3); NILMI 2(1), 11(3)

8.35   LMI 11(4)-(5), 12(4)-(5); NILMI 11(4)-(5),12(4)-(5)

8.37-38 LMI 13; NILMI 13
        www.gov.uk/support-for-mortgage-interest/what-youll-get

Payments, repayments and appeals

How loan payments are paid

8.39   The DWP pays your loan payments:

(a) to your lender if they are approved by the DWP (para 8.41); or

(b) otherwise, to you.

8.40   Your 'lender' means the provider of your mortgage, loan or alternative finance arrangement.

8.41   Most lenders are approved by the DWP, but lenders can also choose not to receive payments from the DWP. Lenders have duties towards you and the DWP: for example, they must apply the money they receive to your account, and pay the DWP a fee of 39p for each payment.

When loan payments are paid

8.42   In all the above cases, the DWP makes payments monthly in arrears. The payment dates don't necessarily match the dates your UC is paid.

Duration of loan payments

8.43   Your loan payments usually begin when your qualifying period is completed (paras 8.18-22). They then continue for as long as you meet all the conditions in table 8.1. For example, they stop if you begin receiving earned income (paras 8.15-16) or if your unearned income becomes so great that you no longer qualify (paras 8.17 and 8.32).

Repaying loan payments

8.44   Your loan payments plus interest (para 8.45) become repayable to the DWP only when:

(a) your home is sold, transferred or disposed of (other than to your partner); or

(b) you die (or in the case of a couple, the last of you who owns your home dies).

But generally speaking you (or your estate) can't be made to repay more than the value of your home. You can also choose to make early repayments at any time, so long as each repayment (other than the final one) is at least £100.

Interest on loan payments

8.45   The DWP charges interest on the loan payments you have received. For each half year (beginning 1st January and 1st July) the DWP uses the most recent weighted average interest rate on conventional gilts [www]. The rate as at 6th April 2018 was 1.5%. Interest ceases when you die (or in the case of a couple, the last of you who owns your home dies), or in any other case when the loan payments are repaid.

8.39-41 LMI 3,17, sch 4; NILMI 3,17,sch 4

8.42   LMI 7; NILMI 7

8.43   LMI 8,9(1)-(3); NILMI 8,9(1)-(3)

8.44-45 LMI 15,16; NILMI 15,16
             www.gov.uk/support-for-mortgage-interest/what-youll-get

Appeals

8.46 Appeals about your entitlement to loan payments and their amount are dealt with in the same way as UC (chapter 14). You can't appeal about when and how payments are made, but you can ask the DWP to reconsider this.

Loan payments if you are on other benefits

8.47 The rules in this chapter have so far been about loan payments for people claiming UC. This section summarises the main differences in the rules about loan payments for people claiming:

(a) SPC (state pension credit); or

(b) a legacy benefit (JSA(IB), ESA(IR) or IS).

Income, capital limit and non-dependants

8.48 If you have claimed SPC or a legacy benefit (rather than UC):

(a) having earned income doesn't by itself stop you getting loan payments, but it reduces your loan payments in the same way as unearned income (para 8.17);

(b) the capital limit is usually £100,000 instead of £200,000 (para 8.33), but apart from that the adjustment for disability adaptations applies in the same way (para 8.34);

(c) if you have one or more non-dependants (para 3.80), deductions are made from your loan payments – these depend on your and your non-dependant's circumstances and there are several exceptions: the rules are similar to those in the *Guide to Housing Benefit* chapter 6.

Qualifying period and loan payment run on

8.49 The other main differences from UC are as follows:

(a) if you have claimed SPC, there is no qualifying period (para 8.18);

(b) if you have claimed a legacy benefit, the qualifying period is 39 weeks, but after gaps in your legacy benefit of no more than 52 weeks you don't have to complete a fresh qualifying period;

(c) if you are on a legacy benefit (not UC or SPC), you qualify for a 'run on' of four extra weeks of loan payments when you start employment or self-employment, so long as it is for at least 30 hours per week and is expected to last at least five weeks.

If you were on SPC or a legacy benefit on 5th April 2018, see also para 8.52.

8.46   DAR99 sch 2 para 5(u)

8.47-49 LMI 2(1) definition: 'legacy benefit' (and LMI generally); NI LMI 2(1)

Transitional rules

People on UC since 5th April 2018

8.50   If you were on UC on 5th April 2018 but didn't yet qualify for owner occupier benefit payments (para 8.2), the continuous period you were on UC counts towards your qualifying period for loan payments (para 8.18).

8.51   If you were on UC on 5th April 2018 and qualified for owner occupier benefit payments (para 8.2) on that date:

(a) you continue to get owner occupier benefit payments in your UC until the end of your assessment period that includes:

- 5th April 2018, if the DWP offered you loan payments by that date, or
- 6th May 2018, if the DWP offered you loan payments by that date (but after 5th April 2018);

(b) you then have six weeks to decide what to do:

- if you accept the offer within the six weeks, you get owner occupier benefit payments for four weeks after your acceptance – and then loan payments after that,
- if you refuse the offer or don't reply to it, you get owner occupier benefit payments until the end of the six weeks or, if earlier, the date of your refusal – and then para 8.29 applies to you.

There are further rules in some cases. In particular, you can continue to get owner occupier benefit payments until 4th November 2018 (or sometimes later) if you need time to have an attorney etc appointed (para 8.29) to make the decision about loan payments.

People on SPC or a legacy benefit since 5th April 2018

8.52   Para 8.50 applies in a similar way to legacy benefits and para 8.51 applies in a similar way to SPC and legacy benefits (but reading 'SPC/legacy benefit' instead of 'UC' and 'benefit week' instead of 'assessment period').

People transferring from a legacy benefit to UC after 5th April 2018

8.53   The following rules apply if:

(a) your date of claim for UC (paras 3.28-32) is on or after 6th April 2018; and

(b) you were on a legacy benefit (JSA(IB), ESA(IR) or IS), or had a partner who was on a legacy benefit, within one month before the date of your claim for UC.

8.54   If you weren't getting loan payments while you were on the legacy benefit, the continuous period you were on the legacy benefit counts towards your qualifying period for loan payments (para 8.18) – and the qualifying period is counted as 39 weeks.

8.55   If you were getting loan payments while you were on the legacy benefit, these continue from when your UC starts (in other words, you don't have to complete a fresh qualifying period).

8.50-52 LMI 19 -20; NILMI 19 -20

8.53-55 LMI 21; NILMI 21

Chapter 9 **Calculating UC**

- The amount of your UC: see paras 9.1-11.
- The standard allowance, child element and two child limit: see paras 9.12-23.
- The work capability, carer and child costs elements: see paras 9.24-45.
- The housing costs element: see paras 9.46-56.
- Housing cost contributions from non-dependants: see paras 9.57-63.
- The benefit cap: see paras 9.64-74.
- Hardship payments if a sanction applies to you: see paras 9.75-83.

The amount of your UC

9.1   This chapter explains how your UC is calculated and how your housing costs are taken into account.

9.2   UC is a monthly benefit. Your entitlement is assessed for each monthly assessment period of your award. For the rules about assessment periods, and when UC starts, changes and ends, see chapters 3 and 11.

The calculation

9.3   The following steps (see paras 9.4-11) give the calculation of UC. Table 9.1 summarises the rules.

Your maximum UC

9.4   Your 'maximum UC' is the total of:

(a) a standard allowance for your basic living needs, or for both of you if you are claiming UC as a couple;

(b) additional amounts (called 'elements') for children and young persons, work capability, carers and childcare costs; and

(c) a housing costs element towards your rent and/or service charges.

These are explained in paras 9.12-63. If you are an owner-occupier or shared owner see chapter 8 for help with your owner-occupier housing costs.

Your income and capital

9.5   The amount of UC you qualify for depends on your income and capital. If you are in a couple, your partner's income and capital are included with yours. This is done even if you are in a couple but claiming UC as a single person (see para 2.8).

9.4   WRA 1(3), 8(2); NIWRO 6(3), 13(2)

9.5   WRA 5; UC 3(3), 18(2), 22(3); NIWRO 10; NIUC 3(2), 18(2), 23(3)

Table 9.1 **Amount of UC**

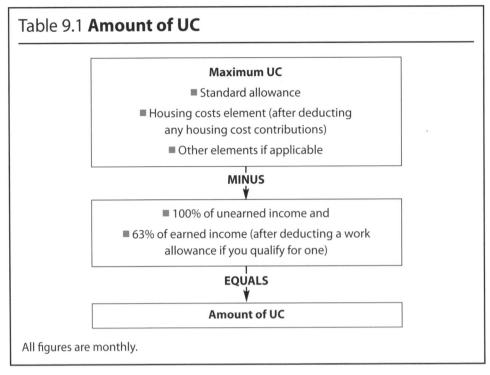

Maximum UC

- Standard allowance
- Housing costs element (after deducting any housing cost contributions)
- Other elements if applicable

MINUS

- 100% of unearned income and
- 63% of earned income (after deducting a work allowance if you qualify for one)

EQUALS

Amount of UC

All figures are monthly.

Capital and the capital limit

9.6   If your capital is over £16,000 you do not qualify for UC. See chapter 10 for how your (and your partner's) capital is assessed and which kinds of capital are counted or ignored.

Income and the amount of UC

9.7   If you have no income, you qualify for maximum UC (see para 9.4).

9.8   If you have income, you qualify for maximum UC minus:

  (a)   the whole of your unearned income; and

  (b)   63% of your earned income (after a work allowance has been deducted if you qualify for one).

See chapter 10 for how your (and your partner's) income is assessed, the work allowance, and which kinds of income are counted or ignored.

Minimum UC

9.9   If you qualify for at least one penny a month you are awarded UC.

T9.1   WRA 5(1)(b),(2)(b), 8(1),(3),(4); UC 22(1), (3); NIWRO 10(1)(b),(2)(b), 13(1),(3),(4); NIUC 23(1), (3)

9.6   WRA 5(1)(a),(2)(a); UC 18(1); NIWRO 10(1)(a),(2)(a); NIUC 18(1)

9.7   WRA 5(1)(b),(2)(b), 8(1)(a); NIWRO 10(1)(b),(2)(b), 13(1)(a)

9.8   WRA 5(1)(b),(2)(b), 8(1),(3),(4); UC 22(1), (3); NIWRO 10(1)(b),(2)(b), 13(1),(3),(4); NIUC 23(1), (3)

9.9   UC 17; NIUC 17

Rounding

9.10 Amounts used in the calculation of UC are rounded to the nearest penny, with halfpennies being rounded upwards.

Other calculation rules

9.11 Your UC can be reduced if:

(a) the 'benefit cap' applies to you (paras 9.64-74);

(b) a sanction applies to you, but in this case you may qualify for a hardship payment (paras 9.75-83);

(c) part of your UC is paid to a third party, for example because of rent, mortgage, utility, child support or other debts (para 12.26);

(d) an overpayment of UC (or related administrative penalty) is recovered (para 13.27); or

(e) an overpayment of another benefit is recovered from your UC.

Examples: Amount of UC

All figures are monthly. None of the claimants have capital.

1. Single renter aged 23, no income

His eligible rent is £400.

Maximum UC

▪ standard allowance	£251.77
▪ housing costs element (eligible rent)	£400.00
▪ total	£651.77
Amount of UC	£651.77

2. Couple over 25, renters, two children aged 3 and 5, unearned income only

Their eligible rent is £1250. Their unearned income is £300 maintenance received by one partner.

Maximum UC

▪ standard allowance	£498.89
▪ two child elements (£277.08 + £231.67)	£508.75
▪ housing costs element (eligible rent)	£1250.00
▪ total	£2257.64
Income deduction	
▪ unearned income £300 x 100%	– £300.00
Amount of UC	£1957.64

9.10   UC 6(1); NIUC 7(1)

3. Couple over 25, renters, no children, earned income only

Their eligible rent is £1300. Their earned income is £2500.

Maximum UC

■ standard allowance	£498.89
■ housing costs element (eligible rent)	£1300.00
■ total	£1798.89

Income deduction

■ earned income £2500 x 63%	– £1575.00

Amount of UC   £223.89

(They don't qualify for a work allowance: see paras 10.13-15 and the examples there.)

Allowances and elements

9.12 This section explains which UC allowances and elements you qualify for. The ones you qualify for are added together to give your maximum UC (see para 9.4).

9.13 Table 9.2 summarises the allowances and elements and gives their amounts.

Standard allowance

9.14 Everyone qualifies for a standard allowance. You get:

  (a) the single rate if you are a single person, or in a couple but claiming UC as a single person (see para 2.8). A lower figure applies if you are under 25;

  (b) the couple rate if you are claiming UC as a couple. A lower figure applies if you are both under 25.

Child element

9.15 You qualify for a child element for each child or young person you are responsible for (see paras 3.72-79):

  (a) if at least one child/young person was born before 6th April 2017, you get

    ■ the higher rate (also called the 'first child' rate) for one child/young person, and

    ■ the lower rate for each of the others;

  (b) otherwise you get the lower rate for each child/young person.

But if you are responsible for more than two children/young persons, you may be affected by the two child limit (para 9.17) or may not be able to claim UC (para 9.22).

9.14   WRA 9; UC 36(1), (3); NIWRO 14; NIUC 38(1), (3)

9.15   WRA 10; UC 24(1), 36(1); UCTP 43; NIWRO 15; NIUC 25(1), 38(1)

Disabled child addition

9.16   You qualify for the disabled child addition for each child or young person who meets one of the following conditions:

(a) you get the higher rate for each child/young person who is:

  ■ entitled to the highest rate of the care component of disability living allowance, or

  ■ entitled to the enhanced rate of the daily living component of personal independence payment, or

  ■ certified as blind or severely sight-impaired by a consultant ophthalmologist;

(b) you get the lower rate for each child/young person who is entitled to disability living allowance or personal independence payment but does not meet the conditions in (a).

You get a disabled child addition for every child/young person who meets these conditions, even if the number of your child elements is affected by the two child limit.

Table 9.2 **UC allowances and elements (2018-19)**

	Monthly amount
Standard allowance	
■ single under 25	£251.77
■ single aged 25 or over	£317.82
■ couple both under 25	£395.20
■ couple at least one aged 25 or over	£498.89
Child element	
■ higher rate	£277.08
■ lower rate	£231.67
Disabled child addition	
■ higher rate	£383.86
■ lower rate	£126.11
Work capability elements	
■ LCWRA element	£328.32
■ LCW element	£126.11
Carer element	£156.45
Childcare costs element	
■ maximum for one child	£646.35
■ maximum for two or more children	£1108.04

9.16   WRA 10; UC 2 definition: 'blind', 24(2), 36(1); NIWRO 15; NIUC 2, 25(2), 38(1)

T9.2   UC 36(1); NIUC 38(1)

The two child limit

9.17   The two child limit is introduced on 6th April 2017. To begin with, it has an interim period which is likely to run until a date in January 2019 (DWP circular U1/2017 page 5). The main rules during and after the interim period are the same (paras 9.18-20) but the transitional rules are different (paras 9.21-23).

How the two child limit works

9.18   The two child works as follows:

(a) you qualify for a child element (para 9.15) for each 'protected' child/young person in your family – this means each one who falls within any of the general or transitional exceptions (paras 9.19-23);

(b) and if there are one or more other children/young persons in your family, you qualify for a child element for:

■ two of them if you don't have any protected children or young persons, or

■ one of them if you have one protected child/young person, or

■ none of them if you have two or more protected children/young persons.

The DWP may tell you the order in which it takes your children/young persons into account. Although this may not match the order they were born in, it doesn't affect the rules given above.

General exceptions to the two child limit

9.19   A child/young person is in an excepted group and so doesn't count towards the two child limit (para 9.18) if he or she:

(a) was born to you or your partner as part of a multiple birth (twins, triplets and so on) – in this case, one child counts towards the two child limit and the other or others are in the excepted group; or

(b) was adopted by (or placed for adoption with) you or your partner – but not if you or your partner are their parent or step-parent or the adoption was directly from outside the British Isles; or

(c) is looked after by you or your partner as a 'friend or family carer' or 'kinship carer' under:

■ formal arrangements made (now or before they reached 16) by social services or a court, or confirmed by you or your partner being entitled to guardian's allowance for them, or

■ informal arrangements (made by you or your partner) if they would otherwise be likely to enter local authority care (in practice a social worker will be asked to confirm this); or

(d) is a child whose parent is under 16, and you or your partner is responsible for both of them; or

---

9.18   UC 24A, 24B; NIUC 25A, 25B

9.19   UC sch 12, NIUC sch 12

(e) was born to you or your partner as a result of non-consensual sexual intercourse with a person who doesn't (or doesn't now) live with you, for example due to rape or controlling or coercive behaviour (see para 9.20); or

(f) is your step-child and (a), (b) or (e) applied to them when you were in a couple with their parent or adoptive parent – but in this case only for as long as you remain on UC with no breaks in your entitlement longer than six months.

9.20   The DWP recognises that non-consensual sexual intercourse is an extremely sensitive issue. It can therefore accept evidence (relating to para 9.19(e)):

(a) from a third party it has approved for this purpose, normally a health professional, registered social worker or specialist charity; or

(b) that the person has been convicted of a relevant offence; or

(c) that the Criminal Injuries Compensation Board has made a relevant award to you; or

(d) from yourself, if you wish to do so.

Transitional exceptions during the interim period

9.21   Until the interim period ends (para 9.17), every child/young person who was born before 6th April 2017 is in an excepted group and so doesn't count towards the two child limit (para 9.18). The general exceptions also apply (para 9.19).

9.22   But until the interim period ends, if you are responsible for more than two children/young persons you can't make a claim for UC unless:

(a) you were on UC within the previous six months (paras 3.45-49); or

(b) you were on UC as a couple within the previous one month and are now claiming UC as a single person.

Instead, you can claim 'legacy' benefits (JSA(IB), ESA(IR), IS, CTC, WTC and HB). These have a two child limit with rules and exceptions that are similar to UC.

Transitional exceptions after the interim period

9.23   After the interim period ends (para 9.17), a child/young person is in an excepted group and so doesn't count towards the two child limit (para 9.18) if he or she:

(a) was born before 6th April 2017; and

(b) was either:

■ included in your UC at the end of the interim period, or

■ included in your child tax credit, JSA(IB) or income support within six months before your UC starts.

The general exceptions also apply (para 9.19).

9.20   UC 2 definition: 'step-parent', sch 12 para 5; NIUC 2, sch 12 para 5
9.21   UCTP 40(1),(2); NIUCTP 41(1),(2)
9.22   UCTP 39; SI 2017/483; NIUCTP 40
9.23   UCTP 40(1),(3),(4), 41; NIUCTP 41(1),(3),(4), 42

Examples: The two child limit

In examples 1-4 UC claims are made during the interim period (para 9.17) and the claimants are then continuously entitled to UC. In examples 5-6 the claims are made after the interim period and the claimants haven't been on UC or a legacy benefit before. All the examples use 'child' to include both children and young persons (paras 3.73-74).

UC claims made during the interim period

1. Two children

A single person has two children. She claims (and qualifies for) UC in March 2017.

- She qualifies for two child elements during and after the interim period.

2. Four children

A couple have three children born before 6th April 2017 and one baby born on or after that date.

- They qualify for three child elements (for the older children) during and after the interim period, but no child element for the baby (para 9.18(b)).

One of the older children then leaves home.

- They qualify for two child elements, but still no child element for the baby (para 9.18(b)).

3. New twins

A couple have one child born before 6th April 2017 and baby twins born on or after that date.

- They qualify for two child elements, during and after the interim period – one for the 'second' twin (para 9.18(a)) and only one more (para 9.18(b)).

4. An adopted child

The couple in example 3 adopt a child.

- They qualify for a third child element during and after the interim period (para 9.18(b)).

UC claims made after the interim period

5. Three children

A single person has three children born before 6th April 2017.

- She qualifies for only two child elements (para 9.23).

6. A child receiving kinship care

A single person in example 5 starts looking after a child as a kinship carer.

- She qualifies for a third child element for that child (para 9.19(c)).

Work capability elements

9.24   There are two work capability elements, called the 'LCWRA' and 'LCW' elements:

(a) you qualify for the LCWRA element if:

- you have 'limited capability for work and work-related activity' (the LCWRA condition): see paras 9.26-27, and

- you have completed a waiting period if you are required to: see paras 9.31-33;

(b) you qualify for the LCW element if:

- you have 'limited capability for work' (the LCW condition): see paras 9.26-27, and

- you claimed UC, ESA, IB, SDA or IS before 3rd April 2017 and meet the conditions in paras 9.29-30.

The amounts are in table 9.2.

9.25   You cannot get the LCWRA and LCW elements at the same time:

(a) if you are a single person (or claiming UC as a single person) you get whichever one you qualify for;

(b) if you are claiming UC as a couple, you get one LCWRA element if at least one of you qualifies for it, or one LCW element if at least one of you qualifies for it (and neither of you qualifies for the LCWRA element).

See para 9.36 for further rules which apply if you also qualify for the carer element.

Who meets the LCWRA or LCW condition

9.26   You can meet the LCWRA condition (limited capability for work and work-related activity) or LCW condition (limited capability for work) if:

(a) the DWP assesses you as doing so in your claim for UC – you (or someone on your behalf) should provide medical evidence about this, and the assessment (which can include medical examination) is based on the extent to which you can carry out a fixed list of activities; or

(b) the DWP has assessed you as meeting an equivalent condition in your claim for ESA, IB, SDA or IS – in ESA, the LCWRA element is called the 'support component' and the LCW element is called the 'work-related activity component'; or

(c) you fall within certain groups who don't have to have an assessment – for example you meet the LCW condition if you are in hospital, and meet the LCWRA condition if you are terminally ill.

Being terminally ill means suffering a progressive disease which is likely to lead to death within six months. If you are terminally ill you can choose whether or not to tell the DWP. If and when you do, you are awarded the LCWRA element back to when you became terminally ill (para 11.30).

9.24   WRA 12; UC 27(1),(2), 36(1); NIWRO 17; NIUC 28(1),(2), 38(1)

9.25   UC 27(4); NIUC 28(4)

9.26   UC 2 definition: 'terminally ill', 27(3), 38-44, schs 6-9; UCTP 19-27; NIUC 2, 28(3), 40-45, schs 6-9

9.27   But if you have earned income (paras10.7-8) which is more than (or equal to) what you would get for working 16 hours a week at the national minimum wage, you don't meet the LCWRA or LCW condition (so you can't get an LCWRA or LCW element) unless:

(a)   you are on disability living allowance, personal independence payment or attendance allowance or a related benefit (para 10.37); or

(b)   you fall within any of the groups who don't have to have an assessment (para 9.26(c)).

The importance of the LCWRA and LCW conditions

9.28   The LCWRA and LCW conditions don't just affect whether you qualify for a work capability element (paras 9.24-27). Amongst other things, they both also affect:

(a)   whether you are eligible for UC is you are aged 16/17 or are a student (tables 2.2 and 2.3);

(b)   which work-related requirements you are expected to carry out (para 2.44 and table 2.4); and

(c)   the UC work allowance (para 10.13).

So it can be important to be assessed for the LCWRA/LCW condition even if it is too late to get an LCW element (paras 9.29-30) or you qualify for a carer element instead (table 9.3).

Additional conditions for the LCW element

9.29   Since 3rd April 2017, the LCW element is abolished for many, but not all, new UC claims. To qualify for the LCW element, at least one of the following must apply to you (and see also para 9.30):

(a)   you were entitled to the LCW element immediately before 3rd April 2017; or

(b)   you became entitled to the LCW element after a waiting period (para 9.31) that began before 3rd April 2017, and/or as a result of providing medical evidence before then; or

(c)   you are on ESA (or national insurance credits instead of ESA) when you claim UC, and are therefore entitled to the LCW element either immediately or at the end of the 13 week 'assessment phase' (para 9.26(b)); or

(d)   you are on IB, SDA or IS due to incapacity for work when you claim UC, and therefore entitled to the LCW element (para 9.26(b)); or

(e)   you meet any of the conditions (a) to (d) in relation to the LCWRA element, and then become entitled to the LCW element instead.

In each case, 'entitlement' includes when this is the result of backdating (para 3.50) or a revision or appeal (chapter 14).

9.27   UC 41(2),(3); NIUC 42(2),(3)

9.29   SI 2017/204 sch 2 paras 9-15

9.30   Once you qualify for the LCW element (para 9.29), you continue to qualify for it for as long as:

(a) you continuously meet either the LCW or LCWRA element: see paras 9.26-27 (but you aren't awarded the LCW element during the periods you meet the LCWRA condition: para 9.25); and

(b) either:

 ▪ you remain continuously on UC (including when you become a couple or a single person: paras 3.5-7), or

 ▪ the only breaks in your UC are due to the level of your earned or unearned income (para 9.8) and are no longer than six months.

When you stop meeting these conditions you can't qualify for the LCW element again.

The LCWRA waiting period

9.31   Unless the exceptions in para 9.32 apply, you cannot get an LCWRA element until you have completed a waiting period:

(a) you have to wait three months beginning with:

 ▪ the first day you provide medical evidence (para 9.26(a)), or

 ▪ if you have earned income and para 9.27 applies to you, the day you claim UC or first ask for the LCWRA component to be included in it;

(b) your LCWRA element is awarded from the beginning of the assessment period following the day those three months end, so because assessment periods are one month, the waiting period can be up to four months.

Before 3rd April 2017, waiting periods applied in the same way to the LCW element.

Example: The LCWRA waiting period

A claimant is awarded UC for the first time from 4th July (she was not previously on ESA, IB, SDA or IS). On 17th July she provides medical evidence that she qualifies for the LCWRA element, and in due course this is accepted.

Her waiting period lasts for three months from 17th July to 16th October, and she qualifies for the LCWRA element from the first day of her next assessment period, which is 4th November (para 9.31).

9.30   SI 2017/204 sch 2 para 8
9.31   UC 28(1),(2); NIUC 29(1),(2)

Exceptions to the waiting period

9.32 The waiting period does not apply to you if:

(a) you are entitled to ESA and it includes the work-related activity component or support component – or this applied on the day before your UC award started but your contributory ESA has now run out; or

(b) you meet similar conditions in relation to a claim for IB, SDA or IS; or

(c) you are terminally ill (see para 9.26); or

(d) you are transferring between the LCW element and the LCWRA element; or

(e) you were getting an LCWRA or LCW element in a previous award of UC which ended because:

- your income became too high. In this case, the gap between the two UC awards must be no longer than six months, or

- you became a couple or stopped being a couple. In this case there must be no gap between the two UC awards.

If you began a waiting period in a previous award of UC but did not complete it, and the award ended for either of the reasons in (e), the waiting period ends on the day it would have ended had that award continued.

UC during a waiting period

9.33 During a waiting period, if the amount of your income means you:

(a) would qualify for UC with the LCWRA or LCW element; but

(b) would not qualify for UC without it,

you are awarded UC of one penny a month.

Carer element

9.34 You qualify for the carer element if:

(a) you are the carer of a severely disabled person (they could be someone in your household, including your partner, or someone outside it) and;

(b) you don't receive any earned income for caring for them; and

(c) either

- you get carer's allowance for this; or

- you meet the conditions for carer's allowance, or you would do except that your earnings are too high. The main condition is that you are regularly and substantially caring for them for at least 35 hours per week.

The amount is in table 9.2. If you are claiming UC as a couple and you each meet the above conditions in relation to a different severely disabled person, you get two carer elements (one each). Further rules are in paras 9.35-36.

9.32   UC 28(3),(4)-(6); UCTP 19-27; NIUC 29(3),(4)-(6)

9.33   UC 28(7); NIUC 29(7)

9.34   WRA 12; UC 29(1)-(3), 30, 36(1); NIWRO 17; NIUC 30(1)-(3), 31, 38(1)

Table 9.3 **Carer element and LCWRA/LCW elements**

This table explains which element(s) you get if you meet the LCWRA or LCW condition (paras 9.24-32) and the carer condition (paras 9.34-35) at the same time. UC law is not completely clear for couples, and other interpretations may be possible in some couple cases.

Single people who meet the LCWRA condition (para 9.25(a))	▪ You get the LCWRA element (but not the carer element).
Single people who meet the LCW condition (para 9.25(a))	▪ You get the carer element (but not the LCW element).

Couples who meet the LCWRA condition (para 9.25(b))	▪ You get the LCWRA element.
	▪ You also get one carer element (never two), but only if:
	   ▪ both of you meet the LCWRA condition and one or both of you meet the carer condition, or
	   ▪ one of you meets the LCWRA condition and the other one meets the carer condition.

Couples who meet the LCW condition (para 9.25(b))	▪ You get two carer elements (but no LCW element) if both of you meet the carer condition. ▪ You get one carer element if one of you meets the carer condition. You also get the LCW element, but only if the other one meets the LCW condition.

Shared care

9.35   Only one person can count as the carer for each severely disabled person. This applies to carer's allowance as well as the carer element. If two or more people meet the conditions for carer's allowance and/or the carer element, you choose who is to count as the carer, or if you do not the DWP chooses. So unless you agree to change who counts as the carer, you can't get the carer element if your partner or anyone else gets carer's allowance or the carer element for the severely disabled person.

Carer element and work capability elements

9.36   If you are a single person (or claiming UC as a single person) you cannot get a carer element and an LCWRA or LCW element at the same time. You get the element which is worth most. If you are claiming UC as a couple there are limits to getting these at the same time. You get the element (or combination of elements) that is worth most but without making you better off than two single people. Table 9.3 gives the rules about this.

T9.3   UC 29(4); NIUC 30(4)

9.35   UC 29(1),(3); NIUC 30(1),(3)

9.36   UC 29(4); NIUC 30(4)

Childcare costs element

9.37 You qualify for the childcare costs element if you meet:

(a) the work condition (see paras 9.38-40); and

(b) the childcare costs condition (see paras 9.41-43).

The amount is 85% of your childcare costs up to a fixed limit (see paras 9.44-45).

The work condition

9.38 If you are a single person you meet the work condition if you:

(a) are in paid work; or

(b) have an offer of paid work that is due to start before the end of your next assessment period; or

(c) ceased paid work in your current assessment period or up to one month before it began; or

(d) are receiving statutory sick, maternity, paternity or adoption pay or maternity allowance.

What counts as paid work is described in para 9.40. For assessment periods, see para 3.39.

9.39 If you are in a couple (even if you are claiming UC as a single person):

(a) both of you must meet the work condition in para 9.38; or

(b) one of you must meet the work condition and the other one must be unable to provide childcare because they:

- have limited capability for work (or for work and work-related activity): see para 9.26, or

- meet the conditions for carer's allowance (whether or not they have claimed it), or would do so except that their earnings are too high (see para 9.34), or

- are temporarily absent from your household (see para 3.68).

Paid work

9.40 'Paid work' means work for which payment is made or expected. But it does not include work which is for a charitable or voluntary organisation or as a volunteer, and for which only expenses are paid or expected.

The childcare costs condition

9.41 You meet the childcare costs condition if you or your partner (if you are claiming UC as a couple) pay childcare charges for a child or young person you are responsible for. This means:

9.37 WRA 12; UC 31; NIWRO 17; NIUC 32
9.38 UC 31(1)(a),(2); NIUC 33(1)(a),(2)
9.39 UC 3(6), 32(1)(b),(2); NIUC 3(5), 33(1)(b),(2)
9.40 UC 2 definition: 'paid work'; NIUC 2

(a)   a child under 16; or

(b)   a young person aged 16, but only in the period before the first Monday in September following their 16th birthday.

This applies even if the number of your child elements is affected by the two child limit.

9.42   Childcare charges only count for these purposes if they are to enable you to:

(a)   continue in paid work; or

(b)   take up paid work, in the situation in para 9.38(b); or

(c)   maintain arrangements you had before you left paid work, in the situations in para 9.38(c) and (d).

9.43   In order to count for these purposes, the childcare charges must be paid to:

(a)   a registered childminder, childcare agency or equivalent (including an approved childcare provider outside Great Britain); or

(b)   an out-of-school-hours (or pre-school age) scheme provided by a school as part of its school activities.

Childcare provided by the child's 'close relative' (see para 4.45) in the child's home, or by the child's foster parent, is not included.

The amount of the childcare element

9.44   The amount of your childcare element is:

(a)   85% of the monthly childcare charges you pay (para 9.45); or

(b)   the maximum amount in table 9.2 (if that is lower than the 85%).

But any amount of your childcare charges is ignored which: the DWP considers excessive for the extent of your or your partner's paid work; or is met by an employer or any other person; or is met by government payments in connection with any work-related activity or training you are undertaking.

9.45   If the 'full service' rules apply to you (para 1.14), childcare changes are taken into account in a particular assessment period if you (or your partner):

(a)   report them to the DWP within that assessment period, or up to 13 months later in special circumstances (para 11.21); and

(b)   paid them:

- in that assessment period, for childcare provided in that assessment period or in the preceding month – in this case, the whole amount is taken into account , or

- in either of the two preceding months, for childcare provided in that assessment period – in this case, only the amount attributable to that assessment period is taken into account (calculated on a daily basis).

9.41   UC 33(1)(a), 35(9); NIUC 34(1)(a), 37(6)

9.42   UC 33(1)(b); NIUC 34(1)(b)

9.43   UC 35; NIUC 37

9.44   UC 34, 36(1); NIUC 35, 38(1)

9.45   UC 33(1)(za),(a); SI 2014/2887 reg 5

If the 'live service' rules apply to you (para 1.14), child care charges are taken into account in a particular assessment period if you (or your partner) report them to the DWP within that assessment period or the following assessment period, and paid them in that assessment period for childcare provided at any time.

Example: Childcare element and amount of UC

Kate is 29 and has a child of 7. She works and pays a registered childminder £500 a month. Her eligible rent is £800 a month and she has no non-dependants. She has no capital, and her earnings (after deducting the work allowance) are £1500 a month.

Maximum UC

▪ Standard allowance	£317.82
▪ Child element (higher rate)	£277.08
▪ Childcare element (85% of £500)	£425.00
▪ Housing costs element (eligible rent)	£800.00
▪ Total	£1819.90

Amount of UC

▪ Maximum UC	£1819.90
▪ Earned income deduction (63% of £1500)	– £945.00
▪ Monthly amount of UC	£874.90

The housing costs element

9.46　　You qualify for a housing costs element if you are liable to pay rent and/or service charges on your home. This is explained in chapter 4. See paras 9.48-56 for how much you qualify for, and table 4.6 if you qualify for a housing costs element for two homes.

9.47　　Your housing costs element is added to the standard allowance and other elements you qualify for to give the amount of your maximum UC: see para 9.4.

The amount of your housing costs element: renters

9.48　　If you are a renter your housing costs element equals:

　(a)　your monthly eligible rent (see paras 5.9 and 6.9);

　(b)　minus any housing cost contributions expected from non-dependants living with you (see paras 9.57-63).

9.49　　If the housing cost contributions are greater than (or equal to) your monthly eligible rent, your housing costs element is nil. No part of the housing cost contributions is ever deducted from your standard allowance or from other elements you qualify for.

9.46　　WRA 11(1),(2); UC 25; NIWRO 16(1),(2); NIUC 26

9.48　　UC 26(1),(2), sch 4 paras 13,14(2), 22, 23; NIUC 27(1),(2), sch 4 paras 12, 13(2), 21,22

9.49　　UC sch 4 para 14(3); NIUC sch 4 para 13(3)

9.50　　UC 26(1),(4)-(6), sch 5 para 4(3); NIUC 27(1),(4)-(6), sch 5 para 4(3)

The amount of your housing costs element: shared owners

9.50 If you are a shared owner your housing costs element equals your monthly eligible rent minus any housing cost contributions (see paras 9.51-52). See chapter 8 for help with your mortgage interest, etc.

The amount of your housing costs element: owners

9.51 If you are an owner-occupier your housing costs element equals only your eligible service charges (see para 4.23). Unlike the rules for renters, there is no deduction for housing cost contributions. See chapter 8 for help with your mortgage interest, etc.

9.52 But if you are an owner-occupier you do not qualify for a housing costs element if you have any kind of earned income (paras 10.7-8). If you are in a couple (even if you are claiming UC as a single person) you do not qualify if either of you has earned income.

Information about rent and service charges

9.53 If you are a social renter (para 5.3) your landlord is usually asked to provide the DWP with details about your rent and service charges. If you are a private renter (para 6.3), you are usually invited to bring these details to an interview with the jobcentre or (for example) your local council.

Converting rent and service charges to a monthly figure

9.54 Because UC is a monthly benefit, rent or service charge payments which are not monthly are converted to a monthly figure:

(a) multiply weekly payments by 52 then divide by 12;

(b) multiply two-weekly payments by 26 then divide by 12;

(c) multiply four-weekly payments by 13 then divide by 12;

(d) multiply three-monthly payments by 4 then divide by 12;

(e) divide annual payments by 12.

These rules apply to rent and service charges in all cases. They do not apply to your loan payments for mortgage interest etc (see para 8.32 instead). The law gives no specific rule for daily payments. But these usually occur only in the types of accommodation where UC cannot be paid towards housing costs (see para 4.11).

Estimating housing costs

9.55 The DWP can agree to estimate the amount of your housing costs if it doesn't have all the information and evidence it needs about them.

Rent-free and service charge-free periods

9.56 If you have rent-free or service charge-free periods (periods during which rent or service charges are not payable), first calculate the annual figure as follows:

9.51   UC 26(1),(3), sch 5 para 9; NIUC 27(1),(3), sch 5 para 9
9.52   UC sch 5 para 4(1),(2); NIUC sch 5 para 4(1),(2)
9.54   UC sch 4 para 7(1),(2), sch 5 para 13(1),(3); NIUC sch 4 para 6(1),(2), sch 5 para 13(1),(3)
9.55   D&A 39(1),(4)

(a) if your payments are weekly, subtract the number of rent-free weeks from 52, and multiply your weekly payment by the result;

(b) if your payments are two-weekly, subtract the number of rent-free two-weeks from 26, and multiply your two-weekly payment by the result;

(c) if your payments are four-weekly, subtract the number of rent-free four-weeks from 13, and multiply your four-weekly payment by the result;

(d) in any other case, add together all the payments you are liable to make over a 12 month period.

Then divide the result by 12.

Housing cost contributions

9.57   This section describes the housing cost contributions which are deducted from your eligible rent to obtain your housing costs element. This applies if you are a renter or a shared owner, but not if you are an owner-occupier (see paras 9.48-52).

Housing cost contributions and non-dependants

9.58   One housing cost contribution is deducted from your eligible rent for each non-dependant you have. If two non-dependants are a couple, this means two deductions (not one between them).

9.59   A non-dependant is usually an adult son, daughter, other relative or friend who lives with you on a non-commercial basis: for the details see paras 3.80-87. A housing cost contribution can be described as the amount they are expected to contribute towards your housing costs.

The amount of the contribution

9.60   In 2018-19 the monthly amount of the housing cost contribution is £72.16. This figure applies to each non-dependant, no matter what income they have. But see paras 9.62-63 for when no contribution applies at all.

9.61   The UC contribution of £72.16 per month contrasts with the HB figures (which are called non-dependant deductions). These vary with the non-dependant's income and can be over £400 (monthly equivalent).

When no contribution applies

9.62   No housing cost contribution applies for any of the non-dependants in your home if:

(a) you are a single person (or claiming UC as a single person) and you are in any of the groups in table 9.4; or

(b) you are a couple and at least one of you is in any of the groups in table 9.4.

9.56   UC sch 4 para 7(2)(d),(3),(3A),(4), sch 5 para 13(4),(4A),(5); NIUC sch 4 para 6(2)(d),(3),(4),(5), sch 5 para 13(4),(5),(6)

9.58   UC sch 4 para 13; NIUC sch 4 para 12

9.60   UC sch 4 para 14(1); NIUC sch 4 para 13(1)

9.62   UC sch 4 para 15(1); NIUC sch 4 para 14(1)

Table 9.4 **No housing cost contributions: your circumstances**

No housing cost contributions apply if you or your partner are:

(a) in receipt of:

- the middle or highest rate of the care component of disability living allowance, or
- the daily living component of personal independence payment, or
- attendance allowance or equivalent benefit (para 10.37);

(b) entitled to any of the above benefits, but not receiving it because of being in hospital; or

(c) certified as blind or severely sight-impaired by a consultant ophthalmologist.

9.63 No housing cost contribution applies for any particular non-dependant in your home who is in any of the groups in table 9.5.

Table 9.5 **No housing cost contributions: non-dependant's circumstances**

No housing cost contribution applies for any non-dependant who is:

(a) under 21 years old;

(b) responsible for a child under 5 years old;

(c) your son, daughter, step-son or step-daughter (or your partner's if you are claiming UC as a couple) and is a member of the armed forces who is away on operations;

(d) in receipt of:

- the middle or highest rate of the care component of disability living allowance, or
- the daily living component of personal independence payment, or
- attendance allowance or equivalent benefit (para 10.37);

(e) entitled to one of the above benefits, but not receiving it because of being in hospital;

(f) in receipt of state pension credit;

(g) in receipt of carer's allowance; or

(h) a prisoner (see para 2.37).

T9.4   UC 2 definition: 'blind', sch 4 para 15(2); NIUC 2, sch 4 para 14(2)

9.63   UC sch 4 para 16(1); NIUC sch 4 para 15(1)

T9.5   UC sch 4 paras 2 definition: 'member of the armed forces', 16(2); NIUC sch 4 paras 2, 15(2)

Examples: Housing cost contributions

All figures are monthly. No-one in these examples (except the younger son in example 2) is in any of the groups in tables 9.4 or 9.5.

1. One non-dependant

Ewan's eligible rent is £600. He has one non-dependant, his daughter aged 30.

■	Eligible rent	£600.00
■	Housing cost contribution	– £72.16
■	Housing costs element	£527.84

2. Two non-dependants

Rosie's eligible rent is £950. She has two non-dependants, her sons aged 20 and 24.

■	Eligible rent	£950.00
■	Housing cost contribution (older son only)	– £72.16
■	Housing costs element	£877.84

3. Two non-dependants who are a couple

Hazel's eligible rent is £700. She has two non-dependants, her son and daughter-in-law.

■	Eligible rent	£700.00
■	Two housing cost contributions (2 x £72.16)	– £144.32
■	Housing costs element	£555.68

The UC benefit cap

9.64   This section describes how the 'benefit cap' can reduce your UC so that the total of your UC and other welfare benefits does not exceed a fixed monthly figure. Exceptions are given in paras 9.68-74. If your UC is reduced because of the benefit cap, you may be able to get a discretionary housing payment from your local council or (in Northern Ireland) welfare supplementary payments (see the *Guide to Housing Benefit*). The Supreme Court has held that the benefit cap does not in general discriminate unlawfully: R (SG and others) v SSWP. The Court of Appeal (R(DA and others) v SSWP) has also decided that it does not discriminate in the case of lone parents with a child aged under two – a decision which is under appeal to the Supreme Court (HB G3/2018).

The amount of the benefit cap

9.65   The monthly amount of the benefit cap is as follows:

(a)   if you are a single person (or claiming UC as a single person) and are not responsible for any children or young persons:

■   £1284.17 in Greater London,

■   £1116.67 elsewhere;

9.64   R (SG and others) v SSWP UKSC (2015) www.bailii.org/uk/cases/UKSC/2015/16.html;
          R (DA and others) v SSWP EWCA [2018] www.bailii.org/ew/cases/EWCA/Civ/2018/504.html

(b) if you are a single person and are responsible for at least one child or young person, or a couple (with or without children/young persons):

- £1916.67 in Greater London,
- £1666.67 elsewhere.

Greater London means the London Boroughs and the City of London.

The amount of the UC reduction

9.66   Table 9.6 shows how the amount of the reduction (if any) is calculated.

Table 9.6 **Calculating UC benefit cap reductions**

For each assessment period of one month:

(a) Add together your and your partner's entitlement to all the following welfare benefits in that month (see para 9.67):

- universal credit
- child benefit
- jobseeker's allowance
- employment and support allowance
- maternity allowance
- bereavement allowance
- widow's pension
- widowed mother's allowance
- widowed parent's allowance

(b) If you qualify for the UC childcare costs element in that month (see para 9.37), subtract its full amount (see para 9.44) from the above total. (Otherwise skip this step.)

(c) If the result exceeds the monthly benefit cap (see para 9.65) your UC for that month is reduced by the amount of this excess.

Notes:

- Step (b) 'protects' the childcare costs element from the UC benefit cap (even if the amount of your UC is less than your childcare costs element). It is described in a more complicated way in the law, but this table gives the correct result.
- Widow's pension, widowed mother's allowance, widowed parent's allowance are paid for deaths occurring before 6th April 2017. Bereavement support payments for deaths occurring after 5th April 2017 are not counted.
- For specified supported accommodation, see also para 4.11.

9.65   UC 80A; NIUC 80A

T9.6   WRA 96; UC 78,79,81

9.67   The calculation in table 9.6 takes account of the welfare benefits shown there, using the amounts before any reductions for sanctions, recoveries of overpayments and administrative penalties, or payments to third parties. But the following are not included:

(a)   any amount of a welfare benefit you do not receive because of the rules about overlapping benefits;

(b)   any ESA you are disqualified from receiving.

Benefits other than UC are calculated and converted to a monthly figure as described in para 10.33. Your partner's benefits are included if you are in a couple (even if you are claiming UC as a single person). But if you become a couple while you are on UC, and your new partner is on HB but not UC, their benefits are not included during the assessment period in which you become a couple.

Benefit cap exceptions

9.68   The benefit cap does not apply to you if:

(a)   you have earned income of at least £542.88 a month: see para 9.69; or

(b)   you qualify for a 'grace period' after leaving paid work or after a reduction in your earned income: see paras 9.70-73; or

(c)   you qualify for certain benefits etc: see para 9.74.

If you have earned income

9.69   The benefit cap does not apply to you in any assessment period of one month in which you have earned income of at least £542.88 for that month. This means employed and/or self-employed earnings assessed as in chapter 10 (but not the kind of notional self-employed earnings in para 10.78). The figure of £542.88 is the monthly equivalent of working 16 hours a week at the national living wage (which is the same as the national minimum wage for people over 25, and is £7.83 per hour from 1st April 2018). It goes up whenever the national living wage goes up. It applies whether you are a single person or in a couple (regardless of your age). And if you are in a couple, your partner's earned income is included (even if you are claiming UC as a single person).

If you qualify for a grace period

9.70   The benefit cap does not apply to you during a 'grace period'. You qualify for a grace period if you had earned income of at least £542.88 a month (see para 9.69) in each of the 12 months before your grace period begins and:

(a)   your earned income reduces below £542.88 a month (or ends) while you are on UC; or

(b)   you or your partner (even if you are claiming UC as a single person) ceased paid work (see para 9.40) before your entitlement to UC began.

The rules in these cases are in paras 9.71-73.

9.67   UC 78(2), 80; UCTP 9; NIUC 78, 80

9.69   UC 6(1A)(za), 82(1)(a),(4); NIUC 7(1A)(za), 82(1)(a),(4); SI 2018/455 reg 2(2)

9.70   WRA 40 definition: 'claimant'; UC 78(2), 82(1)(b),(2)-(4); NIWRO 46; NIUC 78(2), 82(1)(b),(2)-(4)

9.71   If your earned income reduces below £542.88 a month (or ends) while you are on UC (see para 9.70):

(a)   your grace period starts on the first day of the assessment period in which that happens;

(b)   it lasts for nine months (in other words, nine assessment periods).

See example 1.

9.72   If you or your partner ceased paid work before your entitlement to UC began (see para 9.70):

(a)   your grace period starts on the day after you or your partner ceased paid work (if this applies to both you and your partner, use the most recent of these days);

(b)   it lasts nine months – but the benefit cap does not apply to you until the assessment period following the one in which the grace period ends.

See example 2.

9.73   If your entitlement to UC ends before the end of the nine months, your grace period ends when your UC ends.

If you qualify for certain benefits etc

9.74   The benefit cap does not apply to you in any assessment period in which you (or your partner if you are claiming UC as a couple) are in one or more of the excepted groups in table 9.7.

Examples: The UC benefit cap and the grace period

1. A reduction in earned income

A single person has been on UC for over 12 months. She has had earned income of at least £542 per month throughout that time, so no benefit cap has applied to her (see para 9.69). Her assessment periods start on the 23rd of each month. She loses her job on 31st March.

Her grace period (see para 9.71) begins on 23rd March and lasts nine months until 22nd December. The benefit cap applies to her from 23rd December.

2. Losing paid work then claiming UC

A single person has been working for many years with earned income of at least £542 a month. He loses paid work on 15th January. When he claims UC a few weeks later, he is awarded it from 26th February. So his assessment periods begin on the 26th of each month.

His grace period (see para 9.72) begins on 16th January and lasts nine months until 15th October. The benefit cap applies to him from the first day of his next assessment period, which is 26th October.

9.71   UC 82(2)(a); NIUC 82(2)(a)

9.72   UC 82(2)(b); NIUC 82(2)(b)

9.73   UC 82(2); NIUC 82(2)

9.74   UC 83; NIUC 83

Table 9.7 **The UC benefit cap: excepted groups**

(a) You qualify for:
- the LCWRA element in your UC (see para 9.24), or
- the support component in your ESA (see para 9.26), or
- the carer element in your UC (para 9.34).

(b) You are in receipt of:
- personal independence payment,
- disability living allowance,
- carer's allowance,
- guardian's allowance,
- attendance allowance or equivalent benefit (para 10.37),
- industrial injuries benefit,
- a war widow's, widower's, or surviving civil partner's pension,
- a war disablement pension,
- a payment under the Armed Forces and Reserve Forces compensation scheme, or
- a payment from a foreign government similar to any of the last three items;

or are entitled to any of these, but not receiving it because of being in hospital or a care home.

(c) You are responsible for a child or young person who is in receipt of:
- disability living allowance,
- personal independence payment, or
- carer's allowance (young persons only);

or is entitled to either of these, but not receiving it because of being in hospital or a care home.

Notes:

If you are claiming UC as a couple, references to 'you' also include your partner.

Other exceptions to the benefit cap: see paras 9.69-73.

Hardship payments

9.75   This section summarises the hardship payments you may be able to get if your UC is reduced due to a sanction.

Sanctions

9.76   In broad terms, a sanction can apply to you if:

(a) you fail to apply for a vacancy, take up an offer of work or meet another work-related requirement when you are on UC (see paras 2.40-44); or

(b) you lost work or pay voluntarily or for no good reason before claiming UC; or

(c) a sanction is transferred from your JSA or ESA to your UC.

There are detailed rules about how long a sanction lasts. The longest possible period is 1,095 days (three years) if you are aged 18 or over, or 28 days if you are aged 16 or 17.

9.77   The monthly amount of the sanction equals:

(a) the whole of your standard allowance (see table 9.2) if you are aged 18 or over; but

(b) 40% of that if you are aged 16 or 17, or don't have to carry out any work-related requirement or only have to carry out a work-focused interview (para 2.44); but

(c) nil if you have limited capacity for work and work-related activity (see para 9.26).

This is deducted from your UC at a daily rate for each day a sanction applies to you. The daily rate is the monthly amount multiplied by 12 then divided by 365. If you are claiming UC as a couple, half the daily rate applies for each one of you a sanction applies to.

Who qualifies for a hardship payment

9.78   The DWP must award you a hardship payment if:

(a) you are aged 18 or over; and

(b) your sanction equals the whole of your standard allowance (see para 9.77(a)); and

(c) you make an application (see para 9.79); and

(d) you have met any work-related requirements applying to you during the seven days before your application is made; and

(e) the DWP accepts that you are 'in hardship' (see para 9.80).

See paras 9.81-82 for the period and amount.

Applying for a hardship payment

9.79   You can apply for a hardship payment on a form provided for this purpose or in any other manner accepted by the DWP. If you are claiming UC as a couple, either of you may apply. You must provide the information and evidence which is required, and accept that the hardship payment is recoverable (see para 9.83). A separate hardship application is needed for each period (see para 9.81).

9.76   WRA 26, 27; UC 100-113, sch 11; NIWRO 31, 32; NIUC 98-110, sch 11
9.77   UC 90, 91, 111; NIUC 89, 90, 108
9.78   WRA 28, UC 116(1); NIWRO 33, NIUC 111(1)
9.79   UC 116(1)(c)-(e); NIUC 111(1)(c)-(e)

What 'in hardship' means

9.80   You are accepted as being in hardship only if you (or you and your partner if you are claiming UC as a couple):

(a) cannot meet your 'most basic and essential needs' for accommodation, heating, food and/or hygiene, or those of a child or young person you are responsible for; and

(b) cannot do so solely because of the sanction; and

(c) have made 'every effort' to:

- access alternative support to meet or partially meet these needs, and

- stop incurring expenditure which does not relate to them.

The period of the hardship payment

9.81   Each hardship payment covers the period:

(a) from the date you applied (or if later, the date you provided the information and evidence required);

(b) to the day before your next normal monthly payment of UC is due (or if that is seven days or less, to the day before the next but one payment is due).

The amount of the hardship payment

9.82   The amount of your hardship payment is calculated as follows:

(a) start with the amount of UC you lost (as a result of the sanction) in the assessment period before the one in which you made your application;

(b) multiply this by 60%;

(c) multiply the result by 12;

(d) then divide by 365;

(e) then multiply by the number of days in the period your hardship payment covers (see para 9.81).

For sanctions lasting longer than a couple of months or so, the effect of this roundabout calculation is approximately the same as if your sanction was 40% of your standard allowance.

Repaying hardship payments

9.83   Hardship payments are 'recoverable'. This means you are expected to repay them by receiving less UC in the future. But you do not have to repay them during any assessment period in which your earnings (including your partner's if you are claiming UC as a couple) are at least the national minimum wage for your expected hours of work. And once you have had this level of earnings for 26 weeks since a sanction last applied to you, they stop being recoverable altogether.

9.80   UC 116(2),(3); NIUC 116(2),(3)

9.81   UC 117; NIUC 112

9.82   UC 118; NIUC 113

9.83   UC 119; NIUC 114

Chapter 10 **Income and capital for UC**

- General rules about income and capital: see paras 10.1-6.
- Earned income and the work allowance: see paras 10.7-15.
- Employed earnings: see paras 10.16-22.
- Self-employed earnings: see paras 10.23-30.
- Unearned income: see paras 10.31-52.
- Capital: see paras 10.53-72.
- Notional income and capital: see paras 10.73-89.

General rules

10.1   This chapter explains how your income and capital are assessed for UC purposes. It describes which kinds of income and capital are counted and which are 'disregarded' (which means ignored).

10.2   If you have capital over £16,000 you cannot get UC: see para 10.55. Otherwise your income (including assumed income from capital) affects how much UC you get: see paras 10.9 and 10.32. For the UC calculations, see paras 9.3-10.

Whose income and capital are taken into account

10.3   The assessment of your UC takes into account:

(a) your income and capital if you are a single person;

(b) your and your partner's income and capital if you are in a couple.

Your partner's income and capital are included with yours even if you are claiming UC as a single person (see para 2.8). In this chapter, 'your' income and capital includes the income and capital of your partner.

Distinguishing capital from income

10.4   The UC regulations do not provide a definition of income or capital, but the distinction is usually straightforward. For example:

(a) capital includes savings, investments and property, but some capital is disregarded;

(b) income includes earnings, maintenance and benefits, but some income is disregarded.

The rest of this chapter gives the rules for all of these.

10.2   WRA s3, 5; UC 18(1); NIWRO 8, 10, NIUC 18(1)
10.3   UC 18, 22(1),(3); NIUC 18, 23(1),(3)

10.5   A particular payment you receive might be capital (for example an inheritance) or income (for example earnings). This depends on 'the true characteristics of the payment in the hands of the recipient', not what the payment is called by the person paying it: Minter v Hull City Council.

10.6   However, a payment of income can turn into capital. For example, if you receive wages, benefits etc monthly, what you have not spent by the end of the month becomes part of your capital: CH/1561/2005.

Earned income

10.7   Your earned income means your income from:

(a)   employment: see paras 10.16-22;

(b)   self-employment: see paras 10.23-30; and

(c)   any other paid work: see para 10.8.

It can also include notional earnings (see paras 10.74 onwards), but not rent you receive (see paras 10.51 and 10.71-72). For DWP guidance see ADM chapter H3.

10.8   'Any other paid work' means any other work for which payment is made or expected – for example if you are neither employed nor self-employed but someone pays you for a one-off job. It does not include work which is for a charitable or voluntary organisation or as a volunteer, and for which only expenses are paid or expected.

Why earned income is assessed

10.9   Your earned income is taken into account as follows:

(a)   if you qualify for a work allowance (paras 10.13-15):

■   first the work allowance is deducted from your earned income,

■   then your 'maximum UC' is reduced by 63% of the remainder (paras 9.7-8);

(b)   if you don't qualify for a work allowance:

■   your maximum UC is reduced by 63% of your earned income;

(c)   but if you have earned income (no matter how much or how little) you cannot get DWP loan payments or UC towards any owner-occupier payments (see para 8.15).

The examples illustrate this.

10.10   The UC reduction of 63% of earned income is more generous than the reduction in JSA, ESA and IS, which is 100%. This is designed to encourage people to take up employment or become self-employed or increase their earnings.

10.5   Minter v Hull CC 13/10/11 CA (2011) www.bailii.org/ew/cases/EWCA/Civ/2011/1155.html

10.7   UC 52; NIUC 51

10.8   UC 2 definition: 'paid work', 52(a)(iii); NIUC 2 definition: 'paid work', 51(a)(iii)

10.9   UC 22(1),(3), SI 2017/348 1(3); NIUC 23(1),(3)

Assessment periods and monthly amounts

10.11   In each assessment period of one month, the amount of your earned income (from employment or self-employment) is what you actually receive in that month: see paras 3.38-44. But the DWP can:

(a) estimate your earned income in the first assessment period following your UC claim, and/or any assessment period for which you do not provide information;

(b) disregard your earned income in an assessment period in which your employment or self-employment ends (though the DWP doesn't have to: [2015] UKUT 696 (AAC)).

See also paras 10.22, 10.30 and 11.26-27.

Surplus earnings

10.12   If you don't qualify for UC because your earned income (from employment or self-employment) is too high, the excess of your earned income is called 'surplus earnings'. This could affect your future UC if:

(a) the UC full service rules apply to you (para 1.14);

(b) your UC ended on or after 11th April 2018 (8th May in Northern Ireland);

(c) you had at least £2,500 of surplus earnings in the last month in which your UC was assessed; and

(d) you reclaim UC within six month of when your UC ended.

In this case, your surplus earnings are taken into account as earned income (as well as any other income you have) in the first assessment period of your new UC claim. (If you don't qualify, there are detailed rules about what happens if you claim UC again within the six months in (d) above (see ADM memo 11/18).) Because the £2,500 'threshold' in (c) is fairly high, you aren't likely to be affected by surplus earnings unless you are paid annually or six-monthly (etc) rather than monthly or weekly, or unless your earnings vary a great deal from month to month. However, this threshold may be reduced to £300 from April 2019, in which case more people will be affected by surplus earnings.

The work allowance

10.13   You qualify for a work allowance if you or your partner:

(a) are responsible for at least one child or young person (paras 3.72-75); and/or

(b) have limited capability for work or for work and work-related activity (para 9.26).

10.14   The UC work allowance is deducted from your monthly earned income (from employment, self-employment, etc: paras 10.7-8). It can be described as the monthly amount you are allowed to 'keep' before your earned income affects the amount of your UC.

10.15   The amounts of the work allowance are in table 10.1. These apply from 9th April 2018. They apply whether you are single or in a couple. If you are in a couple they apply to your combined earnings (even if you are claiming UC as a single person: para 2.8).

10.11   UC 54; NIUC 53

10.12   UC 54A; SI 2018/65 reg 7; NIUC 54A; NISR 2018/92 reg 7

10.13-14   UC 22(1)(b),(3); NIUC 23(1)(b),(3)

10.15   UC 22(2); SI 2015/1649 reg 1; NIUC 23(2)

Table 10.1 **The UC work allowance (2018-19)**

(a)	Renters in specified supported accommodation (para 4.11)	£409
(b)	Renters in temporary accommodation (para 4.13)	£409
(c)	Other renters	£198
(d)	Shared owners	£198
(e)	Owner occupiers	£409
(f)	People with no housing costs	£409

Amounts are monthly and apply to both single people and couples (paras 10.13-15).

Examples: Earned income, work allowance and housing costs element

In both these examples the claimants are single, over 25 and responsible for one child (but don't qualify for any UC elements apart from that). All figures are monthly.

1. A renter

Penny's monthly eligible rent is £400. Her earned income is £1,000. Deducting her work allowance of £198 gives £802 (para 10.13).
Maximum UC:

■ standard allowance	£317.82
■ child element (higher rate)	£277.08
■ housing costs element (eligible rent)	£400.00
■ total	£994.90
Deduction for earned income: £802 x 63%	– £505.26
Amount of UC	£489.64

2. An owner-occupier

Bob's eligible owner costs are £400. His earned income is £1000. Deducting his work allowance of £409 gives £591.
Maximum UC:

■ standard allowance	£317.82
■ child element (higher rate)	£277.08
■ no housing costs element (paras 9.51-52)	£0.00
■ total	£594.90
Deduction for earned income: £591 x 63%	– £372.33
Amount of UC	£222.57

T10.1   UC 22; NIUC 23; UCTP 5A

Employed earnings

What are employed earnings

10.16 Your 'employed earnings' are your earnings from employment 'under a contract of service' (an employment contract) or 'in an office'. People employed in an office include directors of limited companies, local authority councillors and clergy.

The amount of your employed earnings

10.17 The amount of your employed earnings in an assessment period is:

(a) all the earnings you receive in that period which are subject to income tax (for exceptions see paras 10.18-20); and

(b) repayments and refunds of income tax and national insurance in that period; and

(c) any statutory sick, maternity, paternity or adoption pay you receive in that period;

(d) minus amounts for your income tax, national insurance, pension contributions and payroll giving in that period (see para 10.21).

See also paras 10.13-15 for the work allowance, and paras 10.74-76 for notional earnings.

Excluded earnings

10.18 Employee benefits, such as free use of your employer's facilities, are not included in your earnings whether you pay tax on them or not.

Expenses paid by your employer

10.19 If your employer pays you expenses, these are:

(a) included in your earnings if they are taxable (for example if your employer pays your travel costs between your home and work place);

(b) not included if they are not taxable (for example if your employer pays your travel costs between work places).

Expenses if you are in a service user group

10.20 Expenses you are paid that arise from your participation as a service user are not included in your earnings and are disregarded. This applies if you are a member of the service user group (or the carer of a service user group member), for a body which has a statutory duty to provide health, social care or social housing services or for the DWP in relation to social security, child support or certain employment-training initiatives.

10.16   UC 52(a)(i), 55(1); NIUC 51(a)(i), 55(1)

10.17   UC 55(1),(2),(4),(5); NIUC 55(1),(2),(4),(6)

10.18   UC 55(2); NIUC 55(2)

10.19   UC 55(3)(a); NIUC 55(3)(a)

10.20   UC 53(2), 55(3)(b); NIUC 52(2), 55(3)(b)

Deductions from employed earnings

10.21   The following are deducted from your employed earnings:

(a) tax and national insurance contributions you pay in the assessment period;

(b) tax-deductible pension contributions you make in that period; and

(c) amounts you donate in that period under a PAYE 'payroll giving' scheme approved for tax purposes.

Information used to assess employed earnings

10.22   In most cases, the DWP uses information from HMRC to assess your employed earnings. This is because PAYE law requires most employers to provide details of employees' earnings to HMRC using its Real Time Information system. The DWP counts you as receiving the earnings when it gets this information. But the DWP makes its own decision if this information is likely to be unreliable, or your employer fails to provide it, or you disagree with it. If these arrangements are not in place for some reason, you should report your employed earnings to the DWP each month. The DWP should tell you when you have to do this, and if you fail to follow the reporting instructions your UC could be suspended (para 11.72). See also para 10.12 for when the DWP can estimate your employed earnings.

Self-employed earnings

What are self-employed earnings

10.23   Your 'self-employed earnings' are your earnings from any kind of business which is a 'trade, profession or vocation' where you are not employed by someone else. This applies whether you are a sole trader or in a partnership. For DWP guidance see ADM chapter H4. Note that you may have earnings from both a self-employed activity and employed earnings if you also work for someone else.

The amount of your self-employed earnings

10.24   The amount of your self-employed earnings in an assessment period is:

(a) your business income in that period (see para 10.25);

(b) minus:

- your allowable business expenses in that period (see paras 10.26-28), and

- payments you make to HMRC for your income tax and national insurance and/or tax relievable pension contributions made in that period (see para 10.29), and

- certain unused losses (see para 10.29).

But if this gives a low figure, you can be counted as having a higher amount of earnings: see paras 10.78-81. See also paras 10.13-15 for the work allowance.

10.21   UC 53(1), 55(4A),(5); NIUC 52(1), 55(5),(6)

10.22   AA 159D; UC 54,61; NIAA 159D; NIUC 53,62

10.23   UC 52(a)(ii), 57(1); NIUC 51(a)(ii), 57(1)

10.24   UC 57(2); NIUC 57(2)

Business income

10.25   Your business income is all the income actually received in relation to your business, including:

(a)   money payments (cash, credit transfers, cheques, etc);

(b)   payments in kind (this means in goods, not money);

(c)   repayments and refunds of income tax, national insurance and VAT; and

(d)   the value of assets you sell or stop using for your business (if you earlier claimed them as an allowable expense).

Money owed to you (for example if someone hasn't paid you yet) is not included. Nor are loans or capital payments into your business.

Allowable business expenses

10.26   Your business expenses in the assessment period are allowable only if they are:

(a)   'wholly and exclusively incurred' for the purposes of your business; and

(b)   not 'incurred unreasonably' (i.e. they should be appropriate, necessary and not excessive); and

(c)   not excluded expenses (see para 10.28).

If you pay VAT, you may include this as an allowable business expense. Money you owe (for example if you haven't paid a bill yet) is not allowable. For DWP guidance see ADM paras H4197-4275.

Expenses for mixed purposes

10.27   If you have expenses which are partly for business and partly for private purposes, the identifiable business part is allowable if it meets the conditions in para 10.26. This is done by making a calculation of your business and personal use. But in some situations you can use flat rate allowances instead (and must do this if you use a car for business purposes): see table 10.2.

Excluded expenses

10.28   The following expenses are not allowable:

(a)   any expenditure on non-depreciating assets (including property, shares or assets held for investment);

(b)   losses relating to periods before 11th April 2018 (para 10.29);

(c)   any business entertainment;

(d)   capital repayments on any loan;

(e)   interest payments on any loan taken out for the purpose of your business beyond £41 per month.

The first £41 per month of interest you pay on loans is allowable.

10.25   UC 57(4)-(5); NIUC 57(3)-(4)

10.26   UC 58(1),(2); NIUC 59(1),(2)

10.27   UC 58(1)(b),(4), 59(1); NIUC 59(1)(b),(5), 60(1)

10.28   UC 58(3),(3A); NIUC 59(3),(4)

Table 10.2 **Self-employed expenses: flat rate allowances and adjustments**

If you use a car for your business you can only claim the flat rate allowance in (a) as a business expense; you can't claim any actual expenses for buying or using it. Otherwise, (a) (for other types of vehicle) and (b) and (c) are options; you can choose to use them or can make a calculation of actual business use (para 10.27). All amounts are monthly.

(a) Allowance for business use of a motor vehicle

If you use a motor vehicle for both business and personal purposes, the flat rate allowance for business use depends on your business mileage in the month. It is:

- for a motorcycle, 24p per mile;
- for a car, van or other motor vehicle:
    - 45p per mile for the first 833 miles, plus
    - 25p per mile after that.

(b) Allowance for business use of your home

If you use your home for business purposes, the flat rate allowance for business use depends on the number of hours you spend there on 'income-generating activities' in the month. It is:

- £10 for at least 25 (but not more than 50) hours;
- £18 for more than 50 (but not more than 100) hours;
- £26 for more than 100 hours.

(c) Adjustment for personal use of business premises

This applies to premises you mainly use for business purposes but which you (or you and anyone else) also occupy for personal use. (For example, if your business is running a care home and you live there or stay there.) The flat rate amount is deducted from the total allowable expenses on the premises in the month. It is:

- £350 if one person (you) occupies the premises;
- £500 if two people (including you) do so;
- £650 if three or more people (including you) do so.

Example: Allowable expenses for vehicle use

A self-employed plumber uses his van for both business and personal purposes. In a particular month he drives 2,000 miles, of which 1,500 are for business and 500 are for personal use. His total expenditure for this is £700.

Actual calculation of business use

His business use is ¾ of the total, so his allowable expenses are £525.

Flat rate allowance for business use

His allowable expenses (see table 10.2(a)) are:

■ 833 miles at 45p	£374.85
■ 1,167 miles at 25p	£291.75
■ Total	£666.60

Deductions from self-employed earnings

10.29   The following are deducted from your self-employed earnings:

(a) income tax and class 2 and/or 4 national insurance contributions you pay to HMRC in the assessment period in respect of your trade, profession or vocation; and

(b) tax-deductible pension contributions you make in that period (unless these have already been deducted from any employed earnings you have: see para 10.21); and

(c) 'unused losses' (if the UC full service rules apply to you: para 1.14). These are self-employed business losses you incurred:

■ in an assessment period in your current UC award, or

■ in an assessment period in a previous UC award, so long as the gap between awards was no longer than six months, or

■ in such a gap between awards,

but in each case losses in assessment periods beginning before 11th April 2018 are not deducted.

Information used to assess self-employed earnings

10.30   You should report your self-employed earnings to the DWP each month. The DWP usually expects you to do this between seven days before and 14 days after the end of each assessment period (para 3.38), giving information on:

(a) the business income you actually receive during that assessment period;

(b) the allowable expenses you actually pay out during that assessment period; and

(c) the tax, national insurance and pension contributions you actually pay out during that assessment period.

If you fail to follow the reporting instructions your UC could be suspended (para 11.72). See also para 10.11 for when the DWP can estimate your self-employed earnings.

10.29   UC 53(1), 57(2), 57A; SI 2015/345 para 4; NIUC 52(1), 57(2), 57A
10.30   UC 54, 61(1); NIUC 53, 62(1)

Example: Assessing self-employed earnings

A self-employed plumber provides the following information for a particular month. She used her van wholly for business purposes. She used the flat rate allowance for use of her home (see table 10.2(b)). All her expenses are allowable. So her self-employed earnings are shown below.

Income received		£1,492
Use of van	£314	
Buying in stock for use in trade	£170	
Payment to sub-contractor	£80	
Telephone, postage, stationery	£76	
Advertising, subscriptions	£42	
Use of home	£18	
Tax/NI paid to HMRC	£68	
Total allowable expenses		£768
Self-employed earnings		£724

Unearned income

10.31   Only certain kinds of income count as your 'unearned income'. These are summarised in table 10.3 and further details are in paras 10.34-52. All other kinds of unearned income are disregarded: for some examples see para 10.36.

Why unearned income is assessed

10.32   Your 'maximum UC' is reduced by the whole amount of your unearned income (see paras 9.7-8). Unearned income can also affect the amount of DWP loan payments for owners and shared owners (para 8.17).

Converting unearned income to a monthly figure

10.33   The amount of your unearned income in any UC assessment period of one month is calculated as a monthly figure. Payments which are not monthly are converted to a monthly figure:

  (a) multiply weekly payments by 52 then divide by 12;

  (b) multiply four-weekly payments by 13 then divide by 12;

  (c) multiply three-monthly payments by four then divide by 12;

  (d) divide annual payments by 12.

If your unearned income fluctuates, the monthly amount is calculated over any identifiable cycle, or if there isn't one, over three months or whatever period would give a more accurate result. For student income see table 10.4.

10.31   UC 66; NIUC 66
10.33   UC 73; NIUC 73

Table 10.3 **What counts as unearned income in UC**

(a) Retirement pension income (see para 10.34)

(b) The following social security benefits (see para 10.35):

- jobseeker's allowance (contribution-based);
- employment and support allowance (contributory);
- carer's allowance;
- bereavement allowance (but bereavement support payments payable from 6th April 2017 are disregarded as unearned income - see also Table 10.5 (t));
- maternity allowance;
- widow's pension;
- widowed mother's allowance;
- widowed partner's allowance;
- industrial injuries benefit;
- incapacity benefit;
- severe disablement allowance.

(c) Payments from a foreign government analogous to any of the above.

(d) Maintenance from your current or former spouse or civil partner (see para 10.38).

(e) Student income (see para 10.39).

(f) Training allowances (see para 10.44).

(g) Sports Council awards (see para 10.45).

(h) Some insurance payments (see para 10.47).

(i) Income from an annuity (see para 10.48).

(j) Income from a trust (see paras 10.63-64).

(k) Assumed income from capital (see para 10.56).

(l) Capital treated as income (see paras 10.59-60).

(m) Some kinds of rental income and other taxable income (see paras 10.50-51 and 10.71-72).

In many cases there are further rules and/or disregards. See the paras shown above, and for notional unearned income see para 10.82.

T10.3   UC 66(1)(a)-(m); UCTP 25; NIUC 66(1)(a)-(m)

Example: Unearned income and amount of UC

A couple in their 30s have one child. One partner has JSA(C) of £73.10 a week, which is £316.77 a month. The other has maintenance of £300 a month. So their monthly unearned income is £616.77. (Child benefit is disregarded.) They have no earnings or capital, and their eligible rent is £400.

Maximum UC:

■ standard allowance	£498.89
■ child element (higher rate)	£277.08
■ housing costs element (eligible rent)	£400.00
■ total	£1,175.97
Deduction for unearned income	– £616.77
Amount of UC	£559.20

Retirement pension income

10.34   Retirement pension income counts in full as unearned income. This means any kind of state, occupational or personal retirement pension, including any increase for a partner (but for state pension credit see para 10.36). Periodic payments from the Payment Protection Fund, and foreign state retirement pension, also count in full as unearned income.

Social security benefits

10.35   Table 10.3(b) lists the social security benefits which count as unearned income. They count in full, except for any amount you do not receive because of the rules about overlapping benefits.

Benefits which are disregarded

10.36   Unearned income that is not identified in the UC regulations is disregarded in your UC assessment. Examples of disregarded benefits and other payments are:

(a)   disability living allowance;

(b)   personal independence payment;

(c)   attendance allowance;

(d)   benefits equivalent to attendance allowance (see para 10.37);

(e)   child benefit;

(f)   guardian's allowance;

(g)   council tax rebate;

(h)   working tax credit;

(i)   child tax credit;

10.34   UC 66(1)(a),(da),(la),(2), 67; NIUC 66(1)(a),(da),(la),(2), 67

10.35   UC 66(1)(b); NIUC 66(1)(b)

10.36   UC 66

(j)   housing benefit;

(k)   income support;

(l)   jobseeker's allowance (income-based);

(m) employment and support allowance (income-related);

(n)   state pension credit;

(o)   war pensions;

(p)   fostering and kinship care payments and all the local authority cash benefits in para 18.51;

(q)   monthly bereavement support payments.

In most cases, you cannot get the benefits listed in (h) to (n) at the same time as UC (see paras 1.16-25). Statutory sick, maternity, paternity and adoption pay count as employed earnings: see para 10.17.

10.37   The following benefits are equivalent to attendance allowance:

(a)   increases in industrial injuries benefit for constant attendance or exceptionally severe disablement;

(b)   increases in a war disablement pension for attendance, constant attendance or exceptionally severe disablement;

(c)   an armed forces independence payment; or

(d)   payments for attendance under the Personal Injuries (Civilians) scheme.

Maintenance

10.38   Payments for your or your partner's maintenance (under an agreement or court order) count in full as unearned income, but only if they are paid by your current or former husband, wife or civil partner. All other maintenance (e.g. for a child) is disregarded.

Student income

10.39   You count as having student income if:

(a)   you are a student in full-time advanced or funded education (see paras 2.22-23); and

(b)   you receive:

  ■ a student loan, or a postgraduate master's degree loan or could receive either (see para 10.40), and/or

  ■ a student grant (see paras 10.41-43).

This counts as unearned income. See table 10.4 for when it is taken into account and how to calculate the amount. Any other kinds of student income (for example education maintenance allowances, 16-19 bursary fund payments and hardship fund payments) are disregarded (but for training allowances see para 10.44).

10.37   UC 2 definitions: 'attendance allowance', 'war disablement pension'; NIUC 2

10.38   UC 66(1)(d); NIUC 66(1)(d)

10.39   UC 66(1)(e), 68(1),(6); NIUC 66(1)(e), 68(1),(6)

Student loans

10.40   You are counted as having income from a student loan if you receive such a loan under a government scheme, or you could obtain one by taking reasonable steps to do so. The amount you are counted as receiving is:

(a) the maximum amount of student loan you could obtain by taking reasonable steps to do so (including increases for extra weeks); but

(b) 30% of that maximum amount in the case of a postgraduate master's degree loan; or

(c) nil in the case of a student support loan.

This applies even if your actual loan has been reduced because you, your partner, your parent or anyone else is expected to contribute to it, or because you have a grant.

Student grants

10.41   You are counted as having income from a student grant if you receive any kind of educational grant or award (apart from one you are paid as an under 21-year-old in non-advanced education). This includes grants and awards from government and all other sources.

10.42   If you have income from both a grant and a student loan (see paras 10.40-41), only the following parts of the grant (if you receive them) are counted:

(a) amounts for the maintenance of your partner, child, young person, non-dependant or anyone other than yourself; and

(b) amounts specified in the grant as being towards your rent payments (but only if they are rent payments which can be met by UC: see paras 4.5-8 and 4.21).

In this case the rest of your grant (or all of it if you do not receive either of the above) is disregarded.

10.43   If you have income from a grant but not from a student loan (see paras 10.40-41), the whole of your grant is counted except for any amounts included in it for:

(a) tuition or examination fees;

(b) any kind of disability you have;

(c) term-time residential study away from your educational establishment;

(d) maintaining a home whose costs are not included in your housing costs element and which is not your term-time address;

(e) the maintenance of anyone not included in your or anyone else's UC award;

(f) books and equipment;

(g) travel expenses as a result of your attendance on the course;

(h) childcare costs.

10.40   UC 68(2),(5),(7), 69; NIUC 68(2),(5),(7), 69

10.41   UC 68(3),(4),(7); NIUC 68(3),(4),(7)

10.42   UC 68(3), sch 1 para 2; NIUC 68(3), sch 1 para 2

10.43   UC 70; NIUC 70

Table 10.4 **The monthly amount of student income**

Your student income (from a student loan and/or grant: see paras 10.39-43) is calculated as follows:

- it is averaged over the number of monthly assessment periods described below;
- then £110 is disregarded in each of those assessment periods.

(a) One year or shorter courses

Average student income:

- from the assessment period in which the course starts;
- to the assessment period before the one in which the course ends.

(b) Two year or longer courses with long vacations

For each year, average student income:

- from the assessment period in which:
  - the course starts (first year), or
  - the previous long vacation ends (other years);
- to the assessment period before the one in which:
  - the following long vacation starts, or
  - the course ends (final year).

(c) Two year or longer courses without long vacations

For each year, average student income:

- from the assessment period in which:
  - the course starts (first year), or
  - the year starts (other years);
- to the assessment period before the one in which:
  - the next year starts, or
  - the course ends (final year).

'Long vacation'

This means the longest vacation in any year, but if it is less than one month you do not count as having long vacations.

Training allowances

10.44   Training allowances count as unearned income only if:

(a) they are paid under a government work programme training scheme; and

(b) they are for your living expenses (see para 10.46) or are instead of UC.

T10.4   UC 68(1),(7), 71; NIUC 68(1),(7), 71

10.44   UC 66(1)(f); NIUC 66(1)(f)

Sports Council awards

10.45   Sports Council awards count as unearned income only if they are for your living expenses (see para 10.46).

'Living expenses'

10.46   For the above purpose (paras 10.44-45) living expenses mean the cost of food, ordinary clothing or footwear, household fuel, rent, council tax or other housing costs, for yourself, your partner and any child or young person you are responsible for.

Insurance payments

10.47   Insurance payments count as your unearned income only if they are paid under a policy you took out to insure yourself against:

(a)   losing income due to illness, accident or redundancy; or

(b)   being unable to maintain mortgage payments which (before 6th April 2018) were included in your housing costs element (see para 8.2).

Annuities, trusts, personal injury and compensation

10.48   For the rules about income and capital relating to these, see paras 10.63-67.

Other taxable income

10.49   Other income you have counts as unearned income if:

(a)   it is taxable under specific income tax law (Part 5 of the Income Tax (Trading and Other Income) Act 2005); and

(b)   it is not earned income (see paras 10.7-30).

10.50   For example, this can include royalties, copyright, patent and similar payments, unless these are part of your self-employed (or employed) earnings.

Rent received from a lodger/sub-tenant in your home

10.51   The DWP says (ADM para H5112) that because income from a boarder or sub-tenant is not defined as income for UC purposes it is not taken into account as your unearned income. It stresses that it is not relevant whether the rental income is above or below the HMRC 'rent a room' tax relief limits. If you are self-employed, however, and renting out rooms as part of your business then this income is taken into account as part of your self-employed earnings. See paras 10.71-72 if you receive rent on property other than your home.

10.45   UC 66(1)(g); NIUC 66(1)(g)

10.46   UC 66(2); NIUC 66(2)

10.47   UC 66(1)(h); NIUC 66(1)(h)

10.49   UC 66(1)(m); NIUC 66(1)(m)

10.51   UC 66; NIUC 66

Other unearned income

10.52   The following also count as unearned income:

(a) assumed income from capital: see para 10.56;

(b) some instalments or regular payments of capital: see paras 10.59-60; and

(c) notional unearned income: see para 10.82.

Capital

10.53   All of your capital is taken into account unless it is disregarded. Table 10.5 lists all the kinds of disregarded capital. See paras 10.4-6 for how to distinguish capital from income. For DWP guidance on capital see ADM chapters H1 and H2.

10.54   For example your capital includes:

(a) savings (in cash or in a savings account etc);

(b) investments (shares etc);

(c) property (unless it is disregarded: see table 10.5); and

(d) lump sum payments you receive (for example an inheritance).

It can also include notional capital (see paras 10.83-88).

Why capital is assessed

10.55   Your capital (apart from disregarded capital) is taken into account as follows:

(a) if it is more than £16,000 you are not entitled to UC; otherwise

(b) the first £6,000 is ignored;

(c) the remainder up to £16,000 is counted as providing you with an assumed amount of income (see para 10.56).

Assumed income from capital

10.56   The assumed income from your capital is calculated as follows:

(a) from the total amount of your capital (apart from disregarded capital) deduct £6,000;

(b) then divide the remainder by 250;

(c) each £250 (or part of £250) in excess of £6,000 is treated as producing a monthly income of £4.35;

(d) this gives the monthly amount of your assumed income from capital. It is counted as your unearned income: see paras 10.31-32. (The law calls it the 'yield' from your capital.)

The kinds of capital disregarded in (a) and in para 10.55 are described throughout this chapter. They are the same for both these purposes except in relation to certain annuities and trusts: see paras 10.63-64.

10.53   UC 46(1); NIUC 46(1)

10.54   UC 72(1); NIUC 72(1)

10.55   UC 72(1); NIUC 72(1)

10.56   UC 66(1)(k), 72; NIUC 66(1)(k), 72

Example: Assumed income from capital

A UC claimant has capital, assessed under the rules in this chapter, of £12,085.93.

- The first £6,000 is ignored, leaving £6,085.93.
- There are 25 £250 (or part of) in £6,085.93 (i.e. £6,085.93 divided by 250 = 24.34).
- 25 x £4.35 = £108.75.
- The claimant's assumed monthly income from capital is £108.75.

Table 10.5 **Disregarded capital**

Your home and other premises

In (a) to (e) only one dwelling can be a person's home at any one time. In (a) to (c) there is no time limit.

(a) Your home.

(b) The home of a 'close relative' (see para 4.45) who:

- has 'limited capability for work' (or for 'work and work-related activity'): see para 9.26; or
- has reached state pension credit age: see para 2.10.

(c) The home of your partner if:

- your relationship has not ended; but
- you are not claiming UC as a couple because your circumstances mean you live apart (for example, one of you is in residential care).

(d) A home you intend to occupy if:

- you acquired it within the past six months*; or
- you are taking steps to obtain possession of it, and first sought legal advice about this or began proceedings within the past six months*; or
- you are carrying out essential repairs or alterations to make it fit for occupation, and began doing so within the past six months*.

(e) Your former home if you ceased to occupy it because your relationship with your partner has ended, and:

- they are a lone parent and live in it as their home (in this case there is no time limit); or
- you ceased to occupy it within the past six months*.

(f) A home or any other premises you are taking reasonable steps to dispose of, and began doing so within the past six months*.

T10.5(a)-(t)   UC sch 10 paras 1 to 20 respectively, also para 1(2) for (a) to (e); NIUC sch 10 paras 1 to 19

Business assets

(g) Any assets which are wholly or mainly used for a business you are carrying on (see para 10.23).

(h) Any assets which were wholly or mainly used for a business you ceased within the past six months* if;

  ▪ you are taking reasonable steps to dispose of them; or

  ▪ you ceased business because of 'incapacity' and reasonably expect to begin again when you recover.

Money in a life insurance, pension or funeral plan scheme

(i) The value of a life insurance policy.

(j) The value of an occupational or personal pension scheme.

(k) The value of a funeral plan contract, if its only purpose is to provide a funeral.

Money held for particular purposes

(l) Money deposited with a housing association as a condition of occupying your home.

(m) Money you received within the past six months*, and which you intend to use to buy a home, if:

  ▪ it is the proceeds of the sale of your former home; or

  ▪ it is a grant made to you for the sole purpose of buying a home; or

  ▪ it was deposited with a housing association.

(n) Money you received under an insurance policy within the past six months* because of loss or damage to your home or personal possessions.

(o) Money you received within the past six months* which:

  ▪ is for making essential repairs or alterations to your home or former home: and

  ▪ was given to you (as a grant, loan, gift or otherwise) on condition that it is so used.

Benefits and other payments

(p) A social fund payment you received within the past 12 months.

(q) A payment you received from a local authority within the past 12 months, if it was paid:

  ▪ by social services to avoid taking a child into care or to a child or young person who is leaving or has left care; or

  ▪ to meet anyone's welfare needs relating to old age or disability (for example a community care or direct care payment) apart from any living expenses described in para 10.46.

(r) A payment you received within the past 12 months which was for arrears of (or compensation for late payment of):

- UC; or

- any benefit listed in para 10.36 (a) to (n); or

- any other UK social security benefit which does not count as unearned income in UC.

(s) Any payment made to you as a holder of the Victoria Cross or George Cross. There is no time limit.

(t) An additional payment of bereavement support payment (BSP) for the first month of a BSP period at either the higher (£3,500) or standard (£2,500) rate where it is made within the previous 12 months.

Personal possessions

(u) Your personal possessions. This means any physical assets other than land, property or business assets: R(H) 7/08.

Extending the six-month disregards

*   The DWP can extend any of the six-month disregards in this table if it is reasonable to do so in the circumstances.

Note: see paras 10.65-67 for further disregards relating to personal injury, compensation and independent living payments.

Valuing capital

10.57   Each item of your capital is calculated as follows:

(a) start with its current market or surrender value;

(b) then disregard 10% if selling it would involve costs;

(c) then disregard any debt or charge secured on it.

Example: Valuing capital

A couple own 1,000 shares in a company. Their sell price is currently 34p each.

- Their market value is £340.

- Deduct 10% from this for sale costs, giving £306.

- No debt or charge is secured on them, so their capital value is £306.

If two brothers jointly owned the shares, the capital value of each one's share would be £153.

T10.5(u) UC 46(2); NIUC 46(2)

T10.5(*) UC 48(2); NIUC 48(2)

10.57   UC 49(1); NIUC 49(1)

Jointly held capital

10.58   If you own a capital item jointly with one or more other people, you are assumed to own it in equal shares unless you provide evidence that it should be divided in some other way.

Instalments of capital

10.59   If capital is payable to you in instalments, each instalment counts as capital. But any particular instalment which would take your total capital over £16,000 counts as unearned income (not capital).

Regular payments of capital

10.60   If you receive regular payments of capital which relate to a specific period (and para 10.59 does not apply) these count as unearned income (not capital). For example this applies to payments under an annuity (see para 10.64).

Capital held in a foreign currency

10.61   If you hold capital in a currency other than sterling, any charge or commission for converting it to sterling is disregarded from it.

Capital outside the UK

10.62   The following rules apply if you possess capital in a country outside the UK:

(a) if there is no prohibition in that country against bringing the money to the UK, its market value is the market value in that country;

(b) if there is such a prohibition, its market value is the amount it would raise if it was sold to a willing buyer in the UK.

The rules in paras 10.57-58 and 10.61 then apply.

Annuities and trusts

10.63   An annuity is an investment made with an insurance company which in return pays you a regular amount – for your retirement or for other purposes. A trust is a way of holding capital so that the trustees control it on behalf of one or more beneficiaries. The following annuities and trusts are disregarded in calculating your capital (for all UC purposes):

(a) retirement annuities (table 10.5(j));

(b) annuities and trusts that hold personal injury payments (para 10.65); and

(c) certain government funded trusts (para 10.67).

Income you receive from (a) counts as retirement pension income (para 10.34). Income you receive from (b) or (c) is disregarded (paras 10.64-67).

10.58   UC 47; NIUC 47

10.59   UC 46(1)(a),(4), 66(1)(l); NIUC 46(1)(a),(4), 66(1)(l)

10.60   UC 46(1)(a),(3), 66(1)(l); NIUC 46(1)(a),(3), 66(1)(l)

10.61   UC 49(3); NIUC 49(3)

10.62   UC 49(2); NIUC 49(2)

10.63   UC 66(1)(i),(j),67(l),75; NIUC 66(1)(i),(j),67(l),75

10.64 For all annuities and other trusts:

(a) their capital value is included when deciding whether your total capital is over £16,000 – and if it is over £16,000 you don't qualify for UC (para 10.55), but if it isn't over £16,000, steps (b) to (d) apply;

(b) payments of income you receive from the annuity or trust count as your unearned income;

(c) if you do receive payments of income, the capital value of the annuity or trust is disregarded when calculating your assumed income from capital (para 10.56);

(d) if you don't receive payments of income, the capital value of the annuity or trust is included when calculating your assumed income from capital.

For (b) to (d), regular payments of capital can count as income (para 10.60).

Personal injury payments

10.65 A personal injury payment means money which was awarded to you, or which you (or someone on your behalf) agreed to, as a consequence of a personal injury you had. Personal injury payments are disregarded in calculating your capital if they:

(a) are held in a trust (other capital in the trust deriving from them is also disregarded);

(b) are administered by a court on your behalf, or can only be used under a court's direction; or

(c) were paid to you within the past 12 months. This may allow time for them to be placed in a trust so that (a) then applies.

10.66 Personal injury payments are disregarded in calculating your unearned income if they are:

(a) income paid to you from a trust whose capital value is disregarded under para 10.65(a) or (b); or

(b) regular payments to you under an agreement or court order; or

(c) payments to you from an annuity which was purchased using a personal injury payment.

Compensation and independent living payments

10.67 Payments from government schemes and trusts set up for the following purposes are disregarded in the calculation of both your capital and your income. This means any government scheme or trust which:

(a) compensates you for having been diagnosed with variant Creutzfeldt-Jacob disease; or

(b) compensates you for having been infected with contaminated blood products (examples include the Macfarlane Trust, Eileen Trust, MFET Ltd and the Scottish Infected Blood Support Scheme); or

(c) compensates you because you were interned or suffered forced labour, injury, property loss or loss of a child in the Second World War; or

---

10.64   UC 72(2); NIUC 72(2)

10.65-66   UC 75; NIUC 75

(d)   compensates you for the bombings in London on 7th July 2005 or Manchester on 22nd May 2017, or the terrorist attacks in London on 22nd March 2017 or 3rd June 2017; or

(e)   supports you, if you have a disability, to live independently in your home (for example the Independent Living Funds).

If you are the parent, partner, son or daughter of a person in (a) or (b), payments from the trust or scheme to you, or passed on to you by that person (as a payment or inheritance), are disregarded in most circumstances.

Actual income from capital

10.68   'Actual income from capital' means:

(a)   interest (on a savings account etc);

(b)   dividends (on shares etc);

(c)   rent (on property you rent out); and

(d)   any other 'actual income derived from' your capital.

Paras 10.69-72 give the rules about this.

Income from disregarded capital

10.69   If the capital is disregarded in the assessment of UC (see table 10.5), actual income you receive on it counts as your income. It is usually unearned income (see para 10.49). But if you are self-employed, income you receive on your business assets is included in your self-employed earnings (see para 10.25). For rent see para 10.71.

Income from counted capital

10.70   If the capital is counted in the assessment of UC (see para 10.53), actual income you receive on it counts as your capital from the day it is due. For example this applies to interest you receive on (and leave in) a savings account. For rent see para 10.72.

Rent received on disregarded property

10.71   The rule in para 10.69 means that if you receive rent on a property which is disregarded (see table 10.5 (b) to (f)), the rent counts as your income. Since it is the taxable amount which is taken into account (see para 10.49) the expenses you incur on the property are deducted. For rent from a lodger in your home, see para 10.51.

Rent received on counted property

10.72   The rule in para 10.70 means that if you receive rent on a property which is not disregarded, the rent counts as your capital from the day it is due. But your capital goes down when you pay for expenses you incur on that property. See the example. (If you receive rent from a property business different rules apply: see paras 10.16, 10.23 and 10.87.)

10.67   UC 76; NIUC 76

10.68   UC 72(3); NIUC 72(3)

10.70   UC 72(3); NIUC 72(3)

10.71   UC 66(1)(m); NIUC 66(1)(m)

Example: Rent received on a counted property

A single person owns a house he does not live in. He rents the rooms there to separate tenants through an agency. The house does not fall within any of the capital disregards, and because he has a large mortgage its capital value is not over £16,000 (see para 10.57).

His income from the rent is taken into account as capital (see para 10.72). Each month he receives rent of £900 from which he pays £800 for agency fees, council tax, utility bills and his mortgage. This means his capital goes up by £100 a month.

Notional income and capital

10.73   This section explains when you are counted as having income or capital you do not in fact have. This is called 'notional' income or capital.

Notional earnings: trade disputes

10.74   You are counted as having notional earnings if you withdraw your labour as part of a trade dispute (go on strike). In this case, the amount of your notional earnings is what you would receive if you hadn't done so.

Notional earnings: deprivation

10.75   You are counted as having notional earnings if:

(a) you have deprived yourself of earnings, or your employer has arranged for this; and

(b) the purpose of this was to make you entitled to UC or to more UC. This is assumed to apply to you if you actually became entitled to UC or more UC, and this was a foreseeable and intended consequence of what you or your employer did.

In this case, the amount of your notional earnings is the amount you have deprived yourself of.

Notional earnings: paid less than the going rate

10.76   You are counted as having notional earnings if:

(a) you provide services (see para 10.77) for another person who pays nothing for them, or pays less than would be paid for comparable services in the same location; and

(b) that person's means were sufficient to pay for those services, or pay more for them.

In this case, the amount of your notional earnings is what would be reasonable for the provision of the services.

10.72   UC 72(3); NIUC 72(3)

10.74   UC 2 definition: 'trade dispute', 56; NIUC 2, 56

10.75   UC 52(b), 60(1),(2); NIUC 51(b), 61(1),(2)

10.76   UC 52(b), 60(3); NIUC 51(b), 61(3)

10.77 The rule in para 10.76 does not apply to services you provide:

(a) to a charitable or voluntary organisation, if it is reasonable for you to be paid nothing for them, or less for them; or

(b) as a service user (see para 10.20); or

(c) under a government training or employment programme.

Notional earnings: gainful self-employment

10.78 You are counted as having notional earnings if:

(a) you are in 'gainful self-employment'. This means your business is your main employment and is 'organised, developed, regular and carried on in the expectation of profit'; and

(b) as a condition of getting UC you are required to carry out all the work requirements in para 2.43; and

(c) your own monthly earnings are below your own minimum income floor; and

(d) your combined monthly earnings (if you are in a couple) are below your combined minimum income floors; and

(e) you are not in a UC start-up period, nor in an assessment period containing the first or last day of a start-up period.

For the minimum income floor see para 10.80, and for UC start-up periods see para 10.81. In (c) and (d), monthly earnings mean earnings from this and any other employment or self-employment (after deductions for tax and national insurance). For DWP guidance see ADM paras H4020-57.

10.79 In this case, the amount of your notional earnings is:

(a) the difference between:

- your own monthly earnings, and
- your own minimum income floor; or

(b) if it is lower (and you are in a couple), the difference between:

- your combined monthly earnings, and
- your combined minimum income floors.

The overall effect is that the total of your actual and notional earnings is at least as much as your minimum income floor (or your combined minimum income floors if you are in a couple).

10.77   UC 60(4) ; NIUC 61(4)

10.78   UC 52(b), 62(1), (5), 64; NIUC 51(b), 63(1), (6), 65

10.79   UC 62(1)-(4); NIUC 63(1)-(4)

The minimum income floor

10.80   Your 'minimum income floor' is what you would earn in a month (after deductions for tax and national insurance) for working 35 hours a week at the national minimum wage. But the DWP can agree a lower number of hours applies to you if you have a physical or mental impairment, or have caring responsibilities for a child, a foster child or a person who has a physical or mental impairment. If you are in a couple your partner's minimum income floor is the same, but only one of you can qualify for a lower number of hours for caring for your children.

The UC start-up period

10.81   You qualify for a UC start-up period if:

(a) you began the business which is your main employment within the past 12 months; and

(b) you are taking active steps to increase your earnings from it up to your minimum income floor (see para 10.80); and

(c) you have not begun a UC start-up period for a similar business within the past five years.

The start-up period lasts for 12 months starting from the beginning of the assessment period in which the DWP agrees you are in gainful self-employment (see para 10.78(a)). But it can be brought to an early end if you stop being in gainful self-employment or stop taking steps to increase your earnings.

Example: The UC start-up period

A single person's UC assessment periods start on the 26th of each month. She decides to try self-employment as an illustrator but earns nothing to begin with. She then starts selling work, and the DWP decides on 3rd March 2018 that she is in gainful self-employment.

So a UC start-up period applies to her from 26th February 2018 for 12 months. During the 13 months from 26th February 2018 to 25th March 2019 (see para 10.78(e)), she is not counted as having notional earnings, and only her actual earnings are taken into account.

Notional unearned income: available on application

10.82   You are counted as having notional unearned income equal to any amount which:

(a) would be available to you if you applied for it; but

(b) you haven't applied for.

This rule applies to retirement pension income and any other kind of unearned income listed in table 10.3(c)-(m). But it does not apply to any UK social security benefit.

10.80   UC 62(2)-(4), 85, 88, 90(2)(b),(3); NIUC 63(2)-(4), 84, 87, 89(2)(b),(3)

10.81   UC 63; NIUC 64

10.82   UC 66(1), 74; NIUC 66(1), 74

Notional capital: deprivation

10.83   You are counted as having notional capital if:

(a)   you have deprived yourself of capital; and

(b)   the purpose of this was to make you entitled to UC or to more UC.

In this case, the amount of your notional capital is the amount you have deprived yourself of. See paras 10.84-86 for further details.

Notional capital: exceptions

10.84   The rule in para 10.83 does not apply when you spend capital to:

(a)   pay off or reduce any debt you owe; or

(b)   buy goods or services if this is reasonable in your circumstances.

What deprivation means

10.85   In deciding whether you have deprived yourself of capital, 'the test is one of purpose', and you can only have deprived yourself if obtaining UC formed 'a positive part' of your planning: [2011] UKUT 500 (AAC). If it is clear that you did not (or could not) appreciate what you were doing, or the consequences of it, you cannot count as having deprived yourself: R(H) 1/06. For further examples of how deprivation has been interpreted, see chapter 13 of the *Guide to Housing Benefit*. For DWP guidance see ADM paras H1795-1846.

How notional capital reduces

10.86   If you are counted as having notional capital (see para 10.83), the amount reduces as follows (whether you are on UC or not):

(a)   if your notional capital is more than £16,000, it reduces each month by the amount of UC you would qualify for (if any) in that month without the notional capital;

(b)   if your notional capital is more than £6,000 (but not more than £16,000), it reduces each month by the assumed amount of income it produces: see para 10.56.

Notional capital and earnings: companies

10.87   You are counted as having notional capital and earnings from a company if:

(a)   your relationship to the company is analogous to that of a sole owner or partner; and

(b)   the company carries on a trade or a property business; and

(c)   the company is not an intermediary or managed service company paying you taxable earnings (under Chapter 8 or 9 of Part 2 of the Income Tax (Earnings and Pensions) Act 2003).

10.83   UC 50(1); NIUC 50(1)

10.84   UC 50(2); NIUC 50(2)

10.86   UC 50(3); NIUC 50(3)

10.87   UC 77(1),(5),(6); NIUC 77(1),(5),(6)

10.88   In this case, you are counted as having notional capital equal to the value of the company or your share in it. But the value of company assets used wholly and exclusively for trade purposes is disregarded, and your actual holding in the company is also disregarded. For DWP guidance, see ADM paras H1874-82.

10.89   And you are counted as having notional earnings equal to the income of the company or your share of it. This is calculated using the rules for self-employed earnings (see paras 10.24-30). If it is your main employment the rules about notional earnings from self-employment apply (see paras 10.78-80), but you do not qualify for a UC start-up period (see para 10.81).

10.88   UC 77(2),(3)(a); NIUC 77(2),(3)(a)
10.89   UC 77(3)(b),(c),(4); NIUC 77(3)(b),(c),(4)

Chapter 11 **UC changes**

- Changes of circumstances: see paras 11.3-13.
- When changes of circumstances take effect: see paras 11.14-37.
- Changing wrong decisions: see paras 11.38-46.
- When changed decisions take effect: see paras 11.47-68.
- Suspending, restoring and terminating payments of UC: see paras 11.69-80.

11.1   Your UC can change:

(a) because of a change in your or someone else's circumstances; or

(b) because the DWP changes a decision that was wrong.

For example your UC could increase, reduce or end.

11.2   In the law, changes are also called revisions or supersessions. Table 11.1 explains these terms.

Table 11.1 **Decisions, revisions and supersessions**

Decisions

The DWP makes decisions:

(a) when you claim UC (chapter 3);

(b) when you report a change of circumstances, or the DWP is aware of a change without you reporting it (para 11.5); and

(c) when you ask for a decision to be changed because you think it is wrong, or the DWP realises it is wrong without you asking (para 11.41).

The kinds of decision in (b) and (c) are also called revisions and supersessions. Asking for a decision to be changed is often called 'requesting a reconsideration'.

Revisions

A revision is a decision which alters your UC from the same date (in most cases) as the decision it is altering. Revisions are mainly used when a wrong decision is changed. If they are advantageous to you they often have time limits (paras 11.47-53).

Supersessions

A supersession is a decision which alters your UC from a date later than the date of the decision it is altering. Supersessions are mainly used for changes of circumstances, and sometimes when a wrong decision is changed. If they are advantageous to you they often have time limits (paras 11.14-21 and 11.47-53). A 'closed period supersession' is used when a change of circumstances took place in the past and has already come to an end. It means your UC is altered, but only for that past fixed period (CH/2595/2003).

Changes of circumstances

11.3 This section explains how your UC changes when there is a change in your or someone else's circumstances.

11.4 The DWP can change your UC:

(a) because you or someone else have told it about a change of circumstances (paras 11.7-8); or

(b) on its own initiative (because it is aware of a change of circumstances).

The DWP's decision about the change

11.5 The DWP makes a decision about the change of circumstances. This is also called a 'supersession' or (in a few cases) a 'revision' (table 11.1). But you don't have to use these terms. When you report a change the DWP should treat you as having requested whichever of these is appropriate.

11.6 The DWP's decision could:

(a) increase your UC;

(b) reduce or end your UC; or

(c) change how your UC is paid.

Paras 11.14 onwards give more information about this and explain when the change takes effect.

Duty to tell the DWP about changes

11.7 You have a duty to report any change of circumstances which you might reasonably be expected to know could affect:

(a) your continuing entitlement to UC;

(b) the amount of UC awarded; or

(c) the payment of UC.

These are sometimes called 'relevant changes'. You should tell the DWP as soon as reasonably practicable after the change occurs. If you delay reporting changes that increase your UC, you may end up getting less UC than you could have done (para 11.17).

11.4 D&A 23, sch 1 paras 21,29; NID&A 23, sch 1 paras 21, 29

11.5 SSA 9-10; D&A 12,20(1), 22,23,33(1); NISSO 10, 11,NID&A 12, 20(1), 22,23, 33(1)

11.7 C&P 38(1),(4), D&A 36(9); NIC&P 37(1),(4), NID&A 36(9)

11.8   If you are getting UC as a couple, the above duty applies to both of you. If you are in a couple but getting UC as a single person, it is your duty to report changes relating to both of you. The duty also applies to:

(a)   someone getting UC on your behalf (para 12.5);

(b)   a landlord etc getting UC payments (para 12.11); and

(c)   in appropriate cases, a childcare provider, someone you are caring for, or a pension fund holder (para 3.22).

Kinds of change you should report

11.9   The DWP should explain the kinds of change you need to tell it about. For example:

(a)   changes in your housing costs (see also para 11.23-24);

(b)   changes in your or your partner's income or capital (for earnings and DWP benefits see also paras 11.26 and 11.31);

(c)   other changes relating to you, your benefit unit, non-dependants, or someone you are caring for (chapter 9).

How to tell the DWP about changes

11.10   You should normally be able to tell the DWP about changes via your online account if you have one (para 3.13). If you are told not to use that method, you should be given a contact point you can telephone or write to about changes. In Great Britain you may also be able to report births and deaths by using the Tell Us Once service through the local register office or DWP Bereavement Service.

Information and evidence

11.11   The DWP can ask you for information and evidence about a change of circumstances. The rules are the same as when you made a claim (paras 3.19-20). If you fail to provide this the DWP could suspend payments of your UC (para 11.72).

The DWP's notification to you

11.12   The DWP tells you about decisions changing your UC: see paras 3.34-36. It usually tells you about changes in the amount of your UC at the end of each month (para 11.13) and about other changes when they occur (e.g. about how your UC is paid).

Assessment periods and the 'whole month' approach

11.13   Your UC is awarded for assessment periods of one month and most changes take effect from the beginning of an assessment period (tables 11.2 and 11.3). For further information about assessment periods, see paras 3.38-44.

11.8   C&P 38(1),(4),(7),(8),41; NIC&P 37(1),(4), (7), (8), 38

11.10   C&P 2 definition: 'appropriate office', 38(5),39, sch 2; NIC&P 2, 37(5), sch 1

11.11   C&P 38(2),(3); D&A 33(2),(3); NIC&P 37(2),(3) NID&A 33(2),(3)

When changes of circumstances take effect

11.14   The date from which a change of circumstances alters your UC is called the 'effective date'. The rules about this are summarised in table 11.2. In this section, references to 'you' reporting a change also include when someone else reports it (para 11.8).

Table 11.2 **Changes of circumstances: effective date**

Type of change	Effective date of change
Advantageous changes (changes increasing UC: paras 11.15-17)	
(a) Reported or made within the time limit (the end of the assessment period or in some cases later: para 11.20)	The first day of the assessment period in which the change takes (or took) place
(b) Reported or made outside the time limit	The first day of the assessment period in which the change is reported, or the DWP first takes action to make it (if this is earlier)
Disadvantageous changes (changes reducing or ending UC: paras 11.18-19)	
(c) Whenever reported or made	The first day of the assessment period in which the change takes (or took) place

Notes
- For exceptions see para 11.22.
- In the law, (a) to (c) are all supersessions (table 11.1).

Advantageous changes

11.15   A change is advantageous if it increases your UC.

11.16   If you report the change, or the DWP makes the change, within the time limit (para 11.20), it takes effect from the first day of the assessment period in which the change takes (or took) place.

For exceptions see para 11.22.

11.17   Otherwise, the change takes effect from the first date of the assessment period in which:

(a) you report the change; or

(b) the DWP first takes action to make it (if this is earlier).

For exceptions see para 11.22.

T11.2   D&A sch 1 paras 20,21,29; NID&A sch 1 paras 20,21,29
11.16   D&A sch 1 para 20; NID&A sch 1 para 20
11.17   D&A sch 1 para 21; NID&A sch 1 para 21

Disadvantageous changes

11.18   A change is disadvantageous if it reduces or ends your UC.

11.19   Whenever you report the change, or whenever the DWP makes the change, it takes effect from the first day of the assessment period in which the change takes (or took) place. For exceptions see para 11.22.

Time limit for advantageous changes

11.20   An advantageous change is reported, or made by the DWP, within the time limit if:

(a) you report the change to the DWP within the assessment period in which it takes place; or

(b) you report the change to the DWP up to 13 months after it takes place, and the DWP agrees (para 11.21); or

(c) the DWP first takes action to make the change within the assessment period in which the change takes place.

11.21   When you report a change late (para 11.20(b)), the DWP can only agree to this if:

(a) there are special circumstances why it wasn't practicable for you to report the change earlier – for example if you, your partner or a child or young person were suffering a serious illness or postal services are disrupted (ADM para A4211); and

(b) it is reasonable to allow you extra time – the longer you take the more compelling your reasons have to be.

But the DWP can't take account of ignorance or misunderstanding of the law or the time limits, or of an Upper Tribunal or court interpreting the law in a new way.

Exceptions

11.22   The following kinds of change have rules which are in some cases different from those in paras 11.15-21:

(a) moves and changes in housing costs (paras 11.23-24);

(b) changes in rent officer figures (paras 6.17-18 and 11.63-65);

(c) changes in who your UC is paid to (para 11.25);

(d) changes in earned income (paras 11.26-27);

(e) changes in capability for work (paras 11.28-30);

(f) changes in DWP benefits (paras 11.31-32);

(g) reaching state pension credit age (para 11.33);

(h) qualifying for bereavement run-on because someone has died (paras 11.34-35); and

(i) changes in the law or case law (paras 11.36-37).

See also para 3.5 if you become a couple or a single person while you are on UC.

11.19   D&A sch 1 paras 20,29; NID&A sch 1 paras 20,29

11.20-21   D&A 36; NID&A 36

Examples: changes of circumstances: effective date

1. Starting to pay for childcare costs

Abigail is working and getting UC. Her assessment periods begin on the 26th of each month. She starts paying a childminder to look after her son on 6th June and qualifies for more UC because she is entitled to a childcare costs element. This is an advantageous change (paras 11.15-17) so:

- if she reports this to the DWP on (or before) 25th June, she is within the time limit and her UC increases from 26th May;
- if she reports this on 4th July and doesn't have special circumstances for her delay, her UC increases from 26th June.

2. An increase in capital

Barney is unemployed and getting UC. His assessment periods begin on the 26th of each month. His capital increases on 6th June and he qualifies for less UC. This is a disadvantageous change (paras 11.18-19) so:

- whenever he reports this to the DWP, his UC reduces from 26th May;
- if the increase in his capital is so great that he no longer qualifies for UC, his UC ends on 25th May.

3. A rent increase

Clodagh is getting UC and her assessment periods begin on the 21st of each month. Her rent increases on 1st October and she qualifies for more UC. This is an advantageous change so:

- if she reports this to the DWP on (or before) 20th October, she is within the time limit and her UC increases from 21st September;
- if she reports this on 4th December and doesn't have special circumstances for her delay, her UC increases from 21st November.

4. Size of accommodation needed

Desmond is getting UC and his assessment periods begin on the 21st of each month. His daughter moves out on 1st October and he qualifies for less UC because he is no longer entitled to a bedroom for her. This is a disadvantageous change so:

- whenever he reports this to the DWP, his UC reduces from 21st September.

Moves and changes in housing costs

11.23   You should tell the DWP when you move home or when your housing costs change. You need to report changes in rent even if you are renting from a council or social landlord. The DWP advises that as live service claimants cannot report changes online it also accepts rent change schedules from social landlords [www].

11.23   https://tinyurl.com/UC-guide-for-landlords

11.24 The rules in paras 11.15-21 apply to the above changes, but for changes in rent officer figures see instead paras 6.17-18 and 11.63-65. When a rent increase means you qualify for more UC, your UC increases from the first day of the assessment period in which your rent goes up, so long as you report this on time (para 11.20). But the DWP has wrongly advised some claimants that their UC will increase from the assessment period after that. If this happens to you, see para 11.43 for how to change the DWP's decision.

Changes in who your UC is paid to

11.25 Your UC can be paid to your landlord etc instead of you (para 12.11). If the DWP changes who it is paid to, the change is likely to take effect from the assessment period in which you request this or the DWP decides this. But there could be exceptions in appropriate cases.

Changes in earned income

11.26 You should tell the DWP when you or you or partner start or stop work. But the DWP should be able to take changes in your or your partner's earned income into account automatically – either because you have to provide information about it to the DWP each month, or because the DWP gets the information from HMRC (paras 10.22 and 10.30).

11.27 The rules in paras 11.15-21 apply when you or your partner start or stop work, or your or your partner's earned income increases. But when your or your partner's income reduces, the following applies instead:

(a) if you provide the DWP with any information it needs when required to, your UC increases from the first day of the assessment period in which that reduction takes place;

(b) otherwise the DWP can estimate the amount (para 10.11).

See also paras 3.45-49 if your or your partner's earned income reduces within six months of the DWP saying you don't qualify for UC.

Changes in capability for work

11.28 You should tell the DWP when your or your partner's capability for work changes in a way that affects your entitlement to an LCW or LCWRA element (paras 9.26-28). (Note that the UC LCW element was removed from April 2017 but not if you were already in receipt of it (paras 9.29-30).)

11.29 The rules in paras 11.15-21 apply when your or your partner's capability for work changes. But if:

(a) the change means you no longer qualify for an LCW/LCWRA element, and

(b) you couldn't reasonably have been expected to know you should tell the DWP about the change;

your UC changes from the first day of the assessment period in which the DWP makes its decision. So you haven't been overpaid UC.

11.25   D&A 10, 21, 25; NID&A 10, 21, 25

11.27   D&A sch 1 para 22; NID&A sch 1 para 22

11.29   D&A sch 1 paras 23-25,28,30; NID&A sch 1 paras 23-25,28,30

11.30   Different rules also apply if the DWP has made a decision not to award you an LCW/LCWRA element (the original decision), and then decides to award it because:

(a) it has received new evidence from a healthcare professional etc; or

(b) it has changed its mind about whether you or your partner need an assessment (para 9.26); or

(c) you have told it you or your partner are terminally ill (para 9.26).

In cases (a) and (b) you are awarded the LCW/LCWRA element from when the original decision took effect (or should have). In case (c) you are awarded the LCWRA element from the first day of the assessment period in which you or your partner became terminally ill (or from when your UC began, if this is later). So in all these cases you are awarded arrears of UC.

Changes in DWP benefits

11.31   You shouldn't need to tell the DWP (because it knows already) about changes in your entitlement to any DWP benefit, including when your entitlement starts or stops. This also applies to changes in your partner's, child's or young person's entitlement to a DWP benefit.

11.32   In these cases the rules in paras 11.15-21 don't apply. Instead your UC changes:

(a) from the first day of the assessment period in which the DWP benefit changes (or changed); or

(b) from when your UC began, if this is later.

If this means your UC increases from a date in the past, you are awarded arrears of UC back to then. But if it means your UC reduces or ends from a date in the past, you have been overpaid back to then.

Reaching state pension credit age

11.33   When you or your partner reach SPC age (para 2.10) you can get SPC. You can make an advance claim for SPC at any time in the four months before reaching SPC age. If you do, your UC continues until the day before you or your partner reach SPC age. It is awarded on a daily basis in your last UC assessment period. So if you then qualify for SPC there is no gap between your UC and SPC.

Bereavement run-on

11.34   The bereavement run-on delays the impact of a death on your UC. You qualify for a bereavement run-on if one of the following has died:

(a) your partner if you were claiming UC as a couple;

(b) a child or young person you were responsible for;

(c) a person you were caring for, if you qualified for the UC carer element for caring for them (see para 9.34); or

(d) a non-dependant.

11.30   D&A 5(2)(c),23(2),26(1),(3),35(9), sch 1 para 28; NID&A 5(2)(c),23(2),26(1),(3), 35(9), sch 1 para 28

11.32   D&A 12,21, sch1 para 31; NID&A 12, 21, sch 1 para 31

11.33   D&A sch 1 para 26; NID&A sch 1 para 26

11.34-35   UC 37; NIUC 39

11.35   When you qualify for a bereavement run-on, your maximum UC (see paras 9.12-56) is calculated as though the person had not died during:

(a)   the assessment period containing the date of the death; and

(b)   the next two assessment periods.

But changes in your financial and other circumstances are taken into account in the normal way. The examples illustrate how bereavement run-on works.

Examples: Bereavement run-on

1. Death of a partner

A home owner couple are on UC and their assessment periods start on the 13th of each month. Their maximum UC includes the LCWRA element for one of them (see para 9.26). The partner who qualifies for the LCWRA element dies on 3rd June.

Because of the bereavement run-on, the surviving partner continues to qualify for the LCWRA element up to and including 12th August. But the surviving partner's new financial circumstances are taken into account from 13th May.

2. Death of a non-dependant

A single person renting a housing association flat is on UC and his assessment periods begin on the last day of each month. His mother lives with him (she is his non-dependant) so he qualifies for two bedroom accommodation in calculating his housing costs element (see para 7.8) but his mother is expected to make a housing cost contribution (see para 9.58). His mother dies on 3rd June.

Because of the bereavement run-on, he continues to qualify for two bedroom accommodation until 31st August, and a housing cost contribution continues to be deducted until then.

Changes in the law or case law

11.36   When a change in the law affects your UC, it takes effect on the first day of your assessment period that begins on or after the date given in the Act or regulations making the change.

11.37   Different rules apply to new case law (para 1.44). When an Upper Tribunal or court makes a decision in someone else's case and this affects your own case, the DWP normally changes your UC from the date of that new decision. But there can be exceptions when there are a number of cases about similar matters, and one is used as a 'lead case' for other 'look-alike cases'.

11.36   D&A sch 1 paras 32,33; NID&A 32,33

11.37   SSA 27; D & A 35(5); NISSO 27, NID&A 35(5)

Changing wrong decisions

11.38   This section explains how wrong decisions about your UC are changed, for example if they were based on incorrect facts or applied the law incorrectly.

11.39   When a decision is wrong, the DWP can change it:

(a) because you or someone else have asked it to (paras 11.43-44); or

(b) on its own initiative (because is realises the decision is wrong).

The DWP's original decision

11.40   The decision that is wrong is called the 'original decision'. It could be a decision the DWP made when you claimed UC or when there was a change in your or someone else's circumstances.

The DWP's new decision

11.41   The DWP makes a new decision to replace the original decision. The new decision is also called a 'revision' or 'supersession' (table 11.1). But you don't have to use these terms. When you ask for a decision to be changed the DWP should treat you as having requested whichever of these is appropriate.

11.42   The DWP's new decision could:

(a) increase your UC, or award you UC if the original decision wrongly said you weren't entitled to it;

(b) reduce or end your UC; or

(c) change an overpayment of UC or how it is recovered.

Paras 11.47 onwards give more information about this and explain when the new decision takes effect.

Asking for a decision to be changed

11.43   You can ask for a decision to be changed by contacting the DWP via your online account if you have one (para 3.13) or by telephone or in writing. This is often called 'requesting a reconsideration', and if you wish you can first ask for a written statement of reasons (para 14.9). You should contact the DWP as soon as possible, otherwise you may end up getting less UC than you might have done (para 11.50).

11.44   If you are in a couple, either of you can ask for a decision to be changed. But if you only claimed as a single person, you (rather than your partner) should normally do this. Someone else who is affected by a decision can also ask for it to be changed. For example:

(a) someone claiming UC on your behalf (paras 3.8-10);

(b) a landlord etc if they think your UC should be paid to them (para 12.11); or

(c) someone who has been told an overpayment of UC is recoverable from them (paras 13.19-26).

11.39   D&A 5,8,22; NID&A 5, 8, 22

11.41   SSA 9-10; D&A 5,8,20(1), 22,32, 33(1); NISSO 10-11; NI D&A 5,8, 20(1), 22, 32, 33(1)

11.43   D&A 2 definition: 'appropriate office', 5(1)(b); NID&A 2, 5(1)(b)

11.44   D&A 5(1)(b)

Information and evidence

11.45   When you ask for a decision to be changed you should provide any information and evidence you want the DWP to consider. The DWP can also ask you for information and evidence, and should tell you the time limit for doing this. If you fail to do this within the time allowed, the DWP can just use whatever information and evidence it does have. It could also suspend payments of your UC (para 11.72).

The DWP's notification to you

11.46   The DWP tells you about decisions changing your UC: see paras 3.34-36. If you ask for a decision to be changed, it tells you the new decision or that it has decided not to change the original decision. If someone else asks for a decision to be changed, it tells you and them this. See chapter 14 for how and when you can go on to appeal to a tribunal.

When changed decisions take effect

11.47   When the DWP changes a wrong decision, the date from which its new decision takes effect is called the 'effective date'. The rules about this are summarised in table 11.3. In this section, references to 'you' requesting a change also include when someone else requests it (para 11.44).

Table 11.3 **Changing wrong decisions: effective date**

Type of change	Effective date of new decision
Advantageous changes (changes increasing or awarding UC: paras 11.48-50)	
(a) Requested or made within the time limit (one month or in some cases longer: para 11.53)	The date the original decision took effect (or should have)
(b) Requested or made outside the time limit	The first day of the assessment period in which the change is requested, or the DWP first takes action to make it (if this is earlier)
Disadvantageous changes (changes reducing or ending UC: paras 11.51-52)	
(c) Whenever requested or made	The date the original decision took effect (or should have)

Notes
- For exceptions, see para 11.54.
- In the law, (a) and (c) are revisions and (b) is a supersession (table 11.1).

11.45   C&P 38(2),(3),(4); D&A 20(2),(3),33(2),(3); NIC&P 37(2),(3),(4); NID&A 20(2),(3), 33(2),(3)

T11.3   D&A 5,9(b),21,24,35(2),(4); NID&A 5, 9(b), 21,24, 35(2),(4)

Advantageous changes

11.48   A change is advantageous if the DWP's new decision means:

(a) you qualify for more UC; or

(b) you are entitled to UC (if the original decision said you weren't entitled).

11.49   If you request the change, or the DWP makes the change, within the time limit (para 11.53):

(a) the DWP's new decision takes effect from the date the original decision took effect (or should have);

(b) so you are awarded arrears of UC back to then.

11.50   Otherwise:

(a) the DWP's new decision takes effect from the first day of the assessment period in which:

- ▪ you request the change, or
- ▪ the DWP first takes action to make it (if this is earlier);

(b) so you aren't awarded arrears of UC;

(c) but (a) and (b) only apply if you qualify for more UC (para 11.48(a)); if the original decision said you weren't entitled to UC, you instead need to make a new claim (chapter 3).

For exceptions see para 11.54.

Disadvantageous changes

11.51   A change is disadvantageous if the DWP's new decision means:

(a) you qualify for less UC; or

(b) you are not entitled to UC.

11.52   Whenever you request the change, or whenever the DWP makes the change:

(a) the DWP's new decision takes effect from the date the original decision took effect (or should have);

(b) so you have been overpaid UC back to then.

For exceptions see para 11.54.

Time limit for advantageous changes

11.53   An advantageous change is requested, or made by the DWP, within the time limit if:

(a) you ask the DWP to change a decision within one month of being notified about it (para 3.35); or

(b) you ask for a written statement of reasons (para 14.9) within that month, and then ask the DWP to change the decision within 14 days of:

- ▪ the end of that month, or
- ▪ the DWP providing the written statement (if this is later); or

---

11.49   D&A 5,21; NID&A 5,21

11.50   D&A 24,35(2),(4); NID&A 24, 35(2),(4)

11.52   D&A 9(b),21; NID&A 9(b),21

(c) you ask the DWP to change the decision up to 13 months later than (a) or (b) and the DWP agrees (paras 14.12-15); or

(d) the DWP first takes action to change the decision within one month of notifying you about it.

Exceptions

11.54 Changes to the following kinds of decision have rules which are different from those in paras 11.48-53:

(a) decisions that are wrong because of official error (paras 11.55-60);

(b) decisions about rent officer figures, the benefit cap, sanctions etc (paras 11.61-65);

(c) decisions about overpayments (para 11.66);

(d) decisions you have appealed (para 11.67); and

(e) decisions you can't appeal (paras 11.68).

Examples: Changing wrong decisions: effective date

1. Capital that should be disregarded

Eva has been getting UC since 9th January and her assessment periods begin on the 9th of each month. She realises she forgot to tell the DWP that some of her capital comes from an insurance payment in December for flood damage to her home. She asks the DWP to change her UC and the DWP agrees. This is an advantageous change (paras 11.48-50) so:

- if she requests the change on (or before) 8th February, she is within the time limit and her UC increases from 9th January;

- if she requests the change on 15th February and doesn't have special circumstances for her delay, her UC increases from 9th February.

2. Undeclared earnings

Frank has been getting UC since 9th January and his assessment periods begin on the 9th of each month. The DWP discovers he has been working since before he claimed UC and changes his UC. This is a disadvantageous change (paras 11.51-52) so:

- whenever the DWP makes the change, his UC reduces from 9th January.

3. An official error

Gertrude claimed UC on 9th January. She is a full-time student with a low income. Although she told the DWP when she claimed that she was a foster parent and had a foster child placed with her, the DWP said she wasn't entitled to UC. She asks the DWP to change this decision and the DWP agrees it was wrong because of official error (para 11.57) so:

- whenever she requests the change, she is awarded UC from 9th January.

11.53 D&A 2 definition: 'date of notification', 5(1),6,38(4); NID&A 2, 5(1), 6, 38(4)

Changing decisions that are wrong because of official error

11.55   The DWP should change any decision that is wrong because of official error (para 11.57).

11.56   Whenever you request the change, or whenever the DWP makes the change:

(a)   the DWP's new decision takes effect from the date the original decision took effect (or should have);

(b)   so if the change is advantageous (para 11.48) you are awarded arrears of UC back to then, but if it is disadvantageous (para 11.51) you have been overpaid back to then.

Official errors

11.57   An official error means:

(a)   an error made by a DWP officer, or someone employed by and acting for the DWP, or someone providing services to the DWP (see paras 11.58-60 for examples);

(b)   but not if you or anyone outside the DWP caused or materially contributed to it (e.g. if you didn't give the DWP correct information).

Paras 11.55-56 apply to (a), but paras 11.48-53 apply to (b).

Mistakes of fact

11.58   There is a mistake of fact if the DWP makes a decision in ignorance of, or based on a mistake about, a material fact (a fact that affects your UC). Paras 11.55-56 apply if this is due to official error, otherwise paras 11.48-53 apply.

Errors of law

11.59   There is an error of law if:

(a)   the DWP wrongly applies the law in making a decision;

(b)   but not when it is shown to be an error of law only by an Upper Tribunal or court (in another person's case) interpreting the law in a new way.

Paras 11.55-56 apply to (a), but paras 11.48-53 apply to (b). (For appeals in your own case, see para 11.67.)

Accidental errors

11.60   There is an accidental error if the DWP fails to record, or to put into action, its true intentions (e.g. by mis-entering data on a computer). The DWP can correct an accidental error in a decision, or in a record of a decision, at any time. It must notify you of the correction whether or not it alters your UC, and the correction must be treated as part of the decision or record. Paras 11.48-53 apply if the correction does alter your UC, but the time limit in para 11.53 ignores any period before you are notified of the correction.

11.56   D&A 9(a),21; NID&A 9(a),21

11.57   D&A 2 definitions: 'official error', 'designated authority'; NID&A 2

11.58   D&A 2 definition: 'official error', 9; NID&A 2,9

11.59   D&A 2 definition: 'official error', 9(a); NID&A 2, 9(a)

11.60   D&A 38; NID&A 38

Changing decisions about rent officer figures, the benefit cap, sanctions etc

11.61   The DWP should change any decision that:

(a)   uses a rent officer figure when it shouldn't do, or uses the wrong figure or area (para 11.63);

(b)   applies the benefit cap when it shouldn't do, or calculates it incorrectly (paras 9.64-74);

(c)   applies a sanction when it shouldn't do, or calculates it incorrectly (paras 9.76-82); or

(d)   wrongly reduces or ends your UC under the Fraud Act 2001.

This applies even if you contributed to the decision being wrong (e.g. if you didn't give the DWP correct information).

11.62   Whenever you request the change, or whenever the DWP makes the change:

(a)   the DWP's new decision takes effect from the date the original decision took effect (or should have);

(b)   so if the change is advantageous (para 11.48) you are awarded arrears of UC back to then, but if it is disadvantageous (para 11.51) you have been overpaid UC back to then.

Rent officer figures

11.63   Rent officer figures are used in UC as follows:

(a)   if you are a private renter, the DWP uses rent officer figures and areas (called LHA and BRMA determinations) to calculate your eligible rent (paras 6.15-20);

(b)   if you are a social renter, the DWP can ask the rent officer for a figure (called a housing payment determination) and can choose whether or not to use it in calculating your eligible rent (paras 5.21-26).

Paras 11.59-60 apply if the DWP uses a rent officer figure when it shouldn't do, or uses the wrong figure or area. But see instead para 11.64 if the rent officer corrects a figure, or paras 6.17-18 if your LHA figure changes in April or because your circumstances change.

Corrections to rent officer figures

11.64   The rent officer can reconsider any figure or area used in UC and correct it if they consider it is wrong. This is called a redetermination. The DWP can ask them to do this, or they can do it on their own initiative. If you think the rent officer has got a figure or area wrong, you could try asking them to change it, or asking the DWP to ask them (the law doesn't say that you can or that you can't).

11.65   When a rent officer redetermination means a new figure applies to you:

(a)   if it is higher, the DWP's new decision takes effect from when its original decision took effect (or should have) – so you get arrears of UC back to then;

(b)   if it is lower, the DWP's new decision takes effect from the first day of the assessment period following the one in which the DWP receives the figure from the rent officer – so you haven't been overpaid UC.

In NI analogous rules apply in relation to changes made to determinations by the Northern Ireland Housing Executive.

11.62   D&A 10,14,19,21; NID&A 10,14,19,21

11.65   D&A 19(2),21,30,35(14); NID&A 19(2),21,30, 35(14)

Changing decisions about overpayments

11.66   The DWP can change a decision about:

(a) whether you have been overpaid UC (para 13.1);

(b) the amount of an overpayment (paras 13.7-11);

(c) who it should be recovered from (paras 13.19-26); or

(d) whether it shouldn't be recovered because of hardship etc (paras 13.5-6).

You can ask the DWP to do this at any time, or it can do this at any time on its own initiative. In cases (a) and (b) the DWP's new decision normally takes effect from the date of the decision that meant you were overpaid (paras 13.2-4) – so you should be repaid any amount that was wrongly recovered from you. In cases (c) and (d) the DWP's new decision is likely to take effect from the assessment period in which you request the change or the DWP makes it. But in all of these cases there can be exceptions.

Changing decisions you have appealed

11.67   Chapter 14 explains the rules about appealing to an independent tribunal. Before you appeal you have to ask the DWP to reconsider the decision you want to appeal (paras 11.43-44 and 14.1).

When you appeal, the DWP:

(a) can change the decision before the appeal takes place (paras 14.16-17);

(b) should normally apply the tribunal's decision once the appeal has taken place (paras 14.57 and 14.63).

Changing decisions you can't appeal

11.68   If a decision is of a kind that can't be appealed (table 14.1), you can ask the DWP to change it at any time, or the DWP can change it at any time on its own initiative. The rules for some non-appealable decisions are in paras 11.25, 11.63-65 and 11.66(d). In other cases, the DWP's new decision is likely to take effect from the date the original decision took effect (or should have), or from the assessment period in which it makes the change – but there can be exceptions in appropriate cases.

Suspending, restoring and terminating UC

11.69   This section explains how the DWP can suspend, restore or terminate your UC. The general rules about this are in paras 11.70-76, and the rules for appeals cases are in paras 11.77-79.

Suspending UC

11.70   Suspending UC means that all or part of your UC payments is stopped for the time being. The DWP has told its decision-makers that they should always take account of whether hardship will result before doing this (ADM para A4317).

11.66   D&A 10,21,25,35(2),(4); NID&A 10,21,25,35(2),(4)

11.71   The DWP can suspend all or part of your UC when:

(a) it doubts whether you meet the conditions of entitlement for UC;

(b) it is considering whether to change a decision about your UC (paras 11.4 and 11.39);

(c) it considers there may be an overpayment of UC; or

(d) you don't appear to live at your last notified address.

The DWP can do this straightaway or first ask for information or evidence (para 11.72).

Information and evidence

11.72   When the DWP requires information or evidence, it must notify you of what it requires and how long you have to provide it. It must allow you at least 14 days and can allow longer. The DWP can then suspend all or part of your UC if you don't:

(a) provide the information or evidence within the time allowed; or

(b) satisfy the DWP within that time that it doesn't exist or is impossible to obtain.

Restoring UC

11.73   The DWP must restore payments of your UC when it is satisfied that:

(a) UC is properly payable;

(b) there are no outstanding matters to be resolved; and

(c) you have provided any information or evidence it required, or it doesn't exist or is impossible to obtain.

11.74   Restoring UC means paying the UC that was suspended. The payments should be at the same amount as before; but the rules in paras 11.3-68 apply if there has been a change of circumstances or a decision was wrong.

Terminating UC

11.75   The DWP must terminate your UC if:

(a) it suspended payments of your UC in full;

(b) it required you to provide information or evidence;

(c) more than one month has passed since it required this; and

(d) you haven't provided the information or evidence or satisfied the DWP that it doesn't exist or is impossible to obtain.

The DWP can extend the time limit of one month if this is reasonable (ADM para A4338).

11.76   Terminating UC means you don't get any more payments and your entitlement ends; but the rules in paras 11.3-68 apply if your UC should have stopped from an earlier date. The DWP should notify you when it terminates your UC.

11.71   SSA 22; D&A 44(1),(2)(a); NISSO 22, NID&A 43(1),(2)(a)

11.72   SSA 22; D&A 45; NISSO 22, NID&A 44

11.73   D&A 46(a),(b); NID&A 45(a),(b)

11.75   SSA 23; D&A 47; NISSO 23, NID&A 46

Suspending and restoring UC in appeals cases

11.77   The DWP can suspend all or part of your UC when an appeal is pending against:

(a) a decision of a First-tier Tribunal, Upper Tribunal or court in your own case; or

(b) a decision of an Upper Tribunal or court in another person's case, and it appears to the DWP that the outcome of the appeal could mean your UC should be changed.

11.78   An appeal counts as 'pending' if:

(a)   the DWP has requested a statement of reasons from the First-tier Tribunal and is waiting for this; or

(b)   the DWP is waiting for a decision from the Upper Tribunal or court; or

(c)   the DWP has received the statement of reasons or decision and:

■   is considering whether to apply for permission to appeal,

■   has applied for permission to appeal and is waiting for a decision on this, or

■   has received permission to appeal and is considering whether to appeal; or

(d)   the DWP has made an appeal and it hasn't yet been decided; or

(e)   you or the other person (para 11.77) have made an appeal and it hasn't yet been decided.

In cases (a) to (d) the DWP should keep you informed of its plans.

11.79   The DWP must restore payments of your UC when:

(a)   it runs out of time to request a statement of reasons, apply for permission to appeal, or appeal; or

(b)   it withdraws an application for permission to appeal, or an appeal; or

(c)   it is refused permission to appeal and can't take any further steps to obtain it.

But if the DWP needs information or evidence, the rules in paras 11.72-76 apply.

Changing decisions about suspending, restoring or terminating UC

11.80   You can ask the DWP to reconsider a decision about suspending, restoring or terminating your UC (para 11.43). You can then appeal to a tribunal about a decision to terminate your UC or to alter it when it is restored, but not about a decision to suspend your UC or to restore it without altering it (para 14.18).

11.77   SSA 21; D&A 44(1),(2)(b),(c); NISSO 21, NID&A 43(1),(2)(b),(c)

11.78   SSA 21(3); D&A 44(3)-(5); NISSO 21(3), NID&A 43(3)-(5)

11.79   D&A 46(c),(d); NID&A 45(c),(d)

Chapter 12 **UC payments**

- How, when and to whom UC payments are normally made: see paras 12.1-4 and the payment flexibilities available in Scotland and Northern Ireland – see para 12.18.

- Payment of UC to someone else acting on your behalf: see paras 12.5-6.

- Budgeting, bill payment and the measures introduced by the Government in 2018 to ease your transition onto UC: see para 12.7.

- Arrangements to vary the frequency of payments and for splitting payments between you and a partner: see paras 12.8-10.

- Alternative payment arrangements under which UC may be paid direct to your landlord including the 'trusted partners' arrangement with social landlords: see paras 12.11-17 and the additional powers to make payments to a landlord if you live in Scotland or Northern Ireland: see para 12.18.

- Direct payments to qualifying lenders where your UC included help with the cost of owning your home or where (from 6th April 2018) the DWP is making separate interest bearing loan payments for you: see paras 12.19-25.

- Deductions paid to a third party if you have housing cost, rent or service charge arrears, council tax arrears or certain other debts: see paras 12.26-37.

- Loss of the right to a UC payment if it is not collected and what happens to outstanding payments on the death of the claimant: see paras 12.38-39.

- Payments on account in the form of UC advance payments and budgeting advances: see paras 12.40-49.

How, when and to whom UC is normally paid

Method of payment

12.1   UC is usually paid by direct credit transfer into your bank, building society or other account in monthly payments (but note the payment flexibilities that operate in Scotland and Northern Ireland – para 12.18). During the first stage of transition to UC and subsequent gateway requirements a necessary condition of entitlement was to have a bank, building society or Post Office account or a current account with a credit union. When you first claim UC you are asked for the details of the account you want it paid into. In limited circumstances, if you can't use an account, UC can be paid through the Payment Exception Service (which replaced the Simple Payment Service). This enables you to collect your benefit by using a Simple Payment card at a paypoint outlet which displays the Simple Payment logo [www].

12.1   C&P Regs, 47(1), 46(1), 47(2); SI 2013/386 12(e) (repealed from 16/06/14), SI 2013/983 sch 5 para 7(e)
        www.gov.uk/payment-exception-service

Date of payment

12.2   UC is paid in arrears, normally up to seven days after the last day of your monthly assessment period or as soon as reasonably practicable after that. The additional seven 'waiting days' that many new claimants previously experienced have been abolished from 14th February 2018. If there are delays in deciding or paying your benefit and this is placing you in financial need, you may be able to get a UC advance payment (see para 12.42). Also, the DWP may change the frequency of payment if a single monthly amount causes you problems (see para 12.8 and 12.18).

Example

Brian is entitled to a UC payment for the monthly assessment period from 5th June to 4th July. The DWP should credit his UC to his building society account in the seven days after 4th July and on the same day in each subsequent month.

Where Brian is in financial need but has not had a first payment, or DWP administrative or other delays mean that UC is not paid on the date due, Brian may ask the DWP to make a UC advance payment (para 12.42) at his first Jobcentre interview after applying for UC or by phoning the relevant free UC helpline number.

12.3   The DWP can decide to make a particular credit transfer at other times if it appears appropriate for the purpose of:

(a)   paying arrears of benefit; or

(b)   making a payment at the end of an award or for any similar purpose.

Payment to couples

12.4   If you are in a couple and joint claimants, UC is normally only paid into one account. This can be an account in:

(a)   your name;

(b)   your partner's name; or

(c)   your joint names.

If you can't both agree which account the benefit should be paid into, the DWP can make the decision. This is not an appealable decision. If a single payment to your partner's account or a joint account causes you difficulties, the DWP may decide to split the payment between you (see para 12.9).

12.2   C&P Regs, 45, 47(2)
          UC 19A, 20A, 21(1A), SI 2018/65 3(2)(a), (3), (4), (5)(b)

12.3   C&P Regs, 47(3)

12.4   C&P Regs, 46(1), 47(4)-(6)

Payment to other people on your behalf if you are unable to act

12.5   UC can be paid into a bank or other account in:

(a) an appointee's name – i.e. the name of someone who has been appointed by the DWP to get and deal with your benefit payments – because you are unable for the time being to act – or the name of someone who had previously been appointed to deal with your HB payments by the council and who agrees to be an appointee for UC purposes;

(b) the name of someone who has been authorised to act on your behalf under specific legislation, e.g. an attorney with general power or the power to receive benefit, a deputy appointed by the Court of Protection, a receiver appointed under the Mental Health Act 1983, or in Scotland a judicial factor or any guardian acting or appointed under the Adults with Incapacity (Scotland) Act 2000; or

(c) the joint names of yourself and any of the above.

12.6   Someone who wants to be appointed to get and deal with your UC payments when you're unable to act must be over the age of 18. They should write to the DWP asking to be appointed. The appointment can be ended at any time by the DWP. If the appointee wants to give up the role they must give the DWP a month's written notice.

Budgeting and bill payment

12.7   A single monthly payment of UC which may include money for the rent can be a significant budgeting and bill payment challenge. This is particularly so if the council has previously paid your HB direct to your landlord. And your landlord may be concerned that you will get into rent arrears. The government recognises these problems but says that it wants you to take personal responsibility for your finances and to budget on a monthly basis so that you find it easier to take up monthly paid employment [www]. You may, however, need help dealing with this change. The DWP aims to identify this (in conjunction with other agencies) either when you first become entitled to UC or once an award is made. It can provide you with personal budgeting support in the form of:

(a) money advice – to help you manage your money and pay bills on time;

(b) alternative payment arrangements – such as more frequent payments, payments split between you and a partner, and direct managed payments of the housing element to your landlord.

There has been growing public and political concern with the monthly in arrears payment of UC, delays in payment and related rent arrears. The government has announced the following measures to ease claimants onto the UC scheme:

(a) abolition of waiting days from 14th February 2018 (see para 12.2);

(b) an increase in the amount of UC advance payments and an extension in the period over which they are recovered (see paras 12.42-43);

12.5   C&P Regs, 46(1), 57; NIC&P 41(1), 52

12.6   C&P Regs, 57(3)-(4),(8), NIC&P 52(3)-(4),(8)

(c) if you are moving from HB to UC, an automatic, non-recoverable two-week payment of full HB paid by the council to you early in your first UC assessment period – from 11th April 2018; and

(d) offering you UC managed payments to your landlord when you move from HB to UC, if HB payments are being made direct to your landlord and the UC managed payment criteria are met.

The above measures are outlined in DWP UC Bulletin UC1/2017 [www]. Extra payment flexibilities exist in Scotland and Northern Ireland (see para 12.18).

Alternative payment arrangements

UC paid more often than once a month

12.8   The DWP can pay you more often than once a month if you are having problems budgeting and there is a risk of financial harm to you or your family. The DWP recommends two payments every month in these circumstances but, exceptionally, it may make four [www]. The DWP says that where your UC includes a housing element this more frequent payment of UC should be accompanied by managed payments to your landlord of the housing element [www].

Re-directing and splitting payments between partners

12.9   The DWP can arrange for the UC payable for you and your partner to be paid:

(a) wholly to one of you; or

(b) split between you in such proportion as it thinks appropriate.

12.10   It only does this, however, if it is in the interests of:

(a) both of you;

(b) a child or young person for whom one or both of the you are responsible; or

(c) a severely disabled person – where your UC includes an amount because you have regular and substantial caring responsibilities for that person.

Such re-direction or splitting of payments should be considered in specific situations such as financial abuse where one of you is mismanaging the payments. The DWP says that if it decides to make a split payment, and you have a rental liability, the decision maker must also consider a managed payment of the UC housing element to your landlord.

12.7   SI 2018/65 reg 6(8)
         DWP UC Guidance on personal budgeting support and alternative payment arrangements (April 2018), p3: goo.gl/duHGcU
         DWP UC Bulletin UC1/2017: goo.gl/LHpn98

12.8   C&P Regs, 47(1)
         DWP UC Guidance on personal budgeting support and alternative payment arrangements (April 2018), p10: goo.gl/duHGcU

12.9   C&P Regs, 47(6)

12.10   C&P Regs, 47(6)

Payments of UC to your landlord or someone else

12.11   The DWP can decide to pay your UC either wholly or in part (for example the housing element) to someone else, such as your landlord. The DWP should only do this where it appears necessary to protect your interests or the interests of the other people identified in para 12.10. The DWP provides guidance on paying the UC housing element to your landlord (known as managed payments) in two documents: *UC and rented housing: guide for landlords* (April 2018) [www] and *UC Personal Budgeting Support and Alternative Payment Arrangements* (April 2017) [www]. If an amount for rent is included in your UC and the DWP is considering alternative payment arrangements, it says it gives top priority to paying the housing element direct to your landlord over other alternative arrangements.

12.12   A private landlord normally only knows if you claim UC if you tell them. If your landlord is a social landlord the DWP writes to tell them that you have claimed (in live service areas social landlords get DWP notification UC179 or UC182 if a tenant claims UC). The DWP asks landlords to say if individual tenants are likely to need support. Your landlord can contact the UC Service Centre to tell them about any concerns they have about your financial capability. If when you claim UC the DWP thinks that you need support with budgeting (after for example considering information and evidence supplied by you, your representative or your landlord) it may decide to put in place an alternative payment arrangement including managed payments to your landlord. But just because your HB was paid to your landlord does not necessarily mean that your UC housing element will be. The DWP says that it considers each case on its merits.

12.13   Key factors that the DWP considers in deciding if an alternative payment arrangement is appropriate are set out in the UC Guidance on Personal Budgeting Support [www]. Alternative payment arrangements including managed payments of UC to your landlord (if appropriate) are described as highly likely if you:

(a)   have addiction problems (e.g. drug, alcohol or gambling);

(b)   have learning difficulties (including problems with reading/writing or numbers);

(c)   have severe or multiple debt problems;

(d)   live in temporary or supported accommodation;

(e)   are homeless;

(f)   suffer domestic violence or abuse;

(g)   have a mental health condition;

(h)   are in rent arrears or face eviction;

(i)   are aged 16 or 17; or

(j)   have multiple and complex needs.

An increasing number of social landlords (so called 'trusted partners') [www] are in a DWP scheme under which they identify tenants 'needing' managed payment of the UC housing element to the landlord.[www] The expectation is that the DWP will automatically act on

12.11   C&P Regs, 58(1)
           UC and rented housing: guide for landlords (April 2018): goo.gl/s8pRJ6
           DWP UC Guidance on personal budgeting support and alternative payment arrangements (April 2018), p11: goo.gl/duHGcU

12.12   WRA s. 131 SI 2012/1483 5(1)(g), 5(3A)

these recommendations. All 'trusted partner' landlords are given access to the UC online landlord portal and the enhanced UC service associated with it. If you are a new UC full service claimant. the online portal allows a trusted partner landlord to check if you are claiming UC, verify rent figures and apply for a managed payment. The social landlords expected to become 'trusted partners' in 2017 were identified by the DWP in a House of Commons Library deposited paper [www].

Rent arrears and managed payments of UC to your landlord

12.14   If you, your representative or your landlord tell the DWP that you have rent arrears equal to the amount of one month's rent the DWP may decide to offer you budgeting support and/or pay the housing element of your UC direct to your landlord. If you have rent arrears of an amount equal to 2 months rent your landlord can ask the DWP to consider if managed payments of UC direct to the landlord are appropriate. They can also request that rent arrears be recovered by deduction from your UC – see para 12.33.

12.15   Your landlord may get managed payments of UC by filling in and submitting the appropriate UC47 Rent Arrears Form [www]. To complete this form your landlord needs to know your NI number or your date of birth. They must also provide proof of your rent arrears and a full breakdown of how the amount of rent and the arrears are calculated. Once the DWP gets the completed form and evidence it decides whether to make managed payments to your landlord. Both you and your landlord are told about this decision in writing. It is not appealable but you may ask the DWP to look at it again.

12.16   The DWP also offers an email address for landlords to use for urgent inquiries if you are getting UC live service and your landlord needs an urgent response [www]; or they can telephone 0800 328 9344. If you are getting UC full service you should be able to access information from your online account which you may decide to share with your landlord, or you may provide explicit consent via your account for personal information to be shared with your landlord. Alternatively your landlord can call 0800 328 5644.

DWP periodically reviews alternative payment arrangements

12.17   The DWP looks again at its decision to pay UC direct to your landlord and other alternative payment arrangements periodically. The DWP sets a review date based on your particular circumstances.

Scotland and Northern Ireland

12.18   The Scotland Act 2016 provides the Scottish Government with certain flexibilities (UC Choices) about how or when UC is paid. While the DWP system for alternative payment arrangements continues to operate, in addition if you are a UC applicant/recipient living in Scotland in a full service area (your UC award is managed online) you are offered the following choices through your online account:

12.13   DWP UC Guidance on personal budgeting support and alternative payment arrangements (April 2018): goo.gl/duHGcU
        DWP UC Trusted Partner/Landlord Portal lines to take: goo.gl/Y8DijA
        DWP Registered Social Landlords 2017: goo.gl/kYHr7A

12.15   directpayment.universal-credit.service.gov.uk/
        D&A Regs, sch 3 para 1(n)

12.16   uc.servicecentrehousing@dwp.gsi.gov.uk

- your UC being paid twice-monthly (rather than once a month); and

- any UC housing element being paid direct to your landlord – if you are not already on a DWP alternative payment arrangement or managed payment to your landlord [www].

In Northern Ireland:

- twice-monthly payments in arrears as the default (with payment once a month in arrears if you request this) [www];

- managed payment of the housing element of UC to the landlord as the default – but direct payments would be available to you if you ask and you are not in rent arrears – and certain other conditions are met;

- if you have opted out of direct payments to your landlord but are having difficulty paying the rent your landlord can apply for UC direct payments for rent/rent arrears using form UC47 [www] and sending it to Freepost Universal Credit Northern Ireland.

Direct payment to your lender for mortgage interest etc

12.19 Help with mortgage interest and similar payments to help you purchase your home are now mainly met by DWP loan payments: see chapter 8. But some people still receive UC towards this (para 8.51), and paras 12.20-25 apply in their case.

Information your lender must provide

12.20 When you make a claim for UC, or the housing cost element is to be included in your UC at some other point, your lender should provide the DWP with the following information when asked to do so by the DWP:

(a) the loan interest payments for which you meet the payment condition and the liability condition (see para 4.2);

(b) the amount of the loan;

(c) the purpose for which the loan was made;

(d) the amount outstanding on the loan;

(e) the amount of arrears of loan interest payments due.

12.21 When asked by the DWP, your lender should also tell the DWP about:

(a) any change in the amount of the loan interest payable; and

(b) the amount outstanding on the loan.

12.18   Scotland Act 2016, s29-30, The Universal Credit (Claims and Payments) (Scotland) Regulations SSI 2017/227,
        as amended by SSI 2017/ *Scottish Government, Universal Credit: New choices for people living in Scotland:* goo.gl/9eqezy
        NIC&P 42(1)
        goo.gl/1oU6YM
        NI Form UC47: goo.gl/zJLoMD

12.19   Welfare Reform and Work Act 2016, s18 - 21, SI 2017/725, Welfare Reform and Work (Northern Ireland) Order 2016, NISR 2017/176

12.20   C&P Regs, sch 5, para 11(1)-(2); NIC&P sch 4, 11(1)-(2)

12.21   C&P Regs, sch 5, para 11(3); NIC&P sch 4, para 11(3)

12.22   If your lender gets notice that the loan is going to be redeemed they must tell the DWP about this at once.

The lender must put the direct payments against your loan interest liability

12.23   Where the DWP is making a direct payment to your lender, the lender must apply the amount of the payment towards discharging your liability to make loan interest payments, in respect of which the direct payments are made.

Administration of direct payments to lenders

12.24   The DWP Third Party Payments (TPP) team (part of Payment Resolution Service) based at Norcross act as paying agents. They are responsible for all payments to third party creditors (ADM D4031). In return for getting direct payments of mortgage interest, your lender pays a fee of £0.39 (from 1st April 2017) to the DWP for each transaction.

12.25   There is no right of appeal against a decision to pay mortgage interest payments etc direct to a qualifying lender.

Payment to third parties for certain priority debts

12.26   The DWP can make deductions from your UC to repay certain priority debts (such as rent, utility bills and fines) you owe to a third party. The debts for which deductions can be made include:

(a)   housing costs – not covered by the direct payment arrangements (see para 12.19);

(b)   rent and service charges;

(c)   council tax; and

(d)   several other items including fuel debts, water charges, fines and in NI rates.

12.27   The DWP says (ADM D2022) that it is normally in your interests to make third party deductions if you have:

(a)   a history of persistent mis-spending; or

(b)   a threat of eviction or repossession; and

(c)   no other suitable method of dealing with the debt.

12.28   Deductions are not normally made (ADM D2023) if you:

(a)   show evidence of determination to clear the debt; or

(b)   agree to clear the debt yourself.

12.22   C&P Regs, sch 5, para 11(4); NIC&P sch 4, para 11(3)

12.23   C&P Regs, sch 5, para 6; NIC&P sch 4, para 6

12.24   C&P Regs, sch 5 para 9; NIC&P sch 4, para 9

12.25   D&A Regs, sch 3 para 1(o); NID&A sch 3 para 1(o)

12.26   C&P Regs, sch 6, para 2(1); NIC&P sch 5, para 2(1)

Constraints on third party deductions

12.29   The DWP can't deduct an amount from your UC and pay it to a third party if, in any assessment period, that would:

(a)   reduce the amount payable to you to less than 1p; or

(b)   result in more than three deductions being made, in relation to that assessment period (though there are certain exceptions to this).

12.30   Your consent is not required for the DWP to make deductions for housing costs, rent or service charges. You should, however, be given the opportunity to dispute the liability and the DWP should only make deductions where there is evidence that you are liable to pay the debt (ADM D2026-8).

Third party deductions for arrears of an owner's housing costs

12.31   The DWP may make deductions equal to 5% of the standard allowance from your UC and pay it direct to the creditor where, in any assessment period, you are in debt for any of the following housing costs that have been included in the calculation of your DWP loan payments (chapter 8) or your UC (para 12.19):

(a)   loan interest payments (para 8.8);

(b)   alternative finance payments (para 8.9);

(c)   service charge payments (para 4.23); or

(d)   payments under a shared ownership scheme (para 4.18).

12.32   The DWP says it only does this if it is satisfied that two months' arrears have accrued (ADM D2093). Also a deduction cannot be made under this rule where the item is payable direct to a qualifying lender (see para 12.19).

Third party deductions for arrears of rent and service charges

12.33   If your rent is being met through either UC (or HB because you live in exempt accommodation) the DWP can make deductions of between 10% and 20% from your UC standard allowance (para 9.14) and pay it direct to your landlord to meet arrears of rent, service charges and ineligible service charges. The provision is for a minimum priority deduction of 10%. Whether the deduction can be as high as 20% depends on whether the DWP is making other deductions as the maximum that may normally be deducted from your UC in respect of deductions for arrears, overpayments, repaying advances, child support etc is 40% of your standard allowance. The DWP may, however, exceed this 40% figure to allow it to make a deduction equal to 10% of the standard allowance to pay for rent and service charge arrears.

12.29   C&P Regs, sch 6, para 3(1)(a)-(b), 3(2); NIC&P sch 5, para 3(1)(a)-(b), 3(2)

12.31   C&P Regs, 60, sch 6, para 6(2)-(3); NIC&P 55, sch 5 para 6(2)-(3)

12.32   C&P Regs, 60, sch 6, para 6(5); NIC&P 55, sch 5 para 6(5)

12.33   C&P Regs, reg. 60, sch 6 para 7(1)-(5); NIC&P 55, sch 5 para 7(1)-(5)

12.34 In all cases for these deductions to be payable you must be occupying the accommodation to which the debt relates. Because these deductions may be made where your rent is met through HB in exempt accommodation they can be made for example to cover arrears of ineligible service charges in such accommodation.

12.35 The DWP says it only makes these deductions if satisfied that two months' arrears have accrued (ADM D2120). Also these deductions can only be started if your (and any partner's) earned income in relation to the previous assessment period is not greater than the work allowance (para 10.13 and table 10.1). They must stop if, in relation to the three assessment periods immediately before the date on which the next deduction could otherwise be made, your (and any partner's) earned income is equal to or greater than the work allowance.

12.36 Your landlord may apply for these deduction to be made in the same way as they apply for managed payments of the UC housing element and the same form is used (para 12.15).

Deductions to recover arrears of council tax

12.37 If you have arrears of council tax the authority can make an application to the DWP for deductions to be made from your UC if they have got a liability order or have been granted a summary warrant or decree. The DWP may deduct an amount equal to 5% of your UC standard allowance and pay it to the authority. You must be entitled to UC throughout the assessment period for this deduction to be made. Also a deduction can't be made if a deduction arrangement is already in place to recover arrears of council tax or community charges.

Loss of the right to a UC payment if you fail to get it

12.38 If you (or your appointee, attorney, etc) haven't received your UC payment after 12 months from the date on which your right to the payment arose, you lose the right to that payment (CDLA/2609/2002 and CDLA/2807/2003). But this period may be extended if you write to the DWP after the 12 months are up asking for payment and have continuous good cause (R(S)2/63) from a day within the 12 month period for the late request.

What happens to any UC payment if you die

12.39 Any payment that should have been made to you (unless it has been lost because you didn't get it within 12 months) may be paid or distributed by the DWP among people who are your personal representatives, legatees, next of kin or creditors (all over the age of 16). Where the DWP is satisfied that the payment is needed for the well-being of a child (someone under 16), it may pay it to someone aged 16+ who satisfies the DWP that they will use it for the child's well-being. The 12 month rule still applies (see para 12.38) but here is calculated from the date on which the right to payment arose in relation to these other people. A written application for the payment should be made to the DWP within 12 months from the date of your death – though the DWP may extend this period.

12.34　C&P Regs, sch 6 para 7(4); NIC&P sch 5 para 7(4)

12.35　C&P Regs, sch 6 para 7(6)-(7); NIC&P sch 5 para 7(6)-(7)

12.37　SI 1993 No. 494, 1(2), 2, 3, 5(1A), 8

12.38　C&P Regs, 55; NIC&P 50

12.39　C&P Regs, 56(2)-(8); NIC&P 51(2)-(8)

Payments on account

Two types

12.40   Two types of payments on account of benefit may possibly be available to you:

(a) advances of benefit (UC advances); and

(b) interest free loans – called budgeting advances.

12.41   If the DWP decides to pay you a UC advance or budgeting advance, it also writes to you (and any partner) telling you that:

(a) the advance payment will be deducted from subsequent payments of benefit; and

(b) if it is not deducted in this way you will have to repay it.

The detailed rules regarding these payments are set out in the Social Security (Payments on Account of Benefits) Regulations SI 2013 No 383.

UC advances

12.42   A UC advance may be available if you are in financial need and:

(a) you have made a claim for UC that has yet to be decided but it appears to the DWP likely that you are entitled; or

(b) you haven't had to claim to become entitled to UC but the award has not yet been made; or

(c) UC has been awarded but the first payment has not yet been made; or

(d) a first UC payment has been made but it was for a shorter period than the normal period and a second payment hasn't been received yet; or

(e) you have had a change of circumstance that increases the amount of UC you are entitled to but the award has not yet been altered or the resulting increased payment has not yet been made; or

(f) delays mean that a UC payment hasn't been made on the date due.

The DWP says that the maximum advance it pays in the case of a new UC claim is 100% of your estimated UC payment [www]. You will have up to 12 months to pay back the advance. In exceptional circumstances you can ask for your repayments to be delayed for up to three months.

12.43   Financial need means that there is a serious risk of damage to your health or safety or the health or safety of any partner or child or young person you are responsible for. DWP guidance [www] says that financial need includes if you can't afford to pay your rent or buy food. You can ask for an advance payment by calling the UC helpline or speaking to your work coach [www]. The ability to apply online for advance payments is expected to be available from the spring of 2018. When you ask for a UC advance you should provide as much information and evidence as possible about the circumstances and financial need. Explain how the delay etc is placing at risk your, or your family's, health or safety.

12.41   POA 8, 17; NIPOA 8, 17

12.42   POA 4-6; NIPOA 4-6
         www.gov.uk/guidance/universal-credit-advances

12.43   POA 7; NIPOA 7
         www.gov.uk/guidance/universal-credit-advances

12.44   Advance payments are expected to be paid within five working days or on the same day if you are in immediate need [www]. If the DWP refuses your request for a UC advance there is no right of appeal but you can ask the DWP to reconsider the decision. You should also look into other sources of help such as a discretionary housing payment from the council to help you pay the rent.

Budgeting advances

12.45   You may be able to get an interest free loan in the form of a budgeting advance to help you with one-off expenses such as furniture or household equipment, or expenses related to starting work. You pay back the advance by having the DWP deduct an amount from your monthly UC payments over a 12 month period (this may be extended to 18 months in exceptional circumstances).

12.46   To qualify for a budgeting advance you must have:

(a) been getting UC or a predecessor benefit (IS, JSA(IB), ESA(IR) or pension credit) for a continuous period of at least six months before making the application (except where the expense necessarily relates to getting or keeping a job);

(b) not have earned more than £2,600 in the previous six months (£3,600 for a couple);

(c) repaid any previous budgeting advance and the DWP must be satisfied that the budgeting advance can reasonably be expected to be recovered.

12.47   The minimum amount of budgeting advance payable is £100. The maximum amount is set out in the following table.

Table 12.1 **Maximum amount of budgeting advance**	
Your circumstances	**Maximum amount of budgeting advance**
Single and not responsible for a child or young person	£348
A couple but not responsible for a child or young person	£464
Responsible for a child or young person	£812

12.48   The amount of any budgeting advance you can get is reduced pound for pound by any assessable capital you have above £1,000. If this would reduce the amount to less than £100, then no budgeting advance is payable.

12.49   You can't appeal against a DWP refusal to make a budgeting advance but you can ask for the decision to be reconsidered.

12.44   D&A Regs, sch 3 para 14; NID&A sch 3 para 11
         goo.gl/MEotcv

12.46   POA 12-14; NIPOA 12-14

T12.1   POA 15; NIPOA 12-14

12.48   POA 16; NIPOA 16

12.49   D&A Regs, sch 3 para 14; NID&A, sch 3, para 11

Chapter 13 **UC overpayments**

- Why overpayments occur: see para 13.1.
- How overpayments are created: see paras 13.2-4.
- Recoverability and the DWP's discretion not to recover: see paras 13.5-6.
- Calculation of the recoverable overpayment: see paras 13.7-18.
- People overpayments of UC housing costs and other UC overpayments are recoverable from: see paras 13.19-26.
- Methods of recovery available to the DWP: see paras 13.27-43.

Why overpayments occur

13.1   An overpayment occurs when you are paid more UC than you are legally entitled to. This can happen for a variety of reasons including:

  (a) you give the DWP wrong information, fail to give relevant information or are late in telling the DWP about a change in your circumstances;

  (b) your landlord, employer or someone else gives the DWP incorrect information or fails to provide relevant information they are required to provide;

  (c) the backdating of an income or benefit that affects your UC; or

  (d) the DWP makes a mistake or is late in acting on information.

The creation of UC overpayments

13.2   Once the DWP has awarded and paid you an amount of UC you are normally entitled to that money until:

  (a) it revises or supersedes the awarding decision in accordance with the rules – resulting in you being entitled to less money than you have been paid; or

  (b) an appeal decision means that you are entitled to less money than you have been paid.

13.3   The DWP tells decision makers to make sure that the new entitlement decision revises or supersedes all the awarding decisions which operated during the period of the overpayment. They should be able to produce evidence that the necessary revisions or supersessions have taken place: R(IS) 2/96 (ADM D1032-33). If it is realised after an overpayment decision has been made that there has been no proper alteration of entitlement for all or some part of the overpayment period, the overpayment decision has no force or effect (ADM D1035).

13.1   AA s 71ZB(1)(a), s 71ZB(5); NIAA s69ZB(1)(a), s69ZB(5)

13.2   AA s 71ZB(3); NIAA s 69ZB(3)

Overpayments where there is no requirement for a revision or supersession

13.4   The requirement for a revision or supersession does not apply however where the circumstances of the overpayment do not provide a basis for the awarding decision to be revised or superseded. This is the case, for example, if you have been paid twice by mistake for the same period.

Recoverability

13.5   All UC overpayments that have been properly decided by the DWP are recoverable even if they are caused by the DWP (i.e. are due to official error). Its decision to recover however is a discretionary one.

Discretion not to recover

13.6   The law does not say that the DWP must recover a UC overpayment, only that it may recover such overpayments. The DWP's Benefit Overpayment Recovery Guide (February 2018) [www] says that non-recovery of the debt (a waiver) is considered where there is reasonable evidence that recovery would be detrimental to the health and/or welfare of you or your family or not in the public interest. The guide also says that recovery is only waived on the balance of the amount outstanding and that the DWP does not refund any money already correctly recovered. If you think that repaying the overpayment would be detrimental or not in the public interest you should tell the DWP and ask it not to recover (or not to continue recovering) the overpayment. The DWP says that your request should normally be put in writing. Where you are making the request on financial grounds the DWP is likely to ask you to provide full details of your household income and expenditure. Where you are making the request on health grounds you should say how the recovery of the overpayment is detrimental and include any supporting evidence from a medical practitioner or hospital. If the DWP still decides to recover you cannot appeal this decision but if you think it is failing to take into account relevant factors or being unreasonable you can complain (para 14.3-4). You might also be able to apply for a judicial review, but should get advice on this.

Calculating the overpayment

Establishing the overpayment period

13.7   To work out the amount of the overpayment, the DWP must first establish the start date and the end date of the period for which your UC has been overpaid.

13.4   AA s71ZB(3), OP Regs 5; NIAA s 69ZB(3); NIOP 5

13.5   AA s71ZB(1)(a), OP Regs 3(1); NIAA s69ZB(1)(a); NIOP 3(1)

13.6   AA s71ZB(1)(a); NIAA s69ZB(1)(a)
           DWP Benefit Overpayment Recovery Guide (February 2018), para 8.3 - goo.gl/HZWUfn

Diminution of capital

13.8 The DWP should calculate the amount of the overpayment in a particular way that is 'favourable' to you where:

(a) it occurred because of an error about your capital; and

(b) the overpayment period is three months or more.

13.9 If this applies to you then the DWP, when calculating the recoverable overpayment, should:

(a) at the end of the first three months of the overpayment period – treat your capital as reduced by the amount of UC overpaid during those three months and then use this reduced capital figure to calculate the overpayment after that; and

(b) at the end of each subsequent three month overpayment period – treat your capital as further reduced by the amount of UC overpaid during each three month period and use the resulting reduced capital figures to calculate the overpayments.

This rule reflects the fact that if you had been awarded less UC due to the capital being taken into account you might have used some of it to meet your essential expenditure.

Overpayments of UC housing costs when you move home

13.10 When calculating the recoverable amount of an overpayment caused by you moving home, the DWP has the discretion to subtract an amount equal to your entitlement to UC housing costs on your new home from the amount of the overpayment on your old home. This is done for the same number of assessment periods as you were overpaid UC housing costs on your old home. The DWP can only do this, however, where:

(a) you are not entitled to UC housing costs on your former home because you no longer occupy it; and

(b) the UC housing costs are payable to the same person for both homes.

13.11 Where this rule is used, the DWP treats the same amount as having been paid towards the home you moved into. Again this is for the same number of assessment periods as you were overpaid UC housing costs on your former home.

Additions to the recoverable amount

13.12 In addition to the amount you have been paid above your entitlement, the recoverable sum may be increased by:

(a) recovery of a payment on account (see para 12.41);

(b) recovery of hardship payments;

(c) recovery of penalties imposed as an alternative to prosecution (see para 13.13);

(d) recovery of civil penalties (see para 13.17); and

(e) the costs of court action.

13.9   OP Regs 7; NIOP 7

13.10   OP Regs 9(1)-(2); NIOP 9(1)-(2)

13.11   OP Regs 9(3); NIOP 9(3)

13.12   OP Regs 3; NIOP 3

Administrative penalties

13.13   The DWP may offer you the chance to pay an 'administrative penalty' rather than face prosecution, if:

(a) a UC overpayment was caused by an 'act or omission' on your part; and

(b) there are grounds for bringing a prosecution against you for an offence relating to that overpayment.

The DWP Fraud and Error Service (FES) decides whether to offer an administrative penalty and calculates the amount [www]. You do not have to agree to a penalty. You can opt for the possibility of prosecution instead.

13.14   The DWP's offer of a penalty must be in writing, explain that it is a way of avoiding prosecution, and give other information – including the fact that you can change your mind within 14 days (including the date of the agreement), and that the penalty will be repaid if you successfully challenge it by asking for a reconsideration or appeal. The DWP does not normally offer a penalty (but prosecutes instead) if an overpayment is substantial or there are other aggravating factors (such as you being in a position of trust).

13.15   The amount of the penalty is 50% of the recoverable overpayment. This is subject to a minimum of £350 and a maximum of £5,000 where your act or omission causing the overpayment occurred wholly on or after 1st April 2015. The maximum penalty where the relevant act or omission occurred before that date is £2,000. In NI (at time of writing) the maximum penalty is still set at £2000.

13.16   The DWP may also make an offer of a penalty where your act or omission could have resulted in an overpayment and it thinks there are grounds for bringing a prosecution for a related offence. In these cases the penalty is the fixed amount of £350.

Civil penalties

13.17   The DWP may impose a civil penalty of £50 on you if you:

(a) negligently make an incorrect statement or representation or negligently give incorrect information or evidence relating to a claim or award and fail to take reasonable steps to correct the error; or

(b) without reasonable excuse, fail to provide required information or evidence relating to a claim or award or fail to tell the DWP about a relevant change of circumstance; and

(c) in any of these circumstances this results in the DWP making an overpayment; but

(d) you have not been charged with an offence or cautioned.

The DWP's staff guidance on civil penalties (and when to impose them) is set out in its Advice for Decision Makers (D1271 – 1302) [www].

13.13   AA 115A(1)-(1A); NIAA s109A(1)-(1A)
         DWP Penalties policy: in respect of social security fraud and error (14 August 2017) - goo.gl/2BHc2d

13.14   AA 115A(5)-(6); NIAA s109A(5)-(6)

13.15   AA 115A(3)(a)-(b); art 1(3) of SI 2015/202; NIAA s109A(3)(a)-(b)

13.16   AA 115A(3A); NIAA s109A(3A)

13.17   AA 115C-115D, SI 2012/1990
         DWP ADM Ch D1 - goo.gl/nEcYa1

13.18   The amount of the civil penalty is added to the amount of the recoverable overpayment. If you have been successfully prosecuted for fraud or offered an administrative penalty or caution, the DWP cannot issue you with a civil penalty for the same offence.

People from whom an overpayment may be recovered

13.19   An overpayment is normally recoverable from the person it was paid to (the 'payee') but in specific circumstances it may be recoverable from someone else, either:

(a) in addition to the person paid; or

(b) instead of the person paid.

The DWP says that where an overpayment is recoverable from more than one person then changes in those persons' circumstances or the relationship between them may alter the action taken to recover the debt [www].

Couples

13.20   When an award of UC is made to you jointly with a partner, if an amount is overpaid to one of you it is treated as overpaid to both of you, and so can be recovered from either of you – even the one who didn't get the payment. The DWP says that if you separate from your partner the debt is apportioned 50/50 on separation [www].

Who overpayments of UC housing costs are recovered from

Due to a misrepresentation or a failure to disclose a material fact

13.21   An overpayment of UC housing costs is recoverable from someone who misrepresented or failed to disclose information and not the person who actually got the overpayment where the DWP is satisfied:

(a) that the overpayment occurred because that person misrepresented, or failed to disclose, a material fact (in either case, whether fraudulent or otherwise), and

(b) that person is not the same person who got the overpayment.

13.22   DWP decision makers are advised that where recovery is sought from the landlord under this rule they must be able to show that the landlord has a legal duty to disclose the fact in question (ADM D1170).

On moving home

13.23   If the DWP is satisfied that an overpayment of UC housing costs occurred because you moved home and the overpayment was paid to someone else, e.g. your landlord, the overpayment is recoverable from you as well as that other person.

13.19   AA s 71ZB(2), OP Regs 4; NIAA s69ZB(2), NIOP 4
            DWP Benefit Overpayment Recovery Guide (February 2018), para 2.22 - goo.gl/HZWUfn

13.20   AA s71ZB(6); NIAA s69ZB(6)
            DWP Benefit Overpayment Recovery Guide (February 2018), para 2.22 - goo.gl/HZWUfn

13.21   OP Regs 4(4),(6); NIOP 4(4),(6)

13.23   OP Regs 4(4)-(5); NIOP 4(4)-(5)

Other overpayments of UC housing costs

13.24　　If the DWP is satisfied that an overpayment of UC housing costs occurred for some other reason than you moving home, or someone misrepresenting or failing to disclose a material fact, then the overpayment is recoverable from you and not the person paid. The exceptions to this rule are where:

(a)　the payee was your appointee or someone else such as a landlord getting the payment under an alternative payment arrangement; or

(b)　the overpayment occurred because the amount of the payment was greater than the amount of housing costs you are liable for.

Who other UC overpayments may be recovered from

Appointees and payees under alternative payment arrangements

13.25　　Where the person who was overpaid is your appointee, or someone such as your landlord who received the overpayment under an alternative payment arrangement (see paras 12.11-14), then the overpayment is recoverable from you in addition to the person who got the overpayment (but also note the above paragraphs regarding the recovery of overpaid UC housing costs).

Third parties

13.26　　If the person who received a payment is a third party, such as the landlord in a case of rent arrears direct, then to the extent that the amount overpaid does not exceed the amount payable to that third party an overpayment is recoverable from you instead of that third party.

Methods of recovery

13.27　　The DWP may recover a UC overpayment by any lawful method including sending you a bill for payment and agreeing an instalment payment plan [www]. The following methods are also available:

(a)　deduction from your future UC payments and arrears;

(b)　deduction from other DWP benefits;

(c)　deduction from a landlord's own UC or other DWP benefits;

(d)　adjustment of subsequent payments of benefit;

(e)　deduction from earnings (direct earnings attachment – DEA); or

(f)　through the courts.

The DWP says that where you are unable to repay the overpayment at an agreed rate there are a range of hardship options available including temporary suspension of recovery, reduction in recovery rate or, in exceptional cases, write-off of the debt [www].

13.24　OP Regs 4(7)-(8); NIOP 4(7)-(8)

13.25　OP Regs 4(2); NIOP 4(2)

13.26　OP Regs 4(3); NIOP 4(3)

13.27　AA s71ZB(7); NIAA s69ZB(7)
　　　　DWP Benefit Overpayment Recovery Guide (May 2017), para 5.3-4 - goo.gl/HZWUfn

Table 13.1 **Maximum deduction from UC in the assessment period (2016-17, 17-18 and 18-19)**

Circumstances	You	Maximum deduction (% of the appropriate UC standard allowance)
You have: (a) been found guilty of an offence in relation to the overpayment; (b) made an admission after caution of deception or fraud for the purpose of obtaining benefit; or (c) agreed to pay a penalty as an alternative to prosecution and the agreement has not been withdrawn Recovery of hardship payments	*Single* Under 25 25 or over *Joint claimants* Both under 25 One or both 25 or over	40% £100.71 £127.13 £158.08 £199.56
Your earned income is greater than the work allowance in the calculation of your UC	*Single* Under 25 25 or over *Joint claimants* Both under 25 One or both 25 or over	25% £62.94 £79.46 £98.80 £124.72
Any other case	*Single* Under 25 25 or over *Joint claimants* Both under 25 One or both 25 or over	15% £37.77 £47.67 £59.28 £74.83

T13.1   OP Regs 11(2)-(4); NIOP 11(2)-(4)

Recovery by deductions from your future UC payments

13.28   Overpaid UC recoverable from you may be recovered by deductions from your (or any partner's) future UC payments. This method is limited as follows:

(a) the amount deducted must not be greater than shown in table 13.1;

(b) no deduction should be made that reduces your UC for the assessment period to less than 1p;

(c) the DWP should consider deducting a lower amount where the maximum rate of deduction would cause hardship to you or your family.

13.29   The 'appropriate UC standard allowance' (table 13.1) is the appropriate UC standard allowance included in the award of UC for you, or for you and your partner as joint claimants.

13.30   The limits shown in Table 13.1 do not apply where:

(a) the deduction is from any payment of arrears of UC – except arrears paid following the suspension of payments; or

(b) the recoverable amount is an overpayment of UC housing costs that are being recovered from someone else, e.g. the landlord.

The DWP also identifies other circumstances in which arrears of your UC should not be withheld in full to recover an overpayment [www]. These include arrears for full periods' benefit that has not been paid on time and arrears earmarked for specific expenditure such as housing costs.

Deductions from UC paid to the landlord on your behalf

13.31   The DWP can decided to recover an overpayment from you by making a deduction from the UC it pays to a landlord on your behalf. Where this happens this leaves you with more rent to pay, or rent arrears if you don't. These arrears can lead to your eviction if they are not dealt with.

13.32   If the DWP decides to recover the overpayment from your landlord, it may still recover the overpayment from the on-going UC payments it makes to the landlord on your behalf. A special rule applies if the DWP is recovering from these on-going payments of UC because your landlord has:

(a) been found guilty of an offence relating to the overpayment; or

(b) agreed to pay a penalty as an alternative to prosecution and the agreement has not been withdrawn.

13.33   In these circumstances your rental obligation to the landlord for the same amount is in law considered to be paid off and your landlord cannot put you into rent arrears for this amount.

13.28   OP Regs 10(2)(b), 11(2)-(3), (7); NIOP 10(2)(b), 11(2)-(3),(7)

13.29   OP Regs 11(11); NIOP 11(11)

13.30   OP Regs 11(8)-(9); NIOP 11(8)-(9)

13.31   AA s71ZC(2)(b); NIAA s 69ZC(2)(b)

13.33   AA s71ZC(3), OP Regs 15(1)-(2); NIAA s69ZC(3), NIOP 15(1)-(2)

13.34   The DWP should tell both you and the landlord

(a) that the overpayment it has decided to recover is one to which this rule applies; and

(b) that your landlord has no right in relation to an equivalent sum against you, and that your obligation to the landlord is to be taken as paid off by the amount so recovered.

Deductions from a 'blameless' tenant's UC payments

13.35   If a UC overpayment is recoverable from a landlord the DWP may recover it by deductions from payments to that landlord of another tenant's UC. This is talked about as recovery from a 'blameless' tenant because the tenant had nothing to do with the overpayment. In these cases the blameless tenant's obligation to the landlord is treated by the law as paid off and the landlord cannot in law put the 'blameless' tenant into rent arrears because of this deduction.

Deductions from a landlord's own benefits

13.36   Where UC has been paid to a third party such as your landlord on your behalf, and the DWP decides to recover the overpayment from the landlord, the overpayment may (though this is rare) be recovered from the landlord's personal entitlement to UC or other DWP benefits (table 13.2).

Recovery by deduction from other DWP benefits

13.37   An overpayment of UC may be recovered by deductions from other DWP benefits that you or any partner are getting. Table 13.2 identifies the other DWP benefits from which recovery can be made.

Table 13.2 **DWP benefits from which UC overpayments can be recovered**

(a) UC	(b) incapacity benefit
(c) maternity allowance	(d) widow(er)'s benefits
(e) bereavement benefits	(f) retirement pension
(g) child's special allowance	(h) attendance allowance
(i) invalid care allowance	(j) disability living allowance
(k) industrial injuries benefit	(l) JSA
(m) ESA	(n) state pension
(o) PIP	

13.34   OP Regs 15(3); NIOP 15(3)

13.35   AA s 71ZC(2)(c),(4); NIAA s69ZC(2)(c),(4)

13.36   AA s71ZC(2)(a); NIAA s69ZC(2)(a)

13.37   AA s71ZC(1); NIAA s69ZC(1)

T13.2   AA s71ZC(1), OP Regs 10; NIAA s69ZC(1), NIOP 10

Deductions from earnings

13.38   Overpayments may be recovered by the DWP requiring your employer to make deductions from your earnings without the need for court action. The DWP suggests that this method of recovery is useful for people who no longer get benefit and who will not come to a voluntary agreement to repay the debt [www].

13.39   The DWP should send a notice to both you and your employer before deductions are made. The employer should tell the DWP if they are not in fact your employer or if they think they are exempt from the deduction arrangement because they are a new business or a micro-business. This should be done within ten days of the day after the notice was sent.

13.40   Your employer should tell you the amount of the deductions and pay the amount deducted (excluding that for administrative costs) to the DWP. They must also keep records of the amounts deducted and of people for whom such deductions have been made. You must tell the DWP within seven days if you leave the employment or when you become employed or re-employed. Your employer should also tell the DWP if you are no longer employed by them. It is a criminal offence to fail to make or pay deductions or to provide information. Guides to direct earnings attachments for employers and others are available on the gov.uk website [www].

Recovery through the courts

13.41   UC overpayments are recoverable through the county court in England and Wales and through the sheriff court in Scotland. The DWP tries to recover court costs when there is a court judgment in its favour. It can add these to the recoverable overpayment and recover them by any method by which overpaid UC can be recovered.

Adjustment of benefit

13.42   In certain circumstances the DWP may recover overpayments of UC by adjusting later benefit payments. UC paid but then determined as not payable, can be treated as properly paid and be set against future payments of benefit or against certain payments to third parties.

Time limits on recovery

13.43   In England, Wales and Northern Ireland the DWP/DFC can't use the courts to enforce a recovery (para 13.41) more than six years from the date you were first notified of the decision (para 14.7) but this does not stop the DWP/DFC from recovering the overpayment by other means (such as deductions from your future UC payments: para 13.28). In Scotland the time limit for recovery through the courts is five years from the date you were notified or 20 years by any method.

13.38   AA s71ZD, OP Regs 20; NIAA s69ZD, NIOP 19; www.legislation.gov.uk/uksi/2013/384/pdfs/uksifia_20130384_en.pdf

13.39   OP Regs 19, 24; NIOP 18, 23

13.40   OP Regs 21-22, 23, 30; NIOP 20-21, 22, 29
         DWP Direct Earnings Attachment: an employers' guide (Jan 2018) - goo.gl/bw6Gtt

13.41   AA s71ZE(1)-(3); NIAA s69ZE(1)-(2)

13.42   AA s71ZF; NIAA s69ZF

13.43   Limitation Act 1980 s9, 38(11) (as amended by WRA 108);
         Prescription and Limitation (Scotland) Act 1973 s6, 7 sch 1 para 1(b);
         Limitation (Northern Ireland) Order 1989 art 6, 2(11) (as amended by NIWRO 111)

Chapter 14 **UC appeals**

Overview

Appeals

14.1   You may be able to get a UC decision changed by asking the DWP to look at it again in the light of any additional information, evidence or explanations you can provide. Legally you are applying for a revision of the decision. The DWP refers to the process it carries out when it gets your request as a 'mandatory reconsideration'. Once the DWP has carried out a mandatory reconsideration, and if you don't get the decision you want, you can appeal to the independent First-tier Tribunal [www]. A further appeal (on a point of law and only if you are given permission) then goes to the Upper Tribunal [www]. The administrative arrangements relating to appeals are the responsibility of Her Majesty's Courts and Tribunals Service (HMCTS) [www]. Not all decisions are appealable (but you can ask for any such non-appealable decisions to be revised). The rules relating to, at and beyond the First-tier Tribunal are the same for UC appeals as for HB appeals (and other social security benefits). But note the requirement for a mandatory reconsideration in relation to UC appeals and the fact that once the DWP has carried out a mandatory reconsideration you send your UC appeal direct to HMCTS.

14.2   You may be dissatisfied not with a decision but with the way you, or your claim, have been dealt with, for example a delay by the DWP in making a decision. Non-appealable decisions and delays in making decisions may in certain instances, and as a last resort, be remedied by (a letter warning of) judicial review (but you should seek advice when considering this action).

14.1   SSA s12, D&A 5, 10, 50
        www.gov.uk/social-security-child-support-tribunal
        www.gov.uk/administrative-appeals-tribunal
        www.gov.uk/courts-tribunals/first-tier-tribunal-social-security-and-child-support

Complaints

14.3   If you want to make a complaint, rather than an appeal, you should first contact the DWP office you are dealing with, explain the matter and give them the opportunity to put things right. It is probably best to do this in writing so that you have a record of the action you have taken. If this is unsuccessful the DWP has a formal complaints procedure that may provide a remedy for your problem [www]. If you remain dissatisfied you can escalate your complaint by asking the Independent Case Examiner to look at it (this is a free and independent complaint resolution and examination service provided by the DWP) [www]. If you're still dissatisfied you can ask your MP [www] to send your complaint to the Parliamentary and Health Service Ombudsman (this is also a free and independent service) [www].

14.4   The DWP says that if it gets something wrong it will act quickly to put it right. This might include any of the following: an apology; an explanation; putting things right, or a special payment if something the DWP has done (or not done) has caused injustice or hardship (see DWP (2012) 'Financial Redress for Maladministration') [www].

Who can appeal

14.5   In addition to the claimant (or the claimants in a joint claim) the following also have a right of appeal. An appeal is accepted where it is made by:

(a)   a person appointed by the DWP to act on behalf of someone else;

(b)   anyone e.g. a landlord from whom an amount of benefit is recoverable, but only if their rights, duties or obligations are affected by the decision; and

(c)   a person appointed by the DWP to proceed with a claim of someone who has claimed benefit and subsequently died.

Representatives

14.6   You can ask a representative to act for you. The DWP's guidance for staff 'Working with Representatives' (August 2015) [www] explains its policy on providing information to representatives. In relation to an appeal you (or your representative if they are a legal representative) must send written notification to HMCTS of the representative's name and address. HMCTS should send a copy of that notice to the DWP and any other party. Anything you are allowed to do or required to do under the First-tier Tribunal procedural rules can be done by your representative (except signing a witness statement). The Tribunal and other parties are able to assume that your representative is authorised to act on your behalf until they receive written notification that this is not the case from either you or the representative.

14.3   www.gov.uk/government/organisations/department-for-work-pensions/about/
        complaints-procedure#complaining-about-our-service
        www.gov.uk/government/organisations/independent-case-examiner
        www.parliament.uk/mps-lords-and-offices/mps/
        www.ombudsman.org.uk/

14.4   DWP, Financial Redress for Maladministration (April 2012) – goo.gl/rkK8qM

14.5   SSA, s 12(2); D&A Regs, 49(b), 49(d), 49(a); NISS98 13(2); NID&A 48(b), 48(d), 48(a)

14.6   DWP, Working with Representatives (12 Aug 2015) – goo.gl/1TNgHt
        FTPR 11(2), 11(5)-(6)

The DWP's decision

14.7   You may be told about decisions relating to your UC entitlement via an online account and the DWP also has the power to tell you in person or through the post. Landlords are likely to be notified of any relevant decision by post. A decision notice is treated as given to you on the date that it becomes available for you to view in your online account or it is given or posted to you. The time limit for disputing a decision begins at the point the DWP issues the decision notice.

14.8   The decision notice from the DWP should tell you about:

  (a) its decision;

  (b) your right to request a statement of reasons for the decision – if this is not included;

  (c) the time limit in which you may make an application for the decision to be revised;

  (d) your right of appeal against the decision (and that this can be exercised only if the DWP has considered an application for revision).

Getting a written statement of reasons from the DWP

14.9   The DWP thinks that most UC decision notifications include reasons but if you're dissatisfied with the decision and the DWP haven't explained it you may find it useful to ask for a written statement of reasons. You should do this so that your request gets to the DWP within one calendar month of the date the DWP issued the decision notice. The DWP should provide you with the statement of reasons within 14 days of receipt of your request or as soon as practicable after that.

> ### Example: Calendar month
>
> The DWP issues a decision notice on a claim on 19th November. The one month period is 20th November to 19th December.

Applying for a mandatory revision

14.10   If, having read the decision notice and any explanations offered by the DWP, you remain dissatisfied you can apply for a revision of the decision (a mandatory reconsideration). There is no application form for this. You can ask for the decision to be revised by telephoning the DWP or by putting your request in writing. The telephone number and contact address should be on your decision notice. The DWP's UC Full Service Guidance [www] says that you are able to apply for a revision over the phone, face to face, by putting a note in your journal or in writing. It's usually best to apply in writing, keeping a copy of what you send and a note of the date you send it. However you apply, you should make sure that your application gets to the DWP within one calendar month of the date the DWP notified you of the decision. However, if you asked for a written statement of reasons, and the DWP provided it:

14.7   D&A 3, 4; C&P 3, sch 2; NID&A 3, 4; NIC&P 3, sch 1

14.8   D&A 7(1), 7(3); NID&A 7(1), 7(3)

14.9   D&A 3(1), 7(1), 7(3)(b), 7(4); NID&A 3(1), 7(1), 7(3)(b), 7(4)

14.10   D&A 5(1)(b); NID&A 5(1)(b)
          DWP Universal Credit Full Service Guidance (Sept 2016) goo.gl/QNBRVq

(a) within the one-month period – you have a month and 14 days to get your request to the DWP;

(b) outside the one-month period – you have 14 days from the date on which the DWP provided the statement to you to get your request to the DWP.

14.11   While the DWP may allow a late application for revision (see below), if it doesn't you lose your right to a mandatory reconsideration (see para 14.15). In these circumstances, the DWP should consider whether an 'any time' revision is appropriate because, for example, of a mistake it made in arriving at the original decision (DM A3047).

Allowing a late application for revision

14.12   If you want to get a late application for revision accepted it must satisfy a number of conditions. It should:

(a) include a request for an extension of time in which to apply;

(b) identify the decision that you want changed; and

(c) explain why the extension of time has been needed and identify the special circumstances that stopped you applying within the normal time limit.

Your application must be made within 12 calendar months of the latest date by which the application for revision should have been received by the DWP. This means that your application must be made within 13 calendar months of the date the DWP issued the notification. Before 16/11/2017 a 'drafting flaw' in the regulations gave you a total period of 14 calendar months [www].

14.13   If the DWP is to accept your late application it must be satisfied that:

(a) it is reasonable to grant the extension; and

(b) it was not practicable for you to make the application within the normal time limit due to special circumstances.

14.14   The DWP advises that the term 'special circumstances' is not defined in legislation and should be interpreted broadly (ADM A3055). It indicates that the term can include factors such as:

(a) a death or serious illness;

(b) not being in the UK;

(c) normal postal services being adversely affected;

(d) learning or language difficulties;

(e) difficulty getting evidence or information to support the application; and

(f) ignorance or misunderstanding of the law or time limits.

But these are only examples and the DWP should consider each on its merits.

14.12   D&A 6(1)-(3); NID&A 6(1)-(3)
             Explanatory Memorandum to SI 2017/1015 paras 7.28-30 – goo.gl/BeR2vD

14.13   D&A 6(4)-(5); NID&A 6(4)-(5)

14.15 In deciding whether it is reasonable to grant an extension of time, the DWP must have regard to the principle that the greater the amount of time that has passed between the end of the normal time limit and the actual date of receipt of the application, the more compelling must be your special circumstances for the late application. The DWP Full Service Guidance, however, says that it would be an exceptional case that is not admitted late [www]. Following an Upper Tribunal decision (R(CJ) and SG v SSWP (ESA) [2017] UKUT 0324 (AAC)) if your late application is made within the 13 month period but cannot be admitted the DWP should give you a decision refusing to revise and issue a mandatory reconsideration notice that should include a right of appeal to the tribunal (DWP ADM 21/17 paras 5-7). If you appeal the tribunal should be able to consider the substance of the decision you are concerned with – not just the question of lateness. If you apply for a mandatory reconsideration more than 13 months after the DWP issued the decision, the DWP should give you a decision refusing to revise but without a right of appeal.

DWP's mandatory reconsideration

14.16 The DWP should reconsider the decision you are unhappy with based on the information and evidence it has available and any additional information, evidence and explanations you supply. Make sure you include everything that you want considered because the DWP needn't consider any issue you haven't raised. If the DWP can't change the decision fully in your favour, a decision maker should try to contact you and tell you about this. They should also ask you if you have any other information or evidence that relates to the decision. If you do, they should tell you where to send it to and the time limit for doing this. You normally get one calendar month in which to supply any additional information or evidence but the DWP is able to extend this period if it would be appropriate to do so. The DWP may revise the original decision if it was based on: insufficient evidence, a mistaken view of the facts, or if it reaches a different conclusion about the relevant facts. The DWP may also revise the decision if it was based on an incorrect interpretation of the law [www].

14.17 There is no statutory timescale for the completion of a mandatory reconsideration. Once the DWP has completed the process it sends out two mandatory reconsideration notices. One is for you to keep and the other is for you to send to HMCTS if you want to appeal to the First-tier Tribunal. If the decision has been changed in your favour you should get any benefit owed backdated to the effective date of the revised decision.

Decisions you cannot appeal

14.18 You can appeal most decisions and the DWP's decision notice should tell you if a decision is appealable. There are some decisions, however, that are not appealable. Table 14.1 identifies the main decisions you cannot appeal. You can ask for an 'any time' revision or supersession of such decisions, but if the DWP doesn't agree to do this the only legal remedy is judicial review.

14.15 D&A 6(6); NID&A 6(6)
DWP Universal Credit Full Service Guidance, (Sept 2016) goo.gl/QNBRVq
14.16 SSA 9(1)-(2); D&A 20(2)-(3); NISS98 10(1)-(2); NID&A 20(2)-(3)
14.18 D&A 7(1)(b), 10, 50(2), sch 3; NID&A 7(1)(b), 10, 49(2), sch3

Table 14.1 **Main non-appealable decisions**

1. Decisions about the information or evidence required in connection with a claim.

2. Decisions about appointees where the claimant is unable to act.

3. A decision in default of a nomination by a couple of the assessment period when separate claimants become a couple.

4. A decision to nominate a main carer, where more than one person cares for a disabled person and they cannot agree who should be nominated as the main carer.

5. A decision to award a particular amount of UC dependent upon someone's age.

6. A decision which adopts a rent officer's decision.

7. Suspension of payment of UC.

8. Staying making a decision where decisions/appeals involve issues that arise on appeal in other cases.

9. UC payment arrangements.

10. Making payments by direct credit transfer into a specific bank or other account.

11. Payments of UC to third parties in the claimant's or family's interests including direct payment of housing costs (other than arrears) to a landlord.

12. Payments of mortgage interest direct to lenders.

13. Ending the right to obtain a payment of UC where the claimant has not obtained payment of their benefit after 12 months – except a decision to extend the 12 month period where there is good cause.

14. Arrangements for the payment of UC following the death of the claimant.

15. Deductions for council tax except a decision whether there is an outstanding sum due of the amount to be deducted; whether there is sufficient benefit to make a deduction and on the priority to be given to the deduction.

16. A decision on payments on account, except a decision to offset an advance payment of UC against a future award of benefit.

17. A decision on recovery of overpaid UC except:

    (a) who an overpayment of a housing payment is recoverable from;

    (b) the treatment of capital to be reduced (diminution of capital rule);

    (c) the sums to be deducted in calculating recoverable amounts;

    (d) sums to be deducted where there is a change of dwelling and housing costs are payable to the same person.

    Note however that you can appeal the DWP's decision that led to the overpayment and if successful (or partially successful) establish that there is no overpayment or that it is less than the original amount decided by the DWP.

18. Uprating of the benefit.

T14.1   D&A sch 3; NID&A sch 3

Appealing to the First-tier Tribunal (Great Britain)

14.19   If you are dissatisfied with an appealable decision you can send an appeal in writing to HMCTS. An independent body called the First-tier Tribunal should consider it. In some guides you may see this process referred to as 'direct lodgement' – that is sending it direct to HMCTS unlike, for instance, housing benefit appeals where it is sent to the council which forwards it to HMCTS. If you make an appeal to the tribunal you may see or hear yourself referred to as the 'appellant'. You may also come across the term 'respondent' – this is a reference to the DWP decision-maker (i.e. the maker of the decision you have appealed) and also a reference to anyone else who has a right of appeal (for example the landlord in some overpayment cases). Each of you is a 'party' in the proceedings before the tribunal.

The First-tier Tribunal

14.20   The First-tier Tribunal is an independent tribunal established under the Tribunals, Courts and Enforcement Act 2007. It is divided into a number of chambers. The Social Entitlement Chamber considers UC appeals as well as appeals on other social security benefits and certain other matters. The procedural rules of the Social Entitlement Chamber are set out in The Tribunal Procedure (First-tier Tribunal) (Social Entitlement Chamber) Rules SI 2008 No 2685 (as amended). The rules currently in force are on the Gov.uk website [www].

Making an appeal

14.21   Perhaps the easiest way to appeal is for you (or your representative if you have one) to fill in the appeal form SSCS1. If you use the form and complete it properly this should make sure that you provide all the required information. You can download the form from various government websites [www] or get a paper version from some advice agencies. The form gives you the option of indicating whether you wish to attend a hearing or have your appeal decided on the papers. Many people find attending a face-to-face hearing stressful, but research shows that you are more likely to win your appeal if you do attend. The form also asks you to indicate if there are any times or dates when you will be unavailable to attend a hearing over the next six months and if you have any particular needs such as a requirement for a signer or an interpreter.

14.22   Your appeal should be written in English or Welsh and signed by you or your authorised representative. If you don't use the SSCS1 appeal form you should make sure that your appeal includes:

(a)   your name and address;

(b)   the name and address of your representative (if you have one);

(c)   an address where documents for you can be sent or delivered;

(d)   the name and address of anyone else (not the DWP) who has a right to appeal the decision, for example a landlord in relation to certain overpayment decisions; and

(e)   the reasons why you disagree with the DWP's decision.

14.19   FTPR 1(3)

14.20   Part 1 of the Tribunals, Courts & Enforcement Act 2007, art 6(c) of SI 2010 No 2655, FTPR;
             Social Entitlement Chamber tribunal procedure rules – goo.gl/65bhjo

14.21   SSCS1 Form & associated leaflets – goo.gl/n9bJPb

14.22   FTPR 22(3), 11(2), 11(5)

Also it would be useful to indicate whether you wish to attend a hearing and any times or dates when you would be unavailable to attend over the next six months.

14.23　　If your appeal is going to get to HMCTS later than one calendar month after the date on which you were sent the mandatory reconsideration notices it should also include a request for an extension of time and include the reason why your appeal is not provided in time.

14.24　　You must provide with your appeal:

(a)　a copy of the mandatory reconsideration notice;

(b)　any statement of reasons for the decision that you have; and

(c)　any documents in support of your case which have not already been supplied to the DWP (although additional documents may also be supplied at a later date).

If you have lost your mandatory reconsideration notice you should ask the DWP for a copy before sending in the appeal.

14.25　　If you live in England or Wales send your appeal to: HMCTS, SSCS Appeals Centre, PO Box 1203, Bradford BD1 9WP. If you live in Scotland send your appeal to: HMCTS SSCS Appeals Centre, PO Box 27080, Glasgow G2 9HQ. HMCTS should write back to you acknowledging receipt of your appeal and providing you with a contact telephone number and the address of the HMCTS office that is dealing with it.

14.26　　HMCTS should send a copy of your appeal and any accompanying documents to the DWP (and any other respondent) as soon as reasonably practicable after it gets it.

Time limits for making an appeal

14.27　　You should normally get your appeal to HMCTS within one calendar month after the date on which you were sent the mandatory reconsideration notices. Anything in relation to an appeal that must be done by a particular day should be done by 5pm on that day. If the day on which something must be done is not a working day, it is done in time if it is done by 5pm on the next working day. A 'working day' is any day except a Saturday or Sunday, Christmas Day, Good Friday or a bank holiday.

Allowing a late appeal

14.28　　Where your appeal is not made in time it may nevertheless be treated as in time if it is made within 12 calendar months of the time limit and neither the DWP nor any other respondent objects. The time for bringing the appeal can't be extended beyond this 12 month period.

14.23　FTPR 22(6)

14.24　FTPR 22(4)

14.26　FTPR 22(7)

14.27　FTPR 22(2)(d), 12

14.28　FTPR 5(3)(a), 22(6) 22(8)

14.29   The DWP has the right to object to a late appeal but decision-makers are advised (ADM A5081) that it might not be appropriate to object where there are special circumstances such as:

(a)   a difficulty in getting an appointment with a representative (especially in rural areas);

(b)   problems in writing the appeal if you are a blind person living alone;

(c)   a difficulty in getting an appeal form;

(d)   an allegation that the decision notice was not received;

(e)   an inability to read, write or understand English where you live alone;

(f)   a change of address during the one month appeal period;

(g)   an allegation that an earlier appeal was made; or

(h)   an inability to understand the decision notice where you have a mental disability or learning difficulties and live alone.

Where the DWP does object you should be sent a copy of its objections and invited to comment before the matter is referred to a judge. It is the judge who must decide whether or not the late appeal is to be considered.

The DWP's actions on receipt of the appeal and accompanying documentation

14.30   When the DWP gets the appeal from HMCTS it considers (ADM A5100-A5183) whether:

(a)   the appeal is duly made, e.g. whether the person making the appeal has appeal rights;

(b)   the appeal is outside the First-tier Tribunal's jurisdiction, e.g. made about a non-appealable decision;

(c)   the appealed decision should be revised to your advantage (even though a mandatory reconsideration will have already been done at an earlier stage) – in which case the appeal lapses.

The DWP's response to your appeal

14.31   The DWP must get its response back to HMCTS as soon as reasonably practicable after getting the appeal papers. It should normally do this within 28 calendar days though it may ask HMCTS to extend the time limit in exceptional cases. A tribunal judge decides if an extension to the time limit is agreed to. The DWP's response should provide a comprehensive explanation of the reasons for its decision. It should also normally include copies of all the documents relevant to your case in the DWP's possession. The DWP provides you, and any other party, with a copy of its response at the same time as it is provided to HMCTS. If you have a representative then the DWP should provide your representative with a copy and need not also provide it to you. If you are represented and get a copy of its response from the DWP you should contact your representative as soon as possible to make sure that they have also got a copy.

14.29   FTPR 5(2), 5(3)(a)

14.30   SSA s9(6), D&A 52; NISS98 10(6); NID&A 51

14.31   FTPR 24(1)(c), 24(4)(b), 24(4)(a), 11(6)

Your submission

14.32   You, or your representative (if you have one), can make a written submission and supply further documents in reply to the DWP's response. You should normally get these to HMCTS within one calendar month after the date DWP sent out its response, but request more time if you think you will need it. Submissions, etc, are often submitted late. If relevant they may normally be considered by the tribunal but if other parties have not been given adequate time to consider the material this may lead to the adjournment of a hearing. Also note the warning in para 14.39. HMCTS should send a copy of your submission, etc, to the DWP and any other parties.

The First-tier Tribunal

Membership

14.33   The tribunal that considers your case should never consist of more than three people. It normally consists of just one person – a judge who is legally qualified. But if your appeal is about the work capability assessment the judge is joined by a medically qualified member. In rare instances where the appealed decision raises difficult financial questions (e.g. about company accounts) there may be a member with relevant financial qualifications. Another member may also be present to provide experience or to help with the monitoring of standards (Practice Statement of the Senior President of Tribunals, 'Composition of Tribunals in Social Security and Child Support Cases in the Social Entitlement Chamber on or after 1st August 2013') [www].

Venues

14.34   Your hearing normally takes place at a venue near where you live. HMCTS has 152 venues across England, Wales and Scotland. You can find information on venue locations and the available facilities on the web [www].

The tribunal's functions

14.35   The tribunal's task is to reconsider the decision you have appealed and either change it or confirm it. It should reconsider the decision in a way that is fair and just. It cannot alter the law but must interpret and apply the law to the facts of your case. It cannot award compensation or costs in relation to a UC appeal. It does not have to consider any issue that has not been raised, but it does have the power to do so. The tribunal should not shut its eyes to things if to do so would cause an injustice. In certain instances, this could mean that you end up with a decision that is even less favourable than the one you have appealed. The tribunal can't take into account any factual matters that didn't exist at the time the original appealed decision relates to but it can consider evidence that was not available to the original decision maker that relates to those facts.

14.32   FTPR 24(6)-(7)

14.33   Tribunals Judiciary, Practice Statement: Composition of Tribunals (31 July 2013) – goo.gl/hXjT4f

14.34   Venue locations – goo.gl/LPRnNo

14.35   SSA s12(8)(a)-(b); NISS98 13(8)(a)-(b)

14.36   The tribunal also has the power to make a decision in the form of a consent order. This ends the proceedings and makes such other provisions as you, the DWP and any other parties have agreed to. This may be done at the request of the parties if the tribunal considers it appropriate. Perhaps unfortunately the DWP's presenting officers are advised not to agree to any suggestion of a consent order (ADM A5422).

14.37   The tribunal may also give directions (i.e. instructions on how the appeal should be dealt with). You and the DWP can both ask the tribunal to do this or the tribunal can do it on its own initiative (para14.48).

The appeal hearing

Notice

14.38   HMCTS should give you notice of the time and place of the (oral) hearing. This should be given at least 14 days before the hearing (beginning with the day on which the notice is given and ending on the day before the hearing takes place). If notice has not been given to you, or to someone else it should have been given to, the hearing may go ahead only with everyone's consent or in urgent or exceptional circumstances.

14.39   Where you, the DWP and any other party have all chosen not to have a hearing, and the tribunal also thinks that it is able to decide the matter without a hearing, you won't be notified of the date on which the appeal is considered on the papers. You need to make sure that all relevant submissions and documents are with the tribunal before this happens.

Postponement

14.40   The tribunal may postpone the hearing at any time before it starts but need not do this. If you want a postponement, write to the HMCTS clerk giving the reasons for your request. If it is too late to ask for a postponement you may request an adjournment at the hearing. The tribunal may grant or refuse this request as it thinks fit.

Public or private hearings

14.41   Hearings are normally in public but usually only the people involved are present. There is no pre-publication of the cases listed before the First-tier Tribunal (Social Entitlement Chamber) and in practice administrative and security arrangements at tribunal venues mean that obtaining public access to a hearing is tortuous. The Upper Tribunal has nevertheless held that as hearings take place within reasonable office hours and at a publicly recognised court or tribunal hearing centre they meet the minimum requirement of a public hearing ([2015] UKUT 143 (AAC) at [25]). The tribunal may decide that the hearing (or part of it) should be in private if, for example, sensitive or family matters are to be considered. Certain people such as trainee members or clerks may be present (whether or not the hearing is in private), but they must not take part in the proceedings.

14.36   FTPR 32
14.37   FTPR 5(2)-(3), 6
14.38   FTPR 27-29
14.40   FTPR 5(3)(h), 6
14.41   FTPR 30(1), 30(3)

Deciding to go ahead in someone's absence

14.42   If you or someone else who has a right to be present fails to attend the hearing, the tribunal may, having regard to all the circumstances including any explanations offered, go ahead with the hearing if:

(a) it is in the interest of justice to do so; and

(b) it is satisfied that the absent person was told about the hearing or that reasonable steps were taken to do this.

Your rights at the hearing

14.43   The tribunal sets the procedure at the hearing, but you and the other parties have the right to be present, to be heard and to be represented.

14.44   You may be able to attend a hearing by telephone or via a live link, e.g. a video conference facility, but only where the judge gives permission. You should contact HMCTS about this.

14.45   You may be accompanied to the hearing, for example by a friend or relative. With the tribunal's permission they can help you present your case or act as your representative. This is true even if their name has not been previously notified to HMCTS or the DWP.

Order and conduct of the hearing

14.46   The procedure for the hearing is set by the tribunal within the appropriate legal framework, e.g. the need to ensure that you and the other parties have the opportunity to put your case. Failure to observe proper procedures or each party's rights may leave the tribunal's decision open to appeal on grounds of natural justice or the right to a fair hearing (CJSA/5100/2001).

14.47   The way the tribunal conducts itself varies according to the issues it has to decide. You should expect to have those present introduced and their role explained at the start. The tribunal should also tell you about the procedure it wishes to follow and seek your, and any other parties', agreement to going ahead in this way. You may be asked to start by explaining why you think the decision is wrong. If the DWP's presenting officer is present (they are not always), they may be asked to explain the basis of the decision. At some point the tribunal is likely to question you. This questioning may be assertive and inquisitorial. You may be offered the opportunity to have the final word before the tribunal goes on to consider its decision.

14.42   FTPR 31

14.43   FTPR 2, 5, 11, 28

14.44   FTPR 1(3) definition: 'hearing'

14.45   FTPR 11(7)-(8)

14.46   FTPR 5, 6

14.47   FTPR 2, 5, 6, 8

Directions (instructions) – including directions to postpone or adjourn a hearing

14.48   The tribunal may at any stage of the proceedings:

(a) give the directions it thinks necessary or desirable for the just, effective and efficient conduct of the proceedings; and

(b) direct you, or any other party, to provide items or documents as may be reasonably required.

The judge may, for example, direct the postponement of a hearing or the adjournment of a hearing to allow new evidence to be obtained or considered. The tribunal can decide to do this itself, or you or any other party may make a written application giving reasons for a direction to the clerk before a hearing or by an oral request during the hearing.

14.49   If you are dissatisfied with a direction you may apply for it to be amended, suspended or set aside. But if you fail to comply with one that is in force there is a possibility that your appeal may be struck out (if you have been warned about this). If the DWP fails to comply there is a possibility that it may be barred from the proceedings and may have all issues decided against it.

Withdrawing your appeal

14.50   You can withdraw (end) your appeal application any time before the hearing by writing to HMCTS telling it that you are withdrawing your appeal. You may also withdraw your appeal at the hearing itself if the judge agrees. If this happens the clerk sends a written notice to any party who is not present, telling them that the appeal has been withdrawn. If you, or a respondent (a term which includes your landlord in relation to certain decisions) subsequently decide that you or they want to have your appeal considered after all (reinstated), a written application should be made to HMCTS within one calendar month after the date of the hearing requesting this.

The First-tier Tribunal's decision

14.51   The tribunal reaches a decision once it has considered all the evidence. In reaching its decision the tribunal should:

(a) consider the relevant law including any applicable case law;

(b) identify the relevant facts on the basis of the available evidence; and

(c) where the facts are in doubt or dispute, establish them (if necessary on the balance of probability); and

(d) apply the law to the relevant facts to arrive at a reasoned decision.

14.48   FTPR 5(2)-(3), 6

14.49   FTPR 6(5), 7(2)(c), 8(3), 8(7)

14.50   FTPR 17

Duty to follow precedent

14.52   In its consideration of the legal issues the tribunal must follow the legal points held in past decisions of the Upper Tribunal, the Commissioners and the courts unless the case before the tribunal is distinguishable (R(U)23/59). Northern Ireland decisions are not binding in England, Wales or Scotland but are of persuasive authority (R(I)14/63). Decisions of the First-tier Tribunal itself do not set any precedent and so cannot be cited as authority in subsequent cases.

14.53   There is an order of precedence to Upper Tribunal decisions (including the former Commissioners' decisions) (R(I)12/75(T) and [2009] UKUT 4 (AAC) para 37), as follows:

(a) decisions of the Upper Tribunal where a Three Judge Panel (formerly a Tribunal of Commissioners) heard the case are the most authoritative – whether reported or unreported;

(b) reported decisions come next. For many years these were given serial numbers by the year and identified by having the prefix 'R', e.g. R(H)1/02. However, since 1st January 2010 these are known as the Administrative Appeals Chamber Reports and are indicated (after a reference to the parties) by the year of reporting, e.g. [2010], the abbreviation AACR, and the consecutive reporting number within that year's series, e.g. [2010] AACR 40: this is the 'neutral citation';

(c) then come other decisions. These are identified by the file number, e.g. CH/1502/2004, or since 1st January 2010 by a reference to the parties and a neutral citation e.g. JD v Leeds City Council [2009] UKUT 70 (AAC).

14.54   If there is conflict between two or more decisions the above hierarchy should be applied. If the conflicting decisions are of equal rank, the tribunal is free to choose between them. More recent decisions should be preferred to older decisions. If a more recent unreported decision has fully considered all the earlier authorities, and given reasons for disapproving one or more earlier reported decisions, the tribunal should generally follow the more recent unreported decision (R(IS) 13/01).

14.55   Most Upper Tribunal decisions are available online [www]. By February 2018 seven UC specific judgments were available. If you want to use an unreported decision in support of your case, a copy should, where possible, be sent in advance to HMCTS, otherwise an adjournment may be necessary.

The First-tier Tribunal's decision notice

14.56   If you attend the hearing you may be given the decision on the day. The judge should confirm the decision in writing as soon as practicable after the hearing. You should also be sent information on:

(a) how to apply for a written statement of reasons for the tribunal's decision; and

(b) what you need to do if you want to appeal the decision and the time limits within which this should be done.

14.55   UT decisions prior to Jan 2016 – goo.gl/8eaz8j
         UT decisions made from Jan 2016 onwards – goo.gl/b3M2Rg

14.56   FTPR 33(1)-(2)

Implementing the decision

14.57   The decision notice is the legal document that enables the DWP to correct and pay (or recover) UC in line with the tribunal's decision. The DWP should action the tribunal's decision as soon as practicable. Exceptions to this are where:

(a) an appeal is pending against the decision, in which case the DWP has the discretion to suspend payment in whole or in part; or

(b) the First-tier Tribunal suspends the effect of its own decision pending an application for permission to appeal, and any appeal of the decision.

Getting a 'statement of reasons' for the tribunal's decision

14.58   A statement of reasons sets out the judge's findings of fact and reasons for the decision. If you think you may want to appeal to the Upper Tribunal against the First-tier Tribunal's decision you should ask for a written statement of reasons.

Time limit for application for statement of reasons

14.59   You may apply to the clerk at the hearing for a statement of the reasons for the decision. Otherwise your application to HMCTS should be received within one calendar month of the date the First-tier Tribunal's decision notice was given or sent to you. This tribunal may extend this time limit where it is fair and just to do so but if your application is not made in time the chance of appeal may be lost.

Requirement to supply written statement of reasons

14.60   The tribunal must send a copy of its written statement of reasons to you and every other party within one month of the date the application is received or as soon as practicable after that.

The record of the proceedings

14.61   The judge makes a record of the tribunal's proceedings. The record should indicate the evidence received and submissions made as well as any procedural applications. (Practice Statement, 30th October 2008 [www].) This record, together with the decision notice, and any statement of the reasons for the decision, should be preserved for six months from the latest date of: the tribunal's decision, the production of written reasons, any correction, refusal to set aside or determination of an application for permission to appeal the decision. If there is a delay, for example in providing a statement of reasons, this places a duty on the tribunal to keep the record of proceedings for a minimum of six months after the statement of reasons is actually provided ([2015] UKUT 509 (AAC) at [37]). The record may be evidence to support an appeal to the Upper Tribunal. You can apply in writing to HMCTS for a copy within that six month period. It should be supplied on request.

14.57   D&A 44(1), 44(2)(b), 44(3), 44(4); FTPR 5(3)(l); NID&A 43(1), 43(2)(b), 43(3), 43(4)

14.59   FTPR 34(3)-(4)

14.60   FTPR 34(5)

14.61   Tribunals Judiciary, Practice Statement: Record of Proceedings (30 Oct 2008) – goo.gl/WuLcTQ

If the First-tier Tribunal's decision is wrong

14.62   Once the First-tier Tribunal has made and communicated its decision, the decision may be:

(a) altered if the DWP supersedes it;

(b) corrected, where there is an accidental error;

(c) set aside on certain limited grounds;

(d) appealed on a point of law to the Upper Tribunal.

If the First-tier Tribunal receives an application for permission to appeal it must first consider whether to review the decision (para 14.70).

When may the DWP supersede the decision?

14.63   The DWP may supersede the decision either following an application from you or on its own initiative, where:

(a) the decision was made in ignorance of a material fact; or

(b) the decision was based on a mistake as to a material fact; or

(c) there has been a relevant change of circumstances since it had effect.

When may the decision be corrected?

14.64   The tribunal may correct clerical mistakes, accidental errors such as a typing mistake, miscalculations or omissions at any time. A correction made to a decision or to a record of it is treated as part of the decision or record. Any of the parties to the appeal can ask for a correction to be made. A written notice of the correction should be given to every party as soon as practicable. You do not have a right of appeal against the decision to make a correction or a refusal to make a correction.

When may the decision be set aside?

14.65   If the tribunal decision is 'set aside' this means that it is cancelled and a new tribunal hearing may need to be arranged. You, or any other party, can apply for a decision to be set aside. The tribunal may set aside a decision if it considers that it is in the interests of justice to do so; and

(a) a document relating to the proceedings was not sent to, or was not received at an appropriate time by, a party or a party's representative;

(b) a document relating to the proceedings was not sent to the tribunal at an appropriate time;

(c) a party, or a party's representative, was not present at a hearing; or

(d) there has been some other procedural irregularity.

14.63   D&A 31(a), 23(1); NID&A 31(a), 23(1)

14.64   FTPR 36

14.65   FTPR 37(1)-(2), 5(3)(a)

14.66   If you want to apply for a decision to be set aside you must make a written application to the tribunal so that it is received within one calendar month of the date on which the decision was sent out to you. This time limit may be extended where it is fair and just to do so. Other parties to the appeal should be notified of the application and given the right to make representations. There is a right of appeal against a decision to set aside: [2013] UKUT 170 (AAC).

Appeals to the Upper Tribunal (Great Britain)

14.67   You can appeal against a First-tier Tribunal's decision but only if it made an error of law. If the tribunal's decision was in your favour you should be aware that the DWP and any other party to the proceedings can also apply for permission to appeal.

The Upper Tribunal

14.68   The Upper Tribunal is an independent tribunal established under the Tribunals, Courts and Enforcement Act 2007. The Upper Tribunal is divided into a number of chambers. The Upper Tribunal (Administrative Appeals Chamber) (UT(AAC)) considers appeals against a First-tier Tribunal's decisions on UC. All cases in the Upper Tribunal (AAC) are decided by judges, supported by registrars who deal with procedural matters. The Upper Tribunal is a superior court of record. This means that it gives interpretations of the law which are binding on all decision makers and tribunals. Its judges are barristers, solicitors or advocates of not less than ten years' standing who are specialists in social security law, and have a legal status comparable to that of a High Court judge in their specialised area. The procedural rules of the Upper Tribunal are set out in the Tribunal Procedure (Upper Tribunal) Rules SI 2008 No 2698 (as amended). The procedural rules currently in force together with detailed advice regarding appeals to the Upper Tribunal may be found on the Ministry of Justice and gov.uk websites [www].

Getting permission to appeal and the appeal itself

14.69   If, having considered the First-tier Tribunal's statement of reasons, you think that its decision contains an error of law you may apply to it for permission to appeal. Your application should identify the decision in question and the errors of law in it. The application should normally be received by HMCTS within one calendar month from the date the statement of reasons was sent to you. This time limit may be extended by the First-tier Tribunal but you cannot rely on this. If you are making a late application you should include a request for an extension of time and the reason why the application is late.

14.66   FTPR 37(3)

14.67   FTPR 38, 39, UTPR 21

14.68   TCEA s3, UTPR
         UT procedure rules – goo.gl/JLiAdg
         www.gov.uk/administrative-appeals-tribunal/how-to-appeal

14.69   FTPR 38(2)-(3), 38(5)

14.70   The First-tier Tribunal may:

   (a) decide to review the decision without the need to refer the case onwards – if it is satisfied that there was an error of law in the decision. The case may be re-decided or heard again by a different tribunal;

   (b) give permission for the appeal – in which case you will be able to send it on to the Upper Tribunal;

   (c) refuse permission together with a statement of reasons for refusal – in this case you may then apply (normally within one calendar month) directly to the Upper Tribunal for permission to appeal.

14.71   If the First-tier Tribunal has refused you permission to appeal you can apply directly to the Upper Tribunal for permission. This should be done on form UT1 [www] and should normally be made within one month of receipt of a refusal from the First-tier Tribunal – this period may be extended by the Upper Tribunal but you cannot rely on this. If permission is given then your appeal can go ahead.

14.72   You make your appeal in writing – form UT1 can also be used for this. If you have been given permission to appeal by the First-tier Tribunal your appeal to the Upper Tribunal should normally be received within one calendar month of the date of the letter which came with the decision of the First-tier Tribunal on your application for permission to appeal. The Upper Tribunal may extend (or shorten) this period but you can't rely on this happening. Most appeals to the Upper Tribunal are decided on the papers without a hearing. You may, however, ask for a hearing.

What is an error of law?

14.73   An appeal to the Upper Tribunal can only be made on an error of law. An error of law is where the First-tier Tribunal did one or more of the following:

   (a) failed to apply the correct law;

   (b) wrongly interpreted the relevant Acts or Regulations;

   (c) followed a procedure that breached the rules of natural justice;

   (d) took irrelevant matters into account, or did not consider relevant matters, or did both of these things;

   (e) did not give adequate reasons in the full statement of reasons;

   (f) gave a decision which was not supported by the evidence;

   (g) decided the facts in such a way that no tribunal properly instructed as to the law, and acting judicially, could have reached that decision.

These are examples, not an exhaustive list (R(IS) 11/99).

14.70   TCEA s.9; FTPR 38-40

14.71   UTPR 21, 5(3)(a)
         goo.gl/oTnCu5

14.72   UTPR 23, 5(3)(a)

14.73   TCEA s11(2)

Appeals against the Upper Tribunal's decision

14.74   There is a right to appeal against a decision of the Upper Tribunal to the Court of Appeal or the Court of Session in Scotland (but you should seek advice on this). An appeal can only be made on a point of law. Permission to appeal must be obtained from the Upper Tribunal or, if refused, from the relevant court. The time limit for applying for permission to appeal is three months, but it may be extended. If permission is refused the application may be renewed in the relevant court within six weeks.

14.75   Separately from the above, cases involving European Union law can be referred by the Upper Tribunal direct to the European Court of Justice.

Northern Ireland

14.76   If you want to appeal a UC decision in Northern Ireland you should ask for a mandatory reconsideration by the decision-maker. If your dispute is not resolved you may ask an independent appeal tribunal to consider it by appealing directly to the Appeal Service (TAS (NI)) [www]. A form is available for this purpose (NOA1(SS). TAS (NI) are responsible for the administration of the independent appeal tribunals. If you do not agree with the appeal tribunal's decision on a point of law you may be able to appeal the decision to the NI Social Security Commissioners [www].

14.77   Detailed DfC procedural advice on UC appeals in NI is to be found in Ch A5: of the Advice for Decision Making Guide [www]. The main legislation relating to UC appeals is found in:

■ Universal Credit, Personal Independence Payment, Jobseeker's Allowance and Employment and Support Allowance (Decisions and Appeals) Regulations (Northern Ireland) 2016/221;

■ Social Security (Northern Ireland) Order 1998/1506;

■ The Social Security and Child Support (Decisions and Appeals) Regulations (NI) 1999; and

■ The Social Security Commissioners (Procedure) Regulations (Northern Ireland) 1999.

14.74   TCEA s.13(1)

14.76   NISS98 13, 15
www.communities-ni.gov.uk/topics/appeals-service
Appeal form NOA1(SS) and guidance notes – goo.gl/LiK8UC

14.77   DfC Advice for Decision Making Guide, Ch A5 Appeals – PIP & UC – goo.gl/hphVe2

Chapter 15 **Who can get council tax rebate**

- An overview of the council tax – including valuation and banding: see paras 15.1-7.
- Who is liable for the council tax: see paras 15.8-13.
- Exemptions, disability reductions and discounts: see paras 15.14-23.
- Council tax rebates (CTR): the different kinds of CTR; general rules about CTR schemes and how these vary, nationally, locally and by your age: see paras 15.24-46.
- Basic conditions for council tax rebate: see paras 15.47-57.
- Exclusions from CTR: see paras 15.58-66.
- Absences from home and from Great Britain: see paras 15.67-76.

15.1 This chapter applies only in Great Britain (England, Wales and Scotland), where council tax is the form of local taxation. It describes how liability for council tax (i.e. before any rebate) is determined; and general rules about council tax rebate (CTR) including how CTR schemes vary locally and the basic conditions of entitlement. The footnotes to this chapter give the law in England. The equivalent footnotes for Scotland and Wales can be found in appendix 4 table A, for the parts of this chapter that relate to council tax liability (paras 15.3-23); and appendix 4 table B for the remainder.

Council tax overview

15.2 The council tax is the means by which local people help meet the cost of local public services in Great Britain. It is a tax on residential properties, known as dwellings. In England, Scotland and Wales the same authority that is responsible for the billing and collection of the tax (para 15.5) is also responsible for administering CTR. In two tier council areas in England the billing authority is the district (lower tier) council. Table 15.1 lists the key considerations that arise when considering council tax liability, etc. Fuller details of the council tax are in CPAG's regularly revised *Council Tax Handbook* (11th edition), which covers matters not included in this guide (such as billing, payment, penalties, and so on).

Table 15.1 **Council tax liability: key considerations**

(a) Which dwelling is being considered?

(b) What valuation band does it fall into?

(c) How much is the council tax for that band?

(d) Who is liable to pay the council tax there?

(e) Is the dwelling exempt from council tax altogether?

(f) Do you qualify for a disability reduction?

(g) Do you qualify for a discount?

How your liability is calculated

15.3   Liability for the council tax normally falls on the occupier rather than the owner – although there are exceptions. Your liability is calculated on a daily basis, starting from the day you first occupy the dwelling as your 'sole or main residence' and ending on the day that ceases to be the case. If your dwelling is exempt or if you are entitled to a disability reduction or discount these are also calculated on a daily basis.

Dwellings and valuation bands

15.4   One council tax bill is issued per dwelling unless the dwelling is exempt (para 15.15). A dwelling means a house or a flat, etc, whether lived in or not; but also includes houseboats and mobile homes.

15.5   The amount of tax depends first on which valuation band a dwelling has been allocated to, and this is shown on the bill. The lower the valuation band, the lower the tax. An amount for each band is fixed each year by the local council that issues the bill (the 'billing authority'), and often includes amounts for other bodies (such as a county council, a parish council, the police, etc).

15.6   In England and Scotland, dwellings are valued as at 1st April 1991 and there are eight valuation bands – band A to band H. In Wales, dwellings are valued as at 1st April 2003 and there are nine valuation bands – band A to band I. In each case, band A is the lowest. The valuation list holds details of which band each dwelling is in and it can be viewed online [www].

Increased council tax: unoccupied dwellings

15.7   In England and Wales, council tax liability can be increased for dwellings which have been unoccupied and substantially unfurnished for two years or more. The increase (depending on the individual council) can be up to 50%.

15.3   LGFA 1, 2, 6 Scotland

15.4   LGFA 3, 7; SI 1992/550

15.6   LGFA 5(1),(2)
          http://cti.voa.gov.uk/cti/inits.asp

15.7   LGFA 11A

Who is liable to pay council tax?

The general rule: liability of occupiers

15.8   If you are aged 18 or over, you are normally responsible for paying the council tax for the dwelling where you live as your 'sole or main residence', but there are also exceptions described in the next paragraph. If there are other people who live in the dwelling with you the liability falls on the occupier with the greatest legal interest in the dwelling. So, for example, if you are a home-owner with a lodger, you are liable, not the lodger. Likewise, if you are a tenant (council, housing association or private) with a lodger, you are liable, not the lodger.

Exception: when owners are liable

15.9   For certain types of dwelling, council tax liability falls on the owner rather than on the occupier. In other words, the residents are not liable (but the owner may pass on the cost of paying the council tax when fixing the rent). Liability for council tax falls on the owner if the dwelling is:

   (a)   unoccupied (unless the dwelling is exempt: para 15.15);

   (b)   a 'house in multiple occupation' (para 15.10);

   (c)   in England and Wales, a 'hostel' (para 15.11) that is not a residential care home;

   (d)   a bail or probation hostel;

   (e)   a residential care home including local authority residential home;

   (f)   occupied by residents who are members of a religious community;

   (g)   occupied by a minister of religion; or

   (h)   provided as accommodation for asylum seekers by the Home Office under the asylum support provisions.

15.10   A 'house in multiple occupation' is:

   (a)   a building that has been purpose built or adapted for people who are not all part of the same household;

   (b)   inhabited by two or more residents who have a licence or tenancy to occupy only part of it; or

   (c)   inhabited by two or more residents who have licence to occupy but who are only liable to pay rent for their share.

15.11   A hostel is a building or part of a building used for residential accommodation that is provided in non-self-contained units, together with personal care for people who are elderly, disabled, have a past or present alcohol or drug dependence or a past or present mental disorder.

15.8   LGFA 6(1),(2)

15.9   LGFA 8; SI 1992/551

15.10   SI 1992/551 reg 2 Class C; SI 1993/151; SI 1995/620

15.11   SI 1992/548 art 6

Joint liability of residents

15.12   Except where the owner is liable (para 15.9) you can be jointly liable for the council tax with one or more other occupiers. If you are jointly liable (or 'jointly and severally liable') it means you can be held responsible for paying the full bill (rather than just your 'share'). There are two ways in which you can be jointly liable:

(a) if other people live with you, then all of the residents who possess the same greatest legal interest in the dwelling (para 15.8) are jointly liable for the council tax. For example, if you are a joint owner occupier with your sister, or you jointly rent your home with two friends, they are jointly liable with you;

(b) if (by (a) above) you are liable as the occupier then your partner (provided you live together) is jointly liable with you, even if their legal interest is inferior to yours.

For exceptions see the next paragraph. There are further rules (not in this guide) about joint liability for unoccupied properties.

Students and people with severe mental impairment

15.13   The rule about joint liability (para 15.12) does not apply if;

(a) you are a student or severely mentally impaired (in either case as defined in table 15.2); and

(b) there is at least one other resident in the dwelling with the same legal interest in the dwelling as you who does not fall into either of these two categories.

If all of you have the same legal interest in the dwelling and you all fall into either of these two categories, see paragraph 15.15.

Exemptions, disability reductions and discounts

15.14   This section describes how your council tax bill can be reduced before any claim for CTR is applied. In some cases (if your dwelling is exempt) your liability can be reduced to zero. These exemptions, reductions and discounts depend only on your status and not your income or capital.

Exempt dwellings

15.15   Only dwellings, rather than people, can be exempt from the council tax. If your dwelling is exempt it means your liability (i.e. your council tax bill) is reduced to zero for each day the exemption applies. Your dwelling is exempt from council tax if:

(a) all the residents are students or education leavers aged under 20 (table 15.2);

(b) in England and Wales only, all the occupants are students (though their normal residence is elsewhere);

(c) it is a hall of residence mainly occupied by students;

15.12   LGFA 6, 9; SI 1992/558

15.13   LGFA 9(2)

(d) except where the owner is liable (para 15.9), all the occupiers are severely mentally impaired, including if the only other occupiers are students;

(e) all the residents are aged under 18;

(f) it is armed forces accommodation;

(g) in England and Wales only, it is an annex or other similar self-contained part of the property which is occupied by an elderly or disabled relative of a resident living in the rest of it; or

(h) in Scotland only, it is a dwelling owned by a registered housing association which uses it as a trial flat for a pensioner or a disabled person.

15.16   In addition, various unoccupied dwellings are also exempt. For example, an unoccupied dwelling which is substantially unfurnished is exempt for six months (but see para 15.7) – and there are many other categories.

Disability reductions

15.17   Your council tax bill is reduced if your home qualifies for a disability reduction. The effect of the reduction is to reduce your bill to the amount that would be payable if your home was in the next lowest valuation band, or if your home is in band A, your bill is reduced by one sixth.

15.18   Your home qualifies for a disability reduction if there is at least one disabled resident living there and the property provides:

(a) an additional bathroom or kitchen for use by the disabled person;

(b) an additional room, other than a bathroom, kitchen or toilet, used predominantly to meet the disabled person's special needs (for example, a downstairs room used as a bedroom); or

(c) sufficient floor space to enable the use of a wheelchair required by the disabled person within the dwelling.

15.19   In each case the authority must be satisfied that the facility provided is either essential, or of major importance, for the disabled person (who may be an adult or a child) in view of the nature and extent of the disability. Disability reductions are not limited to specially adapted properties.

Discounts

15.20   Your council tax bill is reduced if:

(a) there is only one 'resident' in your home or only one resident who is not a disregarded person. In this case the discount is always 25%; or

(b) the dwelling is unoccupied or the only residents are all disregarded persons (para 15.21). In this case, the discount can be up to 50% depending on the policy of the local billing authority (but see below).

15.15-16   LGFA 4(1),(2); SI 1992/558

15.17   LGFA 13(1),(4),(6),(7); SI 1999/1004

15.18   SI 1992/554; SI 1993/195

15.20   LGFA 11

A 'resident' means anyone aged 18 or over. Note in the case of (b) if the dwelling is actually unoccupied (rather than occupied by disregarded persons) it could be exempt (para 15.16) or liable for increased council tax (para 15.7) depending on the policy of the billing authority.

15.21   For the purpose of deciding the level of discount, certain residents are disregarded (a 'disregarded person'). The categories of residents who are disregarded include students, apprentices, carers, severely mentally impaired people. The full details are found in table 15.2. Note that disregarded status does not affect your liability to pay council tax.

Table 15.2 **Who is a disregarded person**

Regardless of whether you are liable (or jointly liable) for the council tax, you or anyone else who lives in your home (also referred to as 'you' in this table) is a disregarded person if you are:

(a) **a young person for whom child benefit is payable:** You qualify if you are a young person (para 16.64) for whom child benefit could be paid (i.e. during the child benefit extension period) even if it is not in payment.

(b) **an education leaver aged under 20:** You qualify if you are a former student (as defined in the next category) after your course ends during the period 1st May to 31st October or until you reach age 20 if that occurs earlier.

(c) **a student:** You are a student if you are:

■ on a course of further or higher education in the UK or EU (paras 2.20-22) which lasts for at least one academic or calendar year, and in which you are expected to study at least 21 hours per week for at least 24 weeks per year; or

■ aged under 20 on a course of further education in the UK or EU which lasts at least three months, during which you are expected to study at least 12 hours per week during term times; or

■ a student nurse studying for the first time to be included in parts one to six or eight in the nursing register;

■ a foreign language assistant who is registered with the British Council.

(d) **a youth trainee:** You are a youth trainee if you are aged under 25 and undertaking youth training funded by the Skills Funding Agency in England (or equivalent body in Scotland and Wales).

(e) **an apprentice:** You are an apprentice if you are:

■ in employment for the purpose of learning a trade, profession, vocation or similar; and

---

15.21   LGFA 11(5), sch 1

T15.2(a) LGFA sch 1 para 3

T15.2(b) LGFA sch 1 para 11; DDR 3, Class C

T15.2(c) LGFA sch 1 paras 4, 5; DDO art 4, sch paras 2-7

T15.2(d) LGFA sch 1 para 4; DDO art 4; sch 1 para 8

T15.2(e) LGFA sch 1 para 4; DDO art 4, sch 1 para 1; SI 2006/3396

- studying for an accredited qualification; and
- paid no more than £195 per week.

(f) **a care worker:** You are a care worker if you live with the person you care for so that you can better perform your duties and you:

- are employed by that person to provide care or support for at least 24 hours a week; and
- are paid no more than £44 per week; and
- were introduced to them by a local authority, government department or charity.

(g) **a carer of a severely disabled person:** You qualify as a carer if you :

- live with the person you care for; and
- provide care for at least 35 hours a week; and
- you are not the spouse or partner of the person you care for, or their parent if you care for a child aged under 18; and
- the person you care for is 'entitled' to (para 17.71) either: the daily living component of personal independence payment at any rate (only the enhanced rate in Scotland), attendance allowance at any rate (only the higher rate in Scotland), the middle or higher rate of the care component of disability living allowance (only the higher rate in Scotland), an armed forces independence payment or the highest rate of constant attendance allowance.

(h) **'severely mentally impaired':** You qualify as severely mentally impaired if you have a medical certificate confirming your intelligence and social functioning (however caused) is severely impaired; and receive at least one of the following benefits (or would do but for the fact that you have reached pension age):

- the daily living component of personal independence payment;
- attendance allowance;
- the highest or middle rate of the care component of disability living allowance;
- constant attendance allowance paid with an industrial injury benefit;
- an armed forces independence payment;
- in England and Wales the LCW or LCWRA element of universal credit;
- in Scotland only, universal credit or employment and support allowance;
- incapacity benefit, or severe disablement allowance; or
- income support or JSA(IB) (or your partner is) – but only if it includes a disability premium on the grounds of incapacity for work.

T15.2(f) LGFA sch 1 para 9; DDR reg 2, sch paras 1,2; SI 2006/3395 reg 4

T15.2(g) LGFA sch 1 para 9; DDR reg 2, sch paras 3,4; SI 2013/388 sch para 3; SI 2013/591 sch para 6

T15.2(h) LGFA sch 1 para 2; DDO art 3; SI 2013/388 sch para 12; SI 2013/591 sch para 5; SI 2013/630 reg 55

(i) **a member of a religious community:** You qualify if you are a member of a religious community whose principal occupation includes prayer, contemplation, education or the relief of suffering; and you

  ■ have no income (other than an occupational pension) or capital; and

  ■ are dependent on the community for your material needs.

(j) **a diplomat or member of an international body or visiting forces:** You qualify if you are a member of the international headquarters of certain defence organisations or visiting forces (or in some cases you are the dependant of a person who is).

(k) **a non-British spouse or civil partner:** You qualify if you are the husband, wife or civil partner of an education leaver, a student, or member of an international body (as defined in categories (b), (c) and (j)) who is not permitted to work or claim benefits.

(l) **a long-term hospital patient:** You are a long-term patient if you have been in a care home or NHS hospital for more than 52 weeks (adding together periods where the break between them is four weeks or less) or if your sole or main residence is in a care home or independent hospital.

(m) **a prisoner or detainee:** You are a prisoner or detainee if you are in any kind of detention (whether on bail, on remand or serving a sentence, including members of armed forces under military authority).

How to apply for an exemption, disability reduction or discount

15.22   Your authority is expected to take reasonable steps to find out whether any dwellings in its area qualify for an exemption, disability reduction or discount. It can award these on the basis of information available to it, or you can request it in writing. There is no time limit to obtain an exemption, disability reduction or discount, but your authority can ask you to provide appropriate evidence. Appeals about all these things go first to the authority and then to a Valuation Tribunal: the procedures are the same as for CTR appeals in England (chapter 20).

Other reasons why liability may be lower

15.23   In addition to the disability reductions and discounts mentioned above, your authority can offer a discount for prompt payment or if you agree to pay your bill by one of its preferred payment methods.

T15.2(i)   LFGA sch 1 para 11; DDR 3, Class B

T15.2(j)   LGFA sch 1 para 11; DDR 3, Class A, Class D; Class F

T15.2(k)   LGFA sch 1 para 11; DDR 3, Class A, Class E; SI 1995/620 reg 4

T15.2(l)   LGFA sch 1 paras 6,7; DDO art 6

T15.2(m)   LGFA sch 1 para 1; DDO art 2

Examples: Council tax liability, exemptions and discounts

Unless stated below, none of the following are students, severely mentally impaired, or under 18.

A couple with a lodger

A couple live in a house which the man owns in his name only. They have children in their 20s living at home, and a lodger who rents a room and shares facilities. The couple are jointly liable for the council tax, because the man is the resident with the greatest legal interest in the dwelling and the woman is jointly liable with him by being his partner. There is no reason to suppose they qualify for exemption, or a disability reduction or a discount.

A lone parent

A lone parent owns her home and lives there with her three children, all under 18. The lone parent is solely liable for the council tax, because she is the resident with the greatest legal interest in the dwelling. She is the only (adult) resident so she qualifies for a 25% discount.

Three sharers

Three friends jointly rent a house (in other words all their names are on the tenancy agreement). No-one else lives with them. They are all jointly liable for the council tax, because they are all residents with the greatest legal interest in the dwelling. There is no reason to suppose they qualify for exemption, or a disability reduction or a discount.

The sharers' circumstances change

One of the sharers leaves and is not replaced. One of the others becomes a full-time university student. The remaining non-student resident is now the only liable person (para 15.13), and qualifies for a 25% discount because the student is disregarded when counting the residents (para 15.21).

Council tax rebates (CTR): overview

15.24   This section is about general rules for council tax rebates (CTR). It describes how your entitlement to CTR can vary nationally or locally between one council area and another, the different kinds of CTR and what happens if you are entitled to more than one kind.

15.25   In CTR law a council tax rebate is called a 'council tax reduction' but some councils call it 'council tax support' (or council tax rebate).

15.26   The rules about CTR vary:

  (a) between the different kinds of CTR (paras 15.27-29);

  (b) between pension age and working age claims (para 15.30); and

  (c) between England, Scotland and Wales (paras 15.31-46).

Table 15.3 summarises the main variations. In this and the following chapters, we explain when they could affect you.

Table 15.3 **CTR national variations (2018-19)**

	England	Scotland	Wales
Kinds of CTR available (para 15.27)	P: Main CTR, second adult rebate, local CTR classes and discretionary CTR W: Main CTR, discretionary CTR local CTR classes and second adult rebate locally	Main CTR, Scottish special rebate and second adult rebate	Main CTR, local CTR classes and discretionary CTR
Students (para 15.62)	P: Eligible W: Mainly excluded	P: Eligible W: Mainly excluded	P: Excluded W: Mainly excluded
Date CTR starts/ changes (paras 16.23-26, 19.11)	Monday following date of claim/change	Monday following date of claim/change	Exact date of claim/change
Backdating limit (para 16.33)	P: Three months W: Varies locally up to six months	P: Three months W: One month	P: Three months W: One month or varies locally
Extended reductions (para 19.27)	P: Four weeks W: Four weeks or varies locally	Four weeks	Four weeks or varies locally
Appeals (Chapter 20)	To council then Valuation Tribunal	To council then CTR Review Panel	To council then Valuation Tribunal
Variations from council to council (paras 15.34-46)	P: None W: Several local variations	None	Some local variations

- Entries are simplified. 'P' refers to pension age and 'W' to working age claims (table 15.4). Other entries refer to both groups.
- For other national variations, see in particular tables 17.1-3 (calculation amounts) and paras 15.74-75 (absences outside Great Britain).

The different kinds of CTR

15.27 The different kinds of CTR are:

(a) 'Main CTR' applies in England, Scotland and Wales if you are pension age or working age. It can help you pay your council tax if you have a low income (paras 15.48-49 and 17.5).

(b) 'Second adult rebate' applies in England and Scotland if you are pension age or working age. It applies in all areas in England if you are pension age and in some areas if you are working age. It can help you with your council tax if you live with others who aren't expected to contribute to it (see paras 15.50-51). (In CTR law second adult rebate is called 'alternative maximum council tax reduction'.)

(c) 'Scottish special rebate' applies in Scotland if you are pension age or working age. It can help you pay your council tax if your home is in bands E to H (paras 15.52 and 17.11-14).

(d) 'Local classes of CTR' apply in England and Wales where local councils can create new CTR 'classes' of their own (para 15.53) as part of their local scheme. Local CTR classes are in addition to other kinds of CTR or in England may replace main CTR or second adult rebate (para 15.37).

(e) 'Discretionary CTR' applies in England and Wales if you are pension age or working age. It can help you pay your council tax if you are, or a member of a group that is generally at risk of being, on a low income (paras 15.54-57). It can be paid if you do not qualify for, or in addition to the other kinds of CTR.

In this guide: 'CTR' means any or all of these and the above names are used for the individual kind, and 'scheme' means all of the classes of CTR that can be applied for in your area whether that class is devised locally or from the regulations (para 15.53).

15.28   In England and Wales the regulations (paras 15.33-37, 15.44-45) designate main CTR and second adult rebate as belonging to a particular CTR 'class' (i.e. 'Class A', 'Class B', etc) depending on:

(a) the regulations themselves (i.e. 'prescribed requirements' or default scheme);

(b) the age of the applicant (pension age or working age);

(c) the kind of CTR it is (main or second adult rebate); and

(d) in the case of main CTR, whether the applicant's income exceeds their applicable amount (or not).

The CTR regulations determine how 'financial need' is assessed for each named class (chapters 17, 18).

Which kind of CTR is awarded (the 'better buy')

15.29   If you qualify for more than one kind of CTR (para 15.27(a) to(e)) the following rules apply:

(a) if you are entitled to two or more of main CTR, Scottish special rebate, or second adult rebate, you get whichever one of these is the highest; and

(b) in England and Wales, you can get discretionary CTR in addition to any other kind of CTR award. Discretionary CTR can reduce your bill to nil even if the maximum award for other kinds CTR does not (para 17.4).

15.27   England: LGFA 13A(1)(a)-(c), sch 1A para 2; CTP sch1 paras 2-4
            Scotland: LGFA 80; CTS 14, 14A; CTS60+ 14, 14A
            Wales: LGFA 13A(1)(a)-(c), sch 1B paras 3, 4; CTPW 22-25

15.28   CTP sch 1 paras 2-4; CTR 13-18

15.29   England: LGFA 13A(1)(c); CTP sch 1 para 10(5),(6); CTR 32(5),(6)
            Scotland: CTS 14(3A),(9), 14A(1)(b); CTS60+ 14(3A),(9), 14A(1)(b)
            Wales: LGFA 13A(1)(c)

Pension age vs working age applications

15.30 Table 15.4 explains whether your application for CTR counts as 'pension age' or 'working age' (and this definition cannot be varied). Some CTR rules differ between pension age and working age applications. These are explained throughout this chapter and chapters 16 to 20, and the main differences are summarised in table 15.3.

Table 15.4 **Pension age or working age claim?**

Single claimant/lone parent

(a) On JSA(IB)/ESA(IR)/IS/UC	Working age
(b) Otherwise:	
■ under SPC age	Working age
■ at or over SPC age	Pension age

Couple/polygamous marriage

(c) At least one on JSA(IB)/ESA(IR)/IS/UC	Working age
(d) Otherwise:	
■ applicant under SPC age	Working age
■ applicant at or over SPC age	Pension age

Notes:

■ In (d) in mixed age couples it makes a difference which one of you is the applicant.

■ 'SPC age' means the qualifying age for state pension credit. During 2018-19 this is rising from (approximately) 64½ to 65¼. For full details see appendix 3.

CTR in England: pension age

15.31 In England, the rules for main CTR and second adult rebate are the same for all pension age claims, so there are no variations from one local council's area to another.

15.32 In addition to main CTR and second adult rebate your local council can devise new classes of CTR as part of its local scheme but it is not obliged to do so, and most do not. Any new class must be based on 'financial need' (para 15.53).

15.33 The law sets out the rules for main CTR and second adult rebate (para 15.28) as well as who is pension age and your local council cannot vary these matters. The law is in the 'prescribed requirements' regulations (SI 2012/2885) (appendix 1). In the footnotes, 'CTP' refers to these. Many councils also use the 'default scheme' regulations (para 15.36) as the basis for their local scheme rules.

15.30   CTP 2(1) definition: 'qualifying age for state pension credit', 3; CTR 2(1), 3

15.31   LGFA 13A(2),(3), sch 1A para 2(9); CTP 11(1), 14

15.32   LGFA 13A(2),(3), sch 1A para 2(1)-(4),(8),(9)

15.33   CTP 9, 11(1), 14, sch 1 paras 1-4

CTR in England: working age

15.34   For working age claims in England, local councils can vary rules for main CTR/second adult rebate and/or devise completely new classes of CTR to supplement or replace them (para 15.53).

15.35   The law is in the 'prescribed requirements' regulations (SI 2012/2885) and the 'default scheme' regulations (SI 2012/2886) (appendix 1). The prescribed requirements set out only a few basic rules that must be part of every local scheme but these are limited to:

(a)   who is included in your household;

(b)   what is a 'working age' claim;

(c)   migrants and recent arrivals who must be excluded; and

(d)   certain other minimum standards about the process for making claims, notifying decisions and appealing.

15.36   The 'default scheme' regulations (SI 2012/2886) only applied during the 2013-14 financial year. The schedule to these regulations sets out a complete scheme for main CTR and second adult rebate. Many councils have adopted these rules with only a few minor changes as the basis for their local scheme (on a 'cut and paste' basis) and therefore this guide continues to reference them in the footnotes, where 'CTR' refers to these.

15.37   Apart from the matters set out in the 'prescribed requirements' regulations your council has a wide discretion to vary any of the financial conditions for main CTR or second adult rebate (para 15.38) (or replace with classes of its own) but it cannot add further (non-financial) conditions such as a local residence qualification: R (Winder) v Sandwell MBC.

15.38   As an example of how local councils may vary the financial conditions for main CTR or second adult rebate some have done one or more of the following:

(a)   reduced the amount of council tax that can be met by CTR (para 17.4);

(b)   set a minimum award (para 17.9);

(c)   reduced the upper capital limit;

(d)   increased and/or restructured non-dependant deductions and the income bands;

(e)   varied the assessment of different kinds of income;

(f)   increased the excess income taper above 20%;

(g)   limited or removed entitlement to backdated CTR;

(h)   limited or removed entitlement to second adult rebate;

(i)   set their own rates for some or all of the allowances, premiums and components in the calculation of the applicable amount (table 17.3).

In practice, (a) is the only variation made by many councils. Further information about the different local schemes in England can be found online [www].

15.35   CTP 3-9, 12, 13, 15

15.36   LGFA sch 1A para 4

15.37   LGFA 13A(2), sch 1A para 2(8),(9); CTP 12, 13, 15, sch 7 paras 1-7
         R (Winder) v Sandwell MBC [2014]; www.bailii.org/ew/cases/EWHC/Admin/2014/2617.html

15.38   LGFA 13A(2), sch 1A para 2(2)-(4)
         https://www.counciltaxsupport.org

Local schemes in England: preparation, changes and publicity

15.39   Each year your council must consider whether or not it should revise (or replace) its local scheme (for both pension age and working age applications). Any changes must be confirmed by 11th March in time for the new financial year starting in April. When preparing a new scheme your council must publish a draft and conduct a 'meaningful' consultation with local residents: R (Moseley) v Haringey LBC. If the revised scheme results in a reduction or removal of entitlement it must include transitional rules. Your council must publish its scheme rules including any revisions and you can usually find these on its website.

CTR in Scotland

15.40   In Scotland, the CTR scheme is the same for all pension age claims, and for all working age claims. There are no variations from one local council area to another.

15.41   The law for working age claims is in the CTR regulations SSI 2012/303, and for pension age claims is in the CTR (state pension credit) regulations SSI 2012/319 (appendix 1). In the footnotes and in appendix 4 table B, 'CTS' and CTS60+ refer to these respectively.

CTR in Wales

15.42   In Wales, your council can extend the maximum period of the backdating (paras 16.31 and 16.33) and the length of an extended reduction (para 19.28) but apart from that the rules for main CTR are the same for all working age and pension age claims, so there are no variations from one local council's area to another.

15.43   In addition to main CTR your local council can devise new classes of CTR as part of its local scheme (para 15.27) but it is not obliged to do so, and most do not. Any new class can be based on your personal circumstances or by your membership of a group that is generally considered to be in 'financial need' (e.g. disability, old age, etc.). But a local scheme cannot vary the rules about who is excluded (para 15.58).

15.44   The law sets out the rules for main CTR (para 15.42) (including who is pension age/working age) and your local council cannot vary these matters. The law is in the 'prescribed requirements' regulations (SI 2013/3029) (appendix 1). In the footnotes, 'CTPW' refers to these.

15.45   If in any year your council fails to produce a scheme as required (para 15.46) the 'default scheme' is imposed as its own. The default scheme is identical in almost every aspect to the prescribed requirements. The scheme is set out in the schedule to the 'default scheme' regulations (SI 2013/3035); in the footnotes 'CTRW' refers to these. Some councils use the default scheme as the basis for their own scheme rules.

15.39   LGFA sch 1A paras 3(1),(3), 5(1),(2),(4); R (Moseley) v Haringey LBC [2014]
               www.bailii.org/uk/cases/UKSC/2014/56.html

15.40-41   LGFA 80; CTS 14, 14A; CTS60+ 14, 14A

15.42   LGFA 13A(4), sch 1B paras 2-4; CTPW 11, 14(b), 15(2),(3), 22-25, 32-34

15.43   LGFA 13A(4), sch 1B paras 2-4; CTPW 14(a), 15(1), 28-31

15.44   LGFA 13A(4) sch 1B para 3; CTPW 3, 11, 32, 33

15.45   LGFA sch 1B para 6(1)(e); CTPW 13

15.46   Each year your council must consider whether or not it should revise or replace its local scheme (for both pension age and working age applications). Any changes must be confirmed by 31st January in time for the new financial year starting in April. When preparing a new scheme your council must publish a draft and consult with anyone it considers is likely to have an interest in its operation. If the revised scheme results in a reduction or removal of entitlement it must include transitional rules. Having made a scheme your council must publish its rules, and you can usually find these on the council's website.

CTR basic conditions

15.47   This section describes the basic conditions of entitlement for each kind of CTR (para 15.27(a) to (e)). To get CTR you must meet all the basic conditions for the kind you are applying for. Once you are awarded CTR, your CTR continues until you no longer meet them all, at which point it stops.

Main CTR: basic conditions

15.48   The basic conditions for getting main CTR are described in para 15.49:

(a) in Scotland and Wales these rules are the same in every council area (and cannot be varied);

(b) in England your council can vary some of these conditions if you are working age (but not if you are pension age).

The rules about which conditions can be varied in England are described in paras 15.37-38.

15.49   To get main CTR (anywhere in Great Britain) you must meet all of the following:

(a) you are liable to pay council tax for your sole or main residence (para 15.3);

(b) you have made a valid application for CTR and provided the relevant information or evidence (chapter 16);

(c) you are not absent from your home or Great Britain on any day (paras 15.67-75);

(d) you are not excluded by the rules about:

- the upper capital limit (para 15.60),

- migrants and recent arrivals to the UK (para 15.58), or

- students (para 15.62);

(e) any non-dependant deductions that apply are less than your eligible council tax (para 17.15); and

(f) your income is low enough (para 17.5).

See paras 17.3-10 for how your main CTR is calculated and para 15.29 if you qualify for more than one kind of CTR.

15.46   LGFA sch 1B paras 2(2), 6(1)(c),(f); CTPW 12(1), 13, 17, 18

15.49   CTP 11-15, sch 1 paras 1-3; CTR 12, 20-24, 75

Second adult rebate: basic conditions

15.50 Second adult rebate (SAR) applies only in England or Scotland (para 15.27). There are two types, student SAR and general SAR. You are entitled to (either type of) SAR if:

(a) you meet the conditions in para 15.49(a) to (d);

(b) either:

- ▪ you meet the alternative condition (para 15.51) for student SAR,

- ▪ you are the only person liable to pay council tax on your home (general SAR), or

- ▪ there are two or more people liable to pay council tax (including you) and all of you, or all but one of you, is a disregarded person (table 15.2) (general SAR);

(c) there is at least one 'second adult' (para 16.71) who lives with you;

(d) the income of the second adult, or every second adult is low enough (para 17.32); and

(e) no adults in your home pay you rent on a commercial basis.

If you are a student you are entitled to either type of second adult rebate (you are not excluded from SAR: para 15.58). See paras 17.31-35 for how your SAR is calculated and para 15.29 if you qualify for more than one kind of CTR.

15.51 The alternative condition for student SAR (para 15.50) is:

(a) you are the only person liable to pay council tax on your home and you are a student who isn't eligible for main CTR (para 15.63 and table 15.5), or

(b) there are two or more people liable to pay council tax (including you) and all of you are students who aren't in an eligible group for main CTR (para 15.63 and table 15.5).

Scottish special rebate: basic conditions

15.52 If you live in Scotland you can get Scottish special rebate if you meet all the conditions in para 15.49(a) to (f) except that:

(a) in condition (a) your dwelling must be in bands E to H; and

(b) in condition (f) different figures are used instead of your applicable amount to calculate whether your income is low enough (para 17.14).

See paras 17.11-14 for how your Scottish special rebate is calculated and para 15.29 if you qualify for more than one kind of CTR.

Local classes of CTR

15.53 In England and Wales (for pension age and working age) your council can devise new classes in addition to, or (for working applications in England) to replace, main CTR and/or second adult rebate. But any new class must be based on either your personal 'financial need' (i.e. low income) or by your membership of a group that is generally at risk of being in financial

---

15.50   CTP sch 1 para 4; CTR 15, 18

15.51   CTP sch 3 para 1; CTR sch 4 para 1

15.52   CTS 14A; CTS60+ 14A

15.53   England: LGFA 13A(2),(3), sch 1A para 2(2)-(4),(9)
               Wales: LGFA 13A(4),(5), sch 1B paras 3, 4

need (e.g. disability, old age, care leaver aged under 25, etc). The rules about any local CTR class are those that are published by the council (paras 15.39 and 15.46) (and the law about your council's powers to do this are in the footnotes to this para).

Discretionary CTR: basic conditions and how to apply

15.54   In England and Wales only, your council has a wide discretion to reduce your council tax liability 'to such extent as it thinks fit' and this 'includes the power to reduce an amount to nil'. This is called discretionary CTR and it can be awarded even if you do not qualify for, or in addition to, any other the other kind of CTR award.

15.55   The exclusions that apply to the other kinds of CTR (para 15.58) do not apply to discretionary CTR. However, if you are a migrant who is subject to immigration control discretionary CTR counts as 'public funds' so it may not be safe in terms of your immigration status to apply for it [www]. Your council may inform the Home Office if you apply but they are not obliged to do so. (See paras 15.14-23 for other ways to reduce your council tax.)

15.56   Your council can award discretionary CTR based on your personal circumstances or on your membership of a group (a 'class') that is generally at risk of being on low income (e.g. disabled, pension age, etc).

15.57   Your council must publish its rules for discretionary CTR and how to apply, together with its rules for main CTR (para 15.39). In most council schemes you must apply in writing but if your local scheme allows it can be by telephone or online. If your discretionary CTR is based on your membership of a class (para 15.56) your council can treat your application for main CTR as your application for discretionary CTR.

Who is excluded from CTR

15.58   You are excluded from main CTR, Scottish special rebate and any local CTR class if:

(a) you (and your partner's) capital exceeds the upper capital limit (paras 15.60-61);

(b) you (the applicant) are a full time student (paras 15.64-66), and

  ▪ you live in England or Scotland and you are working age, or

  ▪ you live in Wales (whatever your age);

(c) you (the applicant) are a migrant or recent arrival to the UK who:

  ▪ is subject to immigration control (chapter 22),

  ▪ does not have the right to reside in the UK (chapter 23), or

  ▪ is not habitually resident in the British Isles or the Republic of Ireland (chapter 22).

15.54   LGFA 13A(1)(c),(6)

15.55   England: LGFA 13A(1),(2),(3),(9), Sch 1A paras 1, 2(1),(2),(9)
Wales: LGFA 13A(1)(4),(5),(9), Sch 1B paras 1, 3(1)
https://www.gov.uk/guidance/immigration-rules/immigration-rules-introduction#intro6a

15.56   LGFA 13A(1)(c),(7)

15.57   England: LGFA sch 1A para 2(7); CTP sch 7 para 9; CTR sch 1 para 11
Wales: LGFA sch 1B para 5(1)(c),(2); CTPW 12(1), 16(c), sch 12 paras 11, 13; CTRW 11(c), sch 1 para 11

15.58   England: LGFA sch 1A para 2(9); CTP 11(1), 12(1), 13(1); CTR 13-18, 21-24
Wales: LGFA sch 1B para 3(1); CTPW 14(c), 27-31, CTRW 18-22

For working age CTR in England your council can vary the rules in (a) and (b) but not in any other case in England or Wales. The exclusions (a) and (c) (capital limit and migrants) also apply to second adult rebate.

15.59 If you are a couple the exclusions in para 15.58 (b) and (c) (full time students, migrants and recent arrivals) only apply to you (the applicant), so if only one of you is excluded the other should make the application (para 16.2). But if you are subject to immigration control see para 22.13.

The upper capital limit

15.60 The upper capital limit is £16,000 unless you meet one of the exceptions in para 15.61. But in England if you are working age your council can set a lower figure for the limit or vary the exceptions (para 15.38).

15.61 The upper capital limit does not apply if:

(a) you or your partner are on guarantee credit (this applies to all kinds of CTR); or

(b) you apply for second adult rebate in England and your income is less than (or equal to) your applicable amount (para 17.38).

Who is an eligible student

15.62 In England and Scotland, if you are a pension age student you are eligible for CTR in the normal way (and any income from student loans and grants is disregarded). In Wales, you are not entitled to CTR: there are no exceptions.

15.63 In England, Scotland and Wales, if you are a working age 'full-time student' (paras 15.64-66) you are excluded from main CTR (and any locally devised CTR class) unless you fall into one of the 'eligible groups' in table 15.5, but in England these rules can be varied locally. See also para 15.59 if you are a member of a couple.

15.64 You are a 'student' if you are:

(a) 'attending or undertaking a course of study at an educational establishment'; or

(b) claiming JSA and attending an employment-related qualifying course (but this does not apply if you are receiving a training allowance).

The definition in (a) above is broad enough to cover sandwich courses, those where no grant or loan is available and institutions that provide training and instruction as well as education.

15.65 Once your course has started, you continue to be counted as a student until it finishes or you abandon it. So you are counted as a student during any vacation, periods of work experience or sickness absence that occur within the course. But you do not count as a student at the end of the course or between courses.

15.59   CTP 2(1) definition: 'applicant', sch 8 para 4(1); CTR 2(1), 109(1)

15.60   CTP 11(2); CTR 20, 23

15.61   CTP sch 1 para 13, sch 6 para 27; CTR 35, sch 9 para 27, sch 10 para 49

15.62   CTP Part 2, sch 1 paras 2-4; CTR 24, 74

15.63   CTR 24, 75(1),(2)

15.64-66 CTR 73 definitions: 'course of study', 'full-time course of study', 'full-time student', 'modular course', 'student'

15.66 There is no all-embracing definition of 'full-time' (or 'part-time') but your course always counts as full-time if:

(a) it is a sandwich course (i.e. has a period of work experience);

(b) in England and Wales, it is funded by the Department for Education, Welsh Ministers or Skills Funding and requires more than 16 hours guided learning each week (see the students learning agreement or similar document);

(c) in Scotland, you are studying at a college of further education for a course up to and including Scottish Higher or SCOTVEC level 3 that involves more than 16 hours a week in the classroom or workshop based programmed learning or 21 hours a week of either type of tuition or other structured learning supported by teaching staff (as defined in the document signed by the college).

In any other case your council must decide whether a course is full-time by considering factors such as the nature of the course, including the number of hours you are required to attend, how the institution itself describes it and the amount and nature of any grant or loan you receive. But if you are studying on a modular course you will only count as full-time during the parts of the course that you are registered on as full-time.

Table 15.5 **Students eligible for main CTR**

If you are a working age student (para 15.64) you are eligible for main CTR (and Scottish special rebate) if you are:

(a) on JSA(IB), ESA(IR) or income support (or your partner is);

(b) on a part-time course (para 15.66);

(c) aged under 20, in approved training and you were enrolled or accepted on that course before your 19th birthday;

(d) aged under 21 and your course is at a level up to and including GCSE A Level or BTEC/SCOTVEC National Diploma or National Certificate up to level 3 [www] or you are aged 21 and continuing on such a course;

(e) a lone parent or single person responsible for a foster child placed with you by a local authority or voluntary organisation;

(f) a member of a couple who are responsible for a child or young person (para 16.51);

(g) entitled to a disability premium or a severe disability premium;

(h) assessed by the DWP as having limited work capability for ESA purposes for a period of at least 28 weeks;

(i) assessed in your grant award as entitled to an allowance for deafness; or

T15.5   CTR 75(2)
www.gov.uk/what-different-qualification-levels-mean

> (j) unable to get a grant or student loan following an approved absence from your studies due to illness or providing care. This applies only for the period starting when your illness or caring responsibility ends until the day before you resume your course – and only up to a maximum of one year.
>
> **Notes:**
> - If you are pension age see para 15.62.
> - If you are a member of a couple see para 15.59.
> - See para 15.50 for second adult rebate.

Absence from home and from Great Britain

15.67   This section explains when you can get CTR during a temporary absence from home. Paras 15.68-72 give the general rules, and paras 15.73-75 give the exceptions that can apply to absences outside Great Britain.

Absences from home

15.68   Unless you have sub-let your home, you can get CTR during a period of absence:

(a) for up to 13 weeks during a trial period in a care home (or immediately following that: R(H) 4/06) – so long as you intend to return home if the care home is unsuitable (but the total length of your absence must not exceed 52 weeks); or

(b) for up to 52 weeks, but only if you are absent for one of the reasons in table 15.6 – and you intend to return home within 52 weeks or, in exceptional circumstances, not substantially later; or

(c) for up to 13 weeks during an absence for any other reason, but only if you intend to return to your normal home within 13 weeks.

But councils can vary these rules for working age claims in England (para 15.34). And there are exceptions for absences outside Great Britain (paras 15.73-75).

15.69   To get CTR during any absence from home, you must have an 'intention to return'. It is your own intention and not, say, the intention of a relative or official that counts. However, your hope or wish is not on its own sufficient to amount to an intention: it must be capable of being realised. So if it appears (to an impartial observer) that it is impossible for you to return then you cannot be said to have an intention (CSHB/405/2005).

Counting the length of the absence

15.70   The 13-week and 52-week time limits refer to absences which are continuous: R v Penwith DC HBRB ex parte Burt. So, except if you are a prisoner on temporary release, if you return to and occupy the home, even for a short time, the time is reset to zero and starts to run again.

15.67   CTP sch 1 paras 2-5; CTR 13-19

15.68   CTP sch 1 para 5; CTR 19

15.70   R v Penwith DC HBRB ex p Burt 26/02/90 QBD 22 HLR 292

15.71   Your local council must judge whether your absence is likely to exceed the 13/52 week limit by reference to the date you left the home and then subsequently on a week by week basis. If at any later date it seems likely that the limit will be exceeded, then your entitlement to CTR can be revised and ended from that later date (CH/1237/2004). In Scotland only, you may be entitled to a further four weeks CTR at the end of your claim if you move, are liable for council tax on both your old and new homes, and could not have reasonably avoided dual liability.

Table 15.6 **CTR during an absence of up to 52 weeks**

You can get CTR for up to 52 weeks during an absence from your home (para 15.68) if:

(a) you are a patient in hospital or a similar institution;

(b) you are receiving medical treatment or medically approved care or convalescence;

(c) your absence is because your partner or a child is receiving medical treatment or medically approved convalescence;

(d) you are providing medically approved care to someone;

(e) your absence is to care for a child whose parent or guardian is away from their home to receive medical treatment or medically approved care;

(f) you are receiving care in a care home or independent hospital other than during a trial period (e.g. during a period of respite care);

(g) your absence is because of fear of violence;

(h) you are in prison and have not yet been sentenced (para 15.72);

(i) you are in a probation hostel, or a bail hostel, or bailed to live away from your normal home;

(j) you are a student who is eligible for CTR (e.g. if you have to study away from home for part of your course);

(k) you are following a training course.

Note: In this table and in para 15.74, 'medically approved' means approved by a GP, nurse or similar.

Absences in prison

15.72   If you are in prison but have not been sentenced (for example if you are on remand) you can get CTR for up to 52 weeks. If you are later sentenced this counts as a change of circumstances and your local council must then consider whether you will return home within 13 weeks from the date you first left the home. You can only continue to be entitled if it looks like you will return within 13 weeks from your first day in custody: this time limit is rigid (CH/499/2006 and CH/1986/2009). However, most sentences qualify for remission, so if your sentence is six months or less (ten if you are eligible for Home Detention Curfew) you are likely to be entitled.

15.71   CTP sch 1 para 5(2); CTR 19(2)

T15.6   CTP sch 1 para 5(3),(6); CTR 19(3),(6)

Absences from Great Britain

15.73   You can get CTR during temporary absence from Great Britain, but there are different rules about this in England, Scotland and Wales (paras 15.74-75). In all these cases you can only get CTR if your absence is temporary; so you must have an intention to return, and if you decide later not to return your CTR ends on the date you make that decision.

Absences from Great Britain: CTR in England and Scotland

15.74   For pension age claims in England, or for all claims in Scotland, you can get CTR during a temporary absence from Great Britain:

(a) during your first four weeks (in Scotland, first month) of absence, whatever the reason (and in Scotland only, provided also you were not absent on more than two occasions during the 52 weeks before it began);

(b) during your second four weeks (in Scotland, second month) of absence, but only in connection with the death of a family member or a close relative of your family and it would be unreasonable to expect you to return;

(c) in England, for up to 26 weeks if:

- you are a patient in hospital or similar institution, or

- you are receiving medical treatment or medically approved care or convalescence, or

- your absence is because your partner or child is receiving medical treatment or medically approved convalescence, or

- your absence is because of fear of violence;

(d) in Scotland, for up to six months if it is solely in connection with:

- you or a member of your family are being treated for an illness or physical or mental disability, by a person qualified to provide medical treatment, physiotherapy, or similar related treatment, or

- you are undergoing convalescence or care, which results from treatment for an illness or physical or mental disability you had before you left and which has been medically approved;

(e) for up to 26 weeks (in Scotland, without any time limit) if your absence is due to your or your partner's employment as:

- a member of HM armed forces,

- a mariner with a UK contract of employment,

- a continental shelf worker in EU or Norwegian waters, or

- in Scotland, a Crown servant.

For working age claims in England, local councils can apply the above rules or those in paras 15.67-72.

Absences from Great Britain: CTR in Wales

15.75   For all claims in Wales, the rules in 15.67-72 apply to absences outside Great Britain (as well as absences within Great Britain).

15.74   CTP sch 1 para 5(2)(d),(2E),(2F),(3B)-(3G); reg 3 of SI 2016/1262

Chapter 16 **Applying for council tax rebate**

- Who can apply for council tax rebate: see paras 16.1-5.
- How to apply: see paras 16.6-9.
- The information and evidence needed: see paras 16.10-16.
- How complete and incomplete applications are dealt with: see paras 16.17-22.
- When CTR starts: see paras 16.23-27.
- Backdating applications: see paras 16.28-35.
- Length of award and payment: see paras 16.36-38.
- Who is included in your application: see paras 16.39-71.

Who can apply

16.1   You only get council tax rebate if you apply for it. It is your responsibility to apply but you can ask anyone you like to help you fill in the form. In CTR law you are called the 'applicant'.

Couples

16.2   If you are a couple you or your partner can make the application and whoever does is the applicant. In some circumstances – identified in this guide as they arise (e.g. paras 15.59, 16.32, 17.48) – you are better off if one of you rather than the other is the applicant. You can choose which one of you is going to apply but if you can't agree, the council must choose. Regardless of who is the applicant, in practice both of you may be asked to sign the form.

Unable to act

16.3   If you are unable to act for the time being someone else can apply for CTR on your behalf (paras 16.4-5) and this other person has all the rights and responsibilities that normally belong to you (paras 16.10 and 19.2). (The rules in paras 16.4-5 apply in England and Wales and although they do not appear in Scottish CTR law, similar principles apply.)

16.4   Where one of the following has been appointed to act for you, the council must accept an application from them:

   (a) a receiver or deputy appointed by the Court of Protection;

   (b) an attorney with a general power or a power to apply or, as the case may be, receive benefit;

16.1   England: LGFA sch 1A para 2(5); CTP 15, sch 7 paras 1-7, 10-16, sch 8 para 4; CTR 11, 109, sch 1 paras 1-7, 12-18
        Scotland: CTS 14(3)(c), 83, 84; CTS60+ 14(3)(c), 63, 64
        Wales: LGFA sch 1B para 5(1)(a); CTPW 34, sch 12 paras 1-7, 12-18, sch 13 para 1; CTRW 11, 107, sch 1 paras 1-7, 12-18
16.2   CTP sch 8 para 4(1); CTR 109(1)
16.3   CTP sch 8 para 4(2)-(7); CTR 109(2)-(7)
16.4   CTP sch 8 para 4(2),(4); CTR 109(2),(4)

(c) in Scotland, a judicial factor or any guardian acting or appointed under the Adults with Incapacity (Scotland) Act 2000; or

(d) a person appointed by the DWP to act on your behalf in connection with some other benefit.

16.5   In any other case, the council may accept a written request from someone over 18, or a firm or organisation, to be your 'appointee' – for example, a friend or relative, a social worker or solicitor. In doing this the council should take account of any conflict of interests. Either the council or the appointee can end the appointment by giving four weeks' written notice.

How to apply

Applications made to the council

16.6   You, or someone acting on your behalf (para 16.3), should make your application for CTR to the council that issues your council tax bill (para 15.2). You can apply for CTR in writing (normally on the council's form but it could be a letter) to the council's 'designated office' which is the address identified on the form. The application form must be provided free of charge and give the address of every designated office. Your council may also accept an application by telephone which must be made to the number the council has published for that purpose. If you apply by telephone your council can ask you to approve a written statement of your application.

16.7   In England and Wales many councils also accept online applications. If you apply online your council can ask to keep a written or electronic record of your online application. The online address is often published on your council's (written) form.

16.8   If you make a claim to the DWP for JSA, ESA, IS, UC or pension credit you may be asked if you want to apply for CTR. If you do the DWP may inform the council. But this is not an application for CTR. Your application for CTR should be made direct to the council (DCLG – *Localising council tax support administrative matters – guidance note*, March 2013 paras 10-12) [www].

Amending or withdrawing your application

16.9   Before your application is decided, you may:

(a) amend it: the change is treated as having been made from the outset;

(b) withdraw it: the council does not then have to decide it.

You can amend or withdraw a telephone application on the phone or in writing. If you phone the council may ask you to confirm your amendment or withdrawal in writing. In any other case, you must amend or withdraw your application in writing to the council's designated office (para 16.6).

16.5   CTP sch 8 para 4(3),(5); CTR 109(3),(5)

16.6   CTP 2(1) 'designated office', sch 7 paras 2(a),(c), 3, 6; CTR 2(1), sch 1 paras 2(a),(c), 3, 6

16.7   CTP sch 7 paras 2(b), 11(5),(6); CTR sch 1 paras 2(b), 13(5),(6)

16.8   CTP sch 7 paras 2-3, sch 1 paras 2-3
         https://www.gov.uk/government/publications/localising-support-for-council-tax-guidance-note-on-administrative-matters

16.9   CTP sch 8 para 8; CTR 114

Information and evidence

16.10   You are responsible for providing 'certificates, documents, information and evidence' which is 'reasonably required to determine […] your entitlement' to CTR. This applies when you make an application, and also during the course of your award. The council should only get evidence direct from someone else with your written agreement but you usually give this in the declaration you make when you apply.

16.11   The law does not specify (except as described in paras 16.12-15) what information and evidence is required for any particular aspect of your claim. In practice your council can ask for evidence about your household members and their status, income and capital (if you are not on a passport benefit), and other matters; and expect you to provide original documents rather than copies. In written applications, your signature is a reasonable requirement, and it is common practice for the council to also ask for your partner's signature.

Information and evidence about income and capital

16.12   The following rules (paras 16.13-15) about evidence of income apply to all applications for main CTR in Scotland and Wales and to pension age applications in England. For working age claims in England they apply if your council has adopted the equivalent rule about how your income is assessed (paras 18.5 and 18.59) as part of its local scheme (such as the default scheme rules: para 15.36) and in practice nearly all councils apply the passport benefit rule (para 16.13).

16.13   If you have been lawfully awarded a passport benefit by the DWP, your council must accept this as proof that (at the relevant dates) you meet the income-related conditions to get maximum CTR: R v Penwith DC ex p Menear and R v South Ribble HBRB ex p Hamilton. If you have been lawfully awarded savings credit or UC, your council must use the DWP's figures for income and capital (paras 18.6-7).

16.14   The council cannot ask you for any information or evidence whatsoever about the following types of payment, whether they are made to you, your partner, a non-dependant or a second adult:

(a)   payments from certain Government funded trusts made to a person who was infected with HIV or hepatitis C from NHS blood products (para 18.59), or from the London Bombing Charitable Relief Fund, and in certain cases payment from any of these sources that was made to a relative but passed onto you;

(b)   payments in kind of capital from a charity or from the above sources;

(c)   payments in kind of income from any source.

16.10   CTP sch 8 para 7(4); CTR 113(4)

16.13   R v Penwith DC ex p Menear [1991] 24 HLR 115; www.rightsnet.org.uk/pdfs/R_V_Penwith_DC_exp_Menear.pdf
          R v South Ribble HBRB ex p Hamilton [2000] EWCA Civ 518
          www.bailii.org/ew/cases/EWCA/Civ/2000/518.html

16.14   CTP sch 8 para 7(5),(7); CTR 113(5),(7)

National Insurance numbers

16.15   You must either:

(a) provide your national insurance number and your partner's, along with information or evidence to establish this; or

(b) provide information or evidence to help the council identify it; or

(c) if you don't have a national insurance number, make an application for one and give the information or evidence to assist with this – even if it is highly improbable that one will be granted: CH/4085/2007.

This rule does not apply to your partner if he or she is subject to immigration control (chapter 22) and it is not a legal requirement if you apply for CTR in Scotland, although in practice most Scottish councils will ask for it.

16.16   You can appeal any matter about the requirement to provide a national insurance number, including the evidence the council needs to confirm one: CH/1231/2004; and the consequences for your CTR if the DWP refuses to allocate one: 2009 UKUT 74 (ACC).

Complete and incomplete applications

A complete application

16.17   Your application is complete if it is made:

(a) in writing or online and is on an application form approved by the council and completed in accordance with the instructions on it – including any instructions to provide information and evidence;

(b) in some other written form which the council accepts as sufficient in the circumstances, having regard to the information and evidence provided with it;

(c) by telephone and you provide the information and evidence needed to decide it.

Dealing with complete applications

16.18   If your application is complete (para 16.17) (also sometimes called an 'effective' or 'valid' application) the council must decide it.

Dealing with incomplete applications

16.19   An incomplete application (sometimes called a 'defective' application) is one which the council gets but which does not meet the conditions in para 16.17. The council should give you the opportunity to do whatever is needed to complete it. Depending on the circumstances, this could mean the council:

(a) send you an application form;

(b) return a form to you to complete (e.g. if you missed a question); or

(c) ask you for information and evidence (or further information and evidence).

16.15   CTP sch 8 para 7(2),(3); CTR 113(2),(3)

16.17   CTP sch 7 paras 2-5, 7, 11(5),(7); CTR sch 1 paras 2-5, 7, 13(5),(7)

16.18   CTP sch 8 para 11; CTR 116

In all cases, the council must also inform you of your duty to tell it about relevant changes of circumstances which occur, and say what these are likely to be.

16.20 The council must allow you at least one month to provide what is required (see note, table 16.1), and you must be allowed longer if it is reasonable to do so. If you have applied by telephone, the law expressly allows you more than one reminder, and the month is counted from the last such reminder. In the case of written and online applications, some authorities send a reminder, allowing a further period for the reply. In all these cases, if you do what is required within the time limit, your application is treated as having been complete from the outset.

Deciding incomplete applications

16.21 If you fail to complete a written or online application (para 16.20) within the time limit the council does not have to decide it (and if so there is no decision you can appeal). If you apply by telephone but your application is incomplete the council must decide it (and it may, at its discretion decide an incomplete written or online application) but in doing so it may:

(a) decide that you are not entitled to CTR because you do not satisfy the conditions of entitlement, as you have not provided the necessary information or evidence; or

(b) assume the worst in order to decide it. For example, if your bank statement shows that you withdrew £20,000 three weeks ago, and you refuse to explain this, it might be reasonable to decide that your capital remains at £20,000.

In each case, you may appeal.

Applications not received

16.22 The council can't decide an application that it hasn't received – for example an application form which is lost in the post. An (attempted) telephone application in which you do not answer all the questions, or fail to approve a written statement if asked to do so, is treated as 'not received' – but in this case the council may nonetheless decide it. An (attempted) online application which the council's computer does not accept or which is not in the form approved (para 16.7) is treated as 'not received'. In all these cases, if you apply for CTR again, the council should consider whether the conditions for backdating are met (para 16.28).

When CTR starts

England and Scotland

16.23 Unless the exception in para 16.24 applies, your CTR starts on the Monday following your 'date of application' (para 16.27). Even if your date of application is a Monday, your first day of entitlement is the following Monday. The rules about what counts as your 'date of application' are in table 16.1.

16.19-20 CTP sch 7 paras 4, 5, 7, sch 8 para 5(3)-(5); CTR 110(3)-(5), sch 1 paras 4, 5, 7

16.21-22 CTP sch 7 paras 3(1), 6, 7(2), 11(7), 13(3), sch 8 para 5(3)(b); CTR 110(5)(b), sch 1 paras 3(1), 6, 7(2), 13(7), 15(3)

16.23 CTP sch1 para 45(1); CTR 106(1)

16.24   The exception to the general rule (para 16.23) applies if your 'date of application' falls in the 'reduction week' (para 16.25) that your council tax liability begins (e.g. if you have just moved home). In this case, your entitlement begins on the day your liability for council tax begins, whichever day of the week that falls on.

16.25   In CTR law the 'reduction week' is the period that begins on a Monday and ends on the following Sunday.

Wales

16.26   In Wales your CTR starts on your 'date of application' (para 16.27): there are no exceptions to this rule. The rules about what counts as your 'date of application' are in table 16.1 and further details follow.

Examples: When CTR starts (England and Scotland)

The general rule

A man applies for CTR because his income has reduced. His date of application is Thursday 12th July 2018.

His first day of entitlement to CTR is the Monday following his date of application, which is Monday 16th July 2018.

Applying in the week liability begins: whole weeks

A woman moves into her flat on Monday 2nd July 2018, and is liable for council tax from that very day. Her date of application is Thursday 5th July 2018.

Her first day of entitlement to CTR is the day her liability for council tax begins, which is Monday 2nd July 2018.

Applying in the week liability begins: part weeks

A woman moves into her flat on Saturday 2nd June 2018, and is liable for council tax from that very day. Her date of application is Friday 1st June 2018.

Her first day of entitlement to CTR is the day her liability for council tax begins, which is Saturday 2nd June 2018. In her first week she gets two-sevenths of a week's CTR (for the Saturday and the Sunday).

Applying in the week liability begins: applicant does not move in immediately

A man has been living with relatives (and not liable for council tax there). He gets a tenancy which starts on Monday 28th May 2018. He does not fully move in until Wednesday 30th May 2018, and that is the night he starts sleeping there. His date of application for CTR is Thursday 31st May 2018.

His first day of entitlement to CTR depends on when he first becomes liable for council tax. Practice varies, but it is likely to be Monday 28th May 2018 or Wednesday 30th May 2018.

Note: In Wales your CTR starts on the date of your application (para 16.26).

16.24   CTP sch 1 para 45(2); CTR 106(2)

16.25   CTP 2(1) 'reduction week'; CTR 2(1)

16.26   CTPW sch 1 para 39; sch 6 para 45; CTRW 104

16.27   CTP sch 8 para 5; CTR 110

Date of application

16.27   The date of your application is the date your form (together with any information and evidence) is received at the council's designated office, the date of your telephone call or if you apply online the date recorded by the computer unless the council reasonably decides otherwise. In some cases the date of your application can be earlier than this: see table 16.1.

Table 16.1 **Date of application for CTR**	
Situation	**Date of application**
(a) You told the council that you intend to apply ■ You told the council about your intention to apply; ■ it sent you an application form; and ■ you returned the form within one month of when it was sent out (or longer if the council considers this reasonable). You can tell your council about your intention to apply 'by any means' (e.g. telephone, email, letter text, visiting or sending a friend: CIS/2726/2005).	The date you told the council about your intention to apply.
(b) Following your partner's death or separation ■ You apply within one month of your partner's death or of your separation; and ■ your partner was on CTR at the date of death or separation.	The date of the separation or death.
(c) You claim a passport benefit or UC ■ You, or a partner, claim and are awarded a passport benefit (JSA(IB), ESA(IR), IS or guarantee credit) or UC; and ■ your application gets to the council no more than one month after the passport benefit or UC claim was received by the DWP.	The date your passport benefit or UC starts or your first waiting day if you claim JSA(IB) or ESA(IR).
(d) On a passport benefit when your liability starts ■ You or your partner are getting a passport benefit; and ■ you become liable for council tax for the first time; and ■ your application gets to the council no more than one month after your new liability begins.	The first day of your new liability for council tax.

16.27   CTP sch 7 paras 13-16, sch 8 para 5(1)(f),(g); CTR 110(1)(f),(g), sch 1 paras 15-18

T16.1   CTP sch 8 para 5(1)(a)-(g),(2),(3); CTR 110(1)(a)-(g),(2),(3)

(e) You apply in advance ▪ You apply up to 17 weeks before you reach pension credit age; or ▪ you apply up to 17 weeks before an event that makes you entitled (pension age applications); or ▪ you apply up to 13 weeks before an event which makes you entitled to CTR (working age applications); or ▪ you apply up to eight weeks before you become liable for council tax. But the last two do not apply if you are a migrant or new arrival (para 15.58).	Any date in the week before the reduction week (para 16.25) containing the birthday or event in question.
(f) Delays in the council tax being set You are liable for council tax in Scotland; and your council sets its council tax after 31st March; and you apply within four weeks after the date it is set.	The 1st April in that year (or the reduction week in which your entitlement begins if this is later).
(g) Any other application ▪ If none of the above (a)-(f) apply.	The date your application is received at the designated office or the date your application is backdated to if this is earlier (paras 16.28-35).

Note

In items (b)-(d) the one month time limit cannot be extended. In items (a)-(d) 'one month' means a calendar month, counted as follows (R(IB) 4/02):

▪ if the council sends out a letter on 26th June asking you to provide something, you have provided it within a month if you get it to the council by the end of 26th July;

▪ if the council sends out a letter on 31st January asking you to provide something, you have provided it within a month if you get it to the council by the end of 28th (or 29th) February.

Things sent out by the council (such as requests for information or evidence, decision letters) are counted as being sent out on the date of posting.

Backdating of applications

16.28   In certain circumstances (paras 16.31 and 16.33) the date of your application can be earlier than the date in table 16.1, so that your CTR covers a period before you actually applied for it.

16.29   If you applied for CTR on a form which was (on the balance of probability) received by the council, but then mislaid or not acted on, this is not backdating (because in fact the application was made): if CTR is refused you can request a review on the ground of a mistaken fact (para 19.38).

16.30   It is the date of your application which is backdated so even if you are not currently entitled to CTR you can get a payment for an earlier period. Any award is calculated using the rules which applied at the time for the period it covers. Your entitlement does not need to have been continuous or at the same address (or even, arguably, in the same council's area).

Backdating pension age applications

16.31   If you are pension age (table 15.4) your application covers any period in the three months before the date of your application (table 16.1(a)). You do not have to ask for backdating and you do not have to have 'good cause' (or any reason whatsoever). But in any case this cannot be earlier than:

(a)   the day you reached state pension credit age;

(b)   the day your liability for council tax first started; or

(c)   if you claimed pension credit at the same time (table 16.1(c)), any day earlier than three months before the date you claimed pension credit.

16.32   If you are a couple and only one of you is pension credit age you could have a working age or a pension age application, so whether (or for how long) you qualify for backdating can depend on which of you applies (table 15.4 and para 16.2).

Example: Backdating for a pension age applicant

An applicant aged 73 sends in his first ever application for CTR. It reaches the council on Friday 7th September 2018. He would have qualified for several years for a small amount of CTR had he applied.

His date of application is Friday 8th June 2018, which is three months earlier, and (unless his liability for council tax started in the same reduction week: para 16.24) his CTR starts the following Monday (para 16.23), 11th June 2018 (but see para 16.26 for Wales).

Backdating working age applications

16.33   If you have a working age application (table 15.4), the rules about backdating vary:

(a)   In England, your council can set its own backdating rules (para 15.34) such as the time limit or any other conditions (such as 'good cause'). For example, the default scheme allows backdating for 'good cause' for up to six months, but most councils have reduced this to one month or three months, and some have no backdating (but may consider making a discretionary council tax reduction instead: para 15.54). In practice, most councils adopt the good cause rule (as part of the default scheme: para 15.36) with a maximum limit of one, three or six months.

16.31   CTP sch 8 para 6; CTR 111

16.33   CTP sch 8 para 6(1); CTR 112

(b) In Scotland, application must be backdated for up to six months (prior to 1st April 2018 one month) if you ask for this in writing (whether on the council's application form or separately later); and you 'had continuous good cause for your failure to make an application' (as described in paras 16.34-35).

(c) In Wales, the CTR backdating rules are usually the same as for Scotland but with a time limit of three months. However, your council may extend (but not reduce) this time limit and vary the backdating rules in other ways (table 15.3 and para 15.42).

'Good cause'

16.34   Good cause has been explained by tribunals and courts right back to the late 1940s, and this case law is binding: CH/5221/2001. The following are the main principles.

16.35   Good cause includes 'any fact that would probably have caused a reasonable person to act as the claimant did': merely not knowing that you are entitled is not itself sufficient – you (the applicant) are expected to have taken reasonable steps to find out what your rights may be. But you cannot always be assumed to have an understanding of public administration (CS/371/1949, quoted with approval in CH/450/2004). However, this 'traditional formulation' has been criticised ([2010] UKUT 64 (ACC)) because:

(a) it does not reflect the language of the regulations;

(b) it introduces subjective elements while what is 'reasonable' is objective;

(c) not knowing about CTR is not good cause itself, it may be a factor to be taken into account. The law does not expect you 'to be acquainted with the "rules and regulations".'

Length of award and payment

Length of award (when CTR ends)

16.36   There is no set limit to your CTR award. If there is a change in circumstances (para 19.10) this does not end your award unless the change means you no longer meet all the basic conditions of entitlement (para 15.48-57), the revised amount is nil, or you move outside your council area.

Payments of CTR

16.37   CTR is normally paid as a rebate (credit) to your council tax account so that your overall liability is reduced. Any resulting credit on your council tax account may be refunded. The DCLG advises that this can be done, for example, if you are no longer liable for council tax (*Localising council tax support,* November 2012, para 23).

16.38   However, in England and Wales only, the council may pay CTR directly to you if:

(a) you are jointly liable for council tax; and

(b) awarding CTR as a rebate 'would be inappropriate'.

If you are unable to act, this payment can be made to an appointee, etc.

16.37   England: LGFA 13A(1)(a)
         Wales: LGFA 13A(1)(b), CTPW sch 13 para 10(1); CTRW 116(1)

16.38   CTP sch 8 para 14; CTR 118

Who is included in your application

16.39 This section describes how other people who live with you are categorised (e.g. dependent child, lodger, etc) when assessing your CTR application. This is important because each category affects your CTR assessment in different ways. It describes:

(a) who counts as a member of your family (partners and dependent children);

(b) who counts as your partner;

(c) how and when a child is treated as part of your family;

(d) how fostered and adopted children are treated in your claim;

(e) what happens when your partner or child is absent from the home;

(f) who counts as a non-dependant; and

(g) other occupiers who live with you.

Who is a member of your household

16.40 The members of your household include:

(a) family members:

- you (para 16.43),

- your partner(s) (para 16.46),

- dependent children or young persons (para 16.51);

(b) foster children (para 16.56);

(c) non-dependants (para 16.58).

Other people who live with you

16.41 Other people who live in your home that affect your CTR award may include:

(a) lodgers (with or without board) (para 16.62);

(b) joint tenants or joint owners (para 16.66);

(c) certain carers (para 16.68).

In each case the effect on your CTR award is as described in the appropriate paragraph.

Straightforward cases vs complex households

16.42 In most cases assessing your CTR is fairly straightforward if the only people who live with you are the members of your family (i.e. you, your partner and dependent children). But where your circumstances are more complex such as: responsibility for children is shared; your child has reached age 16; a member of your family lives elsewhere; or other people live with you (e.g. a lodger); there are rules to deal with these situations and how they affect your CTR (see example for a complex household).

Example: People who live with you

The following people live with you in your (large) home.

(a) Your partner and dependent children. They are your (CTR) 'family' (para 16.44).

(b) Your foster child. This child is ignored when assessing your CTR (para 16.56), and so is the income from any fostering allowance you receive (para 18.51).

(c) Your parents and your sister. They are your non-dependants (para 16.58).

(d) Your sister has a partner who lives abroad. Because her partner does not live with you, they are ignored when assessing your CTR.

(e) Your sister's baby. Her baby is ignored in assessing CTR (para 16.61).

(f) A lodger who rents a room from you. Part of the income from the lodger is counted (para 18.53).

Claimant and family

16.43   To assess your CTR claim the law will consider you to be in one of three basic household types:

(a) a single claimant – i.e. if you do not have a partner and are not responsible for a child/young person;

(b) a lone parent – i.e. if you do not have a partner and you are responsible for a child or young person; or

(c) you are a member of a couple or polygamous marriage – whether or not responsible for a child or young person. Only one member of a couple or polygamous marriage can claim (the other member is the claimant's partner).

16.44   A person is a member of your 'family' if they are:

(a) your partner; or

(b) a child or young person you are responsible for (they need not be your son or daughter);

and, in each case, they are also a member of your household (para 16.45).

16.45   The term 'household' is not defined in the law but broadly it means anyone who lives in the same dwelling as part of a larger interdependent unit that is self-sufficient as a whole and independent from other occupiers. For example, a landlady and her family would be one household and her lodger another.

Your partner

16.46   If you are in a couple your partner simply means the other member unless they are absent and not treated as part of your household (para 16.45). Partner includes any member of a polygamous marriage, provided the union took place in a country that allows polygamy; in any other case any second or subsequent partner is a non-dependant.

16.43   CTP 2(1) definitions: 'couple', 'lone parent', 'single applicant', 4; CTR 2(1), 4

16.44   CTP 6; CTR 6

16.46   CTP 2(1) definition: 'partner'; CTR 2(1)

16.47 The term 'couple' refers to married couples and civil partners, and also to two people living together as though they were married or in a civil partnership.

16.48 In deciding whether you live together as though you are married, the first consideration is your intention (for example, if your relationship is one of lodger and landlord you will not normally be considered a couple). If this is unclear, it is decided by looking at your relationship and living arrangements (e.g. stability of your relationship, financial arrangements, how others see you). No single factor is conclusive: what matters is the relationship as a whole (R(SB)17/81).

16.49 If your partner is temporarily living away from your home they will continue to be included as a member of your household. CTR law does not define what temporary absence means in this case, so it must be decided according to the facts in each case.

16.50 If your partner does not count as a member of the household, their needs, income and capital should not be taken into account when calculating your CTR. Any money you receive from them should be treated as maintenance (paras 18.54-55).

Children and young persons

16.51 Any child or young person you are responsible for and who is part of your household counts as a member of your family. A 'child' means someone under the age of 16.

16.52 A 'young person' means someone aged 16-19 who you are getting (or could get) child benefit for because they are in secondary education or their 'child benefit extension period'. Broadly this means any child who is: still at school or sixth form college studying a course up A Level, Scottish Higher or NVQ level 3 and not claiming JSA/IS/ESA in their own right. It also includes some 16-17 year olds who have recently left education or training for up to 20 weeks after they left the course.

16.53 You are treated as being responsible for any child or young person who normally lives with you. This is usually straightforward; and, when it is, whether you receive child benefit (or not) is irrelevant. But if the child spends an equal amount of time in another household (such as when you share responsibility with your ex-partner), or if there is doubt over which household they are living in, they are treated as living with the person who gets the child benefit.

16.54 If a child or young person you are responsible for is temporarily living elsewhere, they continue to be included in your household. CTR law does not define what is meant by temporary absence in this case, so it must be decided according to the facts in each case.

16.55 If you are not responsible for a child or young person (because of the rules above) they are ignored when calculating your applicable amount (chapter 17).

16.47   CTP 4; CTR 4

16.49   CTP 8(1); CTR 8(1)

16.50   CTP 4(1); CTR 4(1)

16.51   CTP 8(1); CTR 8(1)

16.52   CTP 2(1) definition: 'young person', 6(2),(3); CTR 2(1), 6(2),(3)

16.53   CTP 7; CTR 7

16.54   CTP 8(1); CTR 8(1)

16.55   CTP sch 1 para 6; CTR 25, 26

Fostering, adoption, etc

16.56   A child or young person is not counted as a member of your household if they are living with you as your foster child or placed with you for adoption (but once adopted they become part of your household).

16.57   A child is not counted as part of your household if they are absent because they are looked after, or in the care of a local authority. But if that child is still living with you while under supervision they do count as part of your household.

Non-dependants

16.58   In broad terms, a non-dependant is someone who normally lives with you on a non-commercial basis. Typical examples are adult daughters, sons, other relatives and friends.

16.59   Anyone who 'normally resides' with you is a non-dependant, unless they are:

(a) a member of your family (para 16.44);

(b) a foster child or other child who is not counted as part of your household (paras 16.56 and 16.61);

(c) a lodger (para 16.62) and any member of their household;

(d) a joint occupier (para 16.66);

(e) a paid carer in certain circumstances (para 16.68).

'Normally resides' is not defined, so each case must be considered on its own facts.

16.60   A person who is staying with you but who normally lives elsewhere (such as a visitor or friend on holiday) is not normally residing and so is not a non-dependant. But a temporary arrangement could eventually become permanent and so at some point (for example, a homeless friend after six months) the council may decide a change of circumstances has occurred and they have become a non-dependant (CH/4004/2004 and CH/3935/2007).

16.61   The partner of a non-dependant is also a non-dependant (but there is only one non-dependant deduction, if any: para 17.28). If your non-dependant has a child, there is normally no deduction made (table 17.1).

Lodgers

16.62   A lodger is someone who lives with you as a commercial arrangement and pays you (or your partner) 'rent'. CTR rules distinguish between two different types:

(a) a lodger who pays you an inclusive charge for meals as well as their accommodation (sometimes called a 'boarder');

(b) any other lodger (i.e. no meals included), sometimes called a 'sub-tenant'.

16.56   CTP 8(2),(3); CTR 8(2),(3)

16.57   CTP 8(4); CTR 8(4)

16.59   CTP 9(1),(2); CTR 9(1),(2)

16.62   CTP 9(2)(e); CTR 9(2)(e)

16.63 In the first case above (para 16.62(a)), at least one 'meal' must be provided – for example, breakfast every day is enough. The meal must be cooked or prepared, and consumed on the premises; and the cooking or preparation must be done by someone other than the boarder themselves.

16.64 Income from a lodger is taken into account in the assessment of your CTR (para 18.53). The method is more favourable if you provide your lodger with meals.

Lodger vs non-dependant

16.65 Both lodgers and non-dependants may make payments to the claimant and have exclusive occupation of, say, a bedroom. But there are many examples of informal arrangements (such as with family members or friends) where exclusive occupation does not result in a tenancy: [2012] UKUT 114 (AAC). The distinction between a lodger and a non-dependant therefore hinges more on whether there is a tenancy or similar commercial arrangement between the parties.

Joint occupiers

16.66 If you have joint liability for the council tax with someone other than your partner then they are a joint occupier for CTR purposes (para 15.12). It includes both joint owners and joint tenants who are not part of your household, for example they might be your friend, brother, sister, or parent as house-sharers or flat-sharers.

16.67 You, and each other joint occupier, are entitled to CTR in your own right (so long as you meet the conditions in the ordinary way) but you only receive CTR on your share of the bill: see para 17.10 for how this is worked out for main CTR and para 17.35 for second adult rebate.

Carers

16.68 If you receive care from a member of your family, a non-dependant, a lodger or a joint occupier, then they are taken into account in that category. For example, if your nephew comes to care for you, he is taken into account as a non-dependant and there are no further rules.

16.69 Any other resident carer who lives with you will count as a non-dependant unless:

(a) they live with you to look after you or your partner; and

(b) the carer is engaged by a charity or voluntary organisation (not a public or local authority); and

(c) that organisation makes a charge to the claimant or partner for the services provided.

If the carer meets all of the conditions (a)-(c) then they cannot be a non-dependant and so no non-dependant charge can be made. Note that certain other paid carers are a disregarded person in terms of council tax liability (table 15.2) and these two categories may sometimes overlap.

16.65   CTP 9(3); CTR 9(3)

16.66   CTP 9(2)(d),(3); CTR 9(2)(d),(3)

16.69   CTP 9(2)(d),(3); CTR 9(2)(d),(3)

Employees

16.70   If you employ someone who lives in your home (e.g. a nanny or au pair) they are not a non-dependant and have no effect on your main CTR (but they may count as a second adult).

Second adults

16.71   A second adult means someone who lives with you and who:

(a) is aged 18 or over;

(b) is not a member of your family (i.e. a young person (para 16.52);

(c) is not liable for council tax (including someone who is exempt from the normal rules about joint liability: para 15.13);

(d) who does not pay you rent on a commercial basis (para 16.62); and

(e) is not a 'disregarded person' (table 15.2).

Most non-dependants who are not a disregarded person are second adults. It probably includes any care worker who is not disregarded (table 15.2(f)) and domestic staff (para 16.70).

16.70   CTP 9(2)(e); CTR 9(2)(e)

16.71   CTP sch 1 para 4(3), sch 3 para 1(1); CTR 15(3), 18(3), sch 4 para 1(1)

Chapter 17 **Calculating CTR**

- ■ Main CTR: see paras 17.3-10.
- ■ Scottish special rebate: see paras 17.11-14.
- ■ Non-dependant deductions: see paras 17.15-30.
- ■ Second adult rebate: see paras 17.31-35.
- ■ Converting figures to weekly amounts: see paras 17.36-37.
- ■ Applicable amounts: see paras 17.38-77.

17.1　This chapter explains how to calculate main CTR, Scottish special rebate and second adult rebate. The full conditions for getting these and discretionary CTR are in chapter 15.

17.2　If you qualify for more than one of the three main kinds of CTR, you are only awarded whichever is the highest of them. This is sometimes referred to as the 'better buy' (see also para 15.29).

Main CTR

17.3　Main CTR is available to both pension age and working age claimants throughout Great Britain, but only if your capital isn't over the upper capital limit (paras 15.60-61). In all other cases, to calculate main CTR work through the steps in paras 17.4-10.

Maximum rebate

17.4　The starting point is your weekly 'maximum rebate' (also called 'maximum reduction'). This is:

(a) the weekly amount of your council tax (para 17.36) or your share of it if you are a joint occupier (para 17.10) – this is called your 'eligible council tax';

(b) minus any non-dependant deductions that apply to you (para 17.15).

For working age claims in England, your maximum rebate can be lower (para 15.38): for example, it can be limited to a percentage of your council tax (usually between 70% and 90%) or to a particular band. It can't be lower for pension age claims in England or for any claims in Scotland and Wales.

Low income for main CTR

17.5　Your income is low enough to qualify for main CTR if:

(a) you or your partner receive guarantee credit, JSA(IB), ESA(IR) or income support (para 18.5); or

(b) you have no income, or no income apart from UC; or

17.2　CTP sch 1 para 10(5),(6); CTR 32(5),(6)
17.4　CTP sch 1 para 7(1); CTR 29(1)

(c)   your income is less than (or equal to) your 'applicable amount'; or

(d)   your income is greater than your applicable amount but the 'excess income' multiplied by the 'taper' (paras 17.6-7) is less than your maximum CTR.

If any of items (a)-(c) apply then you qualify for maximum rebate (para 17.4). In any other case see para 17.6.

Amount of main CTR: income greater than applicable amount

17.6　　　If your income is more than your applicable amount (para 17.8), the difference between the two is called your 'excess income'. You qualify for:

(a)   maximum rebate (para 17.4);

(b)   minus a fixed percentage (the 'taper': para 17.7) of your excess income.

If the result is zero or negative you do not qualify for CTR and for working age claims in England you do not qualify for CTR if the result is positive but less than your minimum award (para 17.9).

17.7　　　The 'taper' is 20% for pension age claims in England and all claims in Scotland and Wales but for working age claims in England it can be varied (para 15.38) and if it is, it is nearly always higher: in some areas it can be as high as 35%.

How the applicable amount and income are calculated

17.8　　　Your income and applicable amount are calculated as follows:

(a)   if you are on UC,

- you qualify for maximum rebate (para 17.4) if you have no other income,

- otherwise special rules apply about assessing your income (para 18.7) and applicable amount (para17.44);

(b)   in any other case (i.e. you are not on UC),

- your applicable amount is worked out as described in para 17.38 onwards,

- your income is worked out as described in chapter 18.

Minimum award

17.9　　　For pension age claims in England and all claims in Scotland and Wales, you are awarded the amount of CTR you qualify for no matter how small it is. But for working age claims in England your council can set a minimum award (para 15.38): usually between 50p and £5 a week.

Apportionment of main CTR for joint occupiers

17.10　　　If you are jointly liable for council tax your 'eligible council tax' (para 17.4(a)) is the total liability divided by the number of people who are jointly liable (paras 15.12-13) but ignoring any student who is excluded from main CTR (para 15.63). If you have a partner and are jointly

---

17.5　　　CTP sch 1 paras 2(e), 3(e),(f), 10(2),(3), 13; CTR 13(e), 14(f), 16(e), 17(f), 32(2),(3), 35, 37, 40(11), 54(2), sch 8 para 8

17.6-7　　CTP sch 1 paras 3(f), 10(3); CTR 14(f), 17(f), 32(3)

17.8　　　CTP sch 1 paras 6, 14, 15, 37; CTR 25, 26, 28, 36, 37, 38, 57(1), 71, 72

17.10　　CTP sch 1 para 7(3)-(5); CTR 29(3)-(5)

liable with at least one other your share includes your partner's liability. So for example, if you are a couple and you are jointly liable with one other your share would be two thirds (rather than one half).

Examples: Calculating main CTR

(For variations for working age claims in England, see paras 17.4 and 17.7.)

Claimant on a passport benefit

A claimant has no non-dependants: she lives alone. The council tax is £20.00 per week but she qualifies for a 25% weekly discount, reducing her liability to £15.00 per week.

Claimants on JSA(IB), ESA(IR), IS or guarantee credit get maximum rebate – which equals their eligible council tax. So in this case her weekly main CTR is £15.00.

Claimant not on a passport benefit

A couple have no non-dependants. They are not on JSA(IB), ESA(IR), IS or guarantee credit. Their joint weekly income exceeds their applicable amount by £20.00. Their eligible council tax liability is £22.56 per week.

Claimants with excess income get maximum rebate minus 20% of their excess income.

Eligible council tax (maximum rebate)	£22.56
Minus 20% of excess income (20% x £20.00)	£4.00
Equals weekly main CTR	£18.56

Scottish special rebate

17.11 Scottish special rebate is available to both pension age and working age claimants in Scotland, but only if your capital isn't over the upper capital limit (paras 15.60-61). It helps with the extra increase in council tax that was introduced for bands E to H from 1st April 2017. This applies on top of the ordinary annual increase, and is 7½% for band E, 12½% for band F, 17½% for band G and 22½% for band H.

17.12 You can calculate the weekly amount of your extra increase as follows:

(a) start with the weekly amount of your council tax (para 17.36);

(b) divide (a) by:

   ■ 1.075 if your home is in band E,

   ■ 1.125 if your home is in band F,

   ■ 1.175 if your home is in band G,

   ■ 1.225 if your home is in band H;

(c) then subtract (b) from (a).

17.11-14   See appendix 4 table B

Maximum special rebate

17.13	Your maximum special rebate is:

(a)	the weekly amount of your extra increase (para 17.12) or your share of it if you are a joint occupier (para 17.10);

(b)	minus any non-dependant deductions that apply to you (para 17.15).

Amount of special rebate

17.14	To calculate Scottish special rebate, work through the following steps:

(a)	compare your weekly income (chapter 18) to the threshold – this is:

- ■	£321 per week if you are a single claimant, or

- ■	£479 per week if you are a couple (with or without children) or a lone parent;

(b)	if your income is less than (or equal to) the threshold, you qualify for maximum special rebate (para 17.13);

(c)	if your income is more than the threshold, the difference between the two is called the 'excess'. You qualify for:

- ■	maximum special rebate (para 17.13);

- ■	minus 20% of the excess.

Example: Calculating Scottish special rebate

A couple living in Scotland have no non-dependants. Their home is in band E and their council tax is £30 per week. Their joint weekly income exceeds the threshold (£479 per week) by £5.00.

Their 'extra increase' is calculated as follows:

Weekly council tax	£30.00
Minus £30.00 divided by 1.075	£27.91
Equals weekly extra increase	£2.09

Their Scottish special rebate is calculated as follows:

Maximum special rebate	£2.09
Minus 20% of excess (20% of £5.00)	£1.00
Equals weekly special rebate	£1.09

Non-dependant deductions

17.15	A non-dependant is, usually, a grown-up son, daughter, friend or relative who lives with you in your home (para 16.58). When calculating CTR each non-dependant is assumed to contribute towards your council tax. This contribution is called a 'non-dependant deduction' – because it is deducted from your eligible council tax when calculating your main CTR (para 17.4) or Scottish special rebate (para 17.13). This section explains when non-dependant deductions apply, and how much they are.

17.15	CTP 9; CTR 9

17.16 For working age claims in England, the rules in this section can vary (para 15.38): in particular, the rates of deduction in table 17.1 can be higher and/or the rules about when a deduction applies may differ. The rules cannot be varied for pension age claims in England, or for any claims in Scotland or Wales.

When no deductions are made

17.17 There is no deduction for any non-dependant at all (regardless of how many there are or what their income is), if you or your partner:

(a) are severely sight impaired or blind or have recently regained your sight (para 17.75);

(b) receive one of the following benefits,

- the daily living component of personal independence payment,
- attendance allowance,
- the care component of disability living allowance,
- constant attendance allowance paid with an industrial injury or war disablement pension,
- an armed forces independence payment; or

(c) in England and Wales only, you would receive one of the benefits in (b) but for the fact that you have been in hospital for four weeks or more.

When a deduction is made

17.18 For any other adult member of your household:

(a) one deduction is made for each occupier unless,

- that person is not a non-dependant (para 16.59),
- the nil rate charge applies (para 17.19),

(b) if two non-dependants are a couple one deduction is made between them (para 17.28).

When the nil rate deduction applies

17.19 The nil rate deduction applies to any non-dependant in your household who is:

(a) aged under 18;

(b) on income support, income-based JSA, income-related ESA, or state pension credit;

(c) on universal credit on the basis that they do not have any earned income;

(d) a youth trainee receiving a training allowance;

(e) a full-time student;

(f) a patient who has been in hospital for 52 weeks or more;

(g) in Scotland only, a member of the armed forces away on operations; or

(h) a 'disregarded person', other than a student, youth trainee or apprentice (table 15.2 categories (a), (b) and (f)-(m)).

17.17   CTP 2(1) definition: 'attendance allowance', sch 1 para 8(6),(11),(12); CTR 2(1), 30(6)

17.18   CTP 9(2), sch 1 para 8(3),(7),(8); CTR 9(2), 30(3),(7),(8)

17.19   CTP sch 1 para 8(1),(2),(7),(8); CTR 30(1),(2),(7),(8)

The amount of the deduction

17.20   Apart from the nil rate, the amount of the deduction varies depending on whether your non-dependant is working at least 16 hours per week and (if they are) on their gross income. The amounts of the deductions are in table 17.1.

Table 17.1 **Non-dependant deductions: 2018-19**

England

If the non-dependant works at least 16 hours per week and has a gross weekly income of:

- at least £436.90   £11.90
- at least £351.65 but under £436.90   £9.95
- at least £202.85 but under £351.65   £7.90
- under £202.85 per week   £3.90

Any other non-dependant (regardless of income level)   £3.90

(For variations for working age claims see para 15.38).

Scotland

If the non-dependant works at least 16 hours per week and has a gross weekly income of:

- at least £439.00   £12.25
- at least £354.00 but under £439.00   £10.25
- at least £204.00 but under £354.00   £8.10
- under £204.00 per week   £4.05

Any other non-dependant (regardless of income level)   £4.05

Wales

If the non-dependant works at least 16 hours per week and has a gross weekly income of:

- at least £440.00   £13.10
- at least £355.00 but under £440.00   £10.95
- at least £205.00 but under £355.00   £8.70
- under £205.00 per week   £4.35

Any other non-dependant (regardless of income level)   £4.35

Notes:

- 'Working 16 hours': see para 17.22
- 'Gross income': see para 17.25

17.20   CTP 10, sch 1 para 8(1),(2); CTR 10, 30(1),(2)

T17.1   England: SI 2017/1305 reg 8
         Scotland: SSI 2018/69 regs 9,16
         Wales: SI 2018/14 reg 17

Assuming the amount of a non-dependant deduction

17.21   If you don't provide evidence of your non-dependant's circumstances, your council is entitled to make an assumption about which deduction applies, often the highest rate. But this must be reasonable and mustn't be based on an opinion that is unlikely to reflect the non-dependant's actual circumstances (CH/48/2006). If you later provide evidence showing a lower deduction applies, the council must award you arrears of CTR (but see para 19.11 if you delay doing this).

Working at least 16 hours per week

17.22   You count as working at least 16 hours per week if:

(a) you are employed or self-employed in work for which payment is made or expected; and

(b) you work at least 16 hours per week every week, or on average (para 17.23).

The law calls this 'remunerative work'.

17.23   If your hours vary, they are averaged according to any recognisable work cycle as follows:

(a) if none can be identified, over five weeks or whatever period would give a more accurate figure;

(b) if one can be identified (for example you work a regular pattern of shifts), over the whole of that cycle. In this case, the averaging includes periods you don't work;

(c) if the cycle is annual (for example you work in term-times but not school holidays) over the whole year. In this case, the averaging excludes periods you don't work but the result applies throughout the year. (So if you work at least 16 hours every week in term-times, you count as working at least 16 hours per week throughout the year.)

Once you count as working at least 16 hours per week you continue to do so while you are on holiday or absent from work 'without good cause'.

17.24   You do not count as working at least 16 hours per week if you:

(a) are absent from work due to illness, whether or not you are being paid;

(b) are on maternity, paternity, shared parental or adoption leave, with the right to return to work under your contract or under employment law;

(c) are on JSA(IB), ESA(IR) or income support for more than three days in any reduction week;

(d) are absent from work 'with good cause' (for example you are laid off);

(e) are doing unpaid work; or

(f) have no income other than a Sports Council award.

17.21   CTP sch 1 para 8(1)(a); CTR 30(1)(a)

17.22   CTP 10(1),(4); CTR 10(1),(4)

17.23   CTP 10(2)-(5); CTR 10(2)-(5)

17.24   CTP 10(5)-(8); CTR 10(5)-(8)

Gross income

17.25   A non-dependant's 'normal' gross weekly income is taken into account (table 17.1). Because the law says it is the 'normal' amount, short-term variations can be ignored, but longer-term changes are taken into account. For example, a non-dependant who is a school assistant could count as working at least 16 hours per week (para 17.23) but changes in their income may mean different levels of non-dependant deduction in term-times and holidays.

17.26   It is the 'gross' income that is taken into account. Apart from those items that are disregarded (para 17.27) 'gross' is not defined, but in practice it means all of their income before deductions and is likely to include:

(a) employed earnings (before tax, national insurance, etc have been deducted);

(b) self employed net profit (after the deduction of reasonable expenses but before tax, national insurance, etc have been deducted);

(c) social security benefits, pensions and credits (except those in para 17.27);

(d) occupational and private pensions;

(e) rental income;

(f) maintenance;

(g) charitable and voluntary income; and

(h) interest on savings.

17.27   The only items that are not counted as part of a non-dependant's gross income are:

(a) personal independence payment;

(b) attendance allowance;

(c) disability living allowance;

(d) constant attendance allowance paid with an industrial injury or war disablement pension;

(e) an armed forces independence payment; or

(f) any payment from (or originally derived from) the government trusts in para 18.59 (Macfarlane Trust, Skipton Fund, etc).

Examples: Calculating main CTR with non-dependants

(For variations for working age claims in England, see para 17.16.)

Claimant on ESA(IR) with working non-dependant

A claimant living in England is on ESA(IR). Her eligible council tax liability is £19.00 per week. Her 26-year-old son lives with her. He earns £450 per week gross for a 35-hour week.

Claimants on ESA(IR) get maximum rebate, which in this case involves a non-dependant deduction. The son is in remunerative work and the level of his gross income means the highest level of deduction applies (table 17.1).

17.25-26 CTP 10(3), sch 1 para 8(2); CTR 10(3), 30(2)

17.27   CTP sch 1 para 8(9),(10); CTR 30(9)

Eligible council tax	£19.00
Minus non-dependant deduction	£11.90
Equals weekly main CTR	£7.10

Claimant on ESA(IR) with non-dependant on JSA(C)

The son in the previous example loses his job and starts receiving JSA(C).

The lower rate non-dependant deduction applies because he is not in work and receives JSA(C) (which unlike JSA(IB) is not a passport benefit).

Eligible council tax	£19.00
The lower non-dependant deduction applies	£3.90
Equals weekly main CTR	£15.10

Non-dependant couples

17.28 If you have a non-dependant who are a couple, only one deduction is made for them. That is the higher (or highest) of the amounts that would have applied if they were single. For the gross income limits in table 17.1, each of them is treated as having the gross income of both of them.

Non-dependants of joint occupiers

17.29 If you are jointly liable for the council tax with someone else (other than your partner) any non-dependant deduction (if it applies) is apportioned as follows:

(a) If the non-dependant 'normally resides' solely with you (and your family) the whole of the non-dependant deduction is made from your eligible council tax (and any claim for CTR by the other occupiers is entirely unaffected).

(b) If the non-dependant 'normally resides' with both you and the other joint occupiers, then the deduction is shared between you.

(But see para 17.16 for variations for working age claims in England.)

Delayed non-dependant deductions for people aged 65+

17.30 In England and Scotland only, if you or your partner are aged 65 or over and there is a change in your non-dependant's circumstances that causes an increase in rate of deduction applied, the resulting change in your CTR award is delayed until the day 26 weeks after the change actually occurred.

17.28   CTP sch 1 para 8(3); CTR 30(3)

17.29   CTP sch 1 para 8(5); CTR 30(5)

17.30   CTP sch 1 para 46(10)-(13); CTR 107(10)-(13)

Second adult rebate

17.31 If you meet the basic conditions for second adult rebate (SAR) (paras 15.50-51) the amount of award depends on:

(a) the kind of SAR you qualify for (student or general) (para 15.50(b));

(b) the income of one or more 'second adults' in your home (para 17.32).

Note that it is the income of the second adults in you home that determines whether you get SAR: your own income is ignored. For who is a 'second adult' see para 16.71.

What counts as low income for SAR

17.32 To get second adult rebate the income of the second adult(s) must be low enough (para 15.50(d)). Low income means:

(a) For student SAR, the second adult or every second adult;

■ is on state pension credit, JSA(IB), ESA(IR) or income support, or

■ is a student who isn't eligible for main CTR (para 15.63).

(b) For general SAR, the second adult or every second adult;

■ is on state pension credit, JSA(IB), ESA(IR) or income support, or

■ has a gross income (para 17.34) that is less than the upper threshold in table 17.2.

But in England for working age claims these rules and the amounts of second adult rebate (para 17.33) can be varied (para 15.38).

The amount of second adult rebate

17.33 If the income of the second adult(s) (para 17.32) is low enough the amount of SAR you get is:

(a) For student SAR, 100% of your council tax (in every case).

(b) For general SAR, the appropriate amount according to the gross income (para 17.34) of the second adults as set out in table 17.2.

Table 17.2 **Amount of general second adult rebate: 2018-19**

England

Second adult is on JSA(IB)/ESA(IR)/IS/pension credit (or, if there are two or more second adults, all of them are)	25%
In any other case gross weekly income of second adult(s) is:	
under £201.00	15%
at least £201.00 but under £260.00	7½%
at least £260.00	nil

17.31   CTP sch 1 paras 4, 9, 10(4), sch 3; CTR 15, 18, 31, 32(4), sch 4

17.32-33   CTP sch 3 para 1(2); CTR sch 4 para 1(2)

Scotland

Second adult is on JSA(IB)/ESA(IR)/IS/pension credit (or, if there are two or more second adults, all of them are)	25%
In any other case gross weekly income of second adult(s) is:	
under £200.00 per week	15%
at least £200.00 but under £261.00	7½%
at least £261.00	nil

Notes:

- Who counts as a second adult: see para 16.71.
- What counts as gross income: see para 17.34.
- The amount of student SAR: see para 17.33.
- Variations for working age claims in England: see para 15.38.

Second adults' gross income

17.34 The gross income of a second adult (para 16.71) is assessed the same way as the gross income of a non-dependant (paras 17.25-27). If there is more than one second adult the combined income of all of them (and of their partners) is used as the gross income figure. Any income of a non-dependant who is a 'disregarded person' is ignored (since they are not a second adult: para 16.71) unless they are part of a couple where the other member is not a 'disregarded person' in which case the income of that (non-disregarded) member is counted.

SAR for joint occupiers

17.35 If there are any other occupiers who are jointly liable for the council tax with you (other than your partner) your CTR is worked out in the normal way (as if you were not a joint occupier) and before any discount you may be entitled to (see example). The total award is then shared equally between you (in other words, at the end of the calculation instead of at the beginning) for each occupier who claims CTR. (The share is always equal between all the joint occupiers.)

Examples: Calculating second adult rebate

(For variations for working age claims in England, see para 17.32.)

SAR under the general rule

A pension age couple live in England, and the council tax on their home is £16 per week. Their income is too high for them to qualify for main CTR. One of them is severely mentally impaired (table 15.2) and so is a disregarded person. The only person living with them is their son, aged 30, whose gross income is £210 per week.

T17.2 England: SI 2017/1305 reg 13
    Scotland: SSI 2018/69 regs 10,17

17.34 CTP sch 3 paras 2, 3; CTR sch 4 paras 2, 3

17.35 CTP sch 1 para 9(2),(3); CTR 31(2),(3)

They qualify for SAR under the general rule. The level of the son's income means this equals 7½% of their council tax (7½% x £16), which is £1.20 per week.

SAR under the student rule

A working age single claimant lives in England, and the council tax on her home is £24 per week. She is a student who isn't eligible for main CTR. The only people living with her are her parents, who are on state pension credit.

She qualifies for SAR under the student rule. This equals 100% of her council tax, which is £24 per week.

SAR under the general rule for joint occupiers

Two sisters are joint owner occupiers and their gross liability for council tax (i.e. before any discount) is £30.00 per week. Their elderly mother lives with them. Their mother has dementia: she receives attendance allowance and state pension credit and qualifies as a disregarded person on the basis of severe mental impairment. The younger of the two sisters cares for her mother for at least 35 hours per week: she is also a disregarded person (table 15.2).

Both sisters make an application for SAR under the general rule. They are both entitled to £3.75 per week (25% of £30 shared equally between them). They also qualify for a 25% discount because two of the occupiers are disregarded persons. So their council tax liability is £15.00 per week: £30.00 less £7.50 (25%) discount and £7.50 (combined) CTR.

Conversion to weekly amounts

Council tax

17.36   Whenever a weekly figure is needed for council tax liability, the following rules apply:

(a) for annual figures, divide the council tax by the number of days in the financial year (365 or 366) to find the daily figure, and then multiply the daily figure by seven;

(b) for figures which do not relate to a whole year, divide the council tax by the number of days it covers to find the daily figure, and then multiply the daily figure by seven.

Income

17.37   Whenever a weekly income figure is needed, the following rules apply:

(a) for an amount relating to a whole multiple of weeks, divide the amount by the number of weeks it covers;

(b) for an amount relating to a calendar month, multiply the amount by 12 to find the annual figure, then divide the annual figure by 52;

(c) for an amount relating to a year, there are two rules. For working age claims, divide the annual amount by 365 or 366 as appropriate to find the daily figure, and then multiply the daily figure by seven. For pension age claims, simply divide the annual amount by 52;

17.36   CTP sch 1 para 7(1)(b); CTR 29(1)(b)

17.37   CTP sch 1 para 17(1); CTR 40(1), 47, 48, 49, 50(1)

(d) for an amount relating to any other period longer than a week, divide the amount by the number of days it covers to find the daily figure, then multiply the daily figure by seven;

(e) for an amount relating to a period less than a week:

- if the period to which the payment relates straddles two rebate weeks (i.e. includes a Sunday and Monday) the whole amount is taken as income in the second week (i.e. the week starting on the Monday);

- if the period is wholly within the same rebate week, the whole amount is included in the following rebate week (although the law is not entirely clear on this point).

Applicable amounts

17.38 This section describes how your council calculates your applicable amount when assessing your main CTR. It covers:

(a) the basic rules;

(b) the detailed conditions for personal allowances, premiums and components; and

(c) further rules and special cases.

17.39 The terms 'family', 'single claimant', 'lone parent', 'couple', 'partner', 'child' and 'young person' are defined in paras 16.43-55. For 'pension age' and 'working age' see table 15.4.

What is an applicable amount?

17.40 Your applicable amount is a standardised assessment of the minimum income required to meet the basic living needs of you and your family. It is compared with your income (chapter 18) when calculating how much main CTR you are entitled to (paras 17.3-10).

How much is the applicable amount?

17.41 Your applicable amount is the total of:

(a) a personal allowance for yourself (and any partner);

(b) a personal allowance for each child or young person in your family; and

(c) any additional amounts (known as premiums and components) you qualify for.

Your applicable amount always includes a personal allowance but any additional amounts depend on your circumstances. Except as described below, there are no limitations on how many premiums and components can be awarded.

17.42 The figures for 2018-19 are given in table 17.3. Detailed conditions are in the rest of this chapter.

17.43 In England, councils can vary applicable amounts for working age claims (para 15.38). In practice, most of them use the same figures as they use in HB (appendix 2), which are in some cases lower than shown in table 17.3. Applicable amounts can't be varied for pension age claims in England or for any claims in Scotland or Wales.

17.41-42   CTP sch 1 para 6(1), sch 2 paras 1-4, part 4; CTR 25(1)

17.43   CTP 14(2), sch 1 para 6

If you are on universal credit

17.44   If you are on UC, instead of the figures in table 17.3 your applicable amount is:

(a) your maximum UC (para 9.4);

(b) plus in Scotland only, £16.73 for each child/young person in your family.

The DWP provides the council with your maximum UC. This is a monthly figure, and your council converts it to a weekly one by multiplying by 12 and dividing the result by 52.

Table 17.3 **Weekly CTR applicable amounts: 2018-19**

Personal allowances

Single claimant	aged under 25 – on main phase ESA	£73.10
	aged under 25 – on main phase ESA: Wales	£76.10
	aged under 25 – other	£57.90
	aged under 25 – other: Wales	£60.25
	aged 25+ but under pension age	£73.10
	aged 25+ but under pension age: Wales	£76.10
	over pension age but under 65	£163.00
	over pension age – other	£176.40
Lone parent	aged 18+ but under pension age	£73.10
	aged 18+ but under pension age: Wales	£76.10
	over pension age but under 65	£163.00
	over pension age – other	£176.40
Couple	at least one aged 18+ both under pension age	£114.85
	at least one aged 18+ both under pension age: Wales	£119.50
	at least one pension age, both under 65	£248.80
	at least one over pension age – other	£263.80
Children and young persons	for each child/young person	£66.90
	for each child/young person: Scotland	£83.63

Premiums and components

Family premium	at least one child/young person	£17.45
Disability premium	single claimant/lone parent	£33.55
	couple (one/both qualifying)	£47.80
Disabled child premium	each child/young person	£62.86
Enhanced disability premium	single claimant/lone parent	£16.40
	couple (one/both qualifying)	£23.55
	each child/young person	£25.48

Work related activity component	single claimant/lone parent/couple	£29.35
Support component	single claimant/lone parent/couple	£37.65
Carer premium	claimant or partner or each	£36.00
Severe disability premium	single rate	£64.30
	double rate	£128.60

Examples: Applicable amounts

Except for the lone parent in the fourth example, none of the following qualifies for any of the premiums for disability or for carers.

Single claimant in Scotland aged 23

Personal allowance:	
Single claimant aged under 25	£57.90
No additional amounts apply	
Applicable amount	£57.90

Couple with two children in Wales aged 13 and 17

The older child is still at school so still counts as a dependant of the couple (a 'young person').

Personal allowances:	
Couple, at least one over 18, both under pension age	£119.50
Child aged 13	£66.90
Young person aged 17	£66.90
Additional amount: family premium	£17.45
Applicable amount	£270.75

Couple in England aged 59 and 65

Personal allowance:	
Couple, at least one aged 65	£263.80
Applicable amount	£263.80

Disabled lone parent in Scotland with a child aged 6

The lone parent is in receipt of the highest rate of the care component of disability living allowance and so qualifies for a disability premium and enhanced disability premium. She has one child aged 6. Her mother (who lives elsewhere) receives carer's allowance to care for her. So she does not qualify for the severe disability premium.

T17.3   England: SI 2017/1305 reg 12
         Scotland: SSI 2015/46 reg 9(a); SSI 2016/253 reg 8, 15; SSI 2018/69 regs 9,16
         Wales: SI 2018/14 regs 5,10

Personal allowances:	
Lone parent aged over 18 (and under pension age)	£73.10
Child	£83.63
Additional amounts:	
Disability premium (single rate)	£33.55
Enhanced disability premium (single rate)	£16.40
Applicable amount	£206.68

Personal allowances

17.45   Your applicable amount always includes a personal allowance for yourself (if you are single or a lone parent), or for both of you if you are a couple. The amounts are in table 17.3, including rates that apply in Wales. (For polygamous marriages, see para 17.76.)

17.46   A personal allowance is awarded for each child or young person in your family (paras 15.89-95). The two child limit does not apply to main CTR in Scotland and Wales. In England the two child limit applies to pension age claims in the same way as for HB, and also for working age claims if your council adopted the two child rules (paras 15.38-39). See the *Guide to Housing Benefit* for how the two child rule works.

Family premium

17.47   You are awarded a family premium:

(a)   in Wales for any period of your CTR award in which at least one member of your family (para 16.44) is a child or young person;

(b)   in England and Scotland only if:

■   the premium was included in your CTR award on 30th April 2016, and

■   there has been no break in your CTR award since then, and

■   there has been at least one child/young person in your family since then.

Couples and the better off problem: working age components and premiums

17.48   If you are a working age couple and at least one of you has a sickness or disability that affects your fitness to work then you may be entitled to:

(a)   the work-related activity component or support component (para 17.52);

(b)   the disability premium (para 17.58); and

(c)   the enhanced disability premium (para 17.63).

You can only get one component and you can't get a component and the disability premium at the same time but you do not receive the one that is the highest value. What you get is determined by the DWP's assessment of your (or your partner's) fitness for work and which one of you makes the CTR claim (paras 17.49-51).

17.45-46   CTP sch 1 para 6(1)(a),(b),(1A),(1B),(1C), sch 2 paras 1, 2;
                 CTR 25(1)(a),(b), 26(1)(a),(b), sch 2 paras 1, 2, sch 3 paras 1-3; SI 2017/1305 regs 7, 17

17.47   England: SI 2015/2041 regs 2(4)(b), 3; Scotland: SSI 2016/81 regs 2, 5, 18
                 Wales: CTPW sch 2 para 3, sch 7 para 4; CTRW sch 2 para 3, sch 3 para 7

17.49   If both you and your partner have claimed ESA but had different work capability assessments (i.e. work-related activity component and support component) you are better off if your CTR claim is made by the member who qualifies for the support component.

17.50   If both you and your partner have claimed ESA and received the same work capability assessment you get (one lot of) that component.

17.51   If only one of you qualifies for an ESA component (or national insurance credit instead) the member who claims CTR should be:

(a)   if one of you receives the support component, that member;

(b)   if one of you qualifies for a disability premium and the other a work-related activity component, the member who qualifies for the disability premium; or

(c)   if neither of you qualify for a disability premium, the member who receives the work-related activity component.

Example: A 'better off' problem for couples

Information

A working age couple meet the additional condition for a disability premium because one of them receives personal independence payment, but the other partner is on ESA(C).

Entitlement to additions in the applicable amount

This depends on which partner is the CTR claimant.

(a)   If the claimant is on ESA(C):

  their applicable amount does not include a disability premium (at any point), but it does include a work-related activity or support component from the claimant's 14th week on ESA(C).

(b)   If the partner is on ESA(C):

  their applicable amount includes a couple-rate disability premium (from the beginning), but it never includes a work-related activity or support component.

Conclusion

So they are better off if (b) applies to them – by over £5 per week in CTR, during the first 13 weeks on ESA(C) (and by a lower amount after that).

Work-related activity component and support component

17.52   If you are working age and have claimed employment and support allowance (ESA) your CTR applicable amount includes:

(a)   a work-related activity component if the DWP has decided you have 'limited capability for work';

(b)   a support component if the DWP has decided you have 'limited capability for work related activity'.

But if you are a couple the component you get depends on which one of you is the CTR applicant (paras 17.49-51).

17.48-51   CTR 26, sch 3 paras 10(8), 18-20

17.52-54   CTR sch 3 paras 21-24

17.53   Your ESA is divided into: an 'assessment phase' (the first 13 weeks immediately after your claim) and a 'main phase' (the following period). The DWPs decision about your capability for work (and therefore any corresponding component in your CTR) only takes effect during your ESA 'main phase'.

17.54   Identifying the DWPs decision about your capability for work and which component you get is usually straightforward because you get the equivalent component in your (contribution-based) ESA. But you also get a component if:

(a) you get national insurance credits instead of an award of that component because

- you hadn't paid enough national insurance contributions to qualify for ESA, or
- your (contribution-based) ESA has expired because it was paid for the maximum period of one year; or

(b) you have 'limited capability for work' and claimed ESA after 2nd April 2017. In this case your ESA award is paid at the basic rate but you still qualify for the work-related activity component in your CTR.

Transitional addition after transferring to ESA

17.55   You qualify for a transitional addition in your CTR if your disability premium stops because you transfer:

(a) from long-term incapacity benefit, severe disablement allowance or national insurance credits instead of these under the old fitness for work test (para17.61);

(b) to contributory ESA, or national insurance credits instead of this (see para 17.54).

The transitional addition stops you from being worse off when the transfer takes place.

17.56   But you do not qualify for a transitional addition if:

(a) you transfer to income-related ESA; or

(b) you are a couple and you qualify for a disability premium under the rules in para 17.59.

In each case, this is because you can't be worse off (but if (b) applies to you, see para 17.51 to ensure this).

17.57   The transitional addition restores your applicable amount to the value it had immediately before you transferred to contributory ESA or national insurance credits. After that:

(a) any subsequent increase in your applicable amount due to a change in your circumstances or the annual up-rating is deducted from your transitional addition until it is eroded to nil;

(b) your transitional addition ends before it is eroded to nil if your contributory ESA ends or your CTR ends;

(c) but if you start back on CTR within 12 weeks of your previous award, your transitional addition is restored.

Disability premium

17.58   If you are working age you qualify for a disability premium if:

(a) you (or if you are in a couple, the one who claims CTR) must not be on ESA (including during a period of ESA disqualification); and

(b) you (or if you are in a couple, either of you) meet the additional condition in the next paragraph.

If you are in a couple you get the couple rate even if only one of you qualifies and if one of you has also claimed ESA see para 17.51 to ensure you are better off.

17.59   You meet the additional condition for the disability premium if:

(a) you or your partner are severely sight impaired or blind or have recently regained your sight (para 17.75);

(b) you or your partner receive any of the following benefits:

  ▪ personal independence payment,

  ▪ attendance allowance or constant attendance allowance paid with an industrial injury or war disablement pension,

  ▪ disability living allowance,

  ▪ an armed forces independence payment,

  ▪ war pensioner's mobility supplement,

  ▪ the disability element or severe disability element of working tax credit;

(c) you or your partner have an invalid vehicle supplied by the NHS or get DWP payments for car running costs; or

(d) you (the CTR claimant) satisfy the old (pre-ESA) fitness for work test (para 17.61).

17.60   If you were receiving one of the first four benefits in 17.59(b) (PIP/DLA/AA/AFIP) but payment has been suspended solely because you have been in hospital for four weeks you continue to be entitled to the premium.

17.61   If you have been continuously incapable of work for a period that began before 27th October 2008 and have not yet been transferred to ESA you may also qualify for the disability premium: see previous editions of this guide.

Disabled child premium

17.62   The condition for this premium is that a child or young person in your family:

(a) is severely sight impaired or blind or has recently regained their sight (para 17.75);

(b) receives personal independence payment; or

(c) receives disability living allowance.

17.58   CTR schv 3 para 9

17.59-61   CTR sch 3 para 10

17.55-57   CTR sch 3 paras 25-29

17.62   CTP sch 2 para 8; CTR sch 2 para 8, sch 3 para 13

One premium is awarded for each child or young person who qualifies. If the child/young person dies the premium continues for eight weeks following the death. The premium continues while your child is in hospital.

Enhanced disability premium

17.63   This premium can be awarded in respect of any member of your family if you are working age; or in respect of a child or young person if you are pension age. One premium is awarded for each child who qualifies plus one for you (or you and your partner) if you qualify.

17.64   If you are working age you (or you and your partner) qualify if:

(a) you (or, in the case of a couple, either you or your partner) receive the daily living component of personal independence payment (or you would do but for the fact you have been in hospital for four weeks or more);

(b) you (or, in the case of a couple, either you or your partner) receive the highest rate of the care component of disability living allowance (or you would do but for the fact you have been in hospital for four weeks or more); or

(c) you (or, in the case of a couple, the one that claims CTR) qualify for an ESA support component.

And if you are in a couple you are always awarded the couple rate (regardless of whether one or both of you qualify). So if only one of you gets a support component in their ESA(C), you are better off if that one makes the claim for CTR (para 17.51).

17.65   The condition for a child or young person is that they receive the daily living component of personal independence payment (at either rate) or the highest rate of the care component of disability living allowance. The premium continues for eight weeks following the child's death.

Severe disability premium

17.66   You qualify for this premium only if you meet all three conditions:

(a) you receive one of the following qualifying benefits:

   ▪ the daily living component of personal independence payment; or

   ▪ attendance allowance or constant attendance allowance paid with an industrial injury or war disablement pension,

   ▪ the middle or highest rate of the care component of disability living allowance; or

   ▪ an armed forces independence payment,

(b) you must have no non-dependants (but see paragraph 17.68 below for exceptions); and

(c) no-one must be receiving carer's allowance (or in Wales, the UC carer element) in respect of you (but see para 17.67 if you are in a couple, and para 17.69 for exceptions).

If you are single or a lone parent and satisfy all three conditions you get the single rate of the severe disability premium. If you are in a couple see the next paragraph.

17.63-65   CTP sch 2 para 7; CTR sch 2 para 7, sch 3 para 12

17.66-69   CTP sch 2 para 6, CTR sch 2 para 6, sch 3 para 11

17.67 If you are in a couple, a severe disability premium is awarded as follows:

(a) if both of you satisfy all three conditions, you get the double rate;

(b) if both of you satisfy the first two conditions but only one satisfies the third condition, you get the single rate;

(c) if only one of you receives a qualifying benefit but the other one is severely sight impaired, blind or has recently regained sight you qualify for the single rate provided you meet the other two conditions. But in this case the CTR application must be made by the member who receives the qualifying benefit;

(d) if you have been getting the double rate but one of you then loses their qualifying benefit because they have been in hospital for four weeks, you get the single rate from that point.

17.68 In deciding whether you meet condition 17.66(b) you are not excluded from the severe disability premium by any non-dependant who:

(a) is severely sight impaired, blind or who has recently regained their sight (para 17.75);

(b) receives:

- the daily living component of personal independence payment,
- attendance allowance or constant attendance allowance paid with an industrial injury or war disablement pension,
- the middle or highest rate of the care component of disability living allowance, or
- an armed forces independence payment.

17.69 In deciding whether you meet condition 17.66(c):

(a) your carer is entitled to carer's allowance but does not receive it because it is overlapped by other benefits (para 17.71);

(b) a backdated award of carer's allowance is ignored in respect of any period before the first payment is made: in other words the backdated part does not cause an overpayment;

(c) if you are in a couple getting the single rate you continue to get it at the single rate if the member with the carer has been in hospital for four weeks or more, even though their carer will stop receiving carer's allowance;

(d) your carer is treated as receiving carer's allowance if they have lost it as a result of a benefit fraud conviction.

Example: Severe disability premium, etc

A husband and wife are both under pension age and both receive the standard rate of the daily living component of personal independence payment. Neither of them is blind. Their daughter of 17 is in full-time employment and lives with them. Their son lives elsewhere and receives carer's allowance for caring for the husband. No-one receives carer's allowance for the wife.

Disability premium: Because of receiving personal independence payment, they are awarded the couple rate of disability premium.

Enhanced disability premium: Because they get the standard rate of the daily living component of personal independence payment, this cannot be awarded.

Severe disability premium:

- Both receive the appropriate type of personal independence payment.
- Although their daughter is a non-dependant, she is under 18.
- Someone receives carer's allowance for caring for only one of them.

So they are awarded the single rate of severe disability premium (for the second reason in para 17.67).

Carer premium

17.70   The condition for this premium is that you or your partner are 'entitled to' (para 17.71) carer's allowance or you were entitled to it within the past eight weeks. If you are a couple you get one premium if one of you satisfies the condition, two if both of you do.

17.71   You need only to be 'entitled' and not 'in receipt' of carer's allowance. So you still qualify if your carer's allowance is overlapped by another benefit (see examples). You must make a claim for carer's allowance to be entitled to it but once your entitlement has been confirmed it continues for as long as you continue to meet the basic conditions for it and it does not matter if your claim was made before you claimed CTR (CIS 367/2003). But if your carer's allowance is overlapped by your retirement pension you only get the carer premium if the person you are caring for continues to receive attendance allowance (or equivalent qualifying benefit).

17.72   You are treated as still receiving carer's allowance if you lose it as a result of taking part in a government training scheme.

Interaction of carer and severe disability premium

17.73   Although an award of carer's allowance qualifies you for a carer premium, the person you care for may lose their severe disability premium. However, if your carer's allowance is overlapped any severe disability premium in your own claim or the person you care for is unaffected (see second example). If you are a couple who care for each other it is therefore possible to qualify for a severe disability premium (at the single or double rate) and one or two carer premiums at the same time.

17.70   CTP sch 2 paras 5(2), 9; CTR sch 2 paras 5(2), 9, sch 3 paras 8(2), 14

17.71   CTP sch 2 para 5(2), CTR sch 2 para 5(2), sch 3 para 8(2)

17.72   CTR sch 3 para 8(1)(b)

17.73   CTP sch 2 para 11; CTR sch 2 para 11, sch 3 para 16

Examples: Carer premium and overlapping benefits

Claimant over 65

A claimant and her partner are both aged over 80 and in receipt of retirement pension. She looks after her partner who has been in receipt of attendance allowance since 26th January 2018. On 2nd February 2018 she made a claim for carer's allowance and was notified by the DWP that she was entitled to carer's allowance but it could not be paid because it was overlapped by her retirement pension (in other words, payment of the latter prevents payment of the former).

On 30th April 2018 she makes a claim for CTR for the first time and is awarded it from 5th February 2018 (para 16.31). The award includes the carer premium. If her partner subsequently dies, she would no longer be entitled to carer's allowance, but the premium would continue for a further eight weeks.

Claimant under 65

A claimant aged 50 is in receipt of bereavement allowance. He cares for his severely disabled sister who receives the daily living component of personal independence payment. He lives alone in his own flat. He claims carer's allowance and is entitled to it but it cannot be paid because it is overlapped by his bereavement allowance; but he is awarded a carer premium in his CTR. Once he has claimed carer's allowance he remains 'entitled' to it until such time as he no longer meets the conditions for it (e.g. he starts work, or his sister no longer qualifies for PIP) and until that time his entitlement to it continues without the need for a further claim even if there are breaks in his CTR award. Note that his sister would also be entitled to the severe disability premium, because although he is 'entitled' to carer's allowance he is not 'in receipt' of it (para 17.71).

DWP concessionary payments

17.74 For the purpose of any entitlement to any premium (but not a component), if you receive a DWP concessionary payment as compensation for non-payment of any qualifying benefit it is treated as if were that benefit.

Meaning of severely sight impaired, blind or recently regained sight

17.75 In deciding whether a non-dependant deduction applies (para 17.17) or entitlement to certain premiums in this section (paras 17.59, 17.62, 17.66-67) a member of your household is 'severely sight impaired' or 'blind' if they are registered as blind with your council social services department; or in either case for a further 28 weeks from the date they were removed from the register due to them having regained their sight.

17.74 CTP sch 2 para 10; CTR sch 2 para 10, sch 3 para 15

17.75 CTP sch 2 para 6(4),(5); CTR sch 2 para 6(4),(5) sch 3 para 10(1)(a)(vii),(2)

Polygamous marriages

17.76   If you are in a polygamous marriage (para 16.46) you get the appropriate amount in table 17.3 for a couple according to the age of the oldest member in the marriage. You also get a personal allowance for each additional spouse based on the oldest member in the marriage which is calculated by deducting the appropriate rate for a single person from the equivalent rate for a couple. Except for the severe disability premium (para 17.77), all premiums and components are awarded in the same way as for couples.

17.77   In the case of a severe disability premium you receive the double rate if all members in the marriage satisfy all three conditions in para 17.66. You get the single rate if all members of the marriage satisfy the first two conditions but one member has a carer who gets carer's allowance; or if the member who claims CTR satisfies all three conditions and all the other partners in the marriage are severely sight impaired, blind or have recently regained their sight.

17.76   CTP sch 2 para 1(3),(4); CTR 27(2), sch 2 para 1(3),(4)

17.77   CTP sch 2 para 6(2)(b); CTR sch 2 para 6(2)(b), sch 3 para 11(2)(b)

Chapter 18 **Income and capital for main CTR**

- Finding the law and general rules: see paras 18.1-15.
- Social security benefits, tax credits and war pensions: see paras 18.16-23.
- Income from employment and self employment: see paras 18.24-49.
- Other kinds of income: see paras 18.50-62.
- Capital: see paras 18.63-76.

Finding the law and general rules

18.1　　This chapter explains how income and capital are calculated for main CTR and Scottish special rebate (para 15.27). It provides a summary of the most common types of income and capital that are encountered when calculating main CTR; for less common items see para 18.15. It does not cover the rules in England and Wales about any other locally devised CTR class (para 15.27) for which you must refer to your council's published rules (paras 15.39 and 15.46). Nor does it cover the rules about income and capital for second adult rebate, for which see paras 15.60-61 and 17.31-34.

Finding the law

18.2　　The law on how income and capital is treated for main CTR can be difficult to identify because of differences between England, Scotland and Wales and how the law is constructed in each of these countries (para 15.26). In addition:

(a) in all three countries, the rules about how your income and capital is treated depend on whether you are a pension age or a working age claimant;

(b) in England (and to a lesser extent in Wales) your local council is free to set its own rules about how your income and capital are treated for working age claims, but in practice most have adopted the 'default scheme' either in full or in part (paras 18.3-4); and

(c) in England for pension age claims, and in Wales for both working age and pension age claims, your local council must comply with the 'prescribed requirements' when calculating income and capital for main CTR (paras 15.33 and 15.44).

The law about main CTR in England

18.3　　The footnote references in this chapter are to the 'prescribed requirements' and the 'default scheme' for England (paras 15.35-37). Although the default scheme no longer has legal force it is still used by most councils as the basis for their own scheme rules (para 15.36) either in its entirety or by varying individual rules. Although the wording for each individual rule is often identical to the default scheme, most councils use their own numbering system. Whatever the rules your council adopts or how they are numbered, it must publish them (para 15.39).

The law about main CTR in Scotland and Wales

18.4 In Scotland, the rules about income and capital for main CTR and Scottish special rebate are the same for all councils (paras 15.40-41) and cannot be varied locally. In Wales, councils must comply with the prescribed requirements rules about income and capital for main CTR and default scheme rules (which are identical) if they apply. In this chapter the equivalent footnote references for Scotland and Wales (for reasons of space and elegance) are in Appendix 4, table B.

Assessing cases on passport benefits

18.5 Main CTR is calculated by comparing your income with your requirements ('applicable amount'). If you are on a passport benefit your income is taken to be zero, so calculating your requirements is unnecessary and all the other detailed rules in this chapter are irrelevant: you get the maximum award. The passport benefits are:

    (a) income-based jobseeker's allowance;

    (b) income-related employment and support allowance;

    (c) income support; and

    (d) guarantee credit.

Assessing cases for savings credit

18.6 If you receive savings credit only (i.e. without guarantee credit) your council must use the income and capital figures supplied to it by the DWP and none of the other rules about income in this chapter apply. Your savings credit is added to the DWP's income figure plus any tariff income (para 18.65) derived from the DWP's figure for your capital and this total is the income figure used to calculate your CTR). The only uncommon exceptions are if you have earnings from work, maintenance from a partner/former partner or a war pension: the rules are the same as for HB (see *Guide to Housing Benefit* table 13.3 for details).

Assessing cases for universal credit

18.7 If you get UC, your council must use the income (and capital) figure the DWP provides, plus your UC award to calculate your CTR (paras 17.4, 17.6 and 17.44). The total is multiplied by 12 and divided by 52 to convert it to a weekly figure. In Scotland, if there are frequent changes in your UC your council estimates the average DWP figure over a period of up to 52 weeks. Apart from that, in England, Scotland or Wales, no other adjustments are made to the DWP's income figure (e.g. earnings disregards). In England your council can adopt a different rule (para 15.38), and some councils deduct the earned income disregards from the DWP's (converted) earned income figure.

Assessing income and capital: all other cases

18.8 CTR is calculated by comparing your requirements ('applicable amount') with your income only. If you possess capital (e.g. savings) its value is converted into a hypothetical

---

18.5   CTP sch 1 para 13; CTR sch 7 para 14; sch 8 paras 8,9 sch 10 paras 8,9

18.6   CTP sch 1 para 14; CTR 36

18.7   CTR 37

income figure ('tariff income': para 18.65) and this is then added to your other sources of income – unless its value exceeds the upper capital limit (para 18.8).

The upper capital limit

18.9 The upper capital limit is £16,000 and if your capital is above this then you are not entitled to main CTR (even if your income is zero); the only exception is if you are on guarantee credit (paras 15.60-61). But in England for working age claims your council can set a lower capital limit (para 15.38). If your capital is below the upper capital limit, see para 18.65.

Differences in treatment: working age and pension age

18.10 CTR law treats your income differently depending on whether you are a working age or pension age claimant (table 15.4). The approach taken by the law in either case is quite different:

(a) if you are working age every source of income you possess is included in your assessment, unless it is an item that is specifically listed in the law as being disregarded;

(b) if you are pension age nothing counts as income unless the law says it does. Some types of income (as the law acknowledges) are then also disregarded (for example, social security benefits count as income, but disability living allowance is disregarded).

18.11 In broad terms the law treats your capital in the same way whether you are pension age or working age: all of your capital counts unless the law specifically lists it as being disregarded; although there are some differences in the list of items that are disregarded between pension age and working age claims (identified as they arise).

Differences in treatment: earned income and unearned income

18.12 CTR law makes the distinction between:

(a) earned income (i.e. from work as an employee or from self-employment);

(b) unearned income: anything else which is not from work. The list is almost endless but typically it includes social security benefits and pensions, tax credits (and universal credit), private pensions (such as from a former employer), rental income (i.e. if you are a landlord) and maintenance (including maintenance received for a child who lives with you).

As a general rule earned income is treated more generously than unearned income because it is always subject to a disregard (i.e. only part of it is taken into account). Certain less common items of unearned income that qualify for a disregard (war pensions, student income and widows/widowers) are subject to an overall (maximum) limit on the amount disregarded of £20: these are identified as they arise.

18.8   CTP sch 1 paras 15, 24(1)(a),(b); CTR 38, 57(1)(a)(b)

18.9   CTP 11(2), sch 1 para 13; CTR 20, 23, 35

18.10   CTP sch 1 paras 16,17,18,24; CTR 38,39,40,52,54,57

18.11   CTP sch 1 para 31(1); CTR 63(1)

18.12   CTP sch 5 para 12(3); CTR sch 6 para 12(3), sch 8 para 40

Distinguishing income from capital

18.13   In most cases distinguishing between income and capital is fairly straightforward. Capital can usually be distinguished from income because it is made without being tied to a past period and is not intended to form part of a series of payments. Further details about distinguishing income from capital can be found in the *Guide to Housing Benefit,* paras 15.10-11.

Deprivation of income and capital

18.14   As a general rule only income and capital you currently hold count in your assessment. However, there are special rules that can treat you as possessing income or capital you have given away, spent, or in some cases money you would be entitled to but have failed to apply for, if your purpose in depriving yourself of that resource was to increase your CTR award. The rules are the same as for HB: for further details see the *Guide to Housing Benefit,* paragraphs 13.46-57 and 15.56-69.

Less common items of income and capital

18.15   This chapter covers only the most common kinds of income and capital; for less common items and other types of case where special rules apply (in particular, students) see the *Guide to Housing Benefit.* The CTR (default scheme) rules for these less common items and special cases are as described for HB.

Social security benefits, tax credits and war pensions

What counts as social security

18.16   In this section 'social security' means those benefits and pensions you receive from the DWP. It also includes any housing benefit (HB) paid by your local authority. It does not include:

(a)   tax credits paid by HMRC (para 18.21);

(b)   war pensions for disability or surviving partners (para 18.23);

(c)   social benefits paid by your employer (such as statutory sick pay or statutory maternity pay) which are usually treated as earned income (para 18.30);

(d)   other social benefits (whether in cash or in kind) paid by your local authority (e.g. discretionary housing payments, 'supporting people' payments and fostering allowances (paras 18.51);

(e)   private pensions and cash benefits (such as a company pension or insurance scheme).

Social security benefits: the general rule

18.17   The general rule is that any social security benefits and pensions you receive are counted in full as your income for the period they cover (including any arrears: see also para 18.70). The more common benefits covered by this rule include retirement pension; contribution-based JSA or ESA; incapacity benefit and carer's allowance; but it includes other less common benefits as well. The exceptions to this are in the next paragraph.

18.14   CTP sch 1 paras 22(9),34(1); CTR 45(9),56(1),67(1)

18.17   CTP sch 1 paras 16(1),17(7); CTR 39(1),40(7), 49(2)

Social security benefits: exceptions to the general rule

18.18   The exceptions to the general rule that social security benefits and pensions count in full as income are:

(a)   the 'passport benefits' IS, JSA(IB), ESA(IR) and guarantee credit;

(b)   savings credit and universal credit;

(c)   housing benefit;

(d)   disability living allowance and personal independence payments;

(e)   attendance allowance;

(f)   constant attendance allowance (for industrial injury);

(g)   child benefit and guardian's allowance;

(h)   winter fuel, cold weather, funeral and maternity payments (all paid by the social fund);

(i)   a Christmas bonus paid with any DWP benefit;

(j)   widowed parent's allowance; and

(k)   bereavement payment for deaths occurring before 6th April 2017 and bereavement support payment for deaths after 5th April 2017.

For other local authority administered cash benefits (e.g. discretionary housing payments and social services payments) see para 18.51.

18.19   The rules for the benefits and pensions (a)-(k) above are:

(a)   if you receive any of the 'passport benefits' your total income and capital (no matter what other sources of income or capital you have) is treated as being zero;

(b)   if you receive savings credit or universal credit your total income and capital is based on the DWP's figures for these (no matter what other sources of income or capital you have), adjusted only as described in paras 18.6-7;

(c)   all of the benefits (c)-(i) are disregarded in full as income (but you must still declare them in your claim);

(d)   the first £15 of widowed parent's allowance is disregarded (but see para 18.12);

(e)   bereavement payment is a single lump sum and counts as capital. Bereavement support payment is paid as an initial lump sum and ongoing monthly payments: the lump sum counts as capital (and in Scotland is disregarded) and the monthly payments are disregarded as income.

18.20   The amount of your social security benefit that counts as income is the gross figure before any deductions are made to recover an overpayment or to pay someone else (typically to pay off a priority debt such as rent, water or fuel arrears). This applies to any benefit covered by the general rule or any of the exceptions above.

18.19(a) CTP sch 1 para 13; CTR 35, sch 7 para 14, sch 8 paras 8,9, sch 10 paras 8,9

18.19(b) CTP sch 1 para 14; CTR 36, 37

18.19(c) CTP sch 1 para 16(1)(j); CTR 39(1)(j), sch 8 paras 11,14,37,38,42,52,66

18.19(d) CTP 16(1)(j), sch 5 paras 7,8; CTR sch 6 paras 7,8, sch 8 para 21

18.19(e) CTP 16(1)(j)(xiii); CTR 39(1)(j)(xiii); SI 2017/422 art 41, 42

18.20   CTP sch 1 para 16(2); CTR 39(2), 54(3)

Working tax credit (WTC) and child tax credit (CTC)

18.21   Any income you receive from tax credits only counts from the date it is paid. Arrears of tax credits count as capital, but are disregarded for 52 weeks from the date they are paid. If your tax credit award has been reduced to recover an overpayment from the previous year, it is the reduced award that is counted. Once in payment, each instalment counts as income for the period it covers as described in the next paragraph.

18.22   Your tax credit instalment is counted as income for CTR:

(a) any child tax credit counts in full as income if you are working age but is disregarded in full if you are pension age;

(b) except where (c) applies, the whole of your working tax credit is counted as income whether you are pension age or working age;

(c) if your earnings from work are insufficient for you to use up the whole of any child care disregard and/or additional earnings disregard you are entitled to, any balance can be deducted from your working tax credit (see *Guide to Housing Benefit* for details).

War pensions for disablement and surviving partners

18.23   If you have a war pension paid for disablement or as a war widow or widower:

(a) in England and Wales, the first £10 is disregarded as income (but see para 18.12), plus any additional amount allowed by your local authority under a local scheme (which most local authorities have);

(b) in Scotland, the whole of your war pension is disregarded; and

(c) in England, Scotland and Wales the whole of any constant attendance allowance or mobility supplement paid with your war pension is disregarded.

For further details about which types of war pension are included, see the *Guide to Housing Benefit.*

Income from employment and self-employment

18.24   Income from employment or self-employment is generally treated slightly more generously than unearned income (para 18.41).

18.25   Your earnings are always converted into a weekly figure regardless of your cycle of payment. If you are an employee in regular paid employment with a fixed salary or wage (i.e. if your hours of work and/or your earnings do not fluctuate) then calculating your earnings for CTR is straightforward: your weekly gross earnings are calculated using the period immediately before the claim, adjustments are made for tax, etc, and then the appropriate earnings disregard is applied.

18.21   CTP sch 1 paras 16(3),27,31(3), sch 6 paras 18,21; CTR 39(3), 54(5), 59, 63(3), 64(10), sch 9 paras 18,21, sch 10 para 12

18.22   CTP sch 1 paras 16(1)(b), 24(1)(c),(2), sch 5 para 21; CTR 39(1)(b), 57(1)(c),(2), sch 6 para 21, sch 8 para 58

18.23   CTP sch 1 paras 16(1)(e)-(h),(l), sch 5 paras 1-6; CTR 39(1)(e)-(h),(l), sch 6 paras 1-6, sch 8 paras 13-14,20,53-56

18.26 However, if your hours of work or earnings are variable, or are irregular for some other reason (e.g. absence due to sickness, or your pay contains a bonus or overtime), or you are in self-employment, then special rules apply (para 18.28).

Assessment period: employees with regular earnings

18.27 This is the first stage in assessing income from employment. The aim is to select a period which gives the most accurate reflection of your income. If you have been in regular employment for at least two months at the time when you claim, your hours follow a regular pattern, and your earnings are constant, then your assessment period is:

(a) if you are working age and paid weekly, the five weeks before your claim;

(b) if you are pension age and are paid at intervals less than a month apart (e.g. weekly, fortnightly) the last four payments before your claim;

(c) in any other case (e.g. paid monthly) the last two payment months immediately before the claim; or

(d) some other period if this would produce a fairer result.

Assessment period: employees with fluctuating earnings and self-employed

18.28 In any other case (i.e. if hours or earnings fluctuate or you are self-employed) the guiding principle is that the length of the assessment period is the one that produces the most accurate result according to the following guidelines:

(a) if you have only just started work then the assessment period is based on what you have already been paid, so long as this is representative;

(b) if your hours vary over a recognisable cycle, then the period selected is one complete cycle (including periods where no work is done);

(c) if it would be fairer to do so, or there is as yet no evidence of earnings, the gross earnings are estimated from a certificate of actual or estimated earnings;

(d) if you are self-employed and have been for some time, the assessment period is normally the last year's trading accounts;

(e) if you have been self-employed for less than a year, the assessment period is the period that will produce the most accurate assessment;

(f) if you are just setting up a business, DWP guidance for HB recommends that gross income (and expenses) should be estimated. Awards based on an estimate usually only last a short period (say three months) after which a new assessment is made.

Employee gross earnings

18.29 If you are an employee (i.e. not self-employed) the next stage is always to calculate your gross earnings. Your gross earnings are simply your total earnings (para 18.30) less any work expenses.

18.27   CTP sch 1 paras 17(2)-(4), 20; CTR 40(2)-(4),43,47(1)(a)

18.28   CTP sch 1 paras 17(2)-(3),20; CTR 40(2),(3), 43,47(1)(b),(2),(3)

Employee earnings: elements included in your pay

18.30   Your total earnings comprise all the following elements of your pay:

(a) regular pay;

(b) arrears of pay or earnings paid as a lump sum;

(c) pay for overtime;

(d) bonus, tips or commission;

(e) holiday pay;

(f) a retainer;

(g) statutory sick pay;

(h) statutory maternity, paternity, or adoption pay.

Items (e)-(h) only count as your earnings while you are still employed (i.e. you will return to work); different rules apply if your employment has already ended (see *Guide to Housing Benefit,* chapter 14). Any earnings paid that relate to a period that ended before your CTR award starts are disregarded.

Employee expenses and tax refunds

18.31   The following items are not part of your gross earnings:

(a) expenses that are 'wholly, exclusively and necessarily' incurred as a result of your work (except any travel to work or child care costs, which must be included in your pay);

(b) if you are working age, any tax refund on your earnings (this counts as your capital).

If any items in (a) and (b) above have been included in your pay packet along with the rest of your pay then they must be deducted to arrive at your gross earnings.

Self-employment: gross income (business income)

18.32   Income derived from the business counts as your gross income from self-employment. It is calculated over your assessment period (paras 18.27-28). The following items do not count as income:

(a) grants to the business (they count as unearned income or capital, typically voluntary or charitable);

(b) any payment made under the Access to Work scheme (i.e. setting up work if you are disabled);

(c) a payment to the business, including a loan, such as an investment by a relative, entrepreneur or bank. This is capital and it is disregarded as a business asset (para 18.72);

(d) payments from the New Enterprise Allowance (they count as unearned income but are disregarded).

18.30   CTP sch 1 para 18(1), sch 4 para 9; CTR 41(1), 51(1), sch 5 para 9, sch 7 paras 1(b),2

18.31   CTP sch 1 para 18(2); CTR 41(2), 51(2)

18.32   CTP sch 1 para 21(1); CTR 44(1), 53(1)

Self-employment: allowable business expenses

18.33   Next calculate your business expenses over the same assessment period as your business income (para 18.28). The general rule is that a business expense is allowable (and so deducted from the gross income) if:

(a) it is wholly and exclusively incurred for the purpose of the business; and

(b) the authority is satisfied that the amount incurred is reasonable.

A special rule applies for calculating your business expenses if you work as a child minder: two thirds of your earnings are disregarded instead of your actual business expenses.

18.34   Allowable expenditure includes items used in your business that also relate to your private use. In such cases the expenditure is apportioned and so long as the apportionment is reasonable it is allowed. For example, loan repayments (capital and interest) for a family car and expenses for its use (e.g. insurance, VED and fuel). Likewise, if you work from home a proportion of your rent and utility bills are eligible. Any wages you pay your partner out of the business are also allowable (although it will count as their earned income): a different rule applies if you both work in a business partnership (See *Guide to Housing Benefit* for details).

Self-employment: pre-tax profit

18.35   Once you have calculated your business income (para 18.32) and allowable expenses the next stage is to calculate your pre-tax profit. This is simply your business income less allowable business expenses (para 18.33).

Employees and self-employed: net income

18.36   To calculate your net income (called your 'net profit' if you are self-employed) start with your gross earnings if you are an employee (para 18.29), or your pre-tax profit if you are self-employed (para 18.35), and deduct:

(a) income tax (para 18.37);

(b) national insurance contributions (para 18.37); and

(c) half of any contributions you pay into a pension scheme (para 18.39).

In each case the amount deducted is based on the amount paid (or estimated) over the same period used to calculate your gross income (i.e. the assessment period).

Income tax and national insurance

18.37   The amount of income tax and national insurance deducted from your gross earnings/pre-tax profit is:

(a) if you are an employee and your actual gross earnings have been used (i.e. not estimated) then the amount deducted is the actual amount of tax and national insurance paid over that period;

18.33   CTP sch 1 para 29(2)(a),(3),(6),(8); CTR 61(3)(a),(4),(7),(9)

18.34   CTP sch 1 para 29(2)(a),(3),(6); CTR 61(3)(a),(4),(7)

18.36   CTP sch 1 paras 19(1),(2), 29(1),(2); CTR 42(1),(2), 52(1),(3), 61(1),(3)

18.37   CTP sch 1 paras 19(2),(5), 30; CTR 42(2),(5), 52(3),(6),62

(b) if your earnings have been estimated or you are self-employed a notional amount is deducted for income tax based only on your basic personal allowance and the basic rate of tax (see next paragraph) on a pro-rata basis;

(c) if your earnings have been estimated your national insurance is calculated on those earnings on a pro rata basis;

(d) if you are self-employed the amount of national insurance deducted is based on the class 2 (nil or a flat rate amount) and class 4 contributions calculated on a pro rata basis. In both cases, these are notional amounts based on the method set out in the regulations and so may be different from the actual amount paid.

18.38   If you are self-employed, the notional amounts of tax and national insurance deducted (for the tax year 2018-19) are calculated as follows:

(a) for tax, start with annual pre-tax profit and subtract the basic personal allowance (£11,850 for anyone born after 5th April 1948). If there is any remainder, multiply it by 20%. The result is your notional income tax;

(b) for class 2 national insurance, if the annual pre-tax profit is £6,205 or more, the amount of notional class 2 contributions is £153.40;

(c) for class 4 national insurance, start with the pre-tax profit (or £46,350 if the pre-tax profit is greater) and subtract £8,424. If there is any remainder multiply it by 9%. The result is your notional class 2 contributions.

Pension contributions

18.39   Half of any pension contributions paid over the assessment period are also deducted from your gross earnings (even if your earnings are estimated). It includes payments into a company pension or a personal pension. If you are self-employed it only applies to any regular contributions you make (not to a lump sum).

Net weekly earned income

18.40   Your net earned income over your assessment period (i.e. gross income less tax, etc) is converted into a weekly figure: see paragraph 17.37.

Earned income taken into account

18.41   The amount of your earned income that is taken into account for CTR is your net weekly earned income less any earned income disregard that applies. The earnings disregards applied are as follows (in this order):

(a) if your earnings are paid in a foreign currency – any banking charge or commission paid to convert that sum into GB pounds;

(b) the appropriate standard earnings disregard (para 18.42 and table 18.1);

(c) if it applies, the child care disregard; and

(d) if it applies, the additional earnings disregard.

These are all weekly amounts.

18.39   CTP sch 1 paras 19(2),(4), 29(1),(2),(8),(10); CTR 42(2),(4), 52(3),(5),61(1),(3),(9),(11)

18.41   CTP sch 1 paras 19(1), 24(1),(c), sch 4; CTR 42(1), 52(2),57(1)(c), sch 5, sch 7

The standard earnings disregard

18.42 The standard earnings disregard is always deducted from the net weekly earnings – whether or not any or all of the other disregards apply. The deduction is made once only from the total earned income – regardless of how many sources. For example, if you have a partner and you both work, it is deducted only once from your combined earnings.

18.43 The appropriate earnings disregard is the highest amount that applies in your case of the amounts in table 18.1. Table 18.1 gives the rules for the most common circumstances for each level of disregard. The rules are the same as for HB; for less common circumstances that apply for the £20 standard disregard, see *Guide to Housing Benefit*.

Table 18.1 **Standard earned income disregards**

Your standard earned income disregard is the highest of the following that applies. The qualifying criteria in each case are:

£125.50 per week (disabled – permitted work)

You or your partner receive contribution-based ESA (or national insurance credits in lieu of ESA) and the DWP has allowed you to earn up to the amount of this disregard without it affecting your ESA.

£25 per week (lone parent)

You are a lone parent.

£20 per week (disabled, carers, special occupations)

(a) you are working age and entitled to a disability premium or severe disability premium (paras 17.58 and 17.66) or are in receipt of main phase ESA (para 17.53);

(b) you are pension age and in receipt of attendance allowance, or main phase ESA, or you would be entitled to a disability premium but for the fact you are pension age;

(c) you are single or a lone parent and in receipt of carer's allowance;

(d) you are a member of a couple and receive carer's allowance, but only from the earnings of the member who receives the carer's allowance;

(e) you or your partner are employed as either a part-time firefighter, auxiliary coast guard, part-time lifeboat worker or as a member of the Territorial Army.

£10 or £5 per week (any other)

In any other case not mentioned above the disregard is

(a) £10 if you are a member of a couple;

(b) £5 if you are single.

18.43   CTP sch 1 para 19(1), sch 4 paras 1-8; CTR 42(1), 52(2), sch 5 paras 1-8, sch 7 paras 4-12

T18.1   CTP sch 1 para 19(1), sch 4 paras 1-8; CTR 42(1), 52(2), sch 5 paras 1-8, sch 7 paras 4-12

The child care disregard

18.44   The child care disregard is made to any net earnings that remain after the standard disregard has been applied. As far as possible it is made to your earnings, but if the amount is greater than you and your partner's earnings any balance is deducted from your working tax credit. The amount of the disregard is the total of weekly child care costs you pay up to a maximum of:

(a) £175.00 if you have child care costs for one child; or

(b) £300.00 if you have child care costs for two or more children.

You are entitled to the child care disregard if you meet the first and second condition (paras 18.45-46).

18.45   The first condition is that you or your partner pay child care costs to a qualifying child care provider for a child who is:

(a) aged 14 or under;

(b) aged 15 until the first Monday in September after their 15th birthday;

(c) aged 16 until the first Monday in September after their 16th birthday provided they qualify for a disabled child premium.

18.46   The second condition is:

(a) you are a lone parent and you work 16 hours or more each week;

(b) you are part of a couple and you both work at least 16 hours each week;

(c) you are part of a couple and one of you works at least 16 hours and the other is too sick or disabled to work (para 18.47);

(d) you are part of a couple and one of you works at least 16 hours a week and the other is aged 80 or over;

(e) you are part of a couple and one of you works at least 16 hours a week and the other is unable to work because they are in prison.

Working 16 hours a week includes periods when you are on statutory sick pay or, in certain circumstances, statutory maternity pay or certain other benefits paid for sickness or maternity. The full conditions are in the *Guide to Housing Benefit*.

18.47   To satisfy 18.46(c) you or your partner count as too sick or disabled to work if you/they:

(a) receive main phase ESA (para 17.53);

(b) receive disability living allowance, personal independence payment, or attendance allowance (or would but for the fact they are currently in hospital);

(c) receive incapacity benefit at the short-term higher rate or the long-term rate;

(d) receive severe disablement allowance;

18.44   CTP sch 1 para 24; CTR 57

18.45   CTP sch 1 para 25(5),(6); CTR 58(5),(6)

18.46   CTP sch 1 para 25(1),(2); CTR 58(1),(2)

18.47   CTP sch 1 para 25(1)(c),(10); CTR 58(1)(c),(11)

(e) have been accepted by the DWP as being unfit for, or having limited capacity for work for a period of at least 28 weeks (i.e. get national insurance credits); or

(f) have an NHS invalid vehicle (i.e. in lieu of DLA/PIP).

The additional earnings disregard

18.48   In addition to the standard earned income disregard and child care disregard (if it applies) you are entitled to the additional earnings disregard if you meet the conditions in the next paragraph. The rate of the disregard is £17.10 per week. It is deducted from your/your partner's earnings (after the standard and child care disregard) unless the result would be to produce a negative earnings figure, in which case it is deducted from your working tax credit instead.

18.49   You are entitled to the additional earnings disregard if:

(a) you receive the 30 hour element in your working tax credit award;

(b) you work at least 16 hours per week and are responsible for a child (i.e. receive the family premium);

(c) you are working age, work at least 16 hours per week and your applicable amount includes a disability premium, work-related activity component or support component;

(d) you are aged at least 25 and you work for an average of at least 30 hours per week;

(e) you are pension age, and work at least 16 hours per week and meet the conditions for £20 standard earnings disregard.

'You' here also refers to your partner – but they must meet the condition in full themselves (not part by you and part by your partner). For items (b)-(e) whether you work 16 or 30 hours each week is decided in the same way as for a non-dependant.

Other sources of income

Other unearned income

18.50   Almost any other regular payment that is not earnings, a social security benefit, tax credit, war pension or local authority benefit counts as unearned income. It includes private pensions (e.g. a personal pension or company pension); rental income from property or a lodger; maintenance received for your child or from a partner/former partner; regular payments from charities or from a trust or any regular source of income including student income (grant, loan, etc). But it does not include any income generated from any savings or investments you own: they count as your capital (para 18.67).

18.48   CTP sch 1 para 19(1), sch 4 para 10(1),(3), sch 5 para 21; CTR 42(1),52(2), sch 5 para 10(1),(3), sch 6 para 21, sch 7 para 18(1),(3), sch 8 para 58

18.49   CTP sch 4 para 10(2); CTR sch 5 para 10(2), sch 7 para 18(2)

Local authority cash benefits

18.51   Most local authority cash benefits are disregarded as income including:

(a)   discretionary housing payments and the (Scottish) welfare fund;

(b)   payments for housing-related support to help you maintain your tenancy ('Supporting People' payments);

(c)   'local welfare provision' or 'occasional assistance' paid to help you

- meet a crisis and avoid harm; or

- avoid entering institutional care (e.g. prison, residential care, hospital) or becoming homeless; or

- to set up home after leaving institutional care;

(d)   social services payments made to help avoid your child going into care;

(e)   community care payments (including personal budgets and direct payments);

(f)   payments for fostering/kinship, adoption or guardianship.

(If you are pension age they are disregarded because they do not count as income.)

Private pensions and annuities etc

18.52   Private pensions count in full as your income for the period it covers (but remember to convert it into a weekly amount). Private pensions include: public sector pensions (e.g. local government); company pensions; payments from the Pension Protection Fund; personal pensions (including NEST for those automatically enrolled) and regular payments from any annuity.

Income from lodgers or renting other property

18.53   Income from lodgers or renting out property that is not your home is treated as follows:

(a)   disregard any rent received from a family member or non-dependant;

(b)   income from lodgers (people living in your home):

- disregard the first £20.00 for each letting or, if meals are provided, each occupier (e.g. including any child);

- then count only half the remainder as income if you provide meals, or all of the remainder in any other case;

(c)   if you are pension age any income from property other than your home is disregarded in full;

(d)   If you are working age any income from property other than your home:

- if the property is disregarded as capital (table 18.2) deduct from the gross rent any

---

18.51   CTP sch 1 para 16(1), sch 6 paras 21, 29, 29B
CTR sch 1 para 16(1), sch 8 paras 30-34, 37,59,64,65, sch 9 paras 21,29 sch 10 paras 12,23-25,61-64

18.52   CTP sch 1 para 16(1)(c),(d),(x); CTR 39(1)(c),(d),(x), 54(1),(2)

18.53   CTP sch 1 para 16(1)(p),(v), sch 5 paras 9,10; CTR 39(1)(p),(v), 54(1),(2), sch 6 paras 9,10, sch 8 paras 26,27

mortgage payments (interest and capital), council tax and water charges (but nothing else) – the result is your income;

- in any other case, including where the capital value is nil, take the rental income for an appropriate period (e.g. six months, a year) deduct any letting expenses (e.g. agents' fees, repairs, cleaning, council tax, water charges and mortgage repayments, etc). The remainder counts as capital, not as income.

Maintenance received

18.54   If you receive maintenance payments (such as from a former partner) it is counted as follows:

(a) If it is made to support a child the whole amount is disregarded if:

- you are pension age; or
- you are working age and the payment is made by a 'liable relative'.

(b) If it is for an adult then the first £15 from all such payments (whether from one or two or more payments) is disregarded but only if there is a child or young person in your family and either:

- you are working age and the payment is made by your former partner or your partner's former partner; or
- you are pension age and the payment is made by your former spouse/civil partner or your partner's former spouse or civil partner.

18.55   'Liable relative' means:

(a) you or your partner's spouse or civil partner from whom you/they are separated or divorced;

(b) the parent or step-parent of a child/young person in your family (i.e. a child you or your partner get child benefit for);

(c) a person who is making maintenance payments and who for that reason can reasonably be treated as the father (whether or not this has been settled by the court).

Payments from charities and friends etc

18.56   If you receive a regular income from a charity or on a voluntary basis (e.g. from a relative or friend) these are completely disregarded (a different rule applies to a lump sum, i.e. capital).

Payments from a trust

18.57   Regular payments from a private trust (i.e. one where you are named as a beneficiary) count in full as your income unless the payments are for a personal injury (see next paragraph) or, if you are pension age, the trust is discretionary (see *Guide to Housing Benefit* for details).

18.54   CTP sch 1 para 16(1)(o), sch 5 para 20; CTR 39(1)(o), sch 6 para 20, sch 8 paras 49,50

18.55   CTR sch 8 para 50(2)

18.56   CTP sch 1 para 16(1); CTR 39(1),64(7), sch 8 para 19

Personal injury payments

18.58   Payments of income for a personal injury, including payments from a trust, are disregarded in full. For lump sum awards see paragraph 18.75.

Government supported special trust funds

18.59   Payments from certain government-created trusts to compensate you if you have contracted certain diseases are disregarded in full as income and capital (para 18.76) as follows:

(a) if you have contracted Variant Creutzfeldt-Jacob Disease (the Variant Creutzfeldt-Jacob Disease Trust);

(b) if you have been infected through NHS blood products with HIV, haemophilia or hepatitis C (Caxton Fund, Eileen Trust, Macfarlane Trust, MFET Ltd, Skipton Fund, and their successor trusts). In certain circumstances these payments may also be disregarded if you have received the payment from a relative as a gift or inheritance.

18.60   Payments from the independent living fund and London Bombings Charitable Relief Fund are also disregarded as income and capital.

Expenses for voluntary work

18.61   Expenses for unpaid work (whether for a charity, voluntary organisation or friend, etc) are disregarded as are expenses paid to you as a member of a service user group (e.g. a health authority or social landlord).

Student income

18.62   If you are a student there are special rules about how your income from grants, loans and other sources is treated (e.g. elements that are disregarded and the period over which these are calculated). These rules are same as for HB (*Guide to Housing Benefit,* chapter 19) but most students are in any case excluded from CTR (para 15.63).

Capital

18.63   This section describes how your capital is taken into account in the calculation of your CTR. Paragraphs 18.64-69 describe general rules about how your capital is taken into account and valued. Paragraphs 18.70 onwards describe the rules for specific items of capital where the whole or part of its value is disregarded – only the most common items have been included. For less common items see the *Guide to Housing Benefit.*

18.58   CTP sch 5 paras 14,15; CTR sch 6 paras 14,15, sch 8 para 19

18.59   CTP sch 1 para 16(1); CTR 39(1),64(7), sch 8 para 41

18.61   CTP sch 1 para 18(2)(f); CTR 41(2)(f), 51(2)(d), sch 8 paras 5,6

18.62   CTR 24, 75-86

18.64   If your capital is above the 'upper capital limit' then you are not entitled to CTR (para 15.60). If your capital is assessed as being below the 'lower capital limit' then your tariff income is zero (para 18.65) and the amount of CTR you receive is unaffected (i.e. it is calculated using your actual income only). The lower capital limit is:

(a) £6,000 if you are working age;

(b) £10,000 if you are pension age.

18.65   If you have capital that is valued between 'the lower capital limit' and 'the upper capital limit' then your capital is converted into a hypothetical income figure (the 'tariff income') and added to any other income in your assessment. Your tariff income is calculated as follows:

(a) If you are working age deduct £6,000 from the total and divide the remainder by 250.

(b) If you are pension age deduct £10,000 and divide the remainder by 500.

(c) Then, in either case, if the result is not an exact multiple of £1, round the result up to the next whole £1. This is your weekly tariff income.

18.66   Any capital held wholly by you or your partner or both of you together is described in the next two paragraphs. However, if your capital is jointly owned with someone else, you must first work out your share (or deemed share) and then value that share in the same way.

Valuing capital: straightforward cases (savings and cash etc)

18.67   In many cases valuing capital is straightforward. The value of the capital is simply the current cash value. This applies to the following:

(a) any savings (in UK sterling) held in a bank or savings account;

(b) National Savings Certificates. These are valued at their current value rather than the face value purchase price (which can be calculated online [www]);

(c) Premium Bonds (at face value);

(d) any other item held in cash, whether or not in an account.

Valuing items: other than savings

18.68   In any other case, any capital that you own that is not in cash or UK sterling (e.g. property, stocks and shares, foreign currency) is valued as follows:

(a) take the current market value or surrender value of the item;

(b) deduct 10% if selling the item or converting into UK sterling would involve costs;

(c) then disregard any debt or charge secured against it (e.g. a mortgage if the item is property) (but not any other debts you may have such as rent arrears).

18.64-65   CTP sch 1 paras 24(1)(b),37; CTR 57(1)(b),71,72

18.67   CTP sch 1 para 32; CTR 65
           www.nsandi.com/savings-index-linked-savings-certificates-calculator

18.68   CTP sch 1 para 32; CTR 65

Table 18.2 **Capital: the value of your home and former home**

The value of your home or former home can be disregarded as capital. The circumstances are described below.

(a) **The home you occupy.** The value of the dwelling you normally occupy as your home is disregarded in full without any time limit.

(b) **Your partner's home if you are living apart but still a couple.** If you and your partner are currently living as separate households but are still committed to each other (i.e. not divorced, separated or estranged, etc) then the value of their home is disregarded.

(c) **Your home or former home following a relationship breakdown.** if you have divorced your partner or become estranged the value of your former home is disregarded if:

- your ex-partner is now a lone parent and continues to live in the property; or
- in any other case, for up to 26 weeks from the date it ceased to be occupied.

(d) **The home of a disabled or elderly relative.** The value your partner's home or any relative of a family member is disregarded provided they are pension age or incapacitated.

(e) **A home you have recently purchased.** The value of any property you intend to occupy is disregarded for up to 26 weeks or such longer period as is reasonable.

(f) **A home you are taking steps to obtain possession of.** The value of any home you are taking steps to obtain possession of (e.g. from squatters or an abusive ex-partner) is disregarded for up to 26 weeks or such longer period as is reasonable.

(g) **A home that requires repairs etc, to make it fit to live in.** If your home requires essential repairs or alterations to make it fit to live in, it is disregarded for up to 26 weeks from the date you first take steps to make it habitable, or such longer period as is reasonable.

(h) **Money from selling your home (working age).** If you are working age any money from selling your home is disregarded for up to 26 weeks (or longer if it is reasonable) but only if you intend to use it to buy a new home. Money from selling includes money received as compensation for compulsory purchase for the home's market value together with any home loss payment intended to be used for the same purpose.

T18.2(a) CTP sch 6 para 26; CTR sch 9 para 26, sch 10 para 4
T18.2(b) CTP sch 6 para 4(b); CTR sch 9 para 4(b), sch 10 para 7(b)
T18.2(c) CTP sch 6 para 6; CTR sch 9 para 6, sch 10 para 30
T18.2(d) CTP sch 6 para 4(a); CTR sch 9 para 4(a), sch 10 para 7(a)
T18.2(e) CTP sch 6 para 1; CTR sch 9 para 1, sch 10 para 5
T18.2(f) CTP sch 6 para 2; CTR sch 9 para 2, sch 10 para 32
T18.2(g) CTP sch 6 para 3; CTR sch 9 para 3, sch 10 para 33

(i) **Money deposited with a housing association (working age).** If you are working age any money deposited with a housing association to obtain a home is disregarded for as long as it remains deposited, or if that money is refunded for up to 26 weeks or longer if reasonable, but only if it is intended to be used to buy another home.

(j) **Money received for buying a home (pension age).** If you are pension age any payments received for the sole purpose of buying a home are disregarded for one year. This is wider than the rule for working age claims (h). For example, it can include the proceeds from a sale but also money gifted or loaned by a relative for that purpose.

(k) **A property you have rented out.** The value of any home you have rented out counts as capital except:

- if it forms part of a business it is disregarded as a business asset; or

- in any other case, the fact that it is occupied may mean its market value is reduced (i.e. its sale value with a sitting tenant) CH/1953/2003.

Note: These conditions may apply simultaneously – or one after another – so long as the relevant conditions are met.

Valuing capital jointly held

18.69 If you own an item of capital jointly with someone other than your partner, you must first determine your share before valuing it as above. If the item owned is held in distinct known shares (e.g. one person holds a one third share and the other two thirds) then it is your actual share that is valued. It is the market value of your share itself (i.e. what would someone be prepared to pay – knowing the remainder is held by someone else) that is valued, not the whole item pro rata. This may mean that the actual share itself has very little value. In any other case (i.e. if the shares are not known) it is assumed that you and all the other owners each hold an equal share.

Arrears of social security benefits and tax credits

18.70 Arrears of social security benefits count as capital if they are still unspent at the end of the period they were paid for, but arrears of tax credits count as capital from the date the payment is received. However, any capital from tax credits arrears or any of the social security benefits in para 18.18(a)-(f) (and in Scotland bereavement support payments) are disregarded for 52 weeks, or longer if they are large arrears of a passport benefit that was paid late due to official error. 'Large arrears' in this case means £5,000 or more.

T18.2(h) CTR sch 10 para 6

T18.2(i) CTR sch 10 para 14

T18.2(j) CTP sch 6 para 18; CTR sch 9 paras 18,20(a)

T18.2(k) CTP sch 6 paras 5,9,10; CTR sch 9 paras 5,9,10, sch 10 paras 10,11

18.69 CTP sch 1 para 36; CTR 70

18.70 CTP sch 1 para 31(3), sch 6 paras 18,21,22; CTR 63(3),64(10), sch 9 paras 18,21,22, sch 10 para 12

Personal possessions

18.71   The value of any personal possessions (e.g. jewellery, art) you hold is ignored. However, if you are working age and you purchased those items in order to dispose of your capital and increase your CTR award, then they can be taken into account.

Business assets

18.72   The value of the assets of a business that is wholly or partly owned by you are disregarded so long as you are engaged in self-employment in that business – including for up 26 weeks or longer if reasonable if you are unable to work due to sickness. If you have stopped working, the business assets are also disregarded for as long as is reasonably needed for their disposal.

Life insurance and annuities etc

18.73   The surrender value of any life insurance policy you hold is ignored. But any money you receive from the policy counts as your capital. The capital value of any money invested in an annuity is also disregarded (although any income it generates is counted as your income).

Compulsory purchase compensation

18.74   Compensation for the market value of your home is disregarded for up to 26 weeks. Home loss payments count in full as part of your capital unless you intend to use the payment to purchase a new home. (See rules in table 18.2 for both items.)

Compensation for personal injury and special trusts

18.75   If you receive a lump sum payment for a personal injury, including from a trust, the payment is disregarded for up to 52 weeks, or without any time limit if you are pension age. If more than one payment is made, the 52 week time limit runs from the date of the first payment. Any lump sum payments you receive for a personal injury that are held in a trust are disregarded in full without time limit (whether you are pension age or working age).

18.76   If you receive a lump sum from any of the special trusts in paragraph 18.59, it is disregarded in full, including in certain circumstances if it has been passed on to you as a gift or an inheritance from a relative.

18.71   CTP sch 6 para 8; CTR sch 9 para 8, sch 10 para 15

18.72   CTP sch 6 paras 9,10; CTR sch 9 paras 9,10 sch 10 para 11

18.73   CTP sch 6 paras 11,24,32; CTR sch 9 paras 11,24,32

18.75   CTP sch 6 para 17; CTR sch 9 para 17

18.76   CTP sch 6 para 16; CTR sch 9 para 16, sch 10 para 29

Chapter 19 **CTR changes to entitlement**

- Duty to tell the council about changes of circumstances: see paras 19.2-6.
- How changes are dealt with: see paras 19.7-8.
- When changes take effect: see paras 19.9-26.
- Extended reductions and continuing reductions: see paras 19.27-36.
- Reviewing awards of CTR: see paras 19.37-41.
- Fraud and penalties: see paras 19.42-46.

19.1 Your entitlement to CTR can change or end. Decisions change when there is a relevant change in your circumstances, or the circumstances of someone else relevant to your CTR entitlement such as a household member, or in the law itself (paras 19.9-36). They can also change when the council reviews entitlement (paras 19.37-38) or as a result of the disputes and appeals procedures.

Duty to tell the council about relevant changes

19.2 You must tell the council about any 'relevant' change of circumstances. The same duty applies to anyone acting for you (paras 16.3-5). This means any change that you (or the other person) could reasonably be expected to know might affect:

(a) your entitlement to CTR; or

(b) the amount of CTR you get.

This duty to notify begins on the date your application is made, and continues for as long as you are getting CTR. (For time limits etc, see paras 19.5-6.)

19.3 The law lists changes that you must tell the council about and changes that you don't have to notify (summarised in tables 19.1 and 19.2). These are not exhaustive. For example, you should also tell the council of changes in your:

(a) personal details (name, address, etc);

(b) family and household details (which could affect the applicable amount or non-dependant deductions); and

(c) capital and income.

19.2   CTP sch 8 para 9(1),(6); CTR 115(1),(6)

Table 19.1 **Changes you must tell the council about**

The following is a list of the items specifically mentioned in the law. Your duty is wider (paras 19.2-3).

If you are a working age applicant

(a) The end of your (or your partner's) entitlement to JSA(IB), ESA(IR), IS or UC.

(b) Your child or young person stops being a member of the family: e.g. when child benefit stops or they leave your household.

If you are a pension age applicant

(a) A non-dependant moves in or out or their income changes.

(b) Absences exceeding or likely to exceed 13 weeks (or four weeks for absences from Great Britain.

Additional matters if you are on savings credit

(a) Changes affecting any child living with you (other than age) which might affect the amount of CTR.

(b) Changes to your capital which take it (or may take it) above £16,000.

(c) Changes to a non-dependant if their income and capital was treated as being yours.

(d) Changes to a partner who was ignored in assessing savings credit but is taken into account for CTR.

Additional matters if you are on second adult rebate

(a) Changes in the number of adults in your home.

(b) Changes in the total gross incomes of the adults in your home.

(c) The date any adult in your home stops getting JSA(IB), ESA(IR) or IS.

How to tell the council about changes

19.4   You must notify a change to the council – or to someone acting on its behalf. Some councils accept notification by telephone or online, though they can require written rather than telephone notifications, or require written or electronic records to be kept if you make online notifications. In Scotland, authorities can specify an address which you can attend to notify births and deaths. In all other cases, changes must be notified in writing to a 'designated office' (para 16.6).

CTR time limits, etc

19.5   For CTR in England and Wales you should tell the council about relevant changes within 21 days beginning with the day on which the change occurs or as soon as reasonably practicable thereafter. There is no equivalent time limit for CTR in Scotland.

T19.1   CTP sch 8 para 9; CTR 115

19.4   CTP sch 7 para 11, sch 8 para 9(2); CTR 115(2), sch 1 para 11

19.5   CTP sch 8 para 9(2); CTR 115(2)

> # Table 19.2 **Changes you don't have to tell the council about**
>
> ---
>
> (a) Beginnings or ends of awards of pension credit (either kind) or changes in the amount – because it is the DWP's duty to tell the council.
>
> (b) Changes which affect JSA(IB), ESA(IR), UC or IS but do not affect CTR.
>
> (c) Changes in council tax.
>
> (d) Changes in the age of any member of your family or non-dependant.
>
> (e) Changes in the CTR regulations.

19.6 CTR law does not say what happens if you fail to tell the council about a relevant change or (in England and Wales) within the above time limits. In practice, if the change would:

(a) reduce or end your entitlement to CTR – councils are likely to regard an overpayment as having occurred and recover it;

(b) increase your entitlement to CTR – it is arguable that councils should award the arrears (since council tax law does not generally contain time limits for adjusting liability), but you should not rely on this and it is likely to be a matter for tribunals and the courts to decide.

Dealing with changes

Decisions, information and evidence

19.7 The council must decide whether to alter (or end) your entitlement to CTR as a result of the change. It may ask you to provide information and evidence it requires in connection with this. You are responsible for providing this in the same way as when you made your application (para 16.10).

Notifications

19.8 When the council alters (or ends) entitlement to CTR, it must tell you about this within 14 days or as soon as reasonably practicable after that. The notification must include:

(a) its new decision; and

(b) your right to obtain a written statement of reasons and to appeal, etc.

The exception to the above is that in Scotland CTR law contains no duty to notify.

T19.2   CTP sch 8 para 9(3)-(4),(7)-(9): CTR 115(3)-(4),(7)-(9)

19.7   CTP sch 8 para 7(4); CTR 113(4)

19.8   CTP sch 8 para 12(1)(b),(2),(4); CTR 117(1)(b),(2)-(4)

When changes take effect

19.9   This section describes when a change affects your entitlement to CTR. There are two steps involved for the council:

(a)   determining the date the change actually occurred; and

(b)   working out (from that) what date it takes effect in CTR.

The date a change occurs: the general rule

19.10   The starting point is that the date a change actually occurs is the date something new happens (for example, a new baby arrives, a birthday, a change in pay). This is a question of fact.

The date a change takes effect: the general rule

19.11   The date a change takes effect is:

(a)   in CTR in Wales, the exact date the change occurs (whatever day of the week this is);

(b)   in CTR in England and Scotland, the Monday after the date the change occurs. Even if the change occurs on a Monday, CTR changes on the following Monday.

19.12   There are different rules for changes in pension credit. These and other special cases are described below (paras 19.13-36).

Moves and changes in council tax liability

19.13   This rule applies when:

(a)   you move home; or

(b)   your liability for council tax changes.

19.14   The date your council tax goes up (or down) is usually clear. The date a move occurs can be less straightforward. However, it is the date you change your normal home, rather than a date on a letting agreement, etc (R(H) 9/05 para 3.4). All moves and all changes in council tax take effect in CTR on the exact day.

Changes to pension credit

19.15   If a change in either your guarantee credit or savings credit, whether due to a change in your circumstances or due to official error, affects your entitlement to CTR, this takes effect from the date shown in table 19.3.

Changes to UC

19.16   When your entitlement to UC starts, changes or ends, the general rules apply (paras 19.10-12).

19.11   CTP sch 1 para 46(1); CTR 107(1)

19.14   CTP sch 1 para 46(3),(4); CTR 107(3),(4)

19.15   CTP sch 1 para 47; CTR 108

Examples: Moves and changes in liability

Moving within the council's area

A woman moves from one address to another within the council's area on Friday 26th October 2018. She is liable for council tax at her old address up to and including Thursday 25th October 2018 and at her new address from Friday 26th October.

Her CTR changes on and from Friday 26th October (on a daily basis) to take account of her new eligible council tax.

Moving out of the council's area

A man moves out of the council's area on Saturday 12th May 2018. He is liable for council tax at his old address up to and including Friday 11th May.

His CTR ends on the last day of his liability for council tax. In other words, his last day of CTR is Friday 11th May.

Table 19.3 **CTR – When pension credit starts, changes or ends**

The change	When it takes effect in CTR
Pension credit starts, increasing your entitlement to CTR	The Monday following the first day of entitlement to pension credit
Pension credit starts, reducing your entitlement to CTR	The Monday following the date the council gets notification from the DWP about this (or, if later, the Monday following the first day of entitlement to pension credit)
Pension credit changes or ends, increasing your entitlement to CTR	The Monday of the benefit week in which pension credit changes or ends
Pension credit changes or ends, reducing your entitlement to CTR due to a delay by you in notifying a change of circumstances to the DWP	The Monday of the benefit week in which pension credit changes or ends
Pension credit changes or ends, reducing your entitlement to CTR in any other case	The Monday following the date the council got notification from the DWP about this (or, if later, the Monday following the pension credit change or end)
If any of the above would take effect during your 'continuing reduction' period (para 19.35), the change is deferred until afterwards.	

T19.3   CTP sch 1 para 47; CTR 108

Changes to tax credits

19.17   When your entitlement to working tax credit or child tax credit starts, changes or ends, the general rule applies (paras 19.10-12). But because of the way tax credits are paid it can involve counting backwards or forwards from the pay date to work out when the change actually occurs. Table 19.4 explains this and includes examples.

Table 19.4 **CTR – When a tax credit starts, changes or ends**

Four-weekly instalments

The pay date is the last day of the 28 days covered by the tax credit instalment. So if a four-weekly instalment is due on the 30th of the month, it covers the period from 3rd to 30th of that month (both dates included).

For example:

    (a)   if that is the first instalment ever of your tax credit, your CTR changes on the Monday following the 3rd of the month;

    (b)   if that is the first instalment of a new rate of your tax credit, your CTR changes on the Monday following the 3rd of the month;

    (c)   if that is the last instalment of your tax credit, the date the change occurs is the 31st of the month, and your CTR changes on the Monday following the 31st of the month.

Weekly instalments

The pay date is the last day of the 7 days covered by the tax credit instalment.

So if a weekly instalment is due on the 15th of the month, it covers the period from 9th to 15th of that month (both dates included).

For example:

    (a)   if that is the first instalment ever of your tax credit, your CTR changes on the Monday following the 9th of the month;

    (b)   if that is the first instalment of a new rate of your tax credit, your CTR changes on the Monday following the 9th of the month;

    (c)   if that is the last instalment of your tax credit, the date the change occurs is the 16th of the month, and your CTR changes on the Monday following the 16th of the month.

Different rules apply for CTR in Wales: para 19.11.

Changes relating to social security benefits

19.18   The following rules apply when entitlement to a social security benefit starts, changes, ends or is reinstated. They apply to all social security benefits (apart from the credits described in paras 19.15-17) received by you, your partner, or a child or young person.

19.19   The date such a change actually occurs is the first day of your new, different, nil or re-instated entitlement. The date the change takes effect in CTR follows the general rules in para 19.11.

19.18   CTP sch 1 para 46(1),(2); CTR 107(1),(2)

19.20   When a social security benefit is found to have been awarded from a date in the past, any resulting increase in CTR is awarded for the past period (so you get your arrears: see the second example). This is the effect of the general rules (para 19.11).

Changes in income, capital, household membership, etc

19.21   The general rules (paras 19.10-12) apply to all other changes – including changes in income, capital, membership of your family or household, and so on. But see also para 17.30 for when non-dependant deductions may be delayed, and paras 18.17 and 18.70 for when arrears of income are (or are not) taken into account.

19.22   Councils also have a discretion to disregard, for up to 30 weeks, changes in the rates of income tax (including the Scottish basic or other rates) and any personal tax relief, national insurance, the amount of tax payable as a result of an increase in the weekly rate of the basic state retirement pension, plus any additions and the maximum rate of tax credits when these result from a change in the law (e.g. the Budget). This discretion does not apply to CTR in Scotland (and is in any case rarely used).

Starting work

19.23   The general rules (paras 19.10-12) apply when you start work. Their effect is that if you start work on a Monday you get a whole week of CTR (except in Wales) as though you had not started work. You may – after that – also qualify for an extended reduction (para 19.27).

Changes ending CTR

19.24   The general rules (paras 19.10-12) apply to any change of circumstances which means that you no longer satisfy all the basic conditions for benefit – for example if your capital now exceeds the upper limit or your income is now too high to qualify.

Changes in the law: regulations and up-ratings

19.25   When regulations relevant to CTR are amended, the council alters your entitlement to CTR from the date on which the amendment takes effect (unless entitlement reduces to nil, in which case para 19.24 applies).

More than one change

19.26   If more than one change occurs in a case, each is dealt with in turn. But in England and Scotland the following rules apply when changes which actually occur in the same reduction week would have an effect (under the earlier rules in this chapter) in different reduction weeks. In all CTR cases, work out the various days on which the changes have an effect (under the earlier rules): all the changes instead apply from the earliest of these dates.

19.22   CTP sch 1 para 28; CTR 60

19.26   CTP sch 1 para 46(7); CTR 107(7)

Extended reductions

19.27 If you are long-term unemployed and start work an extended reduction (ER) helps you by giving you four weeks' extra CTR. They are like the extended payments you can get in HB, JSA or ESA (and you often get them at the same time).

Entitlement

19.28 You are entitled to an ER if you meet the conditions in table 19.5. Councils in England can vary the ER conditions (para 15.38) and in Wales councils can increase the length of an ER award but cannot reduce it (para 15.42).

19.29 No application is required for an ER. All the matters referred to in table 19.5 are for the council to determine (not the DWP). You must be notified about your entitlement to an ER (or not).

Table 19.5 **Who can get an extended reduction**

Applicants who have been on a 'qualifying income-related benefit'

You are entitled to an extended reduction if:

(a) you or any partner start employment or self-employment, or increase hours or earnings;

(b) this is expected to last for at least five weeks;

(c) you or any partner have been entitled to ESA(IR), JSA(IB), JSA(C) or IS continuously for at least 26 weeks (or any combination of those benefits in that period);

(d) immediately before starting the job, etc, you or your partner were on ESA(IR), JSA(IB) or IS. At this point being on JSA(C) is not enough; and

(e) entitlement to ESA(IR), JSA(IB) or IS ceases as a result of starting the job, etc.

Applicants who have been on a 'qualifying contributory benefit'

You are entitled to an extended reduction if:

(a) you or any partner start employment or self-employment, or increase hours or earnings;

(b) this is expected to last for at least five weeks;

(c) you or any partner have been entitled to ESA(C), IB or SDA continuously for at least 26 weeks (or any combination of those benefits in that period);

(d) immediately before starting the job, etc, you or any partner were on ESA(C), IB or SDA. And neither of you must be on ESA(IR), JSA(IB) or IS; and

(e) entitlement to ESA(C), IB or SDA ceases as a result of starting the job, etc.

19.27   CTP 2(1), definition: 'extended reduction'; sch 1 para 38; CTR 2(1), 87,88,94,95,100

19.28   CTPW 32(3), 33(3)

T19.5   CTP 2(1), definitions: 'qualifying contributory benefit', 'qualifying income-related benefit', sch 1 para 38; CTR 2(1), 87, 88, 94, 95, 100

Period and amount

19.30   An ER is awarded from the date the change (getting a job, etc) takes effect, and it lasts for four weeks (as illustrated in the example). In each of those four weeks, the amount of the ER is the greater of:

(a) the amount awarded in the last full benefit week before the ER started;

(b) the amount which would be your entitlement in that particular week if there were no such thing as ERs. For example, if your non-dependant left home you might qualify for more CTR this way.

19.31   Throughout the ER, all changes in your circumstances are ignored. And no ER is awarded for council tax during any period during which you are not liable for council tax.

19.32   In Scotland only, if you or your partner reach pension age during the ER, the figure used for 19.30 (b) throughout the ER is whichever would have been higher using your entitlement before and after that age.

CTR after an extended reduction

19.33   If you qualify for CTR based on your new income after the end of the ER, this is awarded in the normal way – and there is no requirement for you to make a fresh application for this.

Variations for movers

19.34   If you are are entitled to an ER you are entitled to it even if you move home during the ER. In Great Britain, if the move is to another council's area, the determination, notification and award of the ER is done by the council whose area you are moving out of. That council may liaise with the council whose area you are moving into; and may pay the ER to them or to you.

Example: Extended reduction

An applicant who meets all the conditions for an ER starts work on Monday 2nd July 2018.

His award of CTR continues up to and including Sunday 8th July 2018. His ER covers the period from Monday 9th July 2018 to Sunday 5th August 2018. If he then continues to qualify for CTR after that, the new amount of CTR is awarded from Monday 6th August 2018.

19.30   CTP sch 1 paras 39,40; CTR 89,90,96,97,101,102

19.32   CTS60+ 54

19.33   CTP sch 1 para 42; CTR 92, 99, 104

19.34   CTP sch 1 paras 41,44, sch 6 paras 1,2; CTR 91,98,103,105

Continuing reductions

Entitlement

19.35   Continuing reductions are awarded in CTR whenever the DWP tells the council that:

(a) you are on JSA(IB), ESA(IR) or income support and have now reached pension credit age (table 15.4); or

(b) you have a partner who has claimed pension credit.

Continuing reductions enable the award of CTR to continue without a break while the new entitlement to pension credit (if any) is determined.

Period and amount

19.36   The continuing reduction starts immediately after the last day of entitlement to JSA(IB)/ESA(IR)/IS, and lasts for four weeks plus any extra days to make it end on a Sunday. The amount during that period is calculated by treating you as having no income or capital. And if you move home, your eligible council tax is the higher of the amounts at the old and new addresses; and any non-dependant deductions are based on the circumstances at the new address.

Reviewing awards of CTR

19.37   The council may reconsider any decision it has made about your CTR, and in doing so may ask you to provide information and evidence it reasonably requires (para 16.10).

19.38   A review may show that:

(a) there has been an unreported change of circumstances, in which case the earlier rules apply (paras 19.6-36);

(b) a decision was wrong from the outset. CTR does not have special rules for this but in practice the considerations in paragraph 19.6 are also likely to apply here.

In both the above situations the council must tell you what it has done.

CTR overpayments

19.39   If following a review your award is reduced for any period in the past this will result in an overpayment of your CTR. In the law overpaid CTR is called 'excess CTR'.

19.40   There are no nationally set rules about excess CTR. The DCLG has reframed excess CTR as an underpayment of council tax (*Localising council tax support: administrative matters – guidance note,* paras 29-36 [www]). Where you have paid too little council tax because of excess CTR the council can recover the excess as unpaid council tax (in the absence of limitations in its local scheme). The council tax billing, collection and enforcement rules have been amended to allow these 'adjustments' to CTR.

19.35   CTP sch 1 para 43; CTR 93

19.37   CTP sch 8 para 7(4),(6); CTR 113(4),(6)

19.40   http://tinyurl.com/DCLGNote
         Council Tax (Administration and Enforcement) Regulations 1992 (SI 1992/613)
         Council Tax (Administration and Enforcement) (Scotland) Regulations 1992 (SI 1992/1332)

19.41   Rules for dealing with excess CTR (as opposed to the billing for, or enforcement of, unpaid council tax) may be found in the council's local scheme. There is significant variation between authorities ranging from 'an overpayment is rectified by the amount being clawed back by an adjustment to the council tax bill' to 'the treatment of overpayments of council tax support reflects the former CTB regulations'. The power to devise local schemes has also allowed authorities to make more subtle changes to the considerations previously applicable to excess CTB, e.g. 'no underlying entitlement for periods of overpayment is to be calculated'.

Fraud and penalties

19.42   Authorities have powers to investigate and prosecute CTR fraud. Regulations made under those powers provide English and Welsh authorities with investigatory powers, and create offences, administrative and civil penalties in relation to local CTR schemes.

Administrative penalties

19.43   The council may offer you the chance to pay an 'administrative penalty' rather than face prosecution, if:

    (a)   an 'act or omission' on your part caused excess CTR; and

    (b)   there are grounds for bringing a prosecution against you for an offence relating to that excess CTR.

You do not have to agree to a penalty. You can choose the possibility of prosecution instead.

19.44   The offer of a penalty must be in writing, explain that it is a way of avoiding prosecution, and give other information – including the fact that you can change your mind within 14 days (including the date of the agreement), and that the penalty will be repaid if you successfully challenge it by asking for a reconsideration or appeal. Authorities do not normally offer a penalty (but prosecute instead) if an overpayment is substantial or there are other aggravating factors (such as being in a position of trust). For excess CTR the penalty is 50% of the excess (subject to a minimum of £100 and a maximum of £1,000). In these circumstances the council should calculate the amount of the excess CTR on a daily basis beginning with the first day in respect of which the excess is awarded and ending with the day on which the council knew or ought reasonably to have known that an excess had been awarded.

19.45   An offer of a penalty may also be made where your act or omission could have resulted in excess CTR and there are grounds for bringing a prosecution for a related offence. In these cases the penalty is the fixed amount of £100.

19.42   LGFA ss 14A-14C

19.43   LGFA s.14C, SI 2013/501, 11; SI 2013/588, 13

19.45   SI 2013/501 11(2), (6); SI 2013/588 14(1)-(2)

Civil penalties

19.46   The council can impose a £70 penalty on you if you negligently make an incorrect statement in connection with an application for CTR without taking reasonable steps to correct it, or have been awarded CTR but didn't disclose information or report changes in your circumstances without reasonable excuse. In each case, the action or inaction has to result in excess CTR before a civil penalty can be considered. If you are successfully prosecuted for fraud or offered an administrative penalty or caution, you cannot be issued with a civil penalty for the same offence. The amount of the civil penalties is added to the amount of the excess CTR.

19.46   SI 2013/501, 12, 13; SI 2013/588 16-17

Chapter 20 **CTR appeals and further reviews**

- How to get a written explanation about a CTR decision and how to appeal to the council about it in England and Wales: see paras 20.2-8.

- How to appeal to an independent Valuation Tribunal in England or Wales: see paras 20.9-18.

- How appeals are dealt with by the Valuation Tribunal and what happens afterwards: see paras 20.19-22.

- Applying for an internal review of a CTR decision made by a Scottish council: see paras 20.23-24.

- Applying to the independent Council Tax Reduction Review Panel for a further review of a CTR decision made by a Scottish council, how further reviews are dealt with and what happens afterwards: see paras 20.25-38.

20.1   This chapter describes the different arrangements for appealing CTR decisions that apply in England, Scotland and Wales. See paras 20.2-22 for England and Wales and paras 20.23-38 for Scotland.

CTR appeals in England and Wales

Decision notices should include appeal rights

20.2   The CTR decision letter you get from the council should tell you how to appeal and point you to the appeal rules in your council's local CTR scheme (paras 15.35 and 20.6). In England and Wales CTR law refers to a person who has the right of appeal as a 'person aggrieved' and this reflects the fact that CTR appeals are dealt with in a similar way to appeals about council tax generally.

Getting a written explanation of the council's CTR decision

20.3   You can write to the council to ask for a written statement that sets out the reasons for any decision in its decision letter. Your request should be made within one month of the date of the council's decision letter. The council should send you its written statement of reasons within 14 days – or as soon as reasonably practicable after that.

20.2   CTP sch 8 para 12(4),(7)-(8); CTR 117(4),(7)-(8); CTPW sch 14, para 3, sch 13 para 9(7)-(8); CTRW sch 10, para 3, 115(7)-(8)

20.3   CTP sch 8 para 12(5)-(6); CTR 117(5)-(6); CTPW sch 13 para 9(5)-(6); CTRW 115(5)-(6)

Appealing to the council

20.4   A CTR decision is appealable if it affects:

(a)   your entitlement to a reduction under the scheme; or

(b)   the amount of any reduction that you are entitled to.

20.5   If you want to appeal you should write to the council identifying the matter in dispute. You should also say why you are appealing, e.g. the council has established the wrong facts, considered the wrong law (including the rules in its own local scheme), has misapplied the law to the facts, etc. To avoid any doubt that you are appealing, your letter should ask the council to treat your request as a 'notice of appeal under section 16 of the Local Government Finance Act 1992'.

Time limit to appeal to the council

20.6   CTR law in England (paras 15.35-36) doesn't set a time limit in which your appeal should be made but there may (or may not) be a time limit in your local scheme rules.

20.7   In Wales your appeal should reach the council within one month of the date it issued its decision or, where you requested a statement of reasons, within one month of the date the statement of reasons was issued.

The council's response to your appeal

20.8   The council must consider the matters raised in your appeal. It should then write to you describing the steps it has taken to deal with the grievance. But if it thinks that the grounds for the grievance are not well founded, it should give you its reasons for thinking this.

Appealing to the Valuation Tribunal

20.9   If you are still dissatisfied with the council's response (para 20.8) you can appeal directly to the Valuation Tribunal. You can also do this if the council fails to respond to your appeal within two months from the date the council got it.

20.10   Guidance issued by the Valuation Tribunal in England is clear: you can appeal a decision about discretionary CTR to a valuation tribunal in the same way as any other kind of CTR [www] (and the same is true for Wales).

The Valuation Tribunal for England and the Valuation Tribunal for Wales

20.11   The administrative arrangements for valuation tribunals in England and Wales are slightly different:

(a)   in England, CTR appeals are considered by the Valuation Tribunal for England and administrative arrangements are the responsibility of the Valuation Tribunal Service (paras 20.12-21);

20.4-5   LGFA 16; CTP sch 7 para 8(1); CTR sch 1 para 8; CTPW sch 12 para 8(1); CTRW sch 1 para 8(1)

20.7   CTPW sch 12 para 8(2); CTRW sch 1 para 8(2)

20.8   CTP sch 7 para 8(2); CTR sch 1 para 9; CTPW sch 12 para 9; CTRW sch 1 para 9

20.9   CTP sch 7 para 8(3); CTR sch 1 para 10; CTPW sch 12 para 10; CTRW sch 1 para 10

20.10   Council Tax Guidance Manual para 16.2.9
           https://www.valuationtribunal.gov.uk/wp-content/uploads/2016/01/council-tax-guidance-manual.pdf

(b)	in Wales, appeals are considered by, and administered by, the Valuation Tribunal Service for Wales (paras 20.12-21).

More details can be found online [www]. In both England and Wales a further appeal (on a point of law if given permission) may be considered by the High Court.

20.12	The Valuation Tribunal is a free service and cannot award costs against you or the council. Members of the tribunal are volunteers and don't have to have any special qualifications, but they should have received training. Normally two or three members sit on a hearing. A clerk who is a paid official advises on points of law and procedure.

20.13	In England, a First-tier Tribunal (para 14.19) can act as members of the Valuation Tribunal in a CTR appeal on issues that relate to the assessment of income, capital or the right of residence (and sometimes in other cases involving difficult points of law). In these cases a First-tier Tribunal member sits with a senior member of the Valuation Tribunal to consider the appeal. Most other CTR appeals in England are normally considered by two Valuation Tribunal members.

Appeals about discretionary CTR

20.14	If you appeal a decision about discretionary CTR the tribunal isn't confined to making decisions solely within judicial review principles (due process, reasonableness, proportionality, legality, etc) and can substitute its view for that of the council provided it is 'soundly and solidly based'. Even if the council's decision complies with its own published policy, this does not stop the tribunal from allowing the appeal, although it does make it less likely. (See Council Tax Guidance Manual [www].)

Procedural rules and practice statements/protocols

20.15	The tribunal's procedures are set out in the same regulations that govern appeals about other council tax matters (paras 15.3-23). In England the regulations are supplemented by practice statements and in Wales by practice protocols. The details and further information are:

(a)	In England, the Valuation Tribunal for England (Council Tax and Rating Appeals) (Procedure) Regulations SI 2009 No 2269 (as amended) and (for CTR appeals) SI 2013 No 465. Practice statements can be found online [www]. In particular, Practice Statement VTE/PS/A11 contains important information and standard directions for both you and the council.

(b)	In Wales, the Valuation Tribunal for Wales Regulations SI 2010 No 713 (as amended) (and for CTR appeals) SI 2013 No 547. Practice protocols can be found online [www].

20.11	www.valuationtribunal.gov.uk/
		www.valuation-tribunals-wales.org.uk
		LGFA 136, sch 11 para A18A

20.14	Council Tax Guidance Manual paras 16.2.9, 16.3.3 and 16.4.1 (see footnote 20.10)

20.15	www.valuationtribunal.gov.uk/preparing-for-the-hearing/practice-statements/
		www.valuation-tribunals-wales.org.uk/best-practice-protocols.html

The time limits in which to make your appeal to the tribunal

20.16   You should normally make your appeal to the tribunal within:

(a) the two months following the date the council responded to your initial appeal; or

(b) the four months following the date your initial representation is made if the council fails to respond to it.

Your appeal may be allowed out of time appeal if your failure to make it was due to circumstances beyond your control such as illness, absence from home or bereavement. A practice statement and protocol sets out how your application should be made and the relevant considerations [www].

Making an appeal

20.17   You appeal to the tribunal by writing directly to it. Appeal forms are available online [www]. Further details about how and where to appeal are in table 20.1.

Table 20.1 **How and where to appeal CTR**

England

How:	In writing by post or by email
Where:	Valuation Tribunal CTR Team
	Hepworth House
	2 Trafford Court
	Doncaster DN1 1PN
	appeals@vts.gsi.gov.uk
Contact for administrative matters:	0300 123 1033

Wales

How:	Online form (or downloaded)
Where:	The appropriate regional office (if downloaded)
Contact for administrative matters:	See guidance notes

Scotland

How:	In writing by post. (Download form recommended)
Where:	CTR Review Panel
	4th Floor, 1 Atlantic Quay
	45 Robertson Street
	Glasgow, G2 8JB.
Contact for administrative matters:	0141 302 5840
	CTRRPAdmin@scotcourtstribunals.gov.uk

20.16   SI 2009/2269 reg 21(2)-(3),(6); SI 2010/713 reg 29(1)-(2),(5)
         www.valuationtribunal.gov.uk/wp-content/uploads/2016/02/Practice-Statement-A1-Extension-of-times.pdf
         www.valuation-tribunals-wales.org.uk/best-practice-protocols.html

20.17   www.valuationtribunal.gov.uk/forms/appeal-forms/council-tax-reduction/
         www.valuation-tribunals-wales.org.uk/council-tax-reduction.html

20.18 Your appeal should include the following information:

(a) your full name and address;

(b) the address of the relevant chargeable dwelling – if different from your address;

(c) the relevant council's name – and the date on which your initial appeal was served on it;

(d) the date, (if any) that you were notified of the council's response;

(e) the grounds on which you are aggrieved;

(f) brief reasons why you think that the decision or calculation made by the council is incorrect.

If you have also appealed your HB about the same matter to the First-tier Tribunal, you should tell the Valuation Tribunal about this when you appeal your CTR. In Wales your HB appeal letter should be included with your CTR appeal. The clerk should acknowledge receipt of your appeal within two weeks and send a copy of it to the council.

How appeals are dealt with

20.19 Appeals are normally heard unless you and the council agree agree it can dealt with on the papers and the tribunal considers it appropriate. You should normally be given at least 14 days (in Wales four weeks) notice of the time and place of hearing. In England shorter notice than the 14 days may be given in urgent or exceptional circumstances. Hearings are normally held in public so it is possible for you to attend a hearing as an observer to see a tribunal in action. You may be accompanied to your own hearing by someone else. That other person may act as your representative or otherwise assist you in presenting your case. The tribunal itself decides what form the hearing should take (subject to the rules of natural justice). It may give a decision orally at a hearing.

Decision notice and statement of reasons

20.20 The tribunal should provide you with a notice of its decision as soon as reasonably practicable. It should also explain your right to request a written statement of reasons (if not given with the decision) and any right of appeal. In Wales the decision notice should be accompanied by a statement of reasons.

20.21 In England, if you want to ask for a statement of reasons (and it has not been supplied with the decision notice) the tribunal should get your request within two weeks of the date of its decision notice (although it does have the power to extend this period). The statement of reasons should be sent to you (and the council) within two weeks of the request being made or as soon as reasonably practicable thereafter.

20.18   SI 2009/2269 regs 20A, 28(2); SI 2010/713 reg 30(1),(2),(5)

20.19   SI 2009/2269 regs 2, 29, 30, 31, 36(1); SI 2010/713 regs 33(1),(6); 34(1); 36, 37, 40(2)

20.20   SI 2009/2269 reg 36(2); SI 2010/713 reg 40(3)

20.21   SI 2009/2269 reg 37(3)-(7)

After the decision

20.22   The tribunal has the power to correct clerical mistakes, accidental slips and omissions and also to review its decision in specific circumstances. A further appeal to the High Court may only be made on a point of law (para 14.73). It should normally be made within four weeks of the decision notice being issued or, in England, within two weeks of the statement of reasons being issued if later. You should get legal advice before embarking on this course of action.

Scotland: CTR reviews and further reviews

Asking the council to review its decision

20.23   In Scotland if you are dissatisfied with your council's decision about your CTR you can write to it and ask it to review its decision. Your request should get to the council within two months of the date its decision was sent to you. You should set out what you are dissatisfied with and why.

The council's actions on receipt of your review request

20.24   On receipt of your review request the council should:

(a) consider the issue(s) identified in your request,

(b) decide if it is going to change the decision you are dissatisfied with (this should be done within two months of getting the request from you);

(c) tell you in writing about its decision; and

(d) tell you that if you remain dissatisfied you can request a further review, the address to which this should be sent, and the time period in which this must be done (42 days from the date of the council's letter).

Requesting a further review by the CTR Review Panel

20.25   If you are dissatisfied with the council's decision following its review (para 20.24) you, or your representative, can request a further review by writing directly to the CTR Review Panel (table 20.1). Application forms, are available online [www], or from the Review Panel itself (table 20.1) and the Review Panel strongly recommends that you use the form provided to make your application. Your application must be received within six weeks (42 days) from the date of the council's written response to your review request.

20.26   You can also ask for a further review if the council fails to respond to your initial review request and more than two months have passed since they got it. In these circumstances, your request for a further review should be sent in writing to the council. The council cannot write to

20.22   SI 2009/2269 regs 39, 40; SI 2010/713 regs 43(1)-(2); 42, 44(1)-(2)

20.23   CTS 90A(2)-(3); CTS60+ 70A(2)-(3)

20.24   CTS 90A(4); CTS60+ 70A(4)

20.25   http://counciltaxreductionreview.scotland.gov.uk/index.html
         CTS 90B(1); CTS60+ 70B(1)

20.26   CTS 90B(2)-(3) (5); CTS60+ 70B(2)-(3) (5)

you about any decision on your initial review and must pass on your request for a further review to the CTR Review Panel as soon as possible.

20.27   Your request for a further review should set out the matter(s) you are dissatisfied with, the reasons why and include a copy of the authority's CTR internal review decision notice (if there is one).

The CTR Review Panel

20.28   The Review Panel is appointed by a Scottish Cabinet Secretary. One of the panel must also be appointed as senior reviewer. To be appointed, members of the panel have to be solicitors or advocates with at least five years' experience. A further review is normally carried out by a single member Review Panel, though in particular circumstances a three member Review Panel may undertake the review. Administrative arrangements are by the Scottish Courts and Tribunal Service.

The council's response to your further review application

20.29   If the Review Panel decides that your application is complete and valid, it writes to the council, informing it of your request. The council's response should normally be submitted within six weeks (42 days). It should contain all the material it wishes the Review Panel to consider. The council should also forward a copy of its submission to you at this time. If the Review Panel does not get a response from the council within the six weeks, it has the power to exclude the council from any further participation in the proceedings and allow your application [www].

How further reviews are dealt with

20.30   The responsible panel member:

  (a) decides the procedure to be adopted for the further review (having regard to any guidance issued by the senior reviewer);

  (b) can hold any oral hearing in public or private;

  (c) can ask for, but has no power to require, the production of documents or the attendance of anyone as a witness;

  (d) can refuse to allow a particular person to represent you at an oral hearing if there are good and sufficient reasons for doing so.

20.31   The further review should be by way of an oral hearing unless you, the council and the panel member agree that it should be dealt with on the papers. If the panel member asks you about it being dealt with this way, you and the council must tell them whether you both agree to it or not. You should also tell the panel member if you have disputed the equivalent housing benefit decision and if it has already been decided on appeal.

20.27   CTS 90B(4); CTS60+ 70B(4)

20.28   CTS 90C(1)-(2), 90D(1), 90D(8) ; CTS60+ 70C(1), 70C(8)
         http://counciltaxreductionreview.scotland.gov.uk/

20.29   CTS 90D(4); CTS60+ 70C(4)
         http://counciltaxreductionreview.scotland.gov.uk/documents/LA%20Guidance%20Note.pdf

20.30   CTS 90D(6); CTS60+ 70C(6)

20.31   CTS 90D(2)-(3); CTS60+ 70C(2)-(3)

20.32   If you or the council are asked by the panel member to provide documents or information and fail to respond within the time limits set, the panel member may draw any inference from this failure they see fit. This can include allowing or refusing the further review.

Withdrawing your request for further review

20.33   You can withdraw your request for further review only with the permission of the senior reviewer.

The decision

20.34   The panel member reaches a decision in private after the hearing. The decision can be to allow or reject your request, in full or in part. It is either given on the day or sent out in the post, depending on the circumstances of the case. Any re-calculation of your CTR entitlement is carried out by the council.

20.35   If you had an oral hearing, a letter setting out the panel member's decision is given or posted to you and to the council on the day of the hearing. If your case has been decided on the papers, you should get a letter through the post a day or two after the decision has been made. A copy of the decision is also sent to the council.

20.36   Both you and the council are entitled to a full statement of reasons for the decision. You can request this by writing to the Review Panel, at the address above, within 14 days of the date on which the decision was given. You should quote your CTR RP reference number [www]. You or the council may also request a set-aside of the decision in the interests of justice. This should be done within 14 days of the date the decision was made. You should give reasons for the request. Where a panel member decides to set aside the decision the further review must be carried out again.

After the Review Panel's further review

20.37   The council should carry out any necessary re-calculation of the amount of your CTR entitlement and put into effect the Review Panel's decision as soon as reasonably practicable. Any queries you have about how the decision is implemented should be addressed to the council [www].

20.38   There is no right of appeal against the Review Panel's decision [www] but it would presumably be susceptible to judicial review. You should get legal advice about this.

20.32   CTS 90D(4); CTS60+ 70C(4)

20.33   CTS 90D(5); CTS60+ 70C(5)

20.34   CTS 90D(6)(e); CTS60+ 70C(6)(e)

20.36   CTS 90D(6)(f),(6A)-(6C); CTS60+ 70C(6)(f),(6A)-(6C)
         counciltaxreductionreview.scotland.gov.uk/documents/LA%20Guidance%20Note.pdf

20.37   CTS 90D(7); CTS60+ 70(C)(7)
         http://counciltaxreductionreview.scotland.gov.uk/documents/CTRRP%20FAQ%20-%20Public.pdf

20.38   http://counciltaxreductionreview.scotland.gov.uk/documents/CTRRP%20FAQ%20-%20Public.pdf

Chapter 21 **Rate rebates**

- An overview of domestic rates (including liability and exemptions and so on): see paras 21.2-8.
- The different kinds of rebate schemes for help with rates (UC-related, HB and others): see paras 21.9-19.
- UC-related rate rebates: basic conditions and how to claim: see paras 21.20-28.
- How UC-related rebates are calculated: see paras 21.29-36.
- UC-related rate rebates: claims, payments, changes and appeals: see paras 21.37-46.
- HB rate rebates: basic conditions and how to claim: see paras 21.47-53.
- HB rate rebates: how awards are calculated and making payments: see paras 21.54-63.
- Rate relief (and how to calculate it): see paras 21.64-74.
- Lone pensioner allowance: see paras 21.75-81.

21.1   This chapter applies only in Northern Ireland. It describes how who is liable for domestic rates is decided, how your rates bill is calculated, and the various rebate schemes and other ways your liability can be reduced if you have a low income, a disability or if you are a lone pensioner.

Rates

21.2   Domestic rates are the form of local taxation in Northern Ireland. Rates are a tax on residential properties known as dwellings (which for convenience we also refer to as 'your home'). Responsibility for paying them normally falls on the occupier: see paragraph 21.6. Land and Property Services (an executive agency of the Department of Finance) is responsible for the billing and collection of the tax.

Dwellings and annual rates

21.3   The domestic rate is an annual bill. One rates bill is issued per dwelling, unless the dwelling is exempt (para 21.7). A 'dwelling' means any house, flat, houseboat or mobile home, etc, whether lived in or not.

21.4   The amount of your rates bill depends first on the 'rateable value' of your home set by Land and Property Services (LPS). The rateable value is the open market sale value (capital value) of your home on 1st January 2005 (capped to a maximum of £400,000). If you are a NIHE or registered housing association tenant the capital value is substituted by a 'social sector value', calculated by the DFC based on the rent you pay for your home.

21.2   www.finance-ni.gov.uk/land-property-services-lps

21.3   SI 1977/2157 art 4, 17, sch 5, sch 7

21.4   SI 1977/2157 art 23A, 39, sch 12 paras 7-16; NISR 2007/184; NISR 2009/77

21.5 The amount of annual rates is calculated by multiplying the rateable value (or £400,000 if the cap applies: para 21.4) by the rate in the pound ('rate poundage') for the year. The rateable value and aggregate rate poundage for each district is shown on the bill and can be found on the LPS website.

Liability for rates

21.6 The rates bill goes to the owner or occupier of the dwelling. For example:

(a) if you are a NIHE or housing association tenant the rates bill goes to your landlord, who recovers the cost by increasing the overall amount of rent you pay;

(b) if you are a private tenant the rates bill may go to you, or your landlord may add it to your rent;

(c) if you are an owner occupier the rates bill is sent to you.

Note that if you are a tenant and your landlord has paid the rates bill, then they have in effect included the amount in your rent whether or not it was a conscious decision to do so. In each case you can get a rate rebate whether the bill is paid by you or your landlord.

Table 21.1 **Domestic rates: key considerations**

(a) Which dwelling is being considered?

(b) What is the capital value (or social sector value) for that dwelling?

(c) What is the aggregate rate poundage in that district?

(d) Who is liable for the rates?

(e) Is the dwelling exempt from rates altogether?

(f) Do they qualify for a disability reduction?

(g) Do they live in a UC full service area?

(h) Do they qualify for full or partial HB on their rates?

(i) Do they qualify for rate relief on any remaining rates?

(j) Do they qualify for lone pensioner allowance on any remaining rates?

21.5   SI 1977/2157 art 6(3)

21.6   SI 1977/2157 art 18-21

Exemptions

21.7 Certain dwellings are exempt from rates. This is not automatic – you must make an application to Land and Property Services. An occupied dwelling is exempt if the landlord is a registered charity. There are very few other exemptions and they mainly relate to unoccupied properties.

Disability reductions

21.8 Your rates bill is reduced by 25% if your home has been adapted or extended because of the disability of anyone who lives there. The reduction is not automatic: you must make an application to Land and Property Services.

Rate rebate schemes in Northern Ireland

What are rate rebates

21.9 A rate rebate reduces the amount of rates you pay. The amount you receive depends on your UC/HB award: the higher your UC/HB the higher your rebate (and the lower your bill). Rate rebates are funded by a UK government grant paid to LPS and from money raised through the rates themselves. Further information about rate rebates can be found online [www].

21.10 From 27th September 2017, universal credit (UC) is gradually being introduced in Northern Ireland on an area-by-area basis (paras 1.14-15). For working age claimants in UC full service areas help with rates is through the new rate rebate scheme. In this guide we call this a UC-related rate rebate.

21.11 If you live outside a UC full service area you can get housing benefit (HB). You can also get HB if you live in a UC full service area and you are pension age (whether or not if you get SPC); or if you get a legacy benefit. In either case if you get HB you may also get extra help from rate relief and/or the lone pensioner allowance.

Who can get a UC-related rate rebate

21.12 The phased introduction (by individual Jobcentre Plus offices) of UC in Northern Ireland started on 27th September 2017. Over the following 15 months the number of Jobcentre Plus areas covered by UC is gradually being expanded with the full roll out expected to be completed in December 2018. If you are claiming UC you can also claim a rate rebate. A rate rebate is separate from UC so you will have to make a claim for it (para 21.25). In the law it is called rate relief but in this guide we call it a UC-related rate rebate because you can only get it if you get UC and to avoid confusion with the other kind of rate relief (para 21.64).

21.7   SI 1977/2157 sch 7 para 2

21.8   SI 1977/2157 art 31A

21.9   www.nidirect.gov.uk/rate-rebate-scheme

21.10   NISR 2017/190

21.12   NISR 2017/190 regs 2(1) 'relevant district', 3
        https://www.communities-ni.gov.uk/publications/universal-credit-roll-out-by-postcode

21.13   In areas where UC applies you can get a UC-related rate rebate if:

(a) you are working age (or if you are a couple both you and your partner are);

(b) you do not have an existing HB award; and

(c) you have claimed and have been awarded UC (para 21.14).

If you are a couple and only one of you is working age see para 21.18.

21.14   If you get a legacy benefit and have a change of circumstances that would trigger a claim for UC and you make a claim for it, your HB (for both rent and rates) ends (paras 1.21-26). Once you have claimed UC you cannot get HB again unless you move to outside a UC full service area or reach pension credit age.

Who can get a HB rate rebate

21.15   If you live outside a UC full service area you can get housing benefit (HB) to help with your rates whether you are pension age or working age. You may also get rate relief and/or, if you are aged 70 or over, lone pensioner allowance.

21.16   If you are state pension credit age, or you are a couple and both of you are state pension credit age, you can get housing benefit (HB) to help with your rates. This applies whether you live inside or outside a UC full service area. (If you are a mixed age couple and live in a UC full service area see para 21.18.)

21.17   If you are working age (or if you are a couple, both of you are) and you live in a UC full service area and you can get a HB rate rebate only if you have an existing HB award and have not claimed UC (or had a change of circumstances that would start a claim for UC).

21.18   If you are a mixed age couple and live in a UC full service area you can get a HB rate rebate if you get a legacy benefit or SPC (but see para 21.19). In any other case if only one of you is state pension credit age you claim a UC-related rate rebate.

21.19   If you get a legacy benefit and a change occurs that triggers a UC claim (paras 1.21-26) your HB rate rebate ends and you can only get a UC-related rate rebate. This rule applies even if you do not qualify for UC (para 21.14).

21.13   NIWRO art 9(1)(b); NIUC 3(1); RR 10(1)(c),(d)

21.14   NIUCTP 3(1),(2), 4(1)-(4),(7),(8); NISR 2017/190 reg 24

21.15   NISR 2017/190 regs 2(1) 'relevant district', 3 (and see footnote to para 21.12)

21.16   NIWRO art 9(1)(b); NIUC 3(1); NIUCTP 3(1), 24(4)(a)

21.17   NIUCTP 4(1)-(4),(7),(8)

21.18   NIWRO art 9(1)(b); NIUC 3(1), RR 10(1)(c)

21.19   NIUCTP 4(1)-(4),(7),(8)

Basic conditions for UC-related rate rebates

21.20 This section and the following two sections (paras 21.21-46) describes the rate rebate scheme if you have claimed UC. It does not apply if:

(a) you live outside a UC full service area (paras 21.10-11);

(b) you are single and pension age (para 21.16); or

(c) you are a couple and both of you are pension age (para 21.16).

If you are a mixed age couple see para 21.18.

Conditions of entitlement for a UC-related rate rebate

21.21 You are entitled to a UC-related rate rebate only if you meet all of the following conditions:

(a) you are liable for rates on a dwelling in Northern Ireland (para 21.6);

(b) there is an amount of eligible rates (para 21.29);

(c) you are not excluded from a rebate (para 21.22);

(d) you occupy the dwelling as your home (para 21.23);

(e) you are not entitled to HB unless you live in specified supported accommodation (paras 4.11-12);

(f) you are entitled to universal credit; and

(g) during the 'assessment period' either:

  ▪ your income does not exceed your maximum amount; or

  ▪ the amount by which your income exceeds your maximum amount multiplied by the taper is less than the amount of your eligible rates.

21.22 You are excluded from a rate rebate if:

(a) you live with a resident landlord/owner who is a close relative (para 4.45);

(b) you live in a residential care home, nursing home or independent hospital; or

(c) the LPS has decided that your liability was created to take advantage of the rate rebate scheme; or

(d) you are not entitled to UC because you refused to sign a claimant commitment or you are excluded from UC for any other reason (e.g. if you are a student or migrant).

Apart from (a) to (d) are no other exclusions (e.g. capital limit, etc) as these matters are taken into account when your entitlement to UC is considered.

Getting a UC-related rate rebate on two homes or during an absence

21.23 You can only get a UC-related rate rebate on your only or main residence so you cannot usually get a rebate on more than one dwelling or if you are absent from your home (para 21.21(d)). The only exceptions are the same that apply to the UC housing costs element (paras 4.64-78) (and the law is in the footnotes to this para.)

21.21   SI 1977 No. 2157 art 30A(3)(a) as amended by art 134 NIWRO; RR 10(1)-(3), 28(1)

21.22   RR 10(1)(d), 11(4)

21.23   RR 28-35

Applying for a UC-related rate rebate

Who can apply

21.24   If you have made a claim for UC you can apply for a rate rebate. If you are a couple your application can be made by whichever one of you agree should make it (and if you cannot agree LPS decides). If you are unable to act similar considerations apply as for council tax rebate (paras 16.3-4) (and the law is in the footnote to this para). If the LPS takes the view that you need support to make a claim, it must make appropriate arrangements for you. If you need help to apply, further advice is available online [www].

How to apply

21.25   You must make a separate application to LPS for rate rebate (your UC claim cannot be treated as a claim for rate rebate). You can only apply by creating an online rate rebate account [www].

21.26   Your claim is only complete only if it has been accepted by the computer system it is sent to and complies with all of the instructions given on the online form. If your claim is incomplete LPS must inform you of any defect and give you one month to correct it. It your claim is corrected within the one month it is treated as being complete from the outset.

21.27   To start your online rebate account you only need to supply your name and address and complete the declaration that you agree to the information held by the DFC about your UC claim (para 21.36) being shared with LPS and used to work out if you can get a rate rebate.

Time limit for making a claim

21.28   The time limit for making a claim for rate rebate is three months from the date of your first UC payment but if your claim is late it is nevertheless treated as being made in time if:

 (a)   following the death of your partner you make a claim within one month of your being issued with your next rates bill; or

 (b)   on the last day of the time limit you were unable to make a claim due to a failure of the computer system, provided you make a successful claim within 48 hours of the system becoming available again (paras 21.25-27).

There are no other exceptions no matter what the reason (e.g. for good cause, etc).

21.24   RR 3(1),(4), 4(1)-(6)
        www.nidirect.gov.uk/rate-rebate-scheme

21.25   RR 3(2), sch para 2(6)
        https://www.nidirect.gov.uk/services/create-or-log-in-to-a-rate-rebate-account

21.26   RR 5(6)-(9), sch para 5

21.28   RR 5(1),(3),(4)

Calculating UC-related rebates

Eligible rates

21.29   Your eligible rates is the figure used to calculate your entitlement to rate rebate. It is worked out by the following steps:

(a) start with the annual rates due on your home (after any capping that may apply);

(b) if you are entitled to a disability reduction, use the figure after it has been made;

(c) if you are a joint occupier, or part of your home is used for business, apportion the result (para 21.31);

(d) convert it to a monthly figure:

  ▪ if your rates are charged for the full year, by dividing the annual rates by 12;

  ▪ if your rates are charged for only part of the year, by dividing the total charge for that part by the number of days in that part, multiplying by the number of days in the year and dividing by 12.

The resulting figure is your 'maximum rate rebate'.

21.30   If you are entitled to the maximum award and the calculation in para 21.29(d) results in a surplus or a shortfall in the rates payable, an adjustment is made during the final rebate assessment period so that your total rebate matches the total rates charged for that year.

Apportionment of eligible rates

21.31   Your eligible rates figure is apportioned if:

(a) you occupy only part of a rateable unit (for example, if you are a lodger or live with others in a multi-occupied property). In this case only the proportion of the rates payable for your accommodation is eligible for a rebate;

(b) you are jointly liable to pay rates with one or more other occupiers – for example if you have a joint tenancy (paras 5.11-13);

(c) part of the rateable unit is for business use – such as a flat above a shop. This is done in the same way as for eligible rent for HB (see *Guide to Housing Benefit,* chapter 8).

How a your rate rebate is affected if a non-dependant lives with you

21.32   Unlike HB for rates, no deduction is made from your eligible rates for any non-dependant who lives with you (but a non-dependant may affect the way your eligible rates are apportioned).

21.29   RR 11(1), 12(2)

21.30   RR 12(3)

21.31   RR 11(2),(3)

21.32   RR 2(1) 'maximum amount', 10(3)

How UC awards affect the maximum rebate

21.33   If you claim UC (including if you do not qualify for it) your rate rebate is calculated as follows:

(a) if you are not entitled to UC you are not entitled to a rate rebate;

(b) if you get maximum UC (para 9.4) you also get the 'maximum rebate' (para 21.29);

(c) if your UC award is less than the maximum UC, then your maximum rate rebate is reduced: (para 21.35).

How your capital affects your rebate

21.34   Your capital is assessed by the DFC and is taken account of in the income figure the DFC supplies to calculate your rate rebate (para 21.36). If your capital exceeds the UC capital limit (para 10.55) you do not get any UC and so do not get a rate rebate (paras 9.6 and 21.21(f)).

How rebate is calculated if you do not get maximum UC

21.35   If you do not get maximum UC your maximum rate rebate is reduced by 15% of your 'excess income' (but if this figure is more than (or equal to) your maximum rebate, then you do not get a rate rebate). Your excess income is:

(a) your income (para 21.36); less

(b) your maximum UC as calculated by DFC (para 9.4).

The 15% figure is also known as the 'taper'.

How income is calculated

21.36   If you do not get maximum UC your income is calculated as follows:

(a) your UC award; plus

(b) your UC unearned income; plus

(c) your UC earned income; less

- half your UC work allowance (table 10.1).

All the figures (a)-(c) are supplied by the DFC (and the UC figure is your award before any deductions for overpayments, third party payments or sanctions).

Examples: rate rebate calculation

Claimant on maximum UC

A single claimant aged over 25 is unemployed. His annual rates liability is £750.00. He gets maximum UC (para 9.4).

Maximum UC (para 9.4 and table 9.2)	£317.82
Income: UC	£317.82

Because he gets maximum UC he qualifies for maximum rebate (para 21.33) which is £62.50 per month (£750.00 divided by 12).

21.35   RR 10(3)(b)

21.36   RR 10(7)

Claimant unearned and earned income

A lone parent aged 34 cares for her child aged 7. Her monthly earnings are £542.88 (16 hours per week at the minimum wage). She does not pay for any child care. She receives maintenance from her former partner of £130.00 per month. She pays rent of £325 per month. Her UC award is £544.81. Her annual rates liability is £816.00 (= £68.00 per month).

Maximum UC (single 25+, child, housing costs: para 9.4)	£874.49
Universal credit	£527.22
Unearned income (maintenance: para 10.38)	£130.00
Earned income less half of work allowance (£542.88 – ½ of £198.00)	£443.88
Total income	**£1,101.10**
Excess income (total income less maximum UC)	£226.61
Eligible rates	£68.00
Less 15% of excess income	– £33.99
Monthly rate rebate	**£34.01**

UC rebates: decisions, awards, payments and changes

The monthly basis of assessment

21.37   Your rate rebate is based on a monthly assessment period (in the law it is called the 'attribution period' but in this guide we use the term assessment period). Your first assessment period starts on the date of your claim and continues for one month. After that, each assessment period begins on the same day each month in a similar way to UC. (But unlike the 'whole month' approach of UC, changes are dealt with on a pro-rata basis: para 21.44).

Start date, time limits and backdating

21.38   Your rate rebate starts on the date you first become entitled to it (usually the date you first become entitled to UC).

21.39   The time limit for claiming a rate rebate is three months from the start of your UC award. If you claim within the time limit you do not need to show 'good cause' but you cannot get a rebate for any period more than three months before you claim, no matter what the reason.

How your rebate is paid

21.40   Your rate rebate is usually awarded as a credit to your rates account or, if you are a social renter, to your landlord's rates account. Further information can be found on the rate rebate online page.

21.37   RR 12(2), 21(1)

21.38   RR 5(1)

21.39   RR 5(1),(4)

21.40   See footnote to para 21.9

Reviews and changes of circumstance

21.41   Your rate rebate can be revised if:

 (a)   the decision arose from an error made by LPS, the DFC or the Inland Revenue;

 (b)   the decision was made without knowledge of, or a mistake as to a relevant fact;

 (c)   the UC figures on which your rebate is based are changed or your entitlement to UC ends;

 (d)   you become entitled to HB;

 (e)   there is a change in your eligible rates;

 (f)   there is a change in your occupation of the dwelling, for example, temporary absence etc (para 21.23); or

 (g)   your earned income changes.

Any change of circumstances that results in a revised award is calculated using the latest UC figures.

Table 21.2 **UC rebates: date of revision**

Specific change (increase or decrease)

(a) A change in earned income	The start of the assessment period that immediately follows the anniversary date of claim
(b) UC award ends	The day after your last day of entitlement to UC
(c) Change in rateable value notified within three of revaluation	The date the new rateable value applies from

Other changes resulting in a higher award

(d) Official error or the wrong UC figures	Date of the original decision
(e) Error due to a mistaken fact notified within three months or which the authority already had sufficient information to identify it	
(f) Changes of the kind in para 21.41(d)-(f) that are notified within three months	Date the change occurs
(g) Changes of the kind in para 21.41(d)-(f) that are notified later than three months or that you fail to notify	Date you notify LPS of the change or the date it is first identified

Any other change resulting in a lower award

(h) Error due to mistaken fact	Date of the original decision
(i) Any other change of circumstance (i.e. reduced award)	Date the change occurs

21.41   RR 13(1),(3)

T21.2   RR 14(2)-(7),(9)

How and when revisions are made

21.42   Your award can be revised if there has been a change of circumstances or if it was wrong from the outset. The date your award is revised from depends on the type of change, whether it is advantageous (i.e. results in a higher award), and whether it is reported in time. Table 21.2 gives the rules for when revisions take effect.

21.43   You can request a revision on any grounds within three months of receiving notice of your award (decision notice). If the LPS agrees with your reasons your award is revised from the date of the original decision.

21.44   When your award is revised it is recalculated on a pro-rata basis for the assessment period in which the change occurs (table 21.2). During the assessment period in which the change takes place, there is always a 'before' and 'after' and each part is calculated pro-rata according to the number of days before and after the change and added together (see examples).

Overpayments

21.45   Overpayments are recovered by LPS from you (usually by adding it to your rates account), or from the person responsible for rates on the property, depending on the circumstances.

Appeals

21.46   The only matter about your UC-related rebate that can be appealed to a valuation tribunal is a decision that relates to your occupation of the home (para 21.23). No other matter can be appealed to a tribunal (because your award is based on decisions about your UC) but you can ask for revision, including if your UC is changed as result of your appeal about UC.

Examples: UC-related rebates changes and revised awards

1. Change in the DFC figures

A single claimant is awarded partial UC from 1st April 2018 and claims a rate rebate on the same day. His annual rates liability is £840 so his maximum rebate would be £70.00 per month (£840 divided by 12). Based on the DFC's figures of his unearned income he is awarded a partial rebate of £45.00 per month. On the 15th November his unearned income increases. Based on the new DFC figures his rebate is reduced to £30.00 per month. His rebate for the assessment period 1st-30th November is:

£45.00 x 15/30 + £30 x 15/30 =£37.50 (and then £30.00 per month for each following assessment period).

21.43   RR 14(3)(c)

21.44   RR 16

21.45   RR 23-26

21.46   RR 18

2. Award of HB

A single claimant claims and is awarded rebate on 1st April 2018 when she claims UC. Her rates are £840 per year. On 15th August she reaches pension age and claims pension credit and HB-related rebate. Her HB rate rebate starts on Monday 20th August. Her UC-related rate rebate for the assessment period 1st-31st August is:

£70 x 19/31 = £42.90. (She does not qualify for UC-related rebate from 20th August onwards).

3. Increase in earnings

A single claimant with earned income is awarded a UC-related rebate from 15th June 2018. Based on the DFC's income figures, she is awarded a rebate of £30.00 per month. On 23rd September her earnings increase; based on the new DFC income figures her rebate would be £15.00 per month. Her UC rebate does not change until the next assessment period following the anniversary date of her claim: 15th July 2019.

Basic conditions for HB rate rebates

21.47   This section and the remainder of this chapter describe the rate rebate scheme if you cannot make a claim for UC, for example if you are pension credit age. If you cannot claim UC you can get help with your rates through housing benefit (HB) whether or not you also need help with your rent. If you get HB and still have rates left to pay you can also claim:

(a)   rate relief (para 21.64); and/or

(b)   lone pensioner allowance (para 21.75).

You can also get rate relief or lone pensioner allowance if you cannot get UC but your entitlement to HB is nil (e.g. because your income or capital is too high).

Conditions of entitlement to a HB rate rebate

21.48   You are entitled to a HB rate rebate only if you meet all of the following conditions:

(a)   you must be liable for rates on a dwelling in Northern Ireland;

(b)   your eligible rates must be greater than any non-dependant deductions that apply (i.e. there must be an amount of 'maximum HB') (para 21.58);

(c)   you must occupy the dwelling as your home (para 21.50);

(d)   you must not be excluded from HB (para 21.49); and

(e)   either:

- your income must not exceed your applicable amount, or

- the amount by which your income exceeds your applicable amount multiplied by the taper must be less than your maximum HB.

21.48   NICBA 129(1); NIHB 12(2), 13(3)(b),(6); NIHB60+ 12(2), 13(3)(b),(6)

21.49   You are excluded from HB if:

(a) you could make a claim for UC (even if your award would be nil: table 2.1);

(b) you are migrant or recent arrival;

(c) you have capital more than the upper capital limit;

(d) you live with a resident landlord/owner who is a close relative (para 4.45);

(e) you live in a residential care home, nursing home or independent hospital; or

(f) the LPS has decided that your liability was created to take advantage of the HB scheme.

These exclusions are the same as HB for rent: see *Guide to Housing Benefit* for (a), (c)-(f) and for (b) chapter 22 of this guide.

Getting a HB rate rebate on two homes or during an absence

21.50   You can only get a HB rate rebate on your sole or main residence so you cannot normally get a rebate on more than one home, or for your main home if you are absent from it (para 21.21(d)). The only exceptions are the same that apply to HB for rent: see *Guide to Housing Benefit,* chapter 3 for details.

Making a claim for a HB rate rebate

Who can make a claim

21.51   The general rule is that you can make a claim for HB if you are liable for rates. If you are a couple only one of you makes the claim and you can agree which of you should make it, but in some circumstances the amount you get can depend on who claims. If you are unable to act, someone can claim on your behalf. The law about couples and who should claim if the liable person is incapable are the same as HB for rent: see *Guide to Housing Benefit*, chapter 5.

How to claim

21.52   The rules about how to claim are the same as for HB for rent: see *Guide to Housing Benefit,* chapter 5 (and the law is in the footnotes there).

Where to claim

21.53   The general rule is that if you pay rent you make your claim for rate rebate to the Northern Ireland Housing Executive (NIHE). If you are an owner occupier you claim HB from Land and Property Services. More details and exceptions are in table 21.3.

21.49   NIHB 9, 10, 40, 53(1); NIHB60+ 9, 10, 41

21.50   NIHB 7; NIHB60+ 7

21.51-52 NIHB 8(1), 80; NIHB60+ 8(1), 61

21.53   NIAA 126(3),(6); NIHB 2(1) 'relevant authority'; NIHB60+ 2(1)

Table 21.3 **Which agency administers HB rate rebate**

Land and Property Services	**Northern Ireland Housing Executive (NIHE)**
Owner occupiers	NIHE tenants
Partners of sole owners	Housing association tenants
Former partners of sole owners	Tenants of private landlords
Former non-dependants of sole owners	People with a life interest
	People in co-ownership schemes
	People in rental purchase schemes

The same agency also administers rate relief and lone pensioner allowance.

Calculating HB rate rebate

Eligible rates

21.54   Your eligible rates is the figure used to calculate your entitlement to rate rebate (HB for rates). It is worked out by the following steps:

  (a)   Start with the annual rates due on your home (paras 21.4-5) after any capping that may apply.

  (b)   If you are entitled to a disability reduction (para 21.8), use the reduced rates figure.

  (c)   If you are a joint occupier apportion the result.

  (d)   Convert it to a weekly figure (as described in para 21.55).

Unlike HB for rent, there is no power to restrict the eligible rates if your home is too expensive or too large.

Conversion to weekly figure

21.55   If you do not pay rent, your weekly rates is calculated by dividing your rates bill by the number of days it covers and multiplying by seven. If you pay your rates with your rent, to convert your rates to a weekly figure:

  (a)   for rent due in multiples of weeks, divide by the number of weeks it covers;

  (b)   for rent due calendar monthly, multiply by 12 then divide by 52;

  (c)   for rent due daily, multiply by seven.

Impact of rates changes HB for rent

21.56   If your rent includes an amount for rates (para 21.6), a change in the rates (such as the new amount applying from each April, or following the award of a disability reduction) means your eligible rent changes too. You do not have to tell the NIHE about this change: your HB for rent and rates is revised automatically when the NIHE is advised by LPS.

21.54   NIHB 11(1)(a), 12(3), 78(3); NIHB60+ 11(1)(a), 12(3), 59(3)

21.56   NIHB 12(1),(2); 84(2)(a),(b); NIHB60+; 12(1),(2), 65(2)(a),(b)

Example: Calculation of eligible rates

A dwelling has a capital value of £135,000 in an area where the rate poundage is £0.0057777 per £1 of capital value. Capping does not apply so the annual rates payable are:

$$£135,000 \times 0.0057777 = £780.00$$

The weekly eligible rates (to the nearest 1p) are therefore:

£780.00 ÷ 365 x 7	=	£14.96 if paid separately from rent or
£780.00 ÷ 52	=	£15.00 if paid along with rent.

Apportionment of eligible rates

21.57   Your eligible rates figure is apportioned for the same reasons and in the same way as a UC-related rate rebate: see para 21.31 (and the law is in the footnote for this para).

Calculating rate rebate

21.58   The starting point is your weekly 'maximum benefit'. This is:

(a) your weekly eligible rates;

(b) minus any non-dependant deductions which apply (but if these exceed your eligible rates you do not get HB).

No non-dependant deductions are made if the conditions in table 9.4 apply (except that any rate of the care component is sufficient); in any other case the amounts are in table 21.4.

21.59   You qualify for maximum benefit (para 21.58) if you are on income-based JSA, income-related ESA, income support, guarantee credit, or would be receiving any of these if it were not for a sanction, waiting days or the minimum payment rule.

21.60   If you aren't on one of the 'passport benefits' in para 21.59 then your HB is worked out as follows:

(a) If you have no income, or your income is less than or equal to your applicable amount, you qualify for maximum benefit (para 21.58).

(b) If your income is more than your applicable amount, the difference between the two is called 'excess income'. You qualify for maximum benefit minus 20% of your excess income. (The percentage is called the 'taper'.)

Your applicable amount and your income (including any income from capital) is worked out in exactly the same way as HB for rent: see *Guide to Housing Benefit,* chapters 12-15 (and the law is in the footnotes there).

21.57   NIHB 12(2),(4)-(6), 72(1)(a),(b),(8)(b),(10); NIHB60+; 12(2),(4)-(6), 53(1)(a),(b),(8)(b),(9)

21.58   NIHB 68(u), 72(6); NIHB60+ 48(a), 53(6)

21.60   NIHB 87(2), 88, 89(5); NIHB60+ 68(2), 69, 70(5)

Table 21.4 **HB rate rebates non-dependant deductions: 2018-19**

All the figures in this table are weekly amounts.

If the non-dependant is:

■	on JSA(IB), IS or pension credit (either kind)	Nil
■	on UC without any earned income	Nil
■	on ESA(IR) without a work-related activity or support component	Nil
■	aged under 25 on a training allowance	Nil
■	a full time student (but see note)	Nil
■	a member of the armed forces away on operations	Nil

If the non-dependant works at least 16 hours per week and has gross weekly income of:

■	at least £394	£9.90
■	at least £316 but under £394	£8.25
■	at least £183 but under £316	£6.55
■	under £183	£3.30
	Any other non-dependant (regardless of income level)	£3.30

Note: If you (the claimant) and your partner are aged under 65, the nil rate does not apply during the student's summer vacation if he/she works at least 16 hours a week.

Awarding rate rebate as a credit or as a payment

21.61   A rate rebate is awarded as a credit to your rates account, except only that the NIHE may choose (at its discretion) to pay your HB for rates as an allowance (along with any HB for rent) if:

(a) your rent includes an amount for rates (para 21.6); and

(b) you qualify for HB for rent, or would do but for any non-dependant deduction or the deduction made because you have excess income (i.e. the 'taper': para 21.60).

21.62   When HB is paid as an allowance, it is paid either to you or your landlord following the same rules as HB for rent. But if your total HB (for rent and rates) is £2 per week or less it can be paid four-weekly; and if it is less than £1 per week it can be paid every six months.

Paying rate rebate and rent free weeks

21.63   If you pay your rates with your rent, your HB is only awarded for periods in which rent is due. If a rent-free period begins or ends part way through a benefit week your HB is calculated on a daily basis. For further details about how to calculate your rebate during the year if you have rent free weeks: see *Guide to Housing Benefit,* chapter 6.

T1.4   NIHB 72(1),(2)(f)-(h),(7)(b)-(e),(g),(8)(b),(10); NIHB60+ 53(1),(2)(f)-(h),(7)(b)-(e),(g),(8)(b),(9)

Rate relief

What is rate relief?

21.64   The rate relief scheme was introduced in Northern Ireland on 1st April 2007 when the new system for calculating the rateable value of your home was introduced (para 21.4). Because of the way HB rate rebates are calculated, you get no financial benefit from a change in your rates. The rate relief scheme gives you an extra reduction to compensate for this.

21.65   Rate relief is not part of the HB scheme, and you can qualify for rate relief even if you do not qualify for HB; but since the same information is required for both (para 21.67) a full assessment is always carried out.

Who gets rate relief?

21.66   You cannot get rate relief if you get (or could claim) a UC-related rate rebate.

21.67   If you claim HB you do not need to make a separate claim for rate relief: they are both considered together by the agency you claim HB from (table 21.3). You can get rate relief if you do not get maximum HB but still qualify for an award (para 21.60).

21.68   If you do not qualify for a HB rate rebate but you still have rates to pay, you can claim rate relief separately.

Calculating rate relief

21.69   Rate relief is calculated in the same way as your rate rebate, except that:

(a) your rate relief is worked out on the amount of rates remaining after rate rebate has been granted – but ignoring any non-dependant deductions (table 21.4);

(b) if you have a pension age claim and/or if you qualify for a carer premium your applicable amount is higher (para 21.70);

(c) if you have a pension age claim the upper capital limit is £50,000 (tariff income applies as in HB);

(d) the taper percentage used in the calculation is 12% of your excess income.

Examples of the calculation are given at the end of this chapter.

21.70   Your applicable amount is calculated the same way as HB for rent (para 21.60) except:

(a) the rate of the carer premium is £43.20;

(b) if you or your partner have reached state pension credit age (appendix 3) but are aged under 65 your personal allowance is £187.45 if you are single or a lone parent, £273.68 if you are a couple;

(c) if you or your partner are aged 65+ your personal allowance is £202.86 if you are a single claimant or a lone parent, £290.18 if you are a couple.

21.66-68   RR 38; NISR 2007/203; NISR 2007/204; NISR 2007/244; NISR 2011/43

21.70   NISR 2007/203, reg 17(2)(c); NISR 2007/244; NISR 2011/43

Awarding rate relief

21.71   Your rate relief is used to reduce the amount of rates you pay. If you are an owner occupier or a private tenant, it is credited to your rates account by Land and Property Services. If you are a NIHE or housing association tenant, it is paid to your landlord and so reduces the overall rent and rates you pay.

Reconsiderations and appeals

21.72   The rules about how you can get a written statement of reasons, request a review, or appeal, are the same as HB for rent: see *Guide to Housing Benefit,* chapter 16. Your appeal is dealt with by an appeal tribunal and if you also appeal your HB, both decisions are, as far as possible, dealt with at the same time.

Overpayments of rate relief

21.73   Overpaid rate relief can be recovered in the same circumstances as overpaid HB for rent. The recovery can be made by any lawful method, including:

(a) charging the amount back to your rates account;

(b) deducting it from any ongoing rate relief award you are entitled to.

21.74   Your rates account is not normally recharged if you are a NIHE or housing association tenant, except where it is closed (for example, following a death or a move) and there is sufficient credit on it make the recovery. Any deduction from ongoing entitlement must comply with the same rules about the maximum weekly rate of deduction as for HB for rent (but this does not apply to any lump sum arrears).

Lone pensioner allowance

What is lone pensioner allowance?

21.75   Lone pensioner allowance helps single people over 70 who need further help with their rates. It is similar to a council tax single person discount but applies only to people aged 70 or above. Lone pensioner allowance is not means tested and you may get it whether or not you also get a HB rate rebate or rate relief if you still have rates left to pay.

Who gets lone pensioner allowance?

21.76   You can get lone pensioner allowance if you:

(a) are liable for rates on your main home;

(b) are aged 70 or over;

(c) you live alone (see para 21.77 for exceptions);

(d) you make a claim for it (either alongside your claim for HB/rate relief or separately); and

(e) you are not entitled to, or to make a claim for, a UC-related rate rebate.

21.71   NISR 2007/203; NISR 2007/204

21.72   NISR 2007/203; NISR 2007/204

21.73   NISR 2007/203; NISR 2007/204

21.76-77 RR 38; NISR 2008/124 reg 3, sch

Living alone

21.77   In limited circumstances, even though someone else lives in your household, you can still be treated as living alone and thus qualify for lone pensioner allowance. This applies if:

(a) the person living with you is a resident carer (conditions are similar to those for council tax: see table 15.2(g));

(b) the person living with you is aged less than 18;

(c) you are receiving child benefit for the person who lives with you; or

(d) the person living with you is severely mentally impaired (conditions are similar to those for council tax: see table 15.2(h) but without the need for a qualifying benefit).

Calculating lone pensioner allowance

21.78   If you meet the basic conditions (para 21.76) you receive a flat rate 20% reduction on the rates you have to pay (i.e. after any disability reduction, HB rate rebate or rate relief you qualify for). Examples of lone pensioner allowance calculations are at the end of this chapter.

Awarding lone pensioner allowance

21.79   Like rate relief, lone pensioner allowance reduces the rates you pay on your home. If you are an owner occupier or a private tenant, LPS credits it to your rates account. If you are a NIHE or housing association tenant, it is paid to your landlord and so reduces the overall rent and rates you have to pay.

Overpayments of lone pensioner allowance

21.80   An overpayment of lone pensioner allowance is only likely to occur if you no longer live alone (such as if a new partner moves in) or you no longer have rates to pay on your home (for example, if you move). An overpayment of lone pensioner allowance cannot be recovered from your HB or rate relief unless you agree to this but it can be recovered by any other lawful method. If you are an owner occupier or a private tenant the recovery is usually made by charging the amount back to your rates account. If you are a NIHE or housing association tenant, and the account is now closed (for example following a death or a move) it can be recovered from your rent account provided there is sufficient credit on it to make the recovery. If you later re-qualify for lone pensioner allowance, recovery can be made by deducting the overpayment from any lump sum arrears of your new award.

Appeals

21.81   If you want to appeal a decision about your lone pensioner allowance it is considered by the Valuation Tribunal; you must appeal within 28 days of being notified of the decision. Note that this differs from the usual time limit of one month for both HB and rate relief appeals.

Examples: Rate rebate, rate relief and lone pensioner allowance

A claimant without a non-dependant

A couple in their 40s have no non-dependants. They are not on JSA(IB), ESA(IR) or income support. Their income exceeds their applicable amount by £20 per week. Their eligible rates are £15 per week.

Rate rebate (HB for rates)	£
Eligible rates	15.00
minus 20% of excess income (20% of £20.00)	– 4.00
equals weekly rate rebate	11.00
Rate relief	
Rates due after rate rebate	4.00
minus 12% of excess income (12% of £20.00)	– 2.40
equals weekly rate relief	1.60

A claimant with a non-dependant

A single claimant in her 50s has a non-dependant son living with her. The claimant is not on JSA(IB), ESA(IR) or income support. Her income exceeds her applicable amount by £10 per week. Her eligible rates are £18.00 per week. Her son works full-time with gross income of £450 per week.

Rate rebate (HB for rates)	£
Eligible rates	18.00
minus non-dependant deduction	– 9.90
minus 20% of excess income (20% of £10.00)	– 2.00
equals weekly rate rebate	6.10
Rate relief	
Rates due after rate rebate – ignoring non-dependant deduction	2.00
minus 12% of excess income (12% of £10.00)	– 1.20
equals weekly rate relief	0.80

Lone pensioner allowance

A person aged 72 lives alone and has a weekly rates charge of £18. She does not receive either HB or rate relief.

	£
Weekly rates to pay	18.00
Minus lone pensioner allowance (20% of £18)	– 3.60
Net amount to pay	14.40

If the same person receives £10 per week HB and £2 per week rate relief:

	£
Weekly rates to pay	18.00
Minus HB	– 10.00
Minus rate relief	– 2.00
Rates left to pay	6.00
Minus lone pensioner allowance (20% of £6)	– 1.20
Net amount to pay	4.80

Chapter 22 **Migrants and recent arrivals**

- The rules that apply to migrants: see paras 22.1-8.
- How the decision is made: see paras 22.9-22.
- The immigration control test, asylum seekers and refugees: see paras 22.23-37.
- The habitual residence test: see paras 22.38-52.

22.1 This chapter is about when you are eligible for UC, housing benefit (HB) or CTR if you are a person from abroad. It covers everyone, whether you are from the British Isles, Europe or the rest of the world, and whether you are arriving in the UK for the first time or returning after a time abroad.

Which rules apply

22.2 If you have recently arrived in the UK, there are three main rules which affect whether you are eligible for UC/HB/CTR:

(a) the immigration control test;

(b) the right to reside test; and

(c) the habitual residence test.

Table 22.1 shows when each of those rules apply to you. There are also further rules if you are seeking asylum or a refugee.

Table 22.1 **Migrants and recent arrivals: who can get UC/HB/CTR**

A national of	Test you have to satisfy
The British Isles (para 22.5)	Habitual residence
The EEA (para 22.6)	Right to reside (and in some cases also habitual residence)
Macedonia and Turkey	Right to reside and habitual residence
The rest of the world	Immigration control and habitual residence

22.3 For clarity, this guide treats the above three tests as separate (though in the law they are intertwined: paras 22.17-21). The guide also avoids the term 'person from abroad', because it is often used informally to describe someone who has recently arrived in the UK (whereas in the law it has a narrower meaning).

Eligibility of nationals of different parts of the world

22.4   This section identifies which rules apply to you depending on your nationality, followed by a straightforward example of each.

Nationals of the British Isles (the Common Travel Area)

22.5   The 'British Isles' (a geographical term, roughly meaning all the islands off the North-West of the continent) is also called the 'Common Travel Area'. Both terms mean:

(a)   the United Kingdom (England, Wales, Scotland and Northern Ireland);

(b)   the Republic of Ireland;

(c)   the Isle of Man; and

(d)   the Channel Islands (all of them).

If you are a citizen of any part of the British Isles you only have to satisfy the habitual residence test (paras 22.38-52) to be eligible for UC/HB/CTR.

Nationals of the European Economic Area

22.6   Table 22.2 lists all the countries in the European Economic Area (EEA) plus Switzerland, which UK law treats as being part of the EEA. The EEA includes all of the European Union (EU) states and some others. The EEA includes Croatia, which joined the EU on 1st July 2013. If you are an EEA national, the rules for eligibility are described in chapter 23.

Table 22.2 **The European Economic Area (EEA)**

The EEA states (apart from Ireland and the United Kingdom) are:

Austria	Belgium	Bulgaria
Croatia	Cyprus	Czech Republic
Denmark	Estonia	Finland
France	Germany	Greece
Hungary	Iceland	Italy
Latvia	Liechtenstein	Lithuania
Luxembourg	Malta	Netherlands
Norway	Poland	Portugal
Romania	Slovakia	Slovenia
Spain	Sweden	Switzerland

Nationals of the rest of the world

22.7   In this guide this means any country not mentioned above (paras 22.5-6). It also applies to you if you have applied for asylum or to enter the UK solely on humanitarian grounds, whether or not your application has been determined.

22.6 and T22.2   EEA 2(1) definition: 'EEA state'

22.8   If you are a national of the rest of the world you have to satisfy the immigration control test (paras 22.23-37) and also the habitual residence test (paras 22.38-52) to be eligible for UC/HB/CTR.

> ## Examples: Eligibility for UC
>
> **1. A British citizen**
>
> A British citizen has been living abroad for 12 years. During that time she gave up all her connections in the UK. She has now just come 'home' and has rented a flat here.
>
> The only test that applies to a UK national is the habitual residence test. It is unlikely that she satisfies that test to begin with (unless she was working in an EEA state) but she probably will in (say) three months time. So for the time being she can't get UC.
>
> **2. National of the EEA**
>
> An Italian national has been working in the UK for several years. He has recently taken a more poorly paid job.
>
> He passes the right to reside test because he is working. So he can get UC.
>
> **3. National of the rest of the world**
>
> An Indian national arrived in the UK six months ago to be with her family. She was given leave to enter and remain, and was granted leave by the Home Office without any conditions, in other words her leave did not include a 'no recourse to public funds' condition, so she is able to claim benefits. She now claims UC.
>
> The two tests that apply to a national of the rest of the world are the immigration control test and the habitual residence test. She passes both tests. So she can get UC.
>
> In all three examples the same outcome would also apply to claims for HB or CTR.

Decision-making

22.9   This section covers general matters relevant to this chapter and chapter 23, including decision-making and claims, and how the law and terminology work.

DWP and council decisions

22.10   If you are claiming UC the DWP decides whether you satisfy each of the three tests (para 22.2) and can get UC. If you are claiming HB and/or CTR your council decides this, but the law says you pass the habitual residence and right to reside test if you get one of the following DWP benefits:

(a)   income-based jobseeker's allowance (but see para 23.27 for exceptions);

(b)   income-related employment and support allowance;

(c)   income support;

(d)   state pension credit (guarantee credit or savings credit).

(And in practice your council will also accept that you pass the immigration control test (HBGM para C4.33)).

22.10   HB 10(3B)(k),(l); HB60+ 10(4A)(k); NIHB 10(5)(l),(m); NIHB60+ 10(5)(l); CTP 12(4)(h),(ha)

22.11   The rule in para 22.10 about HB/CTR only applies if the DWP has decided (in full possession of the facts) that you can get JSA(IB)/ESA(IR)/IS/SPC and not, say, where you wrongly continue to get it. If the DWP has decided that you cannot get one of these benefits, your council is not compelled to make the same decision – but a considered decision by the DWP carries weight.

Claims and couples

22.12   If you are a couple you usually claim UC jointly (para 3.3), but if only one of you is eligible that person can get UC as a single person (paras 2.7-8 and 2.34-36). You are eligible if you pass each of the three tests (para 22.2).

22.13   If you are a couple and claiming HB/CTR it can matter which partner makes the claim (because only one of you can be the claimant). The rules in this chapter apply to each partner individually. So if partner A is eligible, but partner B is not, partner A must be the claimant to get benefit. In these cases:

(a)   if the 'wrong' partner claims the council must give you a 'not entitled' decision (but it is good practice to explain this and invite a claim from the other partner);

(b)   if the claim is made by the 'correct' partner, it is assessed (e.g. income, applicable amount, etc) in the usual way, so you get a couple personal allowance even though only one of you is entitled (HBGM para C4·218). But if your partner is subject to immigration control they should get advice before you make a claim, because it may affect their immigration status (para 22.15).

National insurance numbers

22.14   If you are claiming UC you (and your partner) must provide your national insurance number (or have applied for one) to complete your claim (para 3.23).

22.15   If you are claiming HB/CTR and you are:

(a)   single or a lone parent, you must provide your national insurance number (or have applied for one) to complete your claim;

(b)   a couple, the rule in (a) applies to both of you except that:

   ▪   if only one of you needs 'leave' from the Home Office (table 22.3) to be in the UK but does not have it (for example, if you have not applied for it or if it has expired) then the requirement does not apply to that person and the DWP advises councils to assign a dummy number (GM D1·284-286);

   ▪   it is not a requirement of the law if you (or your partner) are claiming CTR in Scotland (para 16.15).

This rule (and the rule in para 22.13) is only about who can get HB/CTR. It does not mean that it is safe for your partner in terms of their immigration status to be part of your HB/CTR claim (the couple personal allowance counts as 'public funds'). The council may inform the Home Office, although it is not obliged to do so (HBGM para C4·219).

20.12   UC 3(1),(3); NIUC 3(2)

22.13   HB 8(1)(b), 10(1); HB60+ 8(1)(b), 10(1); NIHB 8(1)(b), 10(1); NIHB60+ 8(1)(b), 10(1); CTP sch 8 para 4(1)

22.15   HB 4(c); HB60+ 4(c); NIHB 4(c); NIHB60+ 4(c); CTP 15, sch 8 para 7(1)-(3)

Making a claim

22.16   Your online UC claim asks you:

(a) if you are British, Irish or a citizen of different country; and

(b) if you have been out of the UK or Ireland in the past two years,

and most HB/CTR claim forms (whether online or paper) ask similar questions. Both questions are intended to act as a trigger for further investigation in appropriate cases. If you are British/ Irish and have not been out of the UK/Ireland in the past two years the DWP/council will normally assume you pass all three tests (para 22.2).

Law, terminology and how the tests overlap

22.17   The tests used to decide if you can get UC/HB/CTR are contained in a mixture of immigration, European and benefit law as follows.

22.18   The 'immigration control test' (para 22.23) may stop you from getting these benefits (and many others) if you are from outside the EEA depending on your immigration status.

22.19   Benefit law (constrained by European law) then stops certain other people including EEA nationals from getting UC/HB/CTR (and many other benefits):

(a) The 'habitual residence test' (para 22.38) is in UC/HB/CTR law and applies regardless of your nationality. For UC the law treats you as not being in the UK (table 2.1 and para 2.27); for HB/CTR the law treats you as not being liable for rent/rates/council tax. The effect is the same: it means you do not qualify for UC/HB/CTR.

(b) The 'right to reside test' applies if you are an EEA national (table 22.2). It is also in UC/HB/CTR law, but what the right to reside means is in the Immigration (European Economic Area) Regulations 2006 (which apply to the whole of the UK). The law says that if you do not pass this test then you do not pass the habitual residence test (and so, as described in (a), you cannot get UC/HB/CTR).

22.20   If you pass the immigration control test then you also pass the right to reside test. The only exception is if you are a citizen of Macedonia or Turkey in which case to get UC/HB/CTR you must either: have 'leave' (table 22.3) (even if it has a 'no public funds' condition: paras 22.27-28); or be an EEA family member. But if you are from Macedonia/Turkey and only have 'temporary admission' (table 22.3) you cannot get UC/HB/CTR even though you pass the immigration control test (Yesiloz v LB Camden).

22.21   If you pass the right to reside test then in most cases you also pass the habitual residence test – but there are a few exceptions: mainly if you are not in work or if you have retired without having worked in the UK (see paragraphs 23.26-33).

Immigration law terms

22.22   A basic understanding of immigration law terminology is useful (particularly in relation to the immigration control test). Table 22.3 lists the key terms and explains them in a way that is helpful for UC/HB/CTR decision making.

22.18   Immigration and Asylum Act 1999 s115 (applies to the whole of the UK); CTP 13

22.19   UC 9(1),(2); NIUC 9(1),(2); HB 10(1)-(3); HB60+ 10(1)-(3); NIHB 10(1)-(3); NIHB60+ 10(1)-(3); CTP 12(1)-(3)

22.20   Yesiloz v Camden LBC [2009] EWCA Civ 415 www.bailii.org/ew/cases/EWCA/Civ/2009/415.html

Table 22.3 **Simplified immigration law terminology**

Immigration rules

The legal rules approved by parliament which UKIV officers use to decide whether a person should be given permission ('leave') to enter the UK.

UK Immigration and Visas (UKIV)

The Home Office agency responsible for immigration control and determining asylum applications (including asylum support).

Leave and temporary admission

Leave is legal permission to be in the UK. Leave can be for a fixed period (limited leave) or open ended (indefinite leave). Both can be granted with or without a 'no recourse to public funds' condition, and this nearly always applies if you have been given limited leave. Leave can be varied provided the application is made before it has expired (para 22.26).

A person who has been granted open ended leave without any conditions is said to have 'indefinite leave to remain', also known as 'settled status'.

A person who is granted leave because they are the partner of British citizen (or a person with 'settled status') usually gets it in two consecutive blocks of 30 months after which they can apply for settled status.

Temporary admission is not in itself a form of leave, it is merely the discretion allowed by UKIV which allows time for you to do something – such as apply for asylum or leave – without falling foul of the law. Since it is not a form of leave, it does not confer a right to reside.

Public funds

Nearly all tax credits and non-contributory benefits (including UC/HB/CTR and legacy benefits) count as public funds. So does a local authority homelessness duty or acceptance on its housing waiting list.

Sponsorship and maintenance undertaking

These terms go together. Someone (typically a partner or elderly relative) may be granted leave to join a family member on the understanding that this 'sponsor' will provide for their maintenance and/or accommodation.

Some (but not all) sponsors are required to sign a written agreement (a maintenance undertaking) as a condition of granting leave and if they do the person they sponsor cannot get UC/HB/CTR (but see para 22.28 for exceptions).

Illegal entrant and overstayer

These both refer to someone who needs leave to be in the UK but does not have it and has not been granted temporary admission. An illegal entrant is someone who entered the UK without applying for leave and an overstayer is someone who was granted leave which has since expired.

> **Right of abode and right to reside**
>
> 'Right of abode' is a term that describes someone who is entirely free of any kind of immigration control. It applies to all British citizens and some citizens of Commonwealth countries, but not necessarily to other forms of British nationality. Non-British nationals can apply to have this status confirmed in their passport.
>
> 'Right to reside' is a wider term that describes anyone who has legal authority to be in the UK. It therefore includes everyone with the right of abode, plus anyone who has any form of leave (including if your leave is granted with 'no recourse to public funds') or is from the EEA and has a right of residence. 'Right to reside' is sometimes used informally to mean right of abode (because it sounds less archaic).

The immigration control test

22.23   If you are from a country outside the EEA you have to pass the immigration control test to get UC/HB/CTR. (You also have to pass the habitual residence test: paras 22.38-52.)

22.24   The purpose of the test is to stop you getting benefit if:

(a) you require 'leave' (table 22.3) but do not have it – e.g. you are an illegal entrant or overstayer; or

(b) you have been granted leave but with a 'no recourse to public funds' condition (but see paras 22.27-28 for exceptions); or

(c) you have been granted leave as a result of a maintenance undertaking (i.e. you are a sponsored immigrant, but see paras 22.27-28 for exceptions); or

(d) you have been granted temporary admission while your application to the Home Office is being decided – for example if you are an asylum seeker.

People who pass the immigration control test

22.25   You pass the immigration control test regardless of your nationality if:

(a) you hold a passport containing a certificate of entitlement to the 'right of abode' (table 22.3) in the UK;

(b) you have 'indefinite leave to remain' (also called settled status);

(c) you have any form of leave whether limited or indefinite (table 22.3), but only if it doesn't include a public funds condition and/or was given without a maintenance undertaking (table 22.3) – although certain exceptions apply (paras 22.27-28);

(d) you applied for asylum and you have been granted refugee status, humanitarian protection or discretionary leave (paras 22.33-34);

(e) you are not an asylum seeker and you have been granted permission to claim UC/HB/CTR as a victim of domestic violence by the Home Office (para 22.37).

The DWP/council normally needs to see your passport or other Home Office documentation to confirm the above.

22.24   IAA99 115(9); CTP 13(2)

22.26   If you have limited leave you can apply for it to be extended before it expires. Provided your application is made in time and in the correct form, you are still treated as having leave until 28 days after the decision is made on your application, and so you pass the immigration control test until then. Authorities often wrongly terminate benefit in these cases.

Who can get benefit with a 'no public funds' condition

22.27   The general rule is that if your UK visa includes a 'no public funds' condition or was given because your sponsor signed a maintenance undertaking (table 22.3) you fail the immigration control test (para 22.24). The only exceptions are in paragraph 22.28.

22.28   You are not affected by the general rule (para 22.27) and pass the immigration control test (and see also paras 22.20 and 22.29) if:

(a) you are a national of Macedonia or Turkey and have been granted 'leave' by the Home Office – including leave with a 'no public funds' condition: [2015] UKUT 438 (AAC) (but see para 22.20);

(b) you were admitted to the UK as a result of a maintenance undertaking (a 'sponsored immigrant'), but you have been resident for five years or more;

(c) you were admitted to the UK as a 'sponsored immigrant' and have been resident for less than five years and your sponsor (or all of your sponsors if there are more than one) has died;

(d) you are the former partner of a British citizen or of a person with settled status (table 22.3) and have been granted permission to claim UC/HB/CTR under the Domestic Violence Concession (para 22.37).

20.29   In the first three cases you must also actually be habitually resident (paras 22.42-52) to get benefit, but not in the fourth (para 22.40).

Asylum seekers

22.30   You are an asylum seeker if you have applied to be recognised as a refugee (para 22.33) under the United Nations Convention because of fear of persecution in your country of origin (typically on political or ethnic grounds).

22.31   While your asylum application is being processed you fail the immigration control test and are disqualified from UC/HB/CTR (and most other benefits), although there are some limited exceptions (para 22.32). If you are disqualified you may be able to get help with your maintenance and accommodation from the Home Office asylum support scheme.

22.32   The exceptions to the general rule in para 22.31 apply if:

(a) you are a couple and your partner is eligible (paras 22.12-13) (and in this case if you are claiming HB/CTR any payment you get from the Home Office for support counts as income: HBGM para C4.128); or

(b) you have been granted discretionary leave (para 22.33) (e.g. if you are aged under 18 and unaccompanied by an adult: but see para 2.14 for UC); or

(c) you are an EEA national (para 22.6), in which case the rules in chapter 23 apply.

22.26   Immigration Act 1971 s3C

22.28   IAA99 115(1),(3),(9); SI 2000 No. 636 reg 2(1), sch paras 2-4; SI 2013 No 458; NISR 2000 No. 71 reg 2(1), sch paras 2-4; CTP 13(1A)

Refugees and others granted leave on humanitarian grounds

22.33   Following your asylum application the Home Office may:

(a) recognise you as a refugee (i.e. accept your claim for asylum) and grant leave; or

(b) refuse asylum but grant humanitarian protection (which is a form of leave) or discretionary leave (see circular HB/CTB A16/2006 for details of when these might apply); or

(c) refuse asylum and not grant leave.

22.34   If leave is granted it is normally for an initial period of 30 months, and then one further period of 30 months, after which you can normally apply for settled status (table 22.3). If you have been granted refugee status, humanitarian protection or discretionary leave you pass the immigration control test and the habitual residence test (including during your first two periods of limited leave). So you can get UC/HB/CTR from the date your status is confirmed. If you are granted refugee status (but not in other cases), then your dependants are granted leave as well so they are also eligible for UC/HB/CTR.

Evacuees

22.35   An evacuee is someone who has been granted leave to enter the UK outside the normal immigration rules in response to a specific humanitarian crisis (e.g. war, famine, natural disaster). Evacuees are often British nationals without full UK citizenship. In appropriate circumstances, the UK government may grant discretionary leave.

22.36   If you are an evacuee you can get UC/HB/CTR if you:

(a) have discretionary leave; or

(b) have some other form of leave and you are habitually resident. (In previous years specific temporary exceptions have been made to the habitual residence requirement but there are none that currently apply).

Destitution domestic violence concession

22.37   If you were granted limited leave as the partner of a British citizen or a person with settled status (table 22.3) but your relationship has broken down because of domestic violence, you can apply for permission to claim certain benefits including UC/HB/CTR for up to three months while the Home Office considers your application to settle in the UK. This is known as the 'Destitution Domestic Violence Concession' (ADM C1674-76) [www]. If your application for DDVC is approved you can get UC/HB/CTR until your application to settle is decided (para 22.40). The DDVC is not available to EEA family members but in certain circumstances you have a right to reside under the EEA regulations if you have suffered domestic abuse: see para 23.23(e).

22.34   UC 9(4)(d),(e)(i),(f); NIUC 9(4)(d),(e)(i),(f); HB 10(1),(3B)(g),(h)(i),(hh); HB60+ 10(1),(4A)(g),(h)(i),(hh); NIHB 10(1),(5)(g),(h)(i),(i); NIHB60+ 10(1),(5)(g),(h)(i),(i); CTP 12(5)(d),(e)(i),(f)

22.37   UC 9(4)(e)(ii); NIUC 9(4)(e)(ii); 10(3B)(h)(ii); HB60+ 10(4A)(h)(ii); NIHB 10(5)(h)(ii); NIHB60+ 10(5)(h)(ii); CTP 12(5)(e)(ii); rule 289A of the immigration rules www.gov.uk/government/publications/application-for-benefits-for-visa-holder-domestic-violence

The habitual residence test

Who has to pass the habitual residence test

22.38   The habitual residence test applies if you are a national of:

(a)   the British Isles; or

(b)   the rest of the world (apart from the EEA).

It does not normally apply if you are an EEA national unless you are not active in the labour market (e.g. not working or looking for work). All the rules that apply if you are an EEA national including these exceptions are dealt with in chapter 23.

22.39   The purpose of the test is to stop someone claiming benefit immediately they enter the UK (for example, if you are a British citizen but have never lived here or have not lived here for a long time).

Habitual residence: who can get UC/HB/CTR

22.40   To get UC/HB/CTR you must pass the habitual residence test (but see paras 22.12-13 for how it applies if you are a couple). You are exempt from the habitual residence test if:

(a)   you are a former asylum seeker who has been granted by the Home Office;

- refugee status,

- humanitarian protection, or

- discretionary leave (paras 22.25 and 22.33);

(b)   you have been granted leave by the Home Office under the destitution domestic violence concession (para 22.37);

(c)   you are an 'economically active' EEA national (para 23.8) or the family member of an economically active EEA national (para 23.22);

(d)   you have been deported to the UK from another country (para 22.41); or

(e)   for HB/CTR only, you get one of the DWP benefits in para 22.10.

If any of (a)-(e) apply you also pass the right to reside test for that same benefit. In any other case you must actually be habitually resident (paras 22.42-52).

People deported to the UK from another country

22.41   If you are a British citizen, have a right of abode or settled status (table 22.3) and you have been deported or removed to the UK from another country you are exempt from the habitual residence test and can get UC/HB/CTR as soon as you enter the UK.

22.38   UC 9(1); NIUC 9(1); HB 10(2); HB60+ 10(2); NIHB 10(2); NIHB60+ 10(2); CTP 12(2)

22.40   UC 9(4)(a)-(c),(g); NIUC 9(4)(a)-(c),(g); HB 10(3B)(za)-(zc),(g),(h),(hh),(i),(k),(l); HB60+ 10(4A)(za)-(zc),(g),(h),(hh),(i),(k); NIHB 10(5)(za)-(zc),(g),(h),(i),(j),(l),(m); NIHB60+ 10(5)(za)-(zc),(g),(h),(i),(j),(l); CTP 12(5)(a)-(c),(g),(h),(ha)

The meaning of habitual residence

22.42 To get UC/HB/CTR you must be 'habitually resident' in the British Isles (para 22.5). What counts as habitual residence is a 'question of fact' (a phrase used to mean that the term is not defined in the regulations). It is decided by looking at all the facts in your case; no list of considerations can be drawn up to govern all cases. The DWP gives general guidance on this (ADM C1946-70 HBGM paras C4.87-106).

22.43 There are two elements to 'habitual residence':

(a) 'Residence': You must actually be resident, a mere intention to reside being insufficient; and mere physical presence is not residence.

(b) 'Habitual': There must also be a degree of permanence in your residence in the British Isles (HBGM para C4.80), the word 'habitual' implying a more settled state in which you are making your home here. There is no requirement that it must be your only home, or that it is permanent, provided it is your genuine home for the time being.

Losing habitual residence

22.44 Habitual residence can be lost in a single day. This applies if you leave the UK intending not to return but to take up long-term residence in another country.

Gaining habitual residence

22.45 You cannot gain habitual residence in a single day. If you have left another country with the intention to settle in the UK you do not become habitually resident immediately on arrival. Instead there are two main requirements (R(IS) 6/96):

(a) your residence must be for an 'appreciable period of time'; and

(b) you must have a 'settled intention' to live in the UK.

'Appreciable period of time' and 'intention to settle'

22.46 There is no fixed period that amounts to an appreciable period of time (CIS 2326/1995). It varies according to the circumstances of your case and takes account of the 'length, continuity and nature' of your residence (R(IS) 6/96).

22.47 Case law (CIS 4474/2003) suggests that, in general, the period lies between one and three months, and that a decision maker needs 'powerful reasons to justify a significantly longer period'. That time would have to be spent making a home here, rather than merely studying or on a temporary visit.

22.48 As suggested by the DWP (ADM C1965-69 HBGM C4.85-86), factors likely to be relevant in deciding what is an appreciable period of time include:

(a) the length and continuity of your residence;

(b) your reasons for coming to the UK;

(c) your future intentions;

(d) your employment prospects (para 22.49); and

(e) your centre of interest (para 22.50);

although no one factor is absolutely decisive in every case.

22.49 In considering your employment prospects, your education and qualifications are likely to be significant (CIS 5136/2007). An offer of work is also good evidence of an intention to settle. If you have stable employment here it is presumed that you reside here, even if your family lives abroad (ADM C1969).

22.50 Your centre of interest is concerned with the strength of your ties to this country and your intention to settle. As suggested by the DWP (ADM C1966 HBGM C4.105), this can be shown by:

(a) the presence of close relatives;

(b) decisions made about the location of your family's personal possessions (e.g. clothing, furniture, transport);

(c) substantial purchases, such as furnishings, which indicate a long term commitment; and

(d) the membership of any clubs or organisations in connection with your hobbies or recreations.

Temporary absence and returning residents

22.51 Once your habitual residence has been established, the following general principles apply (in each case unless other circumstances over-ride them):

(a) if you are a UK or EEA national (only), it resumes immediately on return from a period of work in another EEA member state (Swaddling v Chief Adjudication Officer);

(b) and, in all cases, it resumes immediately on your return from a single short absence (such as a holiday or visiting relatives).

22.52 In considering whether you regain your habitual residence following a longer absence, or repeated absences, the following points need to be considered:

(a) the circumstances in which your habitual residence was lost;

(b) your intentions – if your absence was always intended to be temporary (even in the case of longer absences) you are less likely to lose your habitual residence than someone who never originally had any intention of returning;

(c) your continuing links with the UK while abroad;

(d) the circumstances of your return. If you slot straight back into the life you had before you left, you are likely to resume habitual residence more quickly.

20.51   Swaddling v Chief Adjudication Officer ECJ C-90/97 www.bailii.org/eu/cases/EUECJ/1999/C9097.html

Chapter 23 **EEA nationals**

- Introduction: see paras 23.1-6.
- EEA nationals and the right to reside: see paras 23.7-33.
- Croatian nationals: see paras 23.34-41.

Introduction

23.1   This chapter is about when you are entitled to UC/HB/CTR if you or a member of your family are a citizen of an EEA member state (an 'EEA national'). EEA member states are listed in table 22.2. This chapter does not apply if you are British or Irish (para 22.5); have settled status (table 22.3); or are a citizen of a European country which is not part of the EEA (para 22.6).

23.2   If you are an EEA national you are entitled to UC/HB/CTR if you are:

(a) 'economically active' (para 23.3) and you have a right to reside (paras 23.7-23); or

(b) you are not economically active, and

- you have a right to reside; and
- you are habitually resident in the British Isles.

The requirement to have a right to reside does not violate your right to family life (Mirga v SSWP) and although it constitutes discrimination it is justifiable and so is lawful (Patmalniece v SSWP). If you are a Croatian national further rules apply (paras 23.34-41). If you are a couple see paras 22.12-13 for how all these rules apply to you.

23.3   'Economically active' means you are working or you are temporarily out of work due to sickness or unemployment. In certain circumstances you can be treated as if you are working if you have worked in the UK for at least one year.

Decision making and terminology

23.4   If you are an EEA national general matters such as making your claim, how the law works, decision making and an explanation of the technical terms used in the law and administration are in paras 22.9-22.

23.5   The law about who can get UC/HB/CTR if you are an EEA national is very complex so case law develops rapidly. How the rules are interpreted is likely to continue changing.

23.6   If you are an EEA national you have to show you have a 'right to reside' in the UK to get UC/HB/CTR. But if you are a worker, a former worker (including if you are temporarily unemployed or retired), self-employed, or the family member of someone who is any of these (paras 23.9-23) you are exempt from this test and can get UC/HB/CTR.

23.2   UC 9(4)(a)-(c); NIUC 9(4)(a)-(c); HB 10(3),(3B)(za)-(zc); HB60+ 10(3),(4A)(za)-(zc);
NIHB 10(3),(5)(za)-(zc); NIHB60+ 10(3),(5)(za)-(zc); CTP 12(5)(a)-(c)
Mirga v SSWP [2016] UKSC 1 www.bailii.org/uk/cases/UKSC/2016/1.html
Patmalniece v SSWP [2011] UKSC 11 www.bailii.org/uk/cases/UKSC/2011/11.html

EEA nationals and the right to reside

23.7   This section (paras 23.8-33) is about whether you can get UC/HB/CTR if you are an EEA national. However, if you are a Croatian the rules in this section only apply if:

(a) you are self-employed (paras 23.9 and 23.36);

(b) you have completed one year employed in authorised work (para 23.39).

For all other rules for Croatians, see paragraphs 23.34-41.

Who has a right to reside

23.8   If you are an EEA national (para 22.6) you have a right to reside if you are:

(a) self-employed (paras 23.9-11);

(b) a worker (paras 23.12-16);

(c) self-employed but temporarily unable to work due to sickness (para 23.17);

(d) a worker with retained worker status while temporarily out of work (para 23.17);

(e) a family member as defined in table 23.1(a)-(c) of the above;

(f)   a retired worker or the family member of a retired worker (para 23.20);

(g) in certain circumstances, a long-term resident, parent with a child in education, student or a self-sufficient person (paras 23.21-33); or

(h) the family member of a person in (g).

Details of each of these categories are given in the following paragraphs. In immigration law, the first six groups are sometimes called 'economically active' because you are engaged in the labour market. If you are economically active, you are entitled to UC/HB/CTR without further conditions. If (g) or (h) apply you must also be habitually resident (paras 22.42-52) to get benefit.

Self-employed people

23.9   If you are an EEA national and you are self-employed you have a right to reside and you are entitled to UC/HB/CTR (including if you are a Croatian national, see para 23.36).

23.10   Your self-employment must be 'real', and have actually begun, but unlike the requirement for workers it seems that the ten-hour threshold (para 23.15) does not apply and your self-employed status can continue even where there is no current work, provided you continue to look for it: [2010] UKUT 451 (AAC). A seller of *The Big Issue* who buys the magazine at half price and sells it has been found to be in self-employment: [2011] UKUT 494 (AAC).

23.11   If you are self-employed you have a legal duty to register with HMRC within three months of starting your business – even if you think you won't earn enough to pay tax/national insurance. However, just because you are registered it does not necessarily mean that HMRC accepts you are self-employed (since their job is to collect money, without perhaps worrying unduly about the niceties of its origins). On the other hand, the fact that you have not registered does not mean that you are not self-employed: CIS/3213/2007.

23.8   EEA 6(1), 14(1); UC 9(2),(4)(a)-(c); NIUC 9(2),(4)(a)-(c); HB 10(3),(3B)(za)-(zc); HB60+ 10(3),(4A)(za)-(zc); NIHB 10(3),(5)(za)-(z); NIHB60+ 10(3),(5)(za)-(zc); CTP 12(3),(5)(a)-(c)

Workers

23.12 If you are an EEA national you have a right to reside and you can get UC/HB/CTR if you are a 'worker' (para 23.13). But if you are a Croatian national, see para 23.34.

23.13 You are a worker if you are currently engaged in remunerative work in the UK, which is

(a) 'effective and genuine'; and

(b) not 'on such a small scale as to be purely marginal and ancillary'.

For this matter 'remunerative' has its ordinary English meaning: broadly payment for services you provide.

23.14 The following are relevant to whether your work is 'effective and genuine':

(a) the period of employment;

(b) the number of hours worked;

(c) the level of earnings; and

(d) whether the work is regular or erratic.

23.15 The number of hours worked is not conclusive of your worker status but it is relevant: CH/3733/2007. The European Commission considers ten hours to be sufficient [www] although this may not be enough when the other factors here are considered – and not doing ten hours does not automatically exclude you. The factors always have to be considered together.

23.16 The fact that your job is poorly paid or the fact the that you have to claim, say, tax credits, is not enough on its own to stop you from qualifying as a worker. You can be a 'worker' even if your work is paid 'cash in hand': [2012] UKUT 112 (AAC).

Examples: Right to reside as worker

A Spanish national works in the UK as a cleaner in a garage for two hours a night on two nights a week. He is mainly in the country to study English. So he probably does not pass the right to reside test as a worker.

An Icelandic national works in the UK as a legal translator doing variable hours (depending on whether it is term time or holiday time) but averaging six hours a week over the year. She has been doing this for three years, and her hourly rate is substantial. It is therefore quite possible that she passes the right to reside test as a worker.

Retaining worker/self-employed status while out of work

23.17 If you are an EEA national (but see para 23.36 if you are Croatian) you can retain your worker or self-employed status (and therefore your right to reside and get UC/HB/CTR) if:

(a) you are temporarily unable to work due to sickness or injury. 'Temporarily' is decided objectively (rather than to your intention): De Brito v Home Secretary;

23.15 http://eur-lex.europa.eu/legal-content/EN/TXT/PDF/?uri=CELEX:52002DC0694&from=on

23.17 EEA 6(2),(2A),(3)-(7); UC 9(4)(a); NIUC 9(4)(a); HB 10(3B)(za); HB60+ 10(4A)(za); NIHB 10(5)(za); NIHB60+ 10(5)(za); CTP 12(5)(a)
De Brito v Home Secretary [2012] www.bailii.org/ew/cases/EWCA/Civ/2012/709.htm
Saint Prix v SSWP [2014] www.bailii.org/eu/cases/EUECJ/2014/C50712.html

(b) you are on sick leave or maternity leave, with the right to return under your contract –
or you stopped work because of pregnancy (or its 'aftermath') and intend to return to
work or start another job within a reasonable period of no more than 52 weeks: Saint
Prix v SSWP and [2015] UKUT 502 (AAC);

(c) you have worked for more than one year and are registered unemployed at the
Jobcentre;

(d) you have worked for less than one year and are registered unemployed at the
Jobcentre in which case your retained status lasts for only six months (after which you
become a jobseeker: para 23.26);

(e) you are involuntarily unemployed and have started vocational training; or

(f) you are voluntarily unemployed in order to follow vocational training relating to your
previous employment.

Item (a) includes self-employment but items (b)-(f) only apply to former employees who have
worked in the UK. In the case of items (c) and (d) (registered unemployed with the Jobcentre),
you must provide evidence that you are seeking work and have a genuine prospect of being
engaged; and in the case of item (c), after six months unemployment the DWP says you must
provide 'compelling evidence' of this, although in reality this means no more than provide
evidence itself: [2016] UKUT 372 (AAC).

23.18   You do not necessarily have to be entitled to ESA to qualify as being 'unable to work
due to sickness or injury' (CIS 4304/2007). Likewise you don't have to qualify for JSA or national
insurance credits to be 'registered unemployed' (CIS 184/2008). Small gaps between leaving
your employment and registering as a jobseeker can be ignored: [2013] UKUT 163 (AAC).

EEA nationals with the permanent right of residence

23.19   If you are an EEA national you have a right to reside and you can get UC/HB/CTR if
you have a 'right of permanent residence' in the UK, as defined by the EEA regulations. You
have this right if:

(a) you are a retired worker (para 23.20) or the family member (table 23.1 (a)-(d)) of a
retired worker; or

(b) you are a 'long-term resident' (para 23.21).

But in the case of (b) you must also be habitually resident.

23.20   You are a retired worker (para 23.19) or the family member of a retired worker if:

(a) you or your family member has retired (at retirement age or at early retirement) after
working in the UK for at least 12 months – and have been continuously resident in the
UK for more than three years. In counting this 12 months, any period of involuntary
unemployment registered with the Jobcentre, or period out of work due to illness,
accident or some other reason 'not of [your] own making', is counted as a period of
employment; or

(b) you have retired (at retirement age or at early retirement) and your spouse or civil
partner is a UK national; or

23.19   EEA 5, 15(1)(a)-(f); UC 9(4)(c); NIUC 9(4)(c); HB 10(3B)(zc); HB60+ 10(4A)(zc); NIHB 10(5)(zc); NIHB60+ 10(5)(zc); CTP 12(5)(c)
23.20   EEA 5(2),(3) 15(1)(c),(d),(e); UC 9(4)(c); NIUC 9(4)(c); HB 10 (3B)(zc); HB60+ 10(4A)(zc); NIHB 10(5)(zc); NIHB60+10(5)(zc); CTP 12(5)(c)

(c) you have ceased working as a result of permanent incapacity; and either

▪ the incapacity is the result of an accident at work or an occupational disease which entitles you to ESA, incapacity benefit, industrial injuries benefit or some other pension payable by a UK institution; or

▪ you have continuously resided in the UK for more than two years; or

▪ your spouse or civil partner is a UK national;

(d) you are a former family member of a deceased worker or self-employed person who has retained the right to reside in the way described in para 23.22(d).

23.21   You are a 'long-term resident' if you have lived in the UK continuously for five years by using your EEA right to reside (and not, for example, as a British citizen): McCarthy v the Home Secretary. A period of residence counts as 'continuous' despite absences if:

(a) in any one year, the total length of your absence(s) from the UK is no more than six months, and this can be longer if your absence is due to compulsory military service; or

(b) the total period of absence is not more than 12 months – so long as the reason is pregnancy, childbirth, serious illness, study, vocational training, a posting in another country, or some other important reason.

Once you have acquired a permanent right of residence it can only be lost after an absence from the UK of more than two years.

EEA family member rights

23.22   If you are the 'family member' of an EEA national who has acquired the right to reside you may also acquire a right to reside (and therefore a right to UC/HB/CTR) through them. You are an EEA family member if you satisfy the conditions in table 23.1. You do not need to be an EEA national yourself (although you can be): instead your rights depend on the status of the person you are accompanying (e.g. worker, self-employed, student). If you are an EEA family member (table 23.1) you have a right to reside if:

(a) the person you are accompanying is a worker, self-employed person, student or a self sufficient person;

(b) the person you are accompanying is a person with a permanent right to reside (para 23.19) (whether through residence or retirement);

(c) you have lived in the UK for a continuous period of five years under a right to reside (whether as a family member or otherwise);

(d) the person you accompanied is a worker or self employed person who has died, and

▪ you were living with them immediately before their death, and

▪ either the worker or self-employed person had lived continuously in the UK for at least the two years immediately before their death or their death was a result of an accident at work or occupational disease; or

(e) you are a former family member with a retained right of residence (para 23.23).

23.21   EEA 3; McCarthy v the Home Secretary [2010] www.bailii.org/eu/cases/EUECJ/2010/C43409_0.html

23.22   EEA 14(2), 15(1)(b),(d),(e); UC 9(2),(4)(b); NIUC 9(2),(4)(b); HB 10(3)(3B)(zb); HB60+ 10(3)(4A)(zb); NIHB 10(3)(5)(zb); NIHB60+ 10(3)(5)(zb); CTP 12(3),(5)(b)

Table 23.1 **Who is an EEA family member**

You are an EEA family member if you accompany an EEA national who is self-employed, a worker, a student or a self-sufficient person and you are:

(a)   their spouse or civil partner (until divorce/dissolution, not mere separation or estrangement);

(b)   a direct descendant of that person (e.g. a child or grandchild) or of their spouse or civil partner, and you are

■   aged under 21; or

■   dependent on him/her or their spouse or civil partner (for example, because you are studying or disabled);

(c)   a dependent direct relative in ascending line (e.g. a parent or grandparent) or of their spouse or civil partner;

(d)   some other family member who has been admitted to the UK on the basis that you are:

■   their partner (in the benefit sense, instead of being their spouse or civil partner); or

■   a dependent household member of that person in their country of origin; or

■   a relative who is so ill that you strictly require personal care from that person.

Note:

If the EEA national you accompany is a student:

■   if you are not their dependent child you do not count as a family member during the first three months of their (i.e. the student's) residence; and/or

■   if you only fall within category (d) you only count as a family member if you have been issued with a residence card, family permit or registration certificate by the Home Office.

Former EEA family members with retained rights

23.23   If you are a former EEA family member you nevertheless retain your family member rights if:

(a)   you are the child of a former EEA worker who is in education in the UK;

(b)   you are the parent who is the primary carer of a former EEA worker's child that is in education in the UK;

(c)   the EEA national you accompanied has died, and

■   you were living with them as their family member for at least one year immediately before they died; and

■   you are not an EEA national yourself;

T23.1   EEA 7(1),(2),(4), 8(2)-(5)

(d) you are the separated spouse or registered civil partner of an EEA worker who is living in the UK but you have not yet divorced (or dissolved your civil partnership);

(e) you are a non-EEA national former spouse/civil partner who has divorced (or had your partnership dissolved) and either:

- your marriage/civil partnership lasted at least three years and you both lived in the UK for at least a year before the marriage ended, or

- there was domestic violence, or

- there is a child from the relationship and either custody or access (you must have one or the other) needs to take place in the UK.

Generally, if you are a partner who is not married or in a civil partnership you lose your family member rights if the relationship ends. However, if the relationship has ended because of domestic violence and your former partner is an EEA national you may be able to get leave to remain or a right to reside: this is a new and complicated area of law.

Primary carer of a child in education in the UK

23.24 If you are the child of an EEA migrant worker and in education in the UK, or you are the child's primary carer (e.g. parent, guardian), you have a right to reside and can get UC/HB/CTR provided that you are also habitually resident. This right to reside is sometimes called an 'Ibrahim/Teixeira' right (after the case that first established it). You qualify if:

(a) the child has started a course of education in the UK, (e.g. primary or secondary school, or beginning a college or university course); and

(b) a parent of that child has been, at some time, an EEA worker (including a Croatian while working on the worker authorisation scheme).

The child and the primary carer (whether they are an EEA citizen or not) has the right to reside until the child completes their education. But you can only acquire this right through being a worker and not as a self-employed person: [2014] UKUT 401 (AAC). But you do not acquire the right to reside if you are subject to immigration control and the other parent has a right to reside in the UK and can care for your child: Hines v Lambeth LBC.

Non-EEA parents of a child who is a UK citizen

23.25 If you are a non-EEA national who is the parent of a child who is a UK citizen you have a right to reside (a 'Zambrano' right) but you cannot use it to qualify for UC/HB/CTR. (The regulations prohibit this and have been upheld as valid by the Court of Appeal but you may qualify for other financial support from social services: Sanneh v SSWP.)

23.23   EEA 10(2)-(6)

23.24   EEA 15(A)(1)-(4),(5); UC 9(2); NIUC 9(2); HB 10(3); HB60+ 10(3); NIHB 10(3); NIHB60+ 10(3); CTP 12(3)
        Harrow LBC v Ibrahim and the Home Secretary www.bailii.org/eu/cases/EUECJ/2010/C31008.html
        Teixeira v Lambeth LBC and the Home Secretary www.bailii.org/eu/cases/EUECJ/2010/C48008.html
        Hines v Lambeth LBC [2014] www.bailii.org/ew/cases/EWCA/Civ/2014/660.html

23.25   EEA 15A(4A); UC 9(3)(b); NIUC 9(3)(c); HB 10(3A)(bb),(e); HB60+ 10(4)(bb),(e); NIHB 10(4)(bb),(e); NIHB60+ 10(4)(bb),(e); CTP 12(4)(b);
        Sanneh v SSWP [2015] www.bailii.org/ew/cases/EWCA/Civ/2015/49.html

EEA job seekers

23.26   You count as an EEA job seeker (as defined by the EEA regulations) if:

(a) either:

- you entered the UK seeking work, or

- you are seeking work immediately after your retained worker status as a registered unemployed person (para 23.17) has expired; and

(b) you can provide evidence that you are seeking employment and have a genuine chance of being engaged.

23.27   If you meet the conditions in para 23.26 you are entitled to register as unemployed. But you cannot get jobseeker's allowance and so be passported to HB (para 22.10) during your first three months' residence or after that so long as you remain a jobseeker, unless you have some other right to reside (paras 23.7-24).

Students and other economically inactive but self-sufficient people

23.28   If you are 'economically inactive' (para 23.2) (including if you are a student) you have a right to reside as an EEA national if you were admitted to the UK on the basis that you were 'self-sufficient' (paras 23.29-33). But you can only get UC/HB/CTR if you are also habitually resident (paras 22.38-52). You must have your own resources to be considered self-sufficient: [2014] UKUT 32 (AAC).

23.29   If you are an EEA student you have the right to reside if:

(a) you are currently studying on a course in the UK;

(b) you signed a declaration at the beginning of the course that you were able to support yourself without social assistance (which means UC and any legacy benefit); and

(c) the declaration was true at the time it was signed and for the foreseeable future; and

(d) you have comprehensive health insurance for the UK (access to NHS treatment is not enough: Ahmad v Home Secretary).

23.30   In practice, this means that if you are an EEA student you are unlikely to get UC/HB/CTR. However, it is possible to get UC/HB/CTR if your circumstances have changed since you started your course (e.g. your source of funds has unexpectedly dried up) – but you will also have to satisfy the rules for students (tables 2.3 and 15.5, for HB see *Guide to Housing Benefit*).

23.31   If you are economically inactive but not a student you have a right to reside if you:

(a) have sufficient resources not to be an 'unreasonable burden' on the benefits system; and

(b) have comprehensive health insurance.

23.32   The fact that your income is so low that you qualify for benefits does not automatically disqualify you but in practice you are likely to be refused UC/HB/CTR. However, whether you are an 'unreasonable burden' is a matter of judgment and discretion (para 23.33).

23.26   EEA 6(1),(4)-(6)

23.27   HB 10(3A)(a),(b),(3B)(l); HB60+ 10(4)(b); NIHB 10(4)(b),(5)(m); NIHB60+ 10(4)(b); SI 2013/3196 Reg 2; NISR 2013/308 Reg 2

23.29   EEA 4(1)(c),(d),(2),(4), 6(1)(d),(e), 14(1); UC 9(2); NIUC 9(2); HB 10(3); HB60+ 10(3); NIHB 10(3); NIHB60+ 10(3); CTP 12(3);
        Ahmad v Home Secretary [2014] www.bailii.org/ew/cases/EWCA/Civ/2014/988.html

23.31   EEA 4(1)(c),6(1)(d),14(1); UC 9(2); NIUC 9(2); HB 10(3); HB60+ 10(3); NIHB 10(3); NIHB60+ 10(3); CTP 12(3)

23.33   DWP guidance suggests that if you have been resident in the UK for some time, the fact that you have been self-sufficient until now is a relevant factor in deciding whether you are an 'unreasonable burden' as is the length of time you are likely to be claiming (HBGM para C4.123). For example, if your funds have been temporarily disrupted you may still qualify.

Croatian nationals

23.34   The remainder of this chapter only applies if you are from Croatia. These rules have applied since 1st July 2013 when Croatia joined the European Union. If you are from Croatia you must have a right to reside to get UC/HB/CTR, but unlike other EEA nationals the circumstances in which you can have a right to reside are more limited because there are restrictions on your right to work and you have limited rights if you lose your job.

Right to reside

23.35   If you are Croatian you have a right to reside (and so can get UC/HB/CTR) if you:

(a) are self-employed (para 23.36);

(b) are employed in authorised work (para 23.37);

(c) have completed your one year qualifying period in authorised work (para 23.39) and have a right to reside that would qualify you for UC/HB/CTR if you were from any other EEA country (paras 23.7-33) (for example, if you were working);

(d) are in paid employment and exempt from worker authorisation in any of the ways listed in table 23.2; or

(e) are, in limited circumstances, a primary carer of a child in education (para 23.24).

Self-employed people

23.36   If you are a Croatian who is self-employed you qualify for UC/HB/CTR in exactly the same way as any other EEA national (paras 23.9-11). There are no further conditions and you do not need Home Office authorisation to run your business. However, you must be currently self-employed; it is not enough that you were self-employed in the past: R (Tilianu) v SSWP. But you may remain self-employed despite the fact that your work has currently dried up ([2010] UKUT 451 (AAC)) – even, in the short term, if you have claimed JSA: [2011] UKUT 96 (AAC).

Authorised work

23.37   If you are a Croatian you can usually only take up work (as an employee) which has been 'authorised' by the Home Office until you have completed 12 months in continuous lawful employment (para 23.40). Authorised work is limited to certain specified occupations and in most cases you must meet other further conditions. Unless the work you propose to do falls into the 'highly skilled' category, the numbers of places that are authorised by the Home Office are subject to strict quotas.

23.38   If you are a Croatian it is not enough for you to have been a worker in the past to get UC/HB/CTR, you must meet one of the conditions in para 23.35.

23.35   EEA 4(1)(a),(b), 6(1)(b),(c); SI 2013 No 1460 regs 2(3),(4),(5), 5

23.36   R (Tilianu) v SSWP [2010] www.bailii.org/ew/cases/EWCA/Civ/2010/1397.html

23.37   SI 2013 No 1460 Reg 5

Completing the 12 month qualifying period

23.39   After you have completed your 12 month qualifying period in lawful employment you are no longer required to be authorised to work and you can acquire the right to reside in exactly the same way as any other EEA national (paras 23.8-33).

23.40   During your qualifying period your employment only counts as 'lawful' if you hold the appropriate authorisation document and are complying with any conditions set out in it (CIS/3232/2006 and CJSA/700/2007).

23.41   You are treated as having completed your 12 month qualifying period if you were in lawful employment at the beginning and end of that period and any intervening periods in which you were not do not, in total, exceed 30 days.

Table 23.2 **Croatians exempt from worker authorisation**

You are a Croatian national who is exempt from worker authorisation if:

(a) you have leave to enter the UK (table 22.3) which is not subject to any condition restricting your employment;

(b) you have worked in the UK in lawful employment for an uninterrupted period (para 23.39) of 12 months (whether that period started on, before or after 1st July 2013 when the work authorisation rules started);

(c) you have dual nationality either as a British citizen or a citizen of another EEA state, other than Croatia;

(d) your partner is either a British citizen or has settled status (table 22.3);

(e) you have acquired a permanent right of residence (para 23.19);

(f) you are a family member (para 23.22) of an EEA national (other than a Croatian who is subject to worker authorisation) who has a right to reside in the UK;

(g) you are the partner or a child aged under 18 of a person who has 'leave' to enter the UK (table 22.3) provided the terms of that leave allows them to work;

(h) you are the spouse/civil partner/partner or direct descendant of a Croatian who is subject to worker authorisation, provided that in the case of a direct descendant you are aged under 21 or dependent on that worker;

(i) you meet the Home Office criteria to enter the UK under the highly skilled migrant programme and hold a registration certificate that states that you have unrestricted access to the UK labour market;

(j) you are a student who works for no more than 20 hours per week and you hold a registration certificate which allows you to work for up to 20 hours per week;

(k) you have been posted to work in the UK by an organisation that is based in another EEA member state; or

(l) you are a diplomat or the family member of a diplomat.

23.40-41   SI 2013 No 1460 Reg 2(3),(4),(5)

T23.2   SI 2013 No 1460 Reg 2(2)-(20); UC 9(2); NIUC 9(2); HB 10(3); HB60+ 10(3); NIHB 10(3); NIHB60+ 10(3); CTP 12(3)

Appendix 1 **UC/CTR legislation**

UC: England, Scotland and Wales

Main primary legislation (Acts)

The Social Security Administration Act 1992

The Welfare Reform Act 2012

The Welfare Reform and Work Act 2016

Main secondary legislation (regulations and orders)

SI 2013/376	The Universal Credit Regulations 2013
SI2017/725	The Loans for Mortgage Interest Regulations 2017
SI 2013/380	The Universal Credit, Personal independence Payment, Jobseeker's Allowance and Employment and Support Allowance (Claims and Payments) Regulations 2013
SI 2013/381	The Universal Credit, Personal Independence Payment, Jobseeker's Allowance and Employment and Support Allowance (Decisions and Appeals) Regulations 2013
SI 2013/382	The Rent Officers (Universal Credit Functions) Order 2013
SI 2013/383	The Social Security (Payments on Account of Benefit) Regulations 2013
SI 2013/384	The Social Security (Overpayments and Recovery) Regulations 2013
SI 2013/386	The Universal Credit (Transitional Provisions) Order 2013
SI 2014/1230	The Universal Credit (Transitional Provisions) Regulations 2014
SI 2012/1483	Social Security (Information-sharing in relation to Welfare Services etc) Regulations 2012
SI 2017/725	The Loans for Mortgage Interest Regulations 2017

Recent amending regulations and orders

The following is a list of regulations and orders amending the main secondary legislation since 1st April 2017. This list is up to date as at 1st April 2018.

SSI 2017/227	The Universal Credit (Claims and Payments) (Scotland) Regulations 2017
SI 2017/348	The Universal Credit (Reduction of the Earnings Taper Rate) Amendment Regulations 2017
SI 2017/376	The Social Security (Restrictions on Amounts for Children and Qualifying Young Persons) Amendment Regulations 2017
SI 2017/422	The Pensions Act 2014 (Consequential, Supplementary and Incidental Amendments) Order 2017
SI 2017/427	The Universal Credit (Tenant Incentive Scheme) Amendment Regulations 2017

SSI 2017/436   The Universal Credit (Claims and Payments) (Scotland) Amendment Regulations 2017

SI 2017/581   The Employment and Support Allowance (Miscellaneous Amendments and Transitional and Savings Provision) Regulations 2017

SI 2017/689   The Social Security (Emergency Funds) (Amendment) Regulations 2017

SI 2017/901   The Social Services and Well-being (Wales) Act 2014 and the Regulation and Inspection of Social Care (Wales) Act 2016 (Consequential Amendments) Order 2017

SI 2017/987   The Social Security (Qualifying Young Persons Participating in Relevant Training Schemes) (Amendment) Regulations 2017

SI 2017/1015   The Social Security (Miscellaneous Amendments No. 4) Regulations 2017

SI 2017/1323   The Rent Officers (Housing Benefit and Universal Credit Functions) (Amendment) Order 2017

SI 2018/65   The Universal Credit (Miscellaneous Amendments, Saving and Transitional Provision) Regulations 2018

SI 2018/281   The Social Security Benefits Up-rating Order 2018

SI 2018/307   The Loans for Mortgage Interest and Social Fund Maternity Grant (Amendment) Regulations 2018

Recent commencement orders

The following is a list of orders bringing UC provisions into force since April 2017. This list is up to date as at 26th April 2018.

SI 2017/584   The Welfare Reform Act 2012 (Commencement No. 19, 22, 23 and 24 and Transitional and Transitory Provisions (Modification)) Order 2017

SI 2017/664   The Welfare Reform Act 2012 (Commencement No. 29 and Commencement No. 17, 19, 22, 23 and 24 and Transitional and Transitory Provisions (Modification)) Order 2017

SI 2017/952   The Welfare Reform Act 2012 (Commencement No. 17, 19, 22, 23 and 24 and Transitional and Transitory Provisions (Modification)) Order 2017

SI 2018/138   The Welfare Reform Act 2012 (Commencement No. 9, 21 and 23 (Amendment), Commencement No. 11, 13, 17, 19, 22, 23 and 24 (Modification), Transitional and Transitory Provisions) Order 2018

SI 2018/532   The Welfare Reform Act 2012 (Commencement No. 17, 19, 22, 23 and 24 Transitional and Transitory Provisions (Modification)) Order 2018

CTR: England, Scotland and Wales

Main primary legislation (Acts)

The Local Government Finance Act 1992

The Local Government Finance Act 2012

Main secondary legislation England

SI 2012/2885	The Council Tax Reduction Schemes (Prescribed Requirements) (England) Regulations 2012
SI 2012/2886	The Council Tax Reduction Schemes (Default Scheme) (England) Regulations 2012
SI 2013/215	Council Tax Reduction Schemes (Transitional Provision) (England) Regulations 2013
SI 2013/501	Council Tax Reduction Schemes (Detection of Fraud and Enforcement) (England) Regulations 2013
SI 1996/1880	Local Authorities (Contracting Out of Tax Billing, Collection and Enforcement Functions) Order 1996
SI 2013/502	Local Authorities (Contracting Out of Tax Billing, Collection and Enforcement Functions) (Amendment) (England) Order 2013
SI 2009/2269	Valuation Tribunal for England (Council Tax and Rating Appeals) (Procedure) Regulations 2009
SI 2013/465	The Valuation Tribunal for England (Council Tax and Rating Appeals) (Procedure) (Amendment) Regulations 2013

Recent amending secondary legislation England

SI 2017/1305	The Council Tax Reduction Schemes (Amendment) (England) Regulations 2017

Main secondary legislation Scotland

SSI 2012/303	The Council Tax Reduction (Scotland) Regulations 2012
SSI 2012/319	The Council Tax Reduction (State Pension Credit) (Scotland) Regulations 2012
SSI 2013/87	Council Tax (Information-sharing in relation to Council Tax Reduction) (Scotland) Regulations 2013

Recent amending secondary legislation Scotland

SSI 2017/326	The Council Tax Reduction (Scotland) Amendment (No. 2) Regulations 2017
SSI 2017/357	The Council Tax Reduction (Scotland) Amendment (No. 2) Amendment Regulations 2017
SSI 2017/69	The Council Tax Reduction (Scotland) Amendment Regulations 2018

Main secondary legislation Wales

SI 2013/3029	The Council Tax Reduction Schemes and Prescribed Requirements (Wales) Regulations 2013
SI 2013/3035	The Council Tax Reduction Schemes (Default Scheme) (Wales) Regulations 2013
SI 1993/255	Council Tax (Demand Notices) (Wales) Regulations 1993
SI 2013/63	Council Tax (Demand Notices) (Wales) (Amendment) Regulations 2013
SI 1996/1880	Local Authorities (Contracting Out of Tax Billing, Collection and Enforcement Functions) Order 1996
SI 2013/695	Local Authorities (Contracting Out of Tax Billing, Collection and Enforcement Functions) (Amendment) (Wales) Order 2013
SI 2013/588	Council Tax Reduction Schemes (Detection of Fraud and Enforcement) (Wales) Regulations 2013
SI 2013/111	Council Tax Reduction Schemes (Transitional Provisions) (Wales) Regulations 2013
SI 2010/713	The Valuation Tribunal for Wales Regulations 2010
SI 2013/547	The Valuation Tribunal for Wales (Wales) (Amendment) Regulations 2013

CTR recent amending secondary legislation Wales

SI 2018/14	The Council Tax Reduction Schemes (Prescribed Requirements and Default Scheme) (Wales) (Amendment) Regulations 2018

UC: Northern Ireland

Main primary legislation (Acts and Orders)

Northern Ireland (Welfare Reform) Act 2015

The Welfare Reform (Northern Ireland) Order 2015 SI 2015 No 2006 (N.I. 1)

The Welfare Reform and Work (Northern Ireland) Order 2016 SI 2016 No 999 (N.I. 1)

Main secondary legislation (statutory rules)

NISR 2016/216 The Universal Credit Regulations (Northern Ireland) 2016

NISR 2017/176 The Loans for Mortgage Interest Regulations (Northern Ireland) 2017

NISR 2016/220 The Universal Credit, Personal Independence Payment, Jobseeker's Allowance and Employment and Support Allowance (Claims and Payments) Regulations (Northern Ireland) 2016

NISR 2016/221 The Universal Credit, Personal Independence Payment, Jobseeker's Allowance and Employment and Support Allowance (Decisions and Appeals) Regulations (Northern Ireland) 2016

NISR 2016/222 The Universal Credit Housing Costs (Executive Determinations) Regulations (Northern Ireland) 2016

NISR 2016/226 The Universal Credit (Transitional Provisions) Regulations (Northern Ireland) 2016

NISR 2016/178 The Welfare Supplementary Payments Regulations (Northern Ireland) 2016

NISR 2016/56 The Social Security (Information-sharing in relation to Welfare Services etc) Regulations (Northern Ireland) 2016

NISR 2017/176 The Loans for Mortgage Interest Regulations (Northern Ireland) 2017

Recent amending regulations and orders

NISR 2017/70 The Housing Benefit and Universal Credit (Size Criteria) (Miscellaneous Amendments) Regulations (Northern Ireland) 2017

2017 No. 142 The Universal Credit (Housing Costs Element for claimants aged 18 to 21) (Amendment) Regulations (Northern Ireland) 2017

NISR 2017/144 The Universal Credit Housing Costs (Executive Determinations) (Amendment) Regulations (Northern Ireland) 2017

NISR 2017/145 The Universal Credit (Benefit Cap Earnings Exception) (Amendment) Regulations (Northern Ireland) 2017

NISR 2017/146 The Universal Credit (Miscellaneous Amendments and Transitional and Savings Provisions) Regulations (Northern Ireland) 2017

NISR 2017/147 The Universal Credit (Reduction of the Earnings Taper Rate) (Amendment) Regulations (Northern Ireland) 2017

NISR 2018/36 The Universal Credit Housing Costs (Executive Determinations) (Amendment) Regulations (Northern Ireland) 2018

NISR 2018/37 The Loans for Mortgage Interest and Social Fund Maternity Grant (Amendment) Regulations (Northern Ireland) 2018

NISR 2018/58   The Social Security Benefits Up-rating Order (Northern Ireland) 2018

NISR 2018/92   The Universal Credit (Persons Required to Provide Information, MIscellaneous Amendments and Saving and Transitional Provision) Regulations (Northern Ireland) 2018

Rate rebates: Northern Ireland

Main primary legislation (Acts and Acts of Northern Ireland Assembly)

The Social Security Contributions and Benefits (Northern Ireland) Act 1992

The Social Security Administration (Northern Ireland) Act 1992

The Rates (Northern Ireland) Order 1977 SI 1977/2157

The Rates (Amendment) (Northern Ireland) Order 2006 SI 2006/2954

The Welfare Reform (Northern Ireland) Order SI 2015/2006

The Welfare Reform and Work (Northern Ireland) Order 2016 SI 2016/999

Main secondary legislation (Statutory Rules and Orders)

NISR 2006/405   The Housing Benefit Regulations (Northern Ireland) 2006

NISR 2006/406   The Housing Benefit (Persons who have attained the qualifying age for state pension credit) Regulations (Northern Ireland) 2006

NISR 2007/203   The Rate Relief (Qualifying Age) Regulations (Northern Ireland) 2007

NISR 2007/204   The Rate Relief (General) Regulations (Northern Ireland) 2007

NISR 2008/124   The Rate Relief (Lone Pensioner Allowance) Regulations (Northern Ireland) 2008

NISR 2017/184   The Rate Relief Regulations (Northern Ireland) 2017

Main amending regulations: rate relief

The following is a list of amendments to the main rate relief regulations from 1st April 2007. (For a list of recent amending legislation to housing benefit see *Guide to Housing Benefit*, appendix1).

NISR 2007/244   The Rate Relief (Qualifying Age) (Amendment) Regulations (Northern Ireland) 2007

NISR 2011/43   The Rate Relief (Amendment) Regulations (Northern Ireland) 2011

Appendix 2 **Selected weekly benefit rates from April 2018**

Attendance allowance

Higher rate	£85.60
Lower rate	£57.30

Bereavement benefits

Widowed parents allowance (standard rate)	£117.10
Bereavement allowance (standard rate)	£117.10
Bereavement support payment (higher rate)	£80.77
Bereavement support payment (lower rate)	£23.08

Child benefit

Only or older/oldest child	£20.70
Each other child	£13.70

Carer's allowance

Claimant	£64.60

Disability living allowance

Care component

Highest rate	£85.60
Middle rate	£57.30
Lowest rate	£22.65

Mobility component

Higher rate	£59.75
Lower rate	£22.65

Employment and support allowance (contributory)

Personal allowances

Under 25/lone parent under 18	£57.90
18 or over/under 25 (main phase)	£73.10
Couple both under 18 with child	£87.50
Couple both over 18	£114.85

Components

Work-related activity	£29.05
Support	£37.65

Guardian's allowance   £17.20

Housing benefit applicable amounts

Personal allowances

Single claimant	aged under 25 – on main phase ESA	£73.10	
	aged under 25 – other	£57.90	
	aged 25+ but under pension age	£73.10	
	over pension age but under 65	£163.00	
	over pension age – other	£176.40	
Lone parent	aged under 18 – on main phase ESA	£73.10	
	aged under 18 – other	£57.90	
	aged 18+ but under pension age	£73.10	
	over pension age but under 65	£163.00	
	over pension age – other	£176.40	
Couple	both under 18 – claimant on main phase ESA	£114.85	
	both under 18 – other	£87.50	
	at least one aged 18+ both under pension age	£114.85	
	at least one pension age, both under 65	£248.80	
	at least one over pension age – other	£263.80	
Plus for each child/ young person		£66.90	

Additional amounts

Family premium	at least one child/young person	£17.45	
Disability premium	single claimant/lone parent	£33.55	*
	couple (one/both qualifying)	£47.80	*
Disabled child premium	each child/young person	£62.86	
Enhanced disability premium	single claimant/lone parent	£16.40	*
	couple (one/both qualifying)	£23.55	*
	each child/young person	£25.48	
Work related activity component	single claimant/lone parent/couple	£29.05	*
Support component	single claimant/lone parent/couple	£37.65	*
Carer premium	claimant or partner or each	£36.00	
Severe disability premium	single rate	£64.30	
	double rate	£128.60	

Only awarded with working age claims

Incapacity benefit

Short-term lower rate (under pension age)	£82.65
Short-term higher rate (under pension age)	£97.85
Long-term rate	£109.60
Increase for age higher rate (under 35)	£11.60
Increase for age lower rate (35-44)	£6.45

Industrial disablement pension

20% disabled	£34.96
For each further 10% disability up to 100%	£17.48
100% disabled	£174.80

Jobseekers allowance (contribution-based)

Aged under 18 to 24	£57.90
Aged 25 or more	£73.10

Maternity and paternity pay and allowance

Statutory maternity, paternity and adoption pay	£145.18
Maternity allowance	£145.18

Personal independence payment

Daily living

Enhanced	£85.60
Standard	£57.30

Mobility component

Enhanced	£59.75
Standard	£22.65

Retirement pension

New state pension (full rate)	£164.35
Old state pension single (basic rate)	£125.95
Old state pension couple (basic rate)	£201.46

Severe disablement allowance

Basic rate   £77.65

Age-related addition

    Higher rate   £11.60

    Middle rate   £6.45

    Lower rate   £6.45

Statutory sick pay

Standard rate   £92.05

Appendix 3 **Qualifying age for state pension credit**

Date of birth	Date qualifying age for state pension credit is reached
Before 6th April 1950	On reaching age 60
6th April 1950 to 5th May 1950	6th May 2010
6th May 1950 to 5th June 1950	6th July 2010
6th June 1950 to 5th July 1950	6th September 2010
6th July 1950 to 5th August 1950	6th November 2010
6th August 1950 to 5th September 1950	6th January 2011
6th September 1950 to 5th October 1950	6th March 2011
6th October 1950 to 5th November 1950	6th May 2011
6th November 1950 to 5th December 1950	6th July 2011
6th December 1950 to 5th January 1951	6th September 2011
6th January 1951 to 5th February 1951	6th November 2011
6th February 1951 to 5th March 1951	6th January 2012
6th March 1951 to 5th April 1951	6th March 2012
6th April 1951 to 5th May 1951	6th May 2012
6th May 1951 to 5th June 1951	6th July 2012
6th June 1951 to 5th July 1951	6th September 2012
6th July 1951 to 5th August 1951	6th November 2012
6th August 1951 to 5th September 1951	6th January 2013
6th September 1951 to 5th October 1951	6th March 2013
6th October 1951 to 5th November 1951	6th May 2013
6th November 1951 to 5th December 1951	6th July 2013
6th December 1951 to 5th January 1952	6th September 2013
6th January 1952 to 5th February 1952	6th November 2013
6th February 1952 to 5th March 1952	6th January 2014
6th March 1952 to 5th April 1952	6th March 2014
6th April 1952 to 5th May 1952	6th May 2014
6th May 1952 to 5th June 1952	6th July 2014
6th June 1952 to 5th July 1952	6th September 2014

6th July 1952 to 5th August 1952	6th November 2014
6th August 1952 to 5th September 1952	6th January 2015
6th September 1952 to 5th October 1952	6th March 2015
6th October 1952 to 5th November 1952	6th May 2015
6th November 1952 to 5th December 1952	6th July 2015
6th December 1952 to 5th January 1953	6th September 2015
6th January 1953 to 5th February 1953	6th November 2015
6th February 1953 to 5th March 1953	6th January 2016
6th March 1953 to 5th April 1953	6th March 2016
6th April 1953 to 5th May 1953	6th July 2016
6th May 1953 to 5th June 1953	6th November 2016
6th June 1953 to 5th July 1953	6th March 2017
6th July 1953 to 5th August 1953	6th July 2017
6th August 1953 to 5th September 1953	6th November 2017
6th September 1953 to 5th October 1953	6th March 2018
6th October 1953 to 5th November 1953	6th July 2018
6th November 1953 to 5th December 1953	6th November 2018
6th December 1953 to 5th January 1954	6th March 2019
6th January 1954 to 5th February 1954	6th May 2019
6th February 1954 to 5th March 1954	6th July 2019
6th March 1954 to 5th April 1954	6th September 2019
6th April 1954 to 5th May 1954	6th November 2019
6th May 1954 to 5th June 1954	6th January 2020
6th June 1954 to 5th July 1954	6th March 2020
6th July 1954 to 5th August 1954	6th May 2020
6th August 1954 to 5th September 1954	6th July 2020
6th September 1954 to 5th October 1954	6th September 2020
6th October 1954 or after	On reaching age 66

Appendix 4: **Equivalent footnote references for Scotland and Wales**

Table A: **Council tax liability**

This table shows the equivalent footnote references in paras 15.1-23 for the law on council tax liability in Scotland and Wales. 'Not Scotland' means there is no equivalent law in Scotland. For abbreviations see the key to footnotes at the front of this guide.

	Scotland	**Wales**
15.3	LGFA 70,71,75	LGFA 1,2,6
15.4	LGFA 72	LGFA 3,7; SI 1992/550
15.6	LGFA 74(1),(2); http://www.saa.gov.uk/	LGFA 5(1A),(3); https://www.gov.uk/council-tax-bands
15.7	Not Scotland	LGFA 12
15.8	LGFA 75	LGFA 6(1),(2)
15.9	LGFA 76; SI 1992/1331	LGFA 8; SI 1992/551
15.10	SI 1992/1331 sch para 3	SI 1992/551 reg 2 class C; SI 1993/151; SI 1995/620
15.11	Not Scotland	SI 1992/548 art 6
15.12	LGFA 75,77,77A	LGFA 6,9; SI 1992/558
15.13	LGFA 77(2)	LGFA 9(2)
15.15-16	LGFA 72(1),(6); SI 1992/728	LGFA 4(1),(2); SI 1992/558
15.17	LGFA 80(1),(4),(6),(7); SI 1992/1335	LGFA 13(1),(4),(6),(7); SI 1999/1004
15.18	SI 1992/1335 reg 3	SI 1992/554; SI 1993/195
15.20	LGFA 79	LGFA 11
15.21	LGFA 79(5), sch 1	LGFA 11(5), sch 1
T15.2(a)	LGFA sch 1 para 3	LGFA sch 1 para 3
T15.2(b)	LGFA sch 1 para 11; SI 1992/1409 reg 3, sch para 3	LGFA sch 1 para 11; DDR 3 class C
T15.2(c)	LGFA sch 1 paras 4,5; SSI 2003/176 art 6,7; SSI 2011/5; SSI 2014/7	LGFA sch 1 paras 4,5; DDO art 4, sch 1 paras 2-7
T15.2(d)	LGFA sch 1 para 4; SSI 2003/176 art 8	LGFA sch 1 para 4, DDO art 4, sch 1 para 8
T15.2(e)	LGFA sch 1 para 4; SSI 2003/176 art 5; SSI 2007/214	LGFA sch 1 para 4, DDO art 4, sch 1 para 1; SI 2007/580

	Scotland	Wales
T15.2(f)	LGFA sch 1 para 9; SI 1992/1409 reg 2(2); SSI 2007/213 reg 2	LGFA sch 1 para 9, DDR reg 2, sch paras 1,2; SI 2007/581
T15.2(g)	LGFA sch 1 para 9; SI 1992/1409 reg 2(3); SSI 2013/65; SSI 2013/142 reg 2	LGFA sch 1 para 9, DDR reg 2, sch paras 3,4; SI 2013/639; SI 2013/1049
T15.2(h)	LGFA sch 1 para 2; SSI 2003/176 art 4; SSI 2008/1879 reg 39; SSI 2013/65; SSI 2013/137 reg 14, SSI 2013/142 reg 8	LGFA sch 1 para 2, DDO art 3; SI 2013/638; SI 2013/1048
T15.2(i)	LGFA sch 1 para 11; SI 1992/1409 reg 3, sch para 2	LGFA sch 1 para 11; DDR reg 3, Class B
T15.2(j)	LGFA sch 1 para 11; SI 1992/1409 reg 3, sch para 1	LGFA sch 1 para 11; DDR reg 3, Class A,D,F
T15.2(k)	LGFA sch 1 para 11; SI 1992/1409 reg 3, sch para 1	LGFA sch 1 para 11; DDR reg 3, Class A,E SI 1995/620 reg 4
T15.2(l)	LGFA sch 1 para 8	LGFA sch 1 paras 6,7; DDO art 6
T15.2(m)	LGFA sch 1 para 1; SSI 2003/176 art 3	LGFA sch 1 para 1; DDO art 2
15.24-76	See table B	See table B

Table B: **Council tax rebates**

This table shows the equivalent footnote references for paras 15.24-76 and chapters 16-20 for CTR law in Scotland and Wales. 'Not Scotland'/'Not Wales' means that there is no equivalent law in that country. 'See text' means the equivalent reference is in the footnote for that paragraph (usually because the law is unique to that country). 'Not WA'/'Not PA' means not working age or not pension age respectively. For abbreviations see the key to footnotes at the front of this guide.

Para	Scotland CTS	CTS60+	Wales CTPW	CTRW
15.1-23	See table A	See table A	See table A	See table A
15.27	See text	See text	See text	See text
15.28	Not Scotland	Not Scotland	22-25	13-16
15.29	See text	See text	See text	See text
15.30	2(1), 12	2(1), 12	2(1) 'pensioner', 3	2(1), 3
15.31-39	Not Scotland	Not Scotland	Not Wales	Not Wales
15.40-41	See text	See text	Not Wales	Not Wales
15.42	Not Scotland	Not Scotland	See text	See text
15.43	Not Scotland	Not Scotland	See text	See text
15.44	Not Scotland	Not Scotland	See text	See text
15.45	Not Scotland	Not Scotland	See text	See text
15.46	Not Scotland	Not Scotland	See text	See text
15.49	14	14	27-31	18-24
15.50	14(1)(b),(6),(7)	14(1)(b),(6),(7)	Not Wales	Not Wales
15.51	sch 2 para 1	sch 5 para 1	Not Wales	Not Wales
15.52	See text	See text	Not Wales	Not Wales
15.54	Not Scotland	Not Scotland	See text	See text
15.55	Not Scotland	Not Scotland	See text	See text
15.56	Not Scotland	Not Scotland	See text	See text
15.57	Not Scotland	Not Scotland	See text	See text
15.58	16, 19, 20, 42	16, 19, 40	See text	See text
15.59	2(1) 14(3), 61	2(1), 14(3), 82	2(1), sch 13 para 1(1)	2(1), 107(1)
15.60	42	40	27, 30	18, 21
15.61	sch 5 para 49	24, sch 4 para 27	sch 1 para 7	32
15.62	14(3)(b)	14(3)(b)	31, sch 11 para 3(1)(a)	22, 72(1)(a)
15.63	14(3)(b), 20(1),(3)	14(3)(b), 20(1),(3)	31, sch 11 para 3(1)(b),(2)	22, 72(1)(b),(2)
15.64-66	52	Not PA	sch 11 para 1	70
T15.5	20(2),(3)	Not PA	sch 11 para 3(2)	72(2)
15.67	5, 14(3)(b), 15	5, 14(3)(b), 15	22-26	13-17
15.68	15	15	26	17
15.70	See text	See text	See text	See text
15.71	5(6)(d), 15(3)	5(6)(d), 15(3)	26(2)	17(2)
T15.6	2(1) 'medically approved', 15(4)	2(1), 15(4)	26(3),(6)	17(3),(6)

Para	Scotland CTS	CTS60+	Wales CTPW	CTRW
15.74	16(1), 17, 18	16(1), 17, 18	Not Wales	Not Wales
16.1	See text	See text	See text	See text
16.2	82	61	sch 13 para 1(1)	107(1)
16.3	Not Scotland	Not Scotland	sch 13 para 1(2)-(7)	107(2)-(7)
16.4	Not Scotland	Not Scotland	sch 13 para 1(2),(4)	107(2),(4)
16.5	Not Scotland	Not Scotland	sch 13 para 1(3),(5)	107(3),(5)
16.6	2(1), 83(1), 84(1),(2)	2(1), 63(1), 64(1),(2)	2(1), sch 12 paras 2(a),(c), 3, 6	2(1), sch 1 paras 2(a),(c), 3, 6
16.7	Not Scotland	Not Scotland	sch 12 paras 2(b), 13(5),(6)	sch 1 paras 2(b), 13(5),(6)
16.8	83(1)	63(1)	sch 12 paras 2-3	sch 1 paras 2-3
16.9	87, 88	67, 68	sch 13 para 6	112
16.10	86(1)	66(1)	sch 13 para 5(4)	111(4)
16.13	See text	See text	See text	See text
16.14	86(2),(3)	66(2),(3)	sch 13 para 5(5),(7)	111(5),(7)
16.15	Not Scotland	Not Scotland	sch 13 para 5(2),(3)	111(2),(3)
16.17	83(1),(6), 84(1),(3)	63(1),(6), 64(1),(4)	sch 12 paras 2-5, 7, 13(5),(7)	sch 1 paras 2-5, 7, 13(5),(7)
16.18	Not Scotland	Not Scotland	sch 13 para 8	114
16.19-20	83(3)-(5), 84(4),(5)	63(3)-(5), 64(4),(5)	sch 12 paras 4, 5, 7, sch 13 para 2(3)-(5)	108(3)-(5), sch 1 paras 4, 5, 7
16.21-22	84(2),(3),(5),(6)	64(2),(3),(5),(6)	sch 12 paras 3(1), 6, 7(2), 13(7), 15(3), sch 13 para 2(3)(b)	108(5)(b), sch 1 para 3(1), 6, 7(2), 13(7), 15(3)
16.23	80(1)	58(1)	Not Wales	Not Wales
16.24	80(2)	58(2)	Not Wales	Not Wales
16.25	2(1)	2(1)	2(1)	2(1)
16.26	Not Scotland	Not Scotland	sch 1 para 39, sch 6 para 45	104
16.27	85	65	sch 12 paras 15-17; sch 13 para 2(1)(f),(g)	108(1)(f),(g), sch 1 paras 15-17
T16.1	85(1)(a)-(e),(2)-(4)	65(1)(a)-(e),(2)-(4)	sch 13 para 2(1)(a)-(g),(2),(3)	108(1)(a)-(g),(2),(3)
16.31	Not WA	62	34(4), sch 13 para 4	109
16.33	85(7),(8)	No equiv	34(4), sch 13 para 4	110
16.37	Not Scotland	Not Scotland	See text	See text
16.38	Not Scotland	Not Scotland	sch 13 para 10(2)-(4)	CTRW 116(2)-(4)
16.43	2(1)	2(1)	2(1), 4	2(1), 4
16.44	2(1) 'family'	2(1)	6	6
16.46	2(1)	2(1)	2(1)	2(1)
16.47	2(1) 'couple'	2(1)	4	4
16.49	11(1)	11(1)	8(1)	8(1)
16.50	2(1) 'couple'	2(1)	4(1)	4(1)
16.51	11(1)	11(1)	8(1)	8(1)
16.52	2(1) 'family', 4	2(1), 4;	2(1), 6(2),(3)	2(1), 6(2),(3)
16.53	10	10	7	7
16.54	11(1)	11(1)	8(1)	8(1)

16.55	21	20	sch 1 para 1, sch 6 para 1	23, 24
16.56	11(2),(3)	11(2),(3)	8(2),(3)	8(2),(3)
16.57	11(4)	11(4)	8(4)	8(4)
16.59	3(1),(2)	3(1),(2)	9(1),(2)	9(1),(2)
16.62	3(2)(e)	3(2)(e)	9(2)(e)	9(2)(e)
16.65	3(3)	3(3)	9(3)	9(3)
16.66	3(2)(d),(3)	3(2)(d),(3)	9(2)(d),(3)	9(2)(d),(3)
16.69	3(2)(d),(3)	3(2)(d),(3)	9(2)(d),(3)	9(2)(d),(3)
16.70	3(2)(e)	3(2)(e)	9(2)(e)	9(2)(e)
16.71	2(1), 'second adult', 14(6),(7), sch 2 para 4	2(1), 14(6),(7), sch 5 para 2	Not Wales	Not Wales
17.2	14(3A), 14A(1)(b)	14(3A), 14A(1)(b)	Not Wales	Not Wales
17.4	47(1)	66(1)	sch 1 para 2(1), sch 6 para 4(1)	27(1)
17.5	14(5), 26, 39(2), sch 4 para 8	14(5), 24	22(e), 23(e),(f), 24(e), 25(e),(f), sch 1 paras 4(2),(3), 7, sch 6 paras 6(2), (3), 9, 17(2), sch 9 para 8	13(e), 14(e),(f), 15(e), 16(e),(f), 29(2),(3), 32, 34, 51(2), sch 7 para 8
17.6-7	14(5)(b)	14(5)(b)	23(f), 25(f), sch 1 para 4(3), sch 6 para 6(3)	14(f), 16(f), 29(3)
17.8	21, 23, 26, 27(1), 51	20, 25, 26, 31(2)	sch 1 paras 1, 8, 9, 31, sch 6 paras 1, 3, 9, 20(1), 33	23, 24, 26, 33, 34, 35, 54(1), 68, 69
17.10	66(2)-(3)	47(2)-(3)	sch 1 para 2(3)-(5), sch 6 para 4(3)-(5)	27(3)-(5)
17.11-14	14A, 66(1A),(1B)	14A, 66(1A),(1B)	Not Wales	Not Wales
17.15	3	3	9	9
17.17	2(1), 67(6)	48(6)	2(1), sch 1 para 3(6), sch 6 para 5(6)	2(1), 28(6)
17.18	3(2), 67(3),(7),(8)	3(2), 48(3),(7),(8)	9(2), sch 1 para 3(3),(7),(8), sch 6 para 5(3),(7),(8)	9(2), 28(3),(7),(8)
17.19	67(1),(2),(7),(8)	48(1),(2),(7),(8)	sch 1 para 3(1),(2),(7),(8), sch 6 para 3(1),(2),(7),(8)	28(1),(2),(7),(8)
17.20	6, 67(1),(2)	6, 48(1),(2)	10, sch 1 para 3(1),(2), sch 6 para 5(1),(2)	10, 28(1),(2)
T17.1	See text	See text	See text	See text
17.21	67(1)(a)	48(1)(a)	sch 1 para 3(1)(a), sch 6 para 5(1)(a)	28(1)(a)
17.22	6(1),(4)	6(1),(4)	10(1),(4)	10(1),(5)
17.23	6(2)-(5)	6(2)-(5)	10(2)-(5)	10(2)-(5)
17.24	6(5)-(8)	6(5)-(8)	10(5)-(8)	10(5)-(8)
17.25-26	6(3), 67(2)	6(3), 48(2)	10(3), sch 1 para 3(2), sch 6 para 5(2)	10(3), 28(2)

Para	Scotland CTS	CTS60+	Wales CTPW	CTRW
17.27	67(9)	48(9)	sch 1 para 3(9), sch 6 para 5(9)	28(9)
17.28	67(3)	48(3)	sch 1 para 3(3), sch 6 para 5(3)	28(3)
17.29	67(5)	48(5)	sch 1 para 3(5), sch 6 para 5(5)	28(5)
17.30	No equiv	59(10)-(13)	Not Wales	Not Wales
17.31	14(6),(7),(8)(c), 78, sch 2	14(6),(7),(8)(c), 56, sch 5	Not Wales	Not Wales
17.32-33	sch 2 para 1	sch 5 para 1	Not Wales	Not Wales
T17.2	See text	See text	Not Wales	Not Wales
17.34	sch 2 paras 2, 3	sch 5 paras 2, 3	Not Wales	Not Wales
17.35	78(2),(3)	56(2),(3)	Not Wales	Not Wales
17.36	66(1)(b)	47(1)(b)	sch 1 para 2(1)(b), sch 6 para 4(1)(b)	27(1)
17.37	33	31(1),(2)	sch 1 para 11(1), sch 6 para 13(1)	37(1), 44, 45, 46, 47(1)
17.41-42	21, sch 1 paras 1-7, 17-19	20, sch 1 paras 2-4, 13	sch 1 para 1(1), sch 2 paras 1-4, part 4, sch 6 para 1(1), sch 7 paras 1-7, 17-20	23, 24, sch 2 , paras 1-4, 12 sch 3 paras 1-7, 17-20
17.43	21	20	32(2), 33(2), sch 1 para 1, sch 6 para 1	23, 24
17.44	23	No equiv	sch 6 para 3	26
T17.3	See text	See text	See text	See text
17.45-46	21(a),(b), sch 1 paras 1-3	20(a),(b), sch 1 paras 1-3	sch 1 para 1(1)(a),(b), sch 2 paras 1, 2, sch 6 para 1(1)(a),(b), sch 7 paras 1, 2	23(1)(a),(b), 24(1)(a),(b) sch 2 paras 1, 2, sch 3 paras 1-3
17.47	See text	See text	sch 2 para 3, sch 7 para 4	sch 2 para 3, sch 3 para 4
17.48-51	sch 1 paras 10(9), 18-20	Not PA	sch 6 para 1(1)(d)-(e), sch 7 paras 10(8), 18-20	24(1)(e),(f), sch 3 paras 10(8), 18-20
17.52-54	sch 1 paras 21-24	Not PA	sch 7 paras 21-24	sch 3 paras 21-24
17.58	sch 1 para 9	Not PA	sch 7 para 9	sch 3 para 9
17.59-61	sch 1 para 10	Not PA	sch 7 para 10	sch 3 para 10
17.55-57	sch 1 paras 25-29	Not PA	sch 7 paras 25-29	sch 3 paras 25-29
17.62	sch 1 para 13	sch 1 para 9	sch 2 para 8, sch 7 para 13	sch 2 para 8, sch 3 para 13
17.63-65	sch 1 para 12	sch 1 para 8	sch 2 para 7, sch 7 para 12	sch 2 para 7, sch 3 para 12
17.66-69	sch 1 para 11	sch 1 para 7	sch 2 para 6, sch 7 para 11	sch 2 para 6, sch 3 para 11
17.70	sch 1 para 10	sch 1 para 7	sch 2 para 9, sch 7 para 14	sch 2 para 9, sch 3 para 14
17.71	sch 1 para 8(2)	sch 1 para 6(2)	sch 2 para 5(2), sch 7 para 8(2)	sch 2 para 5(2), sch 3 para 8(2)
17.72	sch 1 para 8(1)(b)	No equiv	sch 7 para 8(1)(b)	sch 3 para 8(1)(b)
17.73	sch 1 para 16	sch 1 para 12	sch 2 para 11, sch 7 para 16	sch 2 para 11, sch 3 para 16

17.74	sch 1 para 15	sch 1 para 11	sch 2 para 10, sch 7 para 15	sch 2 para 10, sch 3 para 15
17.75	sch 1 para 10(1)(a)(v),(2)	sch 1 para 7(4),(5)	sch 2 para 6(4),(5), sch 7 para 10(1)(a)(vii),(2)	sch 2 para 6(4),(5), sch 3 para 10(1)(a)(vii),(2)
17.76	22	sch 1 para 2(3),(4)	sch 2 para 1(3),(4), sch 6 para 2(2)	25(2), sch 2 para 1(3),(4)
17.77	sch 1 para 11(2)(b)	sch 1 para 7(2)(b)	sch 2 para 1(3),(4), sch 6 para 2(2)(a),(b)	25(2)(a),(b), sch 2 para 1(3),(4)
18.5	sch 3 para 14, sch 4 paras 7,8, sch 5 paras 7,8	sch 1 para 13	sch 1 para 7, sch 8 para 14, sch 9 paras 8,9, sch 10 paras 8,9	32, sch 6 para 14, sch 7 paras 8,9, sch 9 paras 8,9
18.6	Not WA	25	sch 1 para 8	33
18.7	26	Not PA	sch 6 para 9	34
18.8	27(1)(a),(b)	26, 28(1)(a),(b)	sch 1 paras 9, 18, sch 6 para 20(1)(a),(b)	35, 54(1)(a),(b)
18.9	42	24	27, 30, sch 1 para 7	21, 32
18.10	27,35,39	26,27,31	sch 1 paras 10,11,12,18, sch 6 paras 15,17	35,36,37,49,51,54
18.11	43(1)	41(1)	sch 1 para 25(1), sch 6 para 26(1)	60(1)
18.12	sch 4 para 40	sch 3 para 11(3)	sch 4 para 12(3), sch 9 para 40	sch 5 para 12(3), sch 7 para 40
18.14	41(1), 48(1)	38(8), 44(1)	sch 1 paras 16(9),25(1), 31, sch 6 paras 19(1),30(1)	42(9),53(1),64(1)
18.17	31(2)	27(1), 31(6)	sch 1 paras 10(1),11(7), sch 6 para 12(2)	36(1),37(7), 46(2)
18.19(a)	sch 3 para 14, sch 4 paras 7,8, sch 5 paras 7,8	24	sch 1 para 7, sch 8 para 14,sch 9 paras 8,9, sch 10 paras 8,9	32, sch 6 para 14, sch 7 paras 8,9, sch 9 paras 8,9
18.19(b)	26	25	sch 1 para 8, sch 6 para 9	33, 34
18.19(c)	sch 4 paras 10,13, 36,42,51,64	27(1)(j)	sch 1 para 10(1)(j), sch 9 paras 11,14,37,38, 42,52,66	36(1)(j), sch 7 paras 11,14,37,38,42,52,66
18.19(d)	sch 4 para 20	sch 3 paras 6,7	sch 4 paras 7,8, sch 9 para 21	sch 5 paras 7,8, sch 7 para 21
18.19(e)	sch 4 para 20A, sch 5 paras 11(g), 65	27(1)(j)(xv),(xva) sch 4 paras 21(2)(aa), 30B	sch 1 para 10(1)(j)(xiii)	36(1)(j)(xiii)
18.20	39(3)	27(3)	sch 1 para 10(2), sch 6 para 17(3)	36(2), 51(3)
18.21	39(5), 32,45(9), sch 5 para 11	27(4), 30,41(3), sch 4 para 18	sch 1 para 10(3),21,25(3), sch 5 para 18,21(2)(j),(n), sch 6 paras 17(5),27(10), sch 10 para 12	36(3), 51(5), 56, 60(3), 61(10), sch 8 paras 18,21, sch 9 para 12
18.22	27(1)(c),(2), sch 4 para 56	27(1)(b), 28(1)(c),(2), sch 3 para 20	sch 1 para 10(1)(b), 18(1)(c),(2), sch 4 para 21, sch 9 para 58	36(1)(b), 54(1)(c),(2), sch 5 para 21, sch 7 para 58

Para	Scotland		Wales	
	CTS	CTS60+	CTPW	CTRW
18.23	sch 4 paras 12-13, 19,52-55	27(1)(e)-(h),(l), sch3 paras 1-5	sch 1 para 10(1)(e)-(h),(l), sch 4 paras 1-6, sch 9 paras 13-14,20,53-56	36(1)(e)-(h),(l), sch 5 paras 1-6, sch 7 paras 13-14,20, 53-56
18.27	29(1)(a)	31(2),(3)	sch 1 para 11(2)-(4), sch 6 para 10(1)(a)	37(2)-(4),40,44(1)(a)
18.28	29(1)(b),(2),(3), 30(1)	31(2), 34	sch 1 paras 11(2),(3),14, sch 6 paras 10(1)(b), (2),(3),11(1)	37(2),(3), 40,44(1)(b), (2),(3)
18.30	34	32	sch 1 para 12(1), sch 3 para 9, sch 6 para 14(1), sch 8 paras 1(b),2	38(1), 48(1), sch 4 para 9, sch 6 paras 1(b),2
18.31	34(2)	32(2)	sch 1 para 12(2), sch 6 para 14(2)	38(2), 48(2)
18.32	34(1)	32(1)	sch 1 para 15(1), sch 6 para 16(1)	41(1), 50(1)
18.33	37(3)(a),(4),(7),(9)	36(2)(a), (3),(6),(8)	sch 1 para 23(2)(a), (3),(6),(8)	58(3)(a),(4),(7),(9)
18.34	37(3)(a),(4),(7)	36(2)(a),(3),(6)	sch 1 para 23(2)(a),(3),(6)	58(3)(a),(4),(7)
18.36	37(1),(3),(4), 35(1),(3)	36(1),(2),(3)	sch 1 paras 13(1),(2), 23(1),(2), sch 6 para 15(1),(3)	39(1),(2), 49(1),(3), 58(1),(3)
18.37	35(3),(6), 38	33(2),(4), 37	sch 1 paras 13(2),(5),24, sch 6 para 15(3),(6)	39(2),(5), 49(3),(6),59
18.39	35(3),(5), 37(1),(3),(11)	33(2),(5), 36(1),(2),(10)	sch 1 paras 13(2),(4),23(1), (2),(8),(10), sch 6 para 15(3),(5)	39(2),(4), 49(3),(5), 58(1),(3),(9),(11)
18.41	27(1),(c), 35(2), sch 3	28(1)(c), 33(1), sch 2	sch 1 paras 13(1),18(1)(c), sch 3, sch 6 para 15(2), sch 8	39(1), 49(2),54(1)(c), sch 4, sch 6
18.43	35(2), sch 3 paras 4-12	33(1), sch 2 paras 1-8	sch 1 paras 13(1), sch 3 paras 1-8, sch 6 para 15(2), sch 8 paras 4-12	39(1), 49(2), sch 4 paras 1-8, sch 6 paras 4-12
T18.1	35(2), sch 3 paras 4-12	33(1), sch 2 paras 1-8	sch 1 para 13(1), sch 3 paras 1-8, sch 6 para 15(2), sch 8 paras 4-12	39(1), 49(2), sch 4 paras 1-8, sch 6 paras 4-12
18.44	27	28	sch 1 para 18	54
18.45	28(5),(6)	29(5),(6)	sch 1 para 19(5),(6)	55(5),(6)
18.46	28(1),(2)	29(1),(2)	sch 1 para 19(1),(2)	55(1),(2)
18.47	28(1)(c),(11)	29(1)(c),(11)	sch 1 para 19(1)(c),(11)	55(1)(c),(11)
18.48	35(2), sch 3 para 18(1),(3), sch 4 para 56	33(1), sch 2 para 10(1),(3), sch 3 para 20	sch 1 para 13(1), sch 3 para 10(1),(3), sch 4 para 21, sch 6 para 15(2), sch 8 paras 18(1),(3), sch 9 para 58	39(1),49(2), sch 4 para 10(1),(3), sch 5 para 21, sch 6 para 18(1),(3), sch 7 para 58
18.49	sch 3 para 18(2)	sch 2 para 10(2)	sch 3 para 10(2), sch 8 paras 18(2)	sch 4 para 10(2), sch 6 para 18(2)
18.51	sch 4 paras 29-33, 37,57,62-63, sch 5 paras 11,22-23, 25,61-64	27(1), sch 4 paras 21,29	sch 1 para 10(1), sch 5 paras 21,28,sch 9 paras, 30-34,37,59,64-65, sch 10 paras 12,23-24,25,59-62	36(1), sch 7 paras 30-34, 37,59,64,65, sch 8 paras 21,29 sch 9 paras 12,23-25,61-64

18.52	39(1),(2)	27(1),(c),(d),(x)	sch 1 para 10(1)(c),(d),(x), sch 6 para 17(1),(2)	36(1)(c),(d),(x), 51(1),(2)
18.53	39(1),(2), sch 4 paras 25,26	27(1)(p),(v), sch 3 paras 8,9	sch 1 para 10(1)(p),(v), sch 4 paras 9,10, sch 6 para 17(1),(2), sch 9 paras 26,27	36(1)(p),(v), 51(1),(2), sch 5 paras 9,10, sch 7 paras 26,27
18.54	sch 4 paras 48,49	27(1)(o), sch 3 para 19	sch 1 para 10(1)(o), sch 4 para 20, sch 9 paras 49,50	36(1)(o), sch 5 para 20, sch 7 paras 49,50
18.55	49(2)	Not Scotland	sch 9 paras 50(2)	sch 7 para 50(2)
18.56	45(6), sch 4 para 18	27(1)	sch 1 para 10(1), sch 6 para 27(7), sch 9 para 19	36(1),61(7), sch 7 para 19
18.58	sch 4 para 18	sch3 paras 13,14	sch 4 paras 14,15, sch 9 para 19	sch 5 paras 14,15, sch 7 para 19
18.59	45(6), sch 4 para 41	27(1)	sch 1 para 10(1), sch 6 para 27(7), sch 9 para 41	36(1),61(7), sch 7 para 41
18.61	34(2)(d), sch4 paras 4,5	32(2)(f)	sch 1 para 12(2),(f), sch 6 para 14(2)(d), sch 9 paras 5,6	38(2)(f), 48(2)(d), sch 7 paras 5,6
18.62	20, 53-65	Not Scotland	sch 11 paras 3-15	22, 72-84
18.64	27(1)(b), 51	27(2), 28(1)(b)	sch 1 paras 18(1),(b),31, sch 6 para 33	54(1)(b),68,69
18.65	27(1)(b), 51	27(2), 28(1)(b)	sch 1 paras 18(1),(b),31, sch 6 para 33	54(1)(b),68,69
18.67	46	42	sch 1 para 26, sch 6 para 28	62
18.68	46	42	sch 1 para 26, sch 6 para 28	62
18.69	50	46	sch 1 para 30, sch 6 para 32	67
T18.2(a)	sch 5 para 3	sch 4 para 26	sch 5 para 26, sch 10 para 4	sch 8 para 26, sch 9 para 4
T18.2(b)	sch 5 para 6(b)	sch 4 para 4(b)	sch 5 para 4(b), sch 10 para 7(b)	sch 8 para 4(b), sch 9 para 7(b)
T18.2(c)	sch 5 para 30	sch 4 para 6	sch 5 para 6, sch 10 para 30	sch 8 para 6, sch 9 para 30
T18.2(d)	sch 5 para 6(a)	sch 4 para 4(a)	sch 5 para 4(a), sch 10 para 7(a)	sch 8 para 4(a), sch 9 para 7(a)
T18.2(e)	sch 5 para 4	sch 4 para 1	sch 5 para 1, sch 10 para 5	sch 8 para 1, sch 9 para 5
T18.2(f)	sch 5 para 32	sch 4 para 2	sch 5 para 2, sch 10 para 32	sch 8 para 2, sch 9 para 32
T18.2(g)	sch 5 para 33	sch 4 para 3	sch 5 para 3, sch 10 para 33	sch 8 para 3, sch 9 para 33
T18.2(h)	sch 5 para 5	Not Scotland	sch 10 para 6	sch 9 para 6
T18.2(i)	sch 5 para 13	Not Scotland	sch 10 para 14	sch 9 para 14
T18.2(j)	No equiv	sch 4 paras 18,20(a)	sch 5 paras 18,20(a)	sch 8 paras 18,20(a)
T18.2(k)	sch 5 paras 9,10	sch 4 paras 5,9,10	sch 5 paras 5,9,10, sch 10 paras 10,11	sch 8 paras 5,9,10, sch 9 paras 10,11
18.70	45(9)	41(3)	sch 1 para 25(3), sch 5 paras 18,21,22, sch 6 para 27(10), sch 10 para 12	60(3),61(10), sch 8 paras 18,21,22, sch 9 para 12
18.71	sch 5 para 14	sch 4 para 8	sch 5 para 8, sch 10 para 15	sch 8 para 8, sch 9 para 15

Para	Scotland CTS	CTS60+	Wales CTPW	CTRW
18.72	sch 5 para 10	sch 4 paras 9,10	sch 5 paras 9,10, sch 10 para 11	sch 8 paras 9,10 sch 9 para 11
18.73	No equiv	sch 4 paras 11,24,33	sch 5 paras 11,24,31	sch 8 paras 11,24,32
18.75	No equiv	sch 4 para 17	sch 5 para 17	sch 8 para 17
18.76	sch 5 para 29	sch 4 para 16	sch 5 para 16, sch 10 para 29	sch 8 para 16, sch 9 para 29
19.2	89(1),(4)	69(1),(4)	sch 13 para 7(1)	113(1)
T19.1	89	69	sch 13 para 7	113
19.4	89(1)	69(1)	sch 12 para 11, sch 13 para 7(2)	113(2), sch 1 para 11
19.5	89(1)	69(1)	sch 13 para 7(2)	113(2)
19.7	Not Scotland	Not Scotland	sch 13 para 5(1)	111(1)
19.8	Not Scotland	Not Scotland	sch 13 para 9(1)(b),(2)-(4)	115(1)(b),(2)-(4)
19.11	81(1)	59(1)	sch 1 para 40(1),(2), sch 6 para 46(1),(2)	115(1),(5),(6)
19.14	81(2),(3)	59(2),(3)	sch 1 para 40(3),(4), sch 6 para 46(3),(4)	105(3),(4)
T19.3	Not Scotland	60	sch 1 para 41	106
19.15	Not Scotland	60	sch 1 para 41	106
19.18	81(1)	59(1)	sch 1 para 40(1),(2), sch 6 para 46(1),(2)	105(1),(2)
19.22	Not Scotland	Not Scotland	sch 1 para 22, sch 6 para 23	57
19.26	81(7)	59(7)	Not Wales	Not Wales
19.27	68,73	49	sch 1 para 32, sch 6 paras 34,39	2(1), 85,86,92,93,98
19.28	Not Scotland	Not Scotland	See text	See text
19.30	74,75	50,51	sch 1 paras 33,34, sch 6 paras 35,36,40,41	87,88,94,95,99,100
T19.5	2(1), 68,73	2(1), 68	sch 1 para 32, sch 6 paras 34,39	85,86,92,93,98
19.32	Not Scotland	See text	Not Wales	Not Wales
19.33	72,77	53	sch 1 para 36, sch 6 paras 38,43	90,97,102
19.34	71,76	52	sch 1 paras 35,38, sch 6 paras 37,42,44	89,96,101,103
19.35	Not Scotland	55	sch 1 para 37	91
19.37	86(1),(4)	66(1),(4)	sch 13 para 5(4),(6)	111(4),(6)
19.41	Not Scotland	Not Scotland	See text	See text
19.42	Not Scotland	Not Scotland	See text	See text
19.43	Not Scotland	Not Scotland	See text	See text
19.46	Not Scotland	Not Scotland	See text	See text
Ch 20	See text	See text	See text	See text
Ch 22	16(1),(2),(5)(d)-(h), 19(1),(2)	16(1),(2),(5)(d)-(h), 19(1),(2)	28(1),(2),(5)(d)-(g),(l), 29(1),(2)	19(1),(2),(5)(d)-(g),(l), 20(1),(2)
Ch 23	16(3),(4), (5)(a)-(c),(i)	16(3),(4), (5)(a)-(c),(i)	28(3),(4), (5)(a)-(c),(k)	19(3),(4), (5)(a)-(c),(k)

Appendix 5 **Proposed start dates for universal credit full service**

England: North East

County Durham	Peterlee JCP, Seaham JCP	Oct-17
	Bishop Auckland JCP, Consett JCP, Crook JCP, Stanley JCP	Dec-17
	Chester le Street JCP, Durham JCP, Newton Aycliffe JCP, Spennymoor JCP	Jun-18
Darlington	Darlington JCP	Jun-18
Gateshead	Gateshead JCP	Oct-17
	Blaydon JCP	Nov-17
Hartlepool	Hartlepool JCP	Dec-16
Middlesbrough	Middlesbrough East JCP, Middlesbrough JCP	Jul-18
Newcastle upon Tyne	Newcastle Cathedral Square JCP	May-16
	Newcastle East JCP	Feb-17
	Newcastle West JCP	Mar-17
North Tyneside	Killingworth JCP, North Shields JCP, Wallsend JCP, Whitley Bay JCP	May-18
Northumberland	Ashington JCP, Berwick JCP, Cramlington JCP, Morpeth JCP	Jul-18
	Alnwick JCP, Bedlington JCP, Blyth JCP, Hexham JCP	Dec-18
Redcar and Cleveland	Eston JCP, Guisborough JCP, Loftus JCP, Redcar JCP	Aug-18
South Tyneside	Jarrow JCP, South Shields JCP	May-18
Stockton	Billingham JCP, Stockton JCP, Thornaby JCP	Jul-18
Sunderland	Houghton le Spring JCP, Southwick JCP, Sunderland JCP, Washington JCP	Jul-18

England: North West

Allerdale	Workington JCP	Nov-16
Barrow In Furness	Barrow JCP	Jul-18
Blackburn With Darwen	Blackburn JCP, Darwen JCP	Feb-18
Blackpool	Blackpool North JCP, Blackpool South JCP	Dec-18
Bolton	Bolton Great Moor St JCP, Bolton Blackhorse St JCP, Farnworth JCP	Jul-18
Burnley	Burnley JCP	May-17
Bury	Bury JCP, Prestwich JCP	Jul-18
Carlisle	Carlisle JCP	Jul-18
Cheshire East	Crewe JCP	Jul-17
	Congleton JCP, Macclesfield JCP, Wilmslow JCP	Jul-18
Cheshire West and Chester	Chester JCP	Jul-17
	Ellesmere Port JCP, Neston JCP, Northwich JCP, Winsford JCP	Dec-17

Chorley	Chorley JCP	Jul-18
Copeland	Whitehaven JCP	Nov-16
Eden	Penrith JCP	Jul-18
Fylde	St Annes JCP	Dec-18
Halton	Runcorn JCP, Widnes JCP	Jul-16
Hyndburn	Accrington JCP	Feb-18
Knowsley	Belle Vale JCP, Garston JCP	Jun-18
	Huyton JCP, Kirkby JCP	May-18
Lancaster	Lancaster JCP, Morecambe JCP	Jul-16
Liverpool	Belle Vale JCP, Garston JCP	Sep-18
	Edge Hill JCP, Toxteth JCP, Wavertree JCP, Williamson Square JCP	Jul-18
	Everton JCP, Norris Green JCP, West Derby JCP	Dec-18
Manchester	Alexandra Park JCP, Chorlton JCP, Didsbury JCP, Longsight JCP, Rusholme JCP	Oct-17
	Newton Heath JCP, Manchester Town Hall outreach JCP, Openshaw JCP	Nov-17
	Cheetham Hill JCP, Wythenshawe JCP	Jul-18
Oldham	Oldham JCP	Apr-17
Pendle	Colne JCP, Nelson JCP	Aug-18
Preston	Preston JCP	Jul-18
Ribble Valley	Clitheroe JCP	Aug-18
Rochdale	Heywood JCP, Middleton JCP, Rochdale JCP	May-18
Rossendale	Rawtenstall JCP	Aug-18
Salford	Eccles JCP, Irlam JCP, Salford JCP, Worsley JCP	Sep-18
Sefton	Bootle JCP, Crosby JCP, Southport JCP	Oct-17
	Aintree JCP	Sep-18
South Lakeland	Kendal JCP	Sep-18
South Ribble	Leyland JCP	Jul-18
St Helens	Newton-le-Willows JCP, St Helens JCP	Jul-18
Stockport	Stockport JCP	Mar-18
Tameside	Ashton-under-Lyne JCP, Hyde JCP, Stalybridge JCP	Aug-18
Trafford	Altrincham JCP, Stretford JCP	Jul-17
Warrington	Warrington JCP	Feb-17
West Lancashire	Ormskirk JCP, Skelmersdale JCP	Dec-17
Wigan	Ashton in Makerfield JCP, Atherton JCP, Leigh JCP, Wigan JCP	Apr-18
Wirral	Birkenhead JCP, Bromborough JCP, Hoylake JCP, Upton JCP, Wallasey JCP	Nov-17
Wyre	Fleetwood JCP	Dec-18

England: Yorkshire and Humberside

Barnsley	Barnsley JCP, Goldthorpe JCP, Wombwell JCP	Jul-17
Bradford	Bradford Eastbrook Court JCP, Bradford Westfield House JCP, Keighley JCP, Shipley JCP	Jun-18
Calderdale	Brighouse JCP, Halifax JCP, Todmorden JCP	Jun-17

Craven	Skipton JCP	Oct-16
Doncaster	Doncaster JCP, Mexborough JCP, Thorne JCP	Oct-17
East Riding of Yorkshire	Bridlington JCP, Beverley JCP, Goole JCP, Hessle JCP	Jul-18
Hambleton	Northallerton JCP	Oct-16
Harrogate	Harrogate JCP	Jun-16
Hull	Hull Britannia House JCP, Hull Market Place JCP	Dec-18
Kirklees	Batley JCP, Dewsbury JCP, Spen Valley JCP, Huddersfield JCP	Nov-17
Leeds	Guisley JCP, Leeds Eastgate JCP, Leeds Park Place JCP, Morley JCP, Pudsey JCP, Seacroft JCP, Leeds Southern House JCP	Oct-18
North East Lincolnshire	Grimsby JCP, Immingham JCP	Dec-17
North Lincolnshire	Barton JCP, Scunthorpe JCP	Oct-17
Richmondshire	Richmond JCP	Jun-16
Rotherham	Dinnington JCP, Maltby JCP, Rotherham JCP	Jul-18
Ryedale	Ryedale JCP	Jun-16
Scarborough	Scarborough JCP, Whitby JCP	May-18
Selby	Selby JCP	May-18
Sheffield	Chapeltown JCP, Sheffield Bailey JCP, Sheffield Cavendish Court JCP	Jul-18
	Sheffield Eastern Ave JCP, Sheffield Hillsborough JCP, Sheffield Woodhouse JCP	Dec-18
Wakefield	Castleford JCP, Hemsworth JCP, Pontefract JCP, Wakefield JCP	Aug-18
York	York Monkgate JCP	Jul-17

England: East Midlands

Amber Valley	Alfreton JCP, Belper JCP, Heanor JCP	Jun-18
Ashfield	Sutton-in-Ashfield JCP	Aug-18
Bassetlaw	Retford JCP, Worksop JCP	Dec-17
Blaby	Leicester Charles St JCP, Leicester New Walk JCP, Leicester Wellington St JCP	Jun-18
Bolsover	Bolsover JCP, Shirebrook JCP	Aug-18
Boston	Boston JCP	Sep-18
Broxtowe	Beeston JCP	Jul-18
Charnwood	Loughborough JCP	Jul-18
Chesterfield	Chesterfield JCP	Nov-17
Corby	Corby JCP	Feb-17
Daventry	Daventry JCP	Nov-16
Derby	Derby Forester House JCP, Derby Normanton Road JCP	Jul-18
Derbyshire Dales	Matlock JCP	Sep-18
East Lindsey	Skegness JCP, Louth JCP	Jun-18
East Northamptonshire	Rushden JCP	May-18
Erewash	Ilkeston JCP, Long Eaton JCP	May-17
Gedling	Arnold JCP	Jul-18

Harborough	Market Harborough JCP	Nov-16
High Peak	Glossop JCP	Sep-18
Hinckley and Bosworth	Hinckley JCP	Mar-17
Kettering	Kettering JCP	Oct-18
Leicester	Leicester Charles St JCP, Leicester New Walk JCP, Leicester Wellington St JCP	Jun-18
Lincoln	Lincoln JCP	Mar-18
Mansfield	Mansfield JCP	Sep-18
Melton	Melton Mowbray JCP	Nov-16
Newark and Sherwood	Newark JCP	May-18
North East Derbyshire	Clay Cross JCP, Staveley JCP	Jul-18
North Kesteven	Sleaford JCP	Jul-18
North West Leicestershire	Coalville JCP	Feb-18
Northampton	Northampton JCP	Jul-18
Nottingham	Bulwell JCP, Nottingham Central JCP, Nottingham Loxley House JCP	Oct-18
Oadby and Wigston	Leicester Charles St JCP	Jun-18
Rushcliffe	Nottingham Central JCP	Oct-18
Rutland	Stamford JCP	Oct-17
South Derbyshire	Swadlincote JCP	Aug-18
South Holland	Spalding JCP	Apr-18
South Kesteven	Grantham JCP, Stamford JCP	Oct-17
South Northamptonshire	Northampton JCP	Jul-18
Wellingborough	Wellingborough JCP	Aug-18
West Lindsey	Gainsborough JCP	Sep-18

England: West Midlands

Birmingham	Birmingham Broad St JCP, Birmingham City JCP, Birmingham South West JCP, Sutton Coldfield JCP, Washwood Heath JCP, Yardley JCP	Nov-17
	Erdington JCP, Handsworth JCP, Kings Heath JCP, Perry Barr JCP, Selly Oak JCP, Sparkhill JCP	Dec-17
Bromsgrove	Bromsgrove JCP	Sep-18
Cannock Chase	Cannock JCP*	Aug-18
Coventry	Coventry Cofa Court JCP, Coventry Tile Hill JCP	Jul-18
Dudley	Dudley JCP, Halesowen JCP, Stourbridge JCP	Jul-17
East Staffordshire	Burton JCP	Aug-18
Herefordshire	Hereford JCP, Leominster JCP, Ross on Wye JCP	Jun-18
Lichfield	Lichfield JCP	Nov-17
Malvern Hills	Malvern JCP	Sep-18
Newcastle-under-Lyme	Kidsgrove JCP, Newcastle Under Lyme JCP	Dec-18
North Warwickshire	Atherstone JCP	Sep-18
Nuneaton and Bedworth	Bedworth JCP, Nuneaton JCP	Oct-17
Redditch	Redditch JCP	Oct-17

Rugby	Rugby JCP	May-16
Sandwell	Oldbury JCP, Smethwick JCP, Tipton JCP, West Bromwich JCP	Jul-18
Shropshire	Bridgnorth JCP, Market Drayton JCP, Oswestry JCP, Shrewsbury JCP, Whitchurch JCP	May-18
Solihull	Chelmsley Wood JCP, Solihull JCP	Jul-17
South Staffordshire	Cannock JCP	Aug-18
Stafford	Stafford JCP	Aug-18
Staffordshire Moorlands	Buxton JCP, Glossop JCP	May-18
Stoke-on-Trent	Hanley JCP, Longton JCP	Jun-18
Stratford	Stratford-upon-Avon JCP	Dec-16
Tamworth	Tamworth JCP	Nov-17
Telford and Wrekin	Madeley JCP, Telford JCP, Wellington JCP	Jul-18
Walsall	Brownhills JCP, Walsall Bayard House JCP, Walsall Bridle Court JCP, Willenhall JCP	Oct-18
Warwick	Leamington Spa JCP	Oct-18
Wolverhampton	Bilston JCP, Wolverhampton Chapel Court JCP, Wolverhampton Molineaux House JCP	Dec-17
Worcester	Worcester JCP	Oct-18
Wychavon	Evesham JCP	Jul-18
Wyre Forest	Kidderminster JCP	Jul-18

England: East of England

Babergh	Sudbury JCP	Oct-17
Basildon	Basildon JCP	Nov-17
Bedford	Bedford JCP	May-17
Braintree	Braintree JCP, Witham JCP	Oct-17
Breckland	Dereham JCP, Thetford JCP	Jun-18
Brentwood	Brentwood JCP	Nov-17
Broadland	Norwich JCP	Oct-18
Broxbourne	Waltham Cross JCP	Nov-17
Cambridge	Ely JCP	May-18
	Cambridge JCP	Oct-18
Castle Point	Canvey JCP	Jul-18
Central Bedfordshire	Dunstable JCP	Jul-18
	Biggleswade JCP, Leighton Buzzard JCP	Aug-18
Chelmsford	Chelmsford JCP	Dec-18
Colchester	Colchester JCP	Jul-18
Dacorum	Hemel Hempstead JCP	Dec-18
East Cambridgeshire	Ely JCP	Sep-18
East Hertfordshire	Hertford JCP	Oct-18
Epping Forest	Loughton JCP	Dec-18
Fenland	Wisbech JCP	Sep-18
Forest Heath	Mildenhall JCP, Newmarket JCP	Dec-18

Great Yarmouth	Great Yarmouth JCP	Mar-16
Harlow	Harlow JCP	Jul-17
Hertsmere	Borehamwood JCP	Dec-18
Huntingdonshire	Huntingdon JCP	Oct-18
Ipswich	Ipswich JCP, Ipswich 'My go Hub'	Apr-18
King's Lynn and West Norfolk	Kings Lynn JCP	Jul-18
Luton	Luton JCP	Oct-18
Maldon	Chelmsford JCP	Sep-18
Mid Suffolk	Stowmarket JCP	May-18
North Hertfordshire	Letchworth JCP	Oct-18
North Norfolk	Cromer JCP	Oct-18
	Fakenham JCP, North Walsham JCP	Dec-18
Norwich	Norwich JCP	Oct-18
Peterborough	Peterborough JCP	Nov-17
Rochford	Rayleigh JCP	Jul-18
South Cambridgeshire	Cambridge JCP	Jun-18
South Norfolk	Diss JCP	May-18
Southend-on-Sea	Southend JCP	Jul-17
St Albans	St Albans JCP	Nov-17
St Edmundsbury	Bury St Edmunds JCP, Haverhill JCP	Oct-17
Stevenage	Stevenage JCP	Oct-18
Suffolk Coastal	Felixstowe JCP, Leiston JCP, Woodbridge JCP	Oct-18
Tendring	Harwich JCP, Clacton JCP	Jul-18
Three Rivers	Watford JCP	Dec-17
Thurrock	Grays JCP	Oct-17
Uttlesford	Braintree JCP	Oct-17
Watford	Watford JCP	Dec-17
Waveney	Lowestoft JCP	May-16
	Beccles JCP	Oct-17
Welwyn Hatfield	Hatfield JCP	Dec-17

England: London

Barking and Dagenham	Barking JCP, Dagenham JCP	Mar-18
Barnet	Barnet JCP, Edgware JCP, Finchley JCP, Hendon JCP	May-18
Bexley	Bexleyheath JCP	Oct-18
Brent	Harlesden JCP, Willesden JCP	Aug-18
	Kilburn JCP, Wembley JCP	Dec-18
Bromley	Bromley JCP	Jul-18
Camden	Kentish Town JCP	Dec-18
City of London	City Tower JCP	Apr-17
Croydon	Croydon JCP	Mar-16
Ealing	Southall JCP	Oct-17
	Acton JCP, Ealing JCP	Mar-18

Enfield	Edmonton JCP, Enfield JCP, Palmers Green JCP.	May-18
Greenwich	Eltham JCP, Woolwich JCP	Oct-18
Hackney	Dalston JCP, Hackney JCP, Hoxton JCP.	Oct-18
Hammersmith and Fulham	Hammersmith JCP	Jun-16
	Shepherds Bush JCP.	Nov-16
	Fulham JCP, Shepherds Bush JCP.	Dec-16
Haringey	Tottenham JCP, Wood Green JCP.	Oct-18
Harrow	Harrow JCP	Jul-18
Havering	Hornchurch JCP, Romford JCP, Barnsbury JCP.	Jun-18
Hillingdon	Hayes JCP, Uxbridge JCP.	Oct-18
Hounslow	Hounslow JCP.	Mar-16
Islington	Finsbury Park JCP, Highgate JCP	Jun-18
Kensington and Chelsea	North Kensington JCP	Dec-18
Kingston upon Thames	Kingston JCP.	Jun-18
Lambeth	Kennington Park JCP	Oct-16
	Brixton JCP, Stockwell JCP	Feb-18
	Clapham Common JCP, Streatham JCP	Feb-18
Lewisham	Forest Hill JCP, Lewisham JCP	Jul-18
Merton	Mitcham JCP.	Dec-17
Newham	Canning Town JCP, East Ham JCP, Plaistow JCP, Stratford JCP	Jul-18
Redbridge	Redbridge JCP	Jun-18
Richmond upon Thames	Twickenham JCP	Jun-18
Southwark	Peckham JCP (50%)	Oct-16
	Peckham JCP (50%)	Nov-16
Sutton	Sutton JCP	Mar-16
Tower Hamlets	Poplar JCP	Feb-17
	City Tower JCP	Mar-17
Waltham Forest	Leytonstone JCP, Walthamstow JCP	May-18
Wandsworth	Wandsworth JCP	Sep-18
Westminster	Marylebone JCP, Westminster JCP.	Jun-18

England: South East

Adur	Worthing JCP	Jul-18
Arun	Bognor JCP, Littlehampton JCP	Jul-18
Ashford	Ashford JCP	Jun-18
Aylesbury Vale	Aylesbury JCP.	Sep-18
Basingstoke and Deane	Basingstoke JCP.	May-18
Bracknell Forest	Bracknell JCP.	May-18
Brighton and Hove	Hove JCP.	Oct-17
	Brighton JCP	Nov-17
Canterbury	Canterbury JCP, Herne Bay JCP, Whitstable JCP	Jul-18
Cherwell	Banbury JCP	Nov-17
Chichester	Chichester JCP	Jul-18
Chiltern	Chesham JCP	Sep-18

Crawley	Crawley JCP	Jun-18
Dartford	Dartford JCP	Jul-18
Dover	Dover JCP	May-17
East Hampshire	Alton JCP, Bordon JCP	Oct-18
	Petersfield JCP	Aug-18
Eastbourne	Eastbourne JCP	Oct-17
Eastleigh	Eastleigh JCP	Jul-17
Elmbridge Borough Council	Staines JCP, Weybridge JCP	Aug-18
Epsom and Ewell	Epsom JCP	Oct-18
	Weybridge JCP	Aug-18
Fareham	Fareham JCP	Aug-18
Gosport	Gosport JCP	Aug-18
Gravesham	Gravesend JCP	May-18
Guildford	Guildford JCP	Oct-18
Hart	Farnborough JCP	Oct-18
Hastings	Hastings JCP	Dec-16
Havant	Cosham JCP, Portsmouth JCP	Sep-18
	Havant JCP	Aug-18
Horsham	Horsham JCP	Jun-18
Isle of Wight	Newport (IOW) JCP	Sep-18
	Ryde JCP	Oct-18
Lewes	Lewes JCP, Newhaven JCP	Sep-18
Maidstone	Maidstone JCP	Aug-18
Medway	Chatham JCP	May-18
Mid Sussex	Haywards Heath JCP, Horsham JCP	Jun-18
Milton Keynes	Milton Keynes JCP	Dec-18
Mole Valley	Redhill JCP	Oct-18
New Forest	Hythe JCP, Lymington, Ringwood	Sep-18
Oxford	Oxford JCP	Oct-17
Portsmouth	Cosham JCP, Portsmouth JCP	Sep-18
Reading	Reading JCP	Dec-17
Reigate and Banstead	Redhill JCP	Oct-18
Rother	Bexhill JCP	Jul-17
Runnymede	Staines JCP, Weybridge JCP	Aug-18
Rushmoor	Aldershot JCP	Oct-18
Sevenoaks	Gravesend JCP	Feb-18
	Dartford JCP	Jul-18
Shepway	Folkestone JCP	May-18
Slough	Slough JCP	Apr-18
South Buckinghamshire	Slough JCP	Apr-18
	High Wycombe JCP	May-18
	Uxbridge JCP	Sep-18
South Oxfordshire	Didcot JCP	Oct-17
	Reading JCP	Dec-17
Southampton	Southampton JCP	Feb-17

Spelthorne	Staines JCP, Weybridge JCP	Aug-18
Surrey Heath	Camberley JCP	Aug-18
Swale	Sheerness JCP, Sittingbourne JCP	Dec-17
Tandridge	Redhill JCP	Oct-18
Test Valley	Andover JCP	Jul-18
Thanet District Council	Margate JCP, Ramsgate JCP	Jul-17
Tonbridge and Malling	Tonbridge JCP	Aug-18
Tunbridge Wells	Tunbridge Wells JCP	Sep-18
Vale of White Horse	Abingdon JCP	Oct-17
Waverley	Guildford JCP	Jul-18
Wealden	Eastbourne JCP	Oct-17
West Berkshire	Newbury JCP, Reading JCP	Dec-17
West Oxfordshire	Witney JCP	Nov-17
Winchester	Winchester JCP	Jul-18
Windsor and Maidenhead	Maidenhead JCP	Feb/May-18
Woking	Woking JCP	Oct-18
Wokingham	Reading JCP	Dec-17
	Bracknell JCP	Feb-18
Worthing	Worthing JCP	Jul-18
Wycombe	High Wycombe JCP	Sep-18

England: South West

Bath and North East Somerset	Bath JCP	May-16
Bournemouth	Bournemouth JCP	Nov-17
	Winton JCP	Nov-17
Bristol	Bedminster JCP, Bristol Central JCP, Bishopsworth JCP	Jun-18
	Easton JCP, Horfield JCP, Shirehampton JCP	Sep-18
	Kingswood JCP	Jul-18
Cheltenham	Cheltenham JCP	Dec-17
Christchurch	Bournemouth JCP	Nov-17
Cornwall	Bude JCP, Launceston JCP, Liskeard JCP	Dec-17
	Bodmin JCP, Newquay JCP, St Austell JCP, Truro JCP	May-18
	Helston JCP, Penryn JCP, Penzance JCP*, Redruth JCP	Jun-18
Cotswold	Cirencester JCP	Nov-17
East Devon	Honiton JCP	Jul-18
East Dorset	Poole JCP	Oct-17
	Winton JCP	Nov-17
Exeter	Exeter JCP	Sep-18
Forest of Dean	Cinderford JCP, Coleford JCP	Nov-17
Gloucester	Gloucester JCP	Feb-18
Isles of Scilly	Penzance JCP	Jun-18
Mendip	Frome JCP, Wells JCP	Jul-16
Mid Devon	Tiverton JCP	Jul-18
North Devon	Barnstaple JCP	Jul-18

North Dorset	Blandford JCP	Oct-17
North Somerset	Weston-Super-Mare JCP	Jun-17
	Clevedon JCP	Jul-17
Plymouth	Plymouth JCP	Oct-17
	Devonport JCP	Nov-17
Poole	Poole JCP	Oct-17
Purbeck	Poole JCP	Oct-17
Sedgemoor	Bridgwater JCP	May-16
South Gloucestershire	Horfield JCP	Sep-18
	Kingswood JCP, Yate JCP	Oct-18
South Hams	Totnes JCP	Sep-18
South Somerset	Yeovil JCP	Apr-17
Stroud	Stroud JCP	Oct-17
Swindon	Swindon JCP (50%)	Nov-16
	Swindon JCP (50%)	Dec-16
Taunton Deane	Taunton JCP	Oct-16
Teignbridge	Newton Abbot JCP	Sep-18
Tewkesbury	Tewkesbury JCP	Dec-17
Torbay	Brixham JCP, Torquay JCP	Sep-18
Torridge	Bideford JCP	Jul-18
West Devon	Plymouth JCP	Oct-17
	Exeter JCP	Sep-18
West Dorset	Bridport JCP	Dec-17
West Somerset	Minehead JCP	Oct-16
Weymouth and Portland	Weymouth JCP	Dec-17
Wiltshire	Chippenham JCP	May-17
	Salisbury JCP	Jun-17
	Devizes JCP, Trowbridge JCP	Jul-17

Wales

Anglesey	Amlwch JCP, Holyhead JCP, Llangefni JCP	Jun-18
Blaenau Gwent	Abertillery JCP, Ebbw Vale JCP, Tredegar JCP	Jul-18
Bridgend	Bridgend JCP, Maesteg JCP, Porthcawl JCP, Pyle JCP	Jun-18
Caerphilly	Bargoed JCP, Blackwood JCP, Caerphilly JCP	Sep-18
Cardiff	Cardiff Alex House JCP, Cardiff Charles Street JCP	Feb-18
Carmarthenshire	Ammanford JCP, Carmarthen JCP, Llanelli JCP	Jun-18
Ceredigion	Aberystwyth JCP, Cardigan JCP	Sep-18
Conwy	Colwyn Bay JCP, Llandudno JCP	Jun-18
Denbighshire	Rhyl JCP	Apr-18
Flintshire County	Flint JCP, Mold JCP, Shotton JCP	Apr-17
Gwynedd	Bangor JCP, Caernarfon JCP, Dolgellau JCP, Machynlleth JCP, Porthmadog JCP, Pwllheli JCP	Jul-18
Merthyr Tydfil	Merthyr Tydfil JCP	Jun-18
Monmouthshire	Abergavenny JCP, Caldicott JCP, Chepstow JCP	Jun-18
Neath Port Talbot	Neath JCP	Oct-17

Newport	Newport JCP	Nov-17
Pembrokeshire	Haverfordwest JCP, Milford Haven JCP, Pembroke Dock JCP	Sep-18
Powys	Brecon JCP, Llandrindod Wells JCP, Machynlleth JCP, Newtown JCP, Welshpool JCP, Ystradgynlais JCP	Oct-18
Rhondda Cynon Taf	Aberdare JCP, Llantrisant JCP, Mountain Ash JCP, Pontypridd JCP, Porth JCP, Tonypandy JCP, Treorchy JCP	Jul-18
Swansea	Gorseinon JCP, Morriston JCP, Swansea JCP	Dec-17
Torfaen	Cwmbran JCP, Pontypool JCP	Jul-17
Vale of Glamorgan	Barry JCP, Penarth JCP	Oct-18
Wrexham	Wrexham JCP	Oct-17

Scotland

Aberdeen	Aberdeen JCP	Oct-18
Aberdeenshire	Banff JCP, Fraserburgh JCP, Peterhead JCP	Jun-18
Angus	Arbroath JCP, Forfar JCP, Montrose JCP	Nov-17
Argyll and Bute	Campbeltown JCP, Dunoon JCP, Helensburgh JCP, Oban JCP, Rothesay JCP	Sep-18
Clackmannanshire	Alloa JCP	Jun-17
Dumfries and Galloway	Annan JCP, Dumfries JCP, Stranraer JCP	May-18
Dundee	Dundee JCP	Nov-17
East Ayrshire	Cumnock JCP, Kilmarnock JCP	Oct-17
East Dunbartonshire	Kirkintilloch JCP	Nov-16
East Lothian	Musselburgh JCP	Mar-16
East Renfrewshire	Barrhead JCP	Sep-18
Edinburgh	Edinburgh City JCP, High Riggs JCP, Leith JCP, Wester Hailes JCP	Oct-18
Eilean Siar	Stornoway JCP	Sep-18
Falkirk	Falkirk JCP, Grangemouth JCP	Mar-18
Fife	Cowdenbeath JCP, Cupar JCP, Dunfermline JCP, Glenrothes JCP, Kirkcaldy JCP, Leven JCP, St Andrews JCP	Dec-17
Glasgow	Anniesland JCP, Bridgeton JCP, Castlemilk JCP, Drumchapel JCP, Easterhouse JCP, Govan JCP, Langside JCP, Laurieston JCP, Maryhill JCP, Newlands JCP, Parkhead JCP, Partick JCP, Shettleston JCP, Springburn JCP	Dec-18
Highland	Inverness JCP	Jun-16
Inverclyde	Port Glasgow JCP, Greenock JCP	Nov-16
Midlothian	Dalkeith JCP, Penicuik JCP	Mar-17
Moray	Buckie JCP, Elgin JCP, Forres JCP	Jun-18
North Ayrshire	Irvine JCP, Kilbirnie JCP, Saltcoats JCP	Nov-17
North Lanarkshire	Airdrie JCP, Bellshill JCP, Cumbernauld JCP, Motherwell JCP	Apr-18
Orkney Islands	Kirkwall JCP	Sep-18
Perth and Kinross	Blairgowrie JCP, Perth JCP	Jun-18

Renfrewshire	Johnstone JCP, Paisley JCP, Renfrew JCP Sep-18
Scottish Borders	Eyemouth JCP, Galashiels JCP, Hawick JCP Jun-18
Shetland Islands	Lerwick JCP Sep-18
South Ayrshire	Ayr JCP, Girvan JCP Feb-18
South Lanarkshire	Cambuslang JCP, East Kilbride JCP, Hamilton JCP, Lanark JCP, Rutherglen JCP Oct-17
Stirling	Stirling JCP... Jun-17
West Dunbartonshire	Alexandria JCP, Clydebank JCP, Dumbarton JCP Oct-18
West Lothian	Bathgate JCP, Broxburn JCP, Livingston JCP............. May-18

Northern Ireland

Antrim and Newtownabbey	Newtownabbey JCP................................... Sep-18 Antrim JCP... Dec-18
Ards and North Down	Newtonards JCP....................................... Sep-18 Bangor JCP.. Oct-18
Armagh, Banbridge and Craigavon	Armagh JCP... Feb-18 Portadown JCP.. Mar-18 Lurgan JCP... May-18 Banbridge Jun-18
Belfast	Causeway Coast and Glens Limavady JCP .... Sep-17 Ballymoney JCP .... Nov-17 Coleraine JCP .... Dec-17 Shankhill JCP, Falls JCP, Andersontown JCP .... Jun-18 Holywood Road JCP.................................... Sep-18 Shaftesbury Square JCP, Knockbreda JCP................ Oct-18 Corporation Street JCP Nov-18
Derry and Strabane	Strabane JCP, Lisnagelvin JCP.......................... Jan-18 Foyle JCP Feb-18
Fermanagh and Omagh	Omagh JCP, Enniskillen JCP............................. Feb-18
Lisburn and Castlereagh	Ballynahinch JCP...................................... Sep-18 Lisburn JCP Oct-18
Mid and East Antrim	Larne JCP, Carrickfergus JCP .... Oct-18 Ballymena JCP Dec-18
Mid-Ulster	Magherafelt JCP....................................... Dec-17 Dungannon JCP....................................... Mar-18 Cookstown (Molesworth Street) JCP, Cookstown (Fairhill Road) JCP Nov-18
Newry, Mourne and Down	Downpatrick JCP, Newry JCP Kilkeel JCP, Newcastle JCP May-18

Index

References in the index are to paragraph numbers (not page numbers), except that 'A' refers to appendices, 'T' refers to tables in the text and 'Ch' refers to a chapter.

W

Y